T0179838

Information Technology and the World of Work

Daphne G. Taras
James T. Bennett
Anthony M. Townsend
editors

Information Technology and the World of Work

Routledge
Taylor & Francis Group

LONDON AND NEW YORK

First published 2004 by Transaction Publishers

2 Park Square, Milton Park, Abingdon, Oxfordshire OX14 4RN
711 Third Avenue, New York, NY 10017

Routledge is an imprint of the Taylor & Francis Group, an informa business

First issued in hardback 2017

Copyright © 2004 Taylor & Francis

All rights reserved. No part of this book may be reprinted or reproduced or utilised in any form or by any electronic, mechanical, or other means, now known or hereafter invented, including photocopying and recording, or in any information storage or retrieval system, without permission in writing from the publishers.

Notice:
Product or corporate names may be trademarks or registered trademarks, and are used only for identification and explanation without intent to infringe.

Library of Congress Catalog Number: 2004045985

Library of Congress Cataloging-in-Publication Data

Information technology and the world of work / Daphne G. Taras, James T.
  Bennett, Anthony M. Townsend, editors.
        p. cm.
    Includes bibliographical references and index.
    ISBN 0-7658-0820-X (pbk. : alk. paper)
      1. Information technology-Management. 2. Communication in organizations—Technological innovations. 3. Internet. 4. Employees—Effect of technological innovations on. 5. Labor unions—Effect of technological innovations on. 6. Work—Effect of technological innovations on. 7. Industrial relations—Effect of technological innovations on. I. Taras, Daphne Gottlieb, 1956- II. Bennett, James T. III. Townsend, Anthony M., 1973

HD30.2I5282   2004
303.48'33—dc22   2004045985

ISBN 13: 978-0-7658-0820-2 (pbk)
ISBN 13: 978-1-138-52608-2 (hbk)

Contents

Acknowledgments

The papers in this book, with the exception of the Introduction, first appeared in a series of six symposia dealing with various aspects of technology, the workplace, and the relationships between employers, employees, and unions. The papers in these symposia were published in the *Journal of Labor Research*: "E-Voice: Information Technology and Unions" (Vol. XXIII, No. 2, Spring 2002); "Technological Change and Industrial Relations" (XXIII, 3, Summer 2002); "Technological Change and Employment Conditions in Traditionally Heavily Unionized Industries" (XXIII, 4, Fall 2002); "E-Voice: Power and Identity Via Electronic Communication" (XXIV, 1, Winter 2003); "E-Voice and Individual Privacy: Emerging Issues at the Intersection of Technology and Employment" (XXIV, 2, Spring 2003); and "Human Resources and Information Technology" (XXIV, 3, Summer 2003). These symposia were generously supported by grants from the John M. Olin Foundation and the Sunmark Foundation.

1

Introduction

Daphne G. Taras
University of Calgary

James T. Bennett
George Mason University

New technologies have become both a means and an end. They are a means of communication linking individuals and organizations throughout the world. Serving as a medium through which electronic messages are sent, they allow rapid diffusion with few barriers to entry save the cost of hardware and an Internet connection. The Internet in particular has permeated the way companies do business and display their wares, the way consumers shop online, and even the way romances are struck through chat rooms. It has penetrated our daily lives and in only a single generation has become a taken-for-granted element in daily living. Teenagers operate the Internet as though they are the center of a great octopus of live connections reaching out to the information they want, the community of people with whom they develop links, and a great many resources that parents would rather they not access. The Internet is also an end: websites are carefully crafted to draw the eye, open the pocketbook, foster loyalty, and be bookmarked as favorite sites. New technologies have insinuated themselves into our lives at an astonishing pace, but industrial relations academics and professionals have not had many years to reflect on the impact of this movement on important processes within our field. We asked scholars, practitioners, union officials, and lawyers to join us in assembling a book that addresses the intersection of technology and employment.

This book is divided into three sections. Each section consists of a blend of case studies, overviews, practitioner insights, and scholarly reflection. Together, the chapters in each section suggest important questions for both the practice and study of employment.

I. Information Technology and Unions

The first section examines the impact of information technology on unions. Chapters 2 and 3 capture the insights of union insiders Sam Pizzigati, Barbara Yentzer, and Ronald D. Henderson of the National Education Association and Robert E. Lucore of the International Brotherhood of Teamsters. In frank discussions, the authors assess their unions' experiences with new technologies. A quarter-century ago, NEA leadership and staff essentially dismissed high-tech as merely a set of tools, albeit expensive ones, for streamlining NEA's existing operations, from processing memberships to keeping financial records. Today, NEA's top leaders are enormously attentive to computer people. NEA insiders are currently debating the association's digital options with such urgency and earnestness that one might think that the survival of the union depended on the choices they make. Crafting a successful strategy, NEA has learned from the school of hard cyber knocks. Initially, computerization led to efficiencies in administrative tasks such as word processing and designing communications devices such as leaflets. It increased the ability of union staff to access each other and exchange information. Membership records could be consolidated and updated more easily. With e-mail and the Internet came a huge upsurge in the capacity of unions to communicate with members and keep in touch with local affiliates. Then, as technology evolved, the idea of creating a union hub, an Internet site to attract hits from members and potential activists, became paramount. Internet designers created attractive and compelling websites.

One of the main insights from the Pizzigati, Yentzer, and Henderson chapter is that some unions became enamored by the Internet's vast potential but erred initially in treating it as an end product, hoping that "if we build it, they will come." Members didn't come, or to be more precise, they did but not more than a few times and certainly not enough to justify the expenditures on the Internet. To treat the union website as passive and put the onus on members to actively seek it out was the incorrect approach. Years of subsequent learning reveals that the Internet is most effective when it is used as an active channel of communication, when the union uses it to reach out to members with customized messages based on members' interests and demographic clusters. Readers will be fascinated by the historic progression and cogent examples offered by these authors about the role of unions such as the NEA and the Teamsters in the complex and competitive information age.

As we catch our breaths over the rapidity of technological change even within unions, it is helpful to offer empirical findings about the Internet world. In chapter 4, Charles R. Greer presents the findings of in-depth examinations of major union websites, supplemented by a content analysis of sixty-four union websites. Further insights are gleaned from interviews with unions' information technology professionals. Greer finds that political activism and collective bargaining functions are widely posted on websites, but unions make less use of the Web to solicit input from members or establish greater two-way communication. Despite the potential of the Internet, unions predominantly use their institutions' main websites merely to disseminate information.

Chapters 5 and 6 conclude the section on unions with a debate on the effectiveness of the Internet for unions. Two authors have very different perspectives. In chapter 5, Arthur B. Shostak argues that labor's best hope for resurgence rests within a group of cyber-savvy unions that make full use of the new technologies to revitalize organizing, servicing, and political action functions. Written in the "jolts" style of the new "digerati," Shostak clearly acknowledges the segmentation that exists among unions based on their use of new technologies. Cyber-naught unions offer only flat and uninspired messages on the Internet and have little attraction to technology breakthroughs. Cyber Drift unions may have high hopes, but their implementation of technology leads to frustration and crippling infrastructure problems. Shostak hopes that another wave of technological change that emphasizes the transactional potential of the Internet will offer those unions that adopt it a tremendous life-giving infusion (see also Lee, 1997; Taylor, 2001). By contrast, in chapter 6, Gary N. Chaison is unconvinced that harnessing the new technologies will create an appreciable turn-around in labor's fortunes. Indeed, he worries that the attention to technology is diversionary and that scarce organizing resources will be siphoned off to be used for various technology boondoggles. Unions were not early entrants into Internet technologies, and unions have no particular competitive advantage, nor are there any barriers to entry that would preserve union marketing efforts.

Assessing the impact of the Internet on unions is not an easy task. Scholars have just started the task of assembling and analyzing the data, and their findings are not yet conclusive (see, for example, Fiorito, Jarley and Delaney, 2002; Fiorito and Bass, 2002). We began thinking about the effects of the Internet on unions and industrial relations in a rather roundabout way, through a variety of incidents. Last year, Taras needed to speak to the president of a large union whose staff was unionized by a different union and was striking him. She called his office and was informed by a voice messaging system that the support staff was engaged in a lawful strike and would not be operating his office. Unthinkingly, she quickly located his personal e-mail address and sent him a message of some mundane matter or other, that is, would he speak to her university class? It struck Taras afterwards: had she just used the new technologies to break an electronic picket line? We think so now but perhaps can assuage her bruised morals because she was trying to maintain contact with a union president and because she was not yet ready to confront the dilemmas of a new age. We are still not ready, and competing insights are hitting us faster than answers or even solid hypotheses. Through chapters 2 to 6, we seek some empirical grounding in assessing those new developments that clearly engender lively debate and highly speculative approaches.

The new technologies are accessible to many different constituencies — unions, employers, labor boards, courts and tribunals, and the rank-and-file — with few barriers to use. Taras belongs to a faculty union, and there also is a large support staff union on campus. They all operate in a computer Intranet system provided by her university. The last two rounds of bargaining for the support staff in particular were acrimonious, and what was most unusual to our eyes was the extent to which the union members used the Intranet to blast the union. The vitriol appearing on the computer screens put the union on the defensive. The rank-and-file can now communicate with each other directly, without the use of the union as intermediary. The very accessibility of the Intranet to union members is a double-edged sword for unions: while it allows unions direct and unfiltered communication to members to build solidarity, it also empowers dissident factions to make ratification of the recommendations of bargaining committees difficult and challenge the activities of union officials. In the electronic age, union democracy does not necessarily mean life is easier for unions (Finnamore, 2000), and we see this finding also in some of the chapters. While unions such as the United Food and Commercial Workers can use the Internet to promote collective bargaining in campaigns to win Wal-Mart or Borders employees, the Internet can also be turned against union organizing by corporations wishing to campaign directly with employees and even by union members wishing to challenge union officials and reform union processes. For example, see www.heretics.net, www.cupewatch.org, www.ufcw. net, www.reapinc.org. North American companies are using a low-cost "investigator" program that records computer activity by employees and scans for keywords such as "union" or "boss," pinpointing potential union organizing hot spots (Teel, 2000). The Internet also provides a clearinghouse for labor market information of interest to workers, including job postings. The technology is only a proxy: it is as active or passive, good or evil, as those who operate it.

But doesn't the technology itself have its own dynamics? With the lure of the computer on our desks at both home and work, we are much more tempted to drop a line of encouragement or criticism to our own unions than we would have in the past. Back then, we would never have taken the time to write a formal letter or make a face-to-face appointment. But now the barricades have fallen, and there is a new permeability between individuals and their institutions. E-mail has a more informal, chatty, cavalier feel to it than past communication methods. We can and do jump over multiple levels of hierarchy to send a message directly to a top official rather than following a traditional chain of command. Why bother with our shop steward when we can take our cases to the top? Unions are inundated with messages from their constituents, and managing the information flow is a challenge.

Similarly, union members are bombarded by messages from marketers, friends, coworkers, politicians, charities, and so many social causes that the union's message can so easily be lost among all the competing calls on our attention. Some unions that have high hopes that all it takes to mobilize workers is an attractive website will be lost in the dust while others will develop more effective uses of the new technology. Shostak believes that union resurgence will arise from these latter techno-savvy unions. Meanwhile, Chaison reminds us that monitoring and adapting technologies is an expensive and time-consuming task: in expending their resources on technology, unions must not assume the Internet is a substitute for action. Rather, the Internet merely complements traditional union activities, and there is little reason to expect unions to be able to ride this new technology beast to victory.

There are generational issues here as well. Professors frequently ask students to access websites for their research and for class discussion. Employers ask their juniors to locate information. We are startled by the extent to which our young students and employees have harsh criticisms of websites that we find quite satisfactory. They say that the linkages are not easy to follow, that the visual imagery is outdated and embarrassing, that the contents are less than compelling. The standard is high among technology consumers, and there is little tolerance for poor craftsmanship. In order to capture the potential of new technologies, unions (never known for being at the forefront of information age technology) are required to measure up to the highest standards of Internet design. We posit that it is not that unions will gain much by adopting the new technologies, but rather, they will lose a great deal by failing to adopt them. New workers will expect readily accessible and relevant information in electronic form. Unions are being asked to make a rapid transition from the industrial age to the information age just to keep up with the marketplace of ideas. The consequences to unions, beneficial and otherwise, form the core of this dynamic section on employee voice and unions.

II. Individual Employee Power, Identity, and Mobilization

The next five chapters examine the effect of remote communication technology on workers. They ask: to what extent do workers who have ready-access incorporate their new technology into (1) their sense of self-definition and class solidarity; (2) their relationship with their employers; (3) their propensity to unionize; and (4) their job action if unionized?

This section opens with Mark Poster's provocative chapter "Workers as Cyborgs." He argues that networked computing alters the very essence of human labor in ways that cannot be articulated clearly but are discerned at a more instinctual level. For example, cyberspace exists as a work venue, but most humans do not have the capacity to understand it or enter it in any meaningful way. We simply have sensory limitations that prevent us from following the high-speed microworld of the computer. Further, the contested terrain of the worksite, with its power relations and interpersonal rivalries, has moved into the world of information technologies. Companies struggle to find technologies that limit the expression of dissent among workers, but, increasingly, companies acknowledge that they cannot constrain the astonishing capacity of the Web to act as the repository of human expressions. Poster discusses the fascinating consequence of computer technologies, that workers have lost their artisanal "touch" and now work "cognitively rather than sensually." Certainly, a keyboard is more antiseptic than a pen, and a voice-recognition program is not a conversation. But Poster goes further than this simple point, arguing that the digital economy organizes production around the partnership of humans with information machines. The future of this partnership is unknown. As he puts it, "cultural change of this sort is difficult, disorienting and confusing." In this thoughtful postmodern perspective on computer technologies, Poster supplies us with the key insights fueling this discourse on the future of labor in the networked age.

Anthony Townsend's chapter 8 examines how the rise of the electronic village changes the way individuals think about themselves and their class. He identifies that the Internet brings a new opportunity for communication to individuals who are no longer bounded by the reach of their physical environment. Does the ability of individuals to move beyond their neighborhoods to embrace an electronic village create fundamental changes to the notion of class, collective action, and solidarity?

Chapter 9 by Daphne Taras and A. Gesser examines how a Web-based organization offers an effective means by which similarly situated junior lawyers exchange information about their compensation and develop strategies for increasing their bargaining power. The focus is on one of the world's most educated, well-paid, hard-working, and disliked workforces. Their story is not likely to make lawyers more endearing, but it does highlight that even the most elite and well-compensated workers may decry their wretched employment conditions.

In a nutshell, here is the story told by Taras and Gesser: in an abrupt departure from the traditional expectation of feudal loyalty to their mentoring partners, firms, and occupations, legal associates in the world's largest law firms took to the Web to air their grievances. This chapter describes the institutional context that allowed this phenomenon to develop, including the sudden emergence of a free-agency norm, the rapidly diminishing dream of making partnership, and a wage bubble that carried compensation to new levels as traditional law firms struggled to retain legal talent against a competitive onslaught launched by Silicon Valley high-tech firms. Among associates in the behemoth law firms of New York, the pressure for billable hours increased, and their relations with their partners eroded. In this environment, associates became hyper-vigilant about discrepancies among firms. Many associates began to experience anger at their employers and a burning injustice at the entire employment structure of big law firms. The Internet became their mechanism to maximize short-term payoffs as compensation for the barely tolerable working conditions and to pay down the large student loans that had allowed them to become lawyers in the first place. The Internet website, "greedyassociates.com" (GA) is a compelling example of employee self-empowerment. It is an electronic insurrection involving little personal risk and the prospect of considerable reward.

The Taras and Gesser chapter asks whether Internet-based vehicles are a new form of collective organization or merely a new mechanism propping up an old system of individual bargaining among professionals. Clearly, new lawyers adopted the Internet to gather salient information about employment, information that once was available only to employers. But despite some bluster, they are not behaving in concert and rarely are using the techniques that indicate collective action. The GA was not the first step in a movement towards a more permanent organizational structure to represent lawyers. Whether the appropriate collective should be a union, a professional association, or an issue-based lobby group is moot, as the GA became none of those things. Instead, it evolved to be the marketing tool to give a greater number of Internet hits to a legal service and product-distribution firm.

There are many other examples of the use of the Internet by nonunion employees to increase their power and highlight issues of concern to them (described in Diamond and Freeman, 2002). Alliance@IBM (www.allianceibm.org) was formed in 1999 in response to protests over unilateral changes in the company's pension systems. Alliance@IBM has developed a greater organizational structure than the GA site. Alliance has members and subscribers and seems to be developing into a sustainable website that allows enhanced voice among IBM workers. Like the GA, it achieved noteworthy victories. Unlike the GA, it built an alliance with a major national union, the Communication Workers of America, and the website clearly is designed for union organizing. Another example of employees' grassroots action is WashTech (www.washtech.org), also now associated with the CWA union. Whereas Alliance@IBM is based on a group's relationship with a single large employer, WashTech is more like the GA site in that it represents an occupational grouping. WashTech represents Silicon Valley and related high-tech workers. It examined the issue of overtime pay, and it developed direct services to its constituency group, including discounted-cost training courses, contract advice, and legislative advocacy. It delivers an Internet digest of news and maintains a confidential subscriber list. Both Alliance@IBM and WashTech overtly ask their computer users to sign union cards that would count as a precondition to a National Labor Relations Board-scrutinized union election. A union-affiliated website for high-tech workers outside the United States was launched by the Australian New South Wales Labour Council (www.itworkers-alliance.org). The Labour Council secretary admitted that this effort was not part of "attempting to recruit members up front — rather to create a culture that workers will want to be part of . . . " (cited in Diamond and Freeman, from www.itworkers-alliance.org/news/general/7.html). The lawyers' GA site was never attached formally or even informally to union activities or any particular union or professional association, whereas Alliance@IBM, WashTech, and ITWorkers are formally tied to union organizing.

Evidently, there is a great deal of Internet use by employees seeking to improve their knowledge of employment practices and compensation trends, access relevant job market information, and seek other similar employees with whom to communicate. Unions are well aware of these activities. Unions sometimes spearhead them. But to what extent does employee use of the Internet for employment-related purposes portend collective action and indicate a propensity to form groups for the purpose of collective bargaining? Can unions actually harness these developments?

Chapter 10 by Laurie Milton is an important contribution to theory development on union propensity. She examines the identity dimensions of unionization among high-tech workers. She outlines an identity-oriented theory of unionization based on three key points about human behavior: (1) People try to create and sustain social and psychological environments that are consistent with their identities; (2) People evaluate the notion of unionizing according to its compatibility with their self-concepts; and (3) People identify with organizations that preserve their self-concepts. These points stand in marked contrast to the conventional union instrumentality assessments provided in much of the mainstream industrial relations assessments of union propensity. Traditional scholarly treatments usually focus on the capacity of unions to deliver tangible gains in the terms and conditions of employment. Using the conventional union instrumentality arguments in the context of high-tech workers, we might conclude that high-tech workers may not need unions because they have few issues of concern, or the issues of concern may be better addressed through other vehicles. Perhaps these workers already perceive themselves to have a voice at work. Perhaps they dislike adversarial union-management relations. Perhaps they would rather switch than fight: they often find it easier to exit the firm and find another better job in this highly volatile industry than to derail their energies into a struggle to improve employment conditions. In any case, sufficient numbers of high-tech workers have stayed away from unions to keep the industry virtually union-free. Using identity-based treatment, Milton adds a whole other dimension to our understanding of the chasm that exists between high-tech workers and unions and demonstrates the enormous uphill battle faced by unions trying to make inroads among high-tech workers.

Milton examines the employment conditions among high-tech workers and finds that they often lack the opportunity structures to permit collective action. They lack long-term attachment to employers, and their careers are marked by rapid movement that provides new challenges. She then conducted exploratory interviews of eight high-tech workers in four companies. These interviews provided more detailed findings about their occupational attachments, working conditions, and sense of self. High-tech workers claim to be mentally engaged by the tasks at hand and lack the time and inclination to divert their attention to other matters within the scope of unions. They have a strong sense of individual self-efficacy in negotiating employment conditions and terms and believe in their job mobility. Although the adrenaline rush of the high-tech industry has been shattered by the industry's doldrums, these workers retain an occupational image based on merit, creativity, and pride in their work.

High-tech workers were effusive about their self-concept as free agents (or in their own vernacular, "e-lancers") and spoke at length about their occupational attachment. By contrast, when asking questions about unions, Milton was met with "silence," even "prolonged silence." Eventually she was told about those aspects of unions that are impossible for high-tech workers to reconcile with their self-concept. Unions were described by high-tech workers as stodgy, inflexible and anti-creative. But here is her main point: unions were viewed as antithetical and possibly damaging to high-tech workers' self-image. Support for unions would be "tantamount to killing a dream." Not only would they be unlikely to unionize, Milton demonstrates that there is so much identity incompatibility that high-tech workers would *avoid* unionizing.

Hence for high-tech workers, the union propensity continuum is not from neutral to positive (as in conventional union instrumentality tests), or from no perceived utility to high perceived utility (as labor economists might label the points). An identity-based analysis allows us to examine union propensity on a new and fuller continuum that captures a range from repulsion to attraction. Perhaps future research might even determine whether there are multiple distinct constructs that exist within the union propensity realm, and one of the most important of the constructs surely should be based on worker identity and self-concept. Against this theory-building backdrop, we can return to our earlier discussion of GA and the union-supported websites such as WashTech and Alliance@IBM to assess the fit between the self-concept of the target audience and the message disseminated in the website. Milton argues that the success of the effort is directly related to its appeal to the core of the workers' identity. The better the match, the greater the appeal, and the more successful the vehicle at mobilizing its audience.

Chapter 11 by Vicki Barnett is a superb case study that could be used to explore Milton's identity-based theorizing. Barnett was a participant in a lengthy, bitter, and unusually technologically savvy strike among Canadian journalists. The chapter is a first-person account of the use and impact of technology during a strike that ultimately failed to achieve a first collective agreement. Reading the Barnett chapter immediately after Milton's elucidation of an identity perspective is a rare treat. The extent to which editorial workers found the means and methods to create identity congruence between their occupational affiliation as journalists and their collective action as strikers is a clear affirmation of Milton's thesis.

In the *Herald* strike described by Barnett, journalists saw themselves as "professional communicators." On strike for the first time in a bargaining unit newly-certified by the large national Communications, Energy and Paperworkers Union (CEP), they were able to harness their journalistic talents and energies and the norms of their profession. They had tremendous comfort with technology and with communication going into the strike. Their "in-house expertise" led to the development and maintenance of a professional-quality strike website. They created a "cyber picket line" among journalists and used the technology to maintain solidarity in this nasty labor dispute. Barnett describes the use of the Web, e-mail, cell phone, and even Globo lights, all in pursuit of bargaining power against an employer who had the resources and resolve to break the union.

As Barnett wrote, it is difficult to win when employees get into a war with someone who buys his ink by the barrel and newsprint by the ton. There was little of a level playing field between the *Herald* workers and the communication chain — although Barnett does not elaborate on this point, modern technology also aided the employer greatly. The newspaper was able to continue operations by filling the news hole with wire copy from other newspapers in the chain and from subscriptions to international wire services. In addition, replacement workers filled any remaining void in local coverage. The striking journalists' only hope was to persuade the public to boycott the *Herald*, and towards this end, they made the most of modern technology. Electronic communication also was used to raise solidarity among strikers, demoralize those who crossed the picket line, and expose the foibles of management. (We see evidence in other settings of use of the Internet to post names of workers who cross picket lines. See Bodor, 2000 for a description of the Massachusetts Nurses Association's use of technology and the "Scabs Exposed" website). In the end, despite the journalists' union's valiant fight over many months, the union suffered an ignominious defeat. There was no first contract; the union won no bargaining rights. The *Herald* journalists today are nonunion, and only a vestige of the striking workers remains employed at the *Herald*. But among committed strikers, there was tremendous pride in the journalistic craft, a certain pleasurable wiliness, and an enhancement of the communications crafts with the adoption of new techniques. The CEP Union itself learned new techniques that might be put to use in strikes elsewhere with a greater likelihood of achieving negotiated contracts.

Perhaps the Taras and Gesser and the Barnett chapters are extreme cases of ill-will in the employment relationship, but we think not. Employees do not mobilize in large numbers and spend their time posting messages on the Web without considerable provocation. As a vehicle for the expression of voice, the Internet allows for new levels of rancor, and we see this in so many protest-based Internet sites. This point is in contrast to some of the assertions made by those who market products on the Web. For example, online dispute resolution systems (e.g. www.cybersettle.com) provide mediation and arbitration services, offering security, privacy, and a blind bidding system to settle disputes without face-to-face interaction. The company that first developed this system asserts in its advertising that "Because Cybersettle participants communicate only via the Internet, personality conflicts, posturing, and positioning are eliminated." Both the Taras and Gesser and the Barnett chapters would dispute this naïve view of Internet-based communication. Depending on the wishes of the message poster, the Internet can broadcast to the world the degree to which parties in a dispute are willing to draw harsh lines around positions and ridicule and damage each other. The gloves can come off as easily on the Internet as in person.

III. Information Technology and Employers: Emerging Policy and Privacy Issues

"You can observe a lot just by watching," said Yogi Berra. At one time, employees worked in physical proximity to "the boss," whose close supervision and monitoring were thought to be essential to ensure the proper pace and conduct of work. Employees were watched. They were coached, trained, rebuked, disciplined, praised, promoted, or discharged. If they told the boss "to go to hell" — one of the important motivations for unionization — they could be fired.

Much has changed and much has not. "The boss" may be a complex assortment of wires and microscopic circuitry. The span of supervision may have increased exponentially from a handful of subordinates to hundreds or even thousands of workers in remote locations. But the desire, the will, and the ability to monitor employee performance persist as a central feature of the employment relationship. And employees still react to protect themselves from intrusiveness. They personally may not tell the boss where to go, but they certainly ask their unions and their lawyers to impart this message.

There are legal and moral issues. We asked our chapter contributors to be oracles, commentators, and analysts. What are the big issues? How has the always-delicate balance that exists between the employed and their employers adapted to the new technologies? We also asked our contributors to grapple with identifying what actually is new about these technologies. Why are they different than, say, the telephone or fax (both of which also are subject to abuse)? What are the unique legal and public policy issues?

Anthony Townsend and James Bennett begin this section in chapter 12 by introducing the main issues. They posit that information and telecommunication technologies are not merely helpful tools to raise productivity and enhance information exchange. Rather, "they actually *become* the work environment." They also absorb many private uses into the employer-sponsored system, leaving a permanent Web-trail of usage and content. Legal issues also differentiate new technologies. In particular, because employer-operated systems are exempt from privacy protections, there is the potential for invasive surveillance. Townsend and Bennett establish the remarkable level of intrusion that has become commonplace in employment settings and argue that the current situation cannot continue unabated. They predict that remediation (either by statute or through employee action) will establish a more "livable equilibrium between legitimate organizational interests in employee activities and employee expectations regarding an acceptable level of individual privacy." They also discuss the role of the union movement in responding to concerns about privacy rights and monitoring.

In chapter 13, Dennis Nolan claims that the use of computers to monitor employee performance merely is an extension of earlier methods of observing employees at work. Old wine in new bottles is the theme. But he points out the important differences that make the new technologies significantly more intrusive. First, they challenge our notion of proportionality. Employer ability to put employees under surveillance extends well beyond any reasonable just cause standard. In the old days of close supervision by a human, there was a limit to how many employees could be observed or how many Pinkerton guards could be hired. By contrast, networked computers allow almost instantaneous monitoring of vast numbers of people engaged in multitudes of different activities. Second, the new technologies cross hierarchy boundaries. Professionals, long exempt from close scrutiny, are now using computerized billing methods and also are being monitored for their productivity. Third, there is not yet sufficient discretion and sensitivity within modern Internet screening to sensibly conduct the task of sorting information. All kinds of people are caught in randomly cast nets. The negative consequences of clumsy screening may well negate the benefits. Fourth, the new technologies are particularly adept at catching employees accessing pornography, and the thrust of employer response seems to be directed at allegedly immoral behavior. Whereas private sexually oriented behavior was quite difficult for employers to monitor using conventional means, it is now exceedingly easy to track access to pornographic websites, passing offensive e-mails, and the other detritus of technological use.

Nolan asks questions as well about why employers engage in wholesale investigations and restrictions. He contrasts the public reasons (e.g., profitability concerns, security issues, fear of vicarious liability) with the private reasons (e.g., curiosity, morality, and union avoidance). Adding credence to his concerns that employers are using technology to regulate morality is the instructive fact that few employees are dismissed for simply wasting work time by repeated use of Internet games or virtual shopping. By contrast, punishment is meted out swiftly when sex is involved. Perhaps, as Nolan argues, sex is a special category of sin. But Nolan also warns us that the "search for a single explanation is unfairly reductionist. No doubt most employers act out of a host of motives, some real, some exaggerated, some questionable, and some quite unconscious." Nolan then addresses the state of American law, policy, and employer behavior using an analysis of relevant cases and statutes. Given the pervasiveness of the new technologies and the laws, what is an employee's reasonable expectation of privacy? Savvy employees know that the answer is "not much." And "given the state of the law, it would be a strange employer indeed that opted to protect employee privacy rather than to invade it." These days, employers are urged by their lawyers to adopt extremely restrictive and intrusive electronic communications policies. Nolan recommends a more balanced approach in which employers adopt greater restraint while employees are made aware of employers' expectations and methods.

Chapter 14 by David Corry and Kim Nutz addresses the struggle between privacy rights and management rights that underpins the employment terrain. Their review of jurisprudence is based on the Canadian setting, but some issues extend well beyond national borders. Employers naturally wish to prevent new forms of employee misconduct — or rather, old forms (such as harassment, inappropriate sexuality at the workplace, and so on) in new guises, enabled by technology. In tone, the Corry and Nutz chapter is more employer focused; this is unremarkable given that these authors practice on the management side of the labor law bar in one of Canada's largest law firms. This chapter provides a helpful overview of the legal issues, including the onus on employers to provide a workplace free from discrimination and harassment. Clearly, free access to technology allows employee behavior that ranges from only slightly vexatious to highly odious and even criminal. They review additional important issues, such as the confidentiality protection necessary for employers to maintain trade secrets and other proprietary information. The use of new technologies is pulling fields of law such as copyright, intellectual property, and defamation into the labor law arena. The authors describe a great many cases and fact situations that challenge or extend traditional jurisprudence. Corry and Nutz then turn their attention to the development and content of workplace policies — with emphasis on the importance of clear and concise policies, communicated to employees with warnings as to penalties for violations — and to the broader Canadian public policy approach. Internet-based union organizing in the context of Canadian statutes and corporate Internet use policies is a perplexing topic. Canadian labor boards are struggling to find the delicate balance that exists between free speech for both employees and employers and union organizing.

Sometimes, the larger social context also spills over onto the employment stage. The role of technology in the post 9/11 security-conscious world and the use of computer records to investigate various stock market scandals both have cascading effects on employment relations. Homeland security employees (many of them unionized) are being hired by the thousands. New technology is no respecter of status when the political mood swings sharply against corporate executives suspected of engaging in illegal activities. Top bosses are caught making inappropriate use of the Internet; illegal stock trades are recorded; insider information is captured, and executives are discovered accessing pornography in violation of corporate policies.

To illustrate the theme that management policies have adapted to new technologies with considerable vigor (particularly since they enable an old and entrenched practice of monitoring performance), we created Table 1. It contrasts the actual employment policies of an American firm in 1833 with an amalgam of contemporary practices. The issues are similar. However, the contemporary setting incorporates an expansive statutory framework, as the three last chapters describe. Carefully reading Table 1 makes us wonder whether we have moved very far from the company town or village life. Perhaps we now live in technology-enabled virtual company towns.

These chapters leave no doubt that employees can have little expectation of privacy when accessing the new technologies. But employees often err. The best illustration of this point is the interface between technology and sex. Do the new technologies, their placement on personal desks and at home, create the illusion of privacy? For example, websites are freely accessed for pornography by a great number of people. Whereas calling a 900 number for pornographic phone calls results in an identifiable financial charge, a "networked personal computer" (is this an oxymoron?) seems to lull the user into a false sense of security. The pervasiveness of technology, and its extension into all facets of life, is a recurrent issue.

The second major theme that emerges from this third section is that technology enables its owners to do what they have always done, only to a greater scale (although not necessarily better). Employers monitor employee performance, as they have always done. Unions organize and engage in political activities, as they have always done. And employees continue to use paid time and employer-provided equipment to meet their work requirements and engage in non-work activities. Although each author identified unique features of the new technologies, none isolated any particularly revolutionary uses in the employment arena. Each author grappled with the delicate balance among such values as productivity, trust, privacy, and freedom.

Among the many questions that remain open for investigation are:

- With such enormous strides in the ability to gather information and monitor access, how do we distinguish between legitimate versus nonlegitimate uses for employers, employees, and unions? What is the appropriate balance?
- Are the gains to unions of using new technologies offset by the ability of employers and individual employees to make countervailing use of the same technologies? Is the technology enhancing collective action and changing behavior, or is it merely allowing us to do what we have always done, only faster?
- What are the best employer policies and practices that respect employees while ensuring productive use of paid time?
- To what extent are new technologies being used to regulate morality? Should they be used this way?
- What is the role of unions in the interface between employees and employers? What are unions' own needs in using technology to mobilize workers?
- Are new legal doctrines developing, or are we merely extending the existing reasoning into a new domain?
- What are the appropriate public policy responses? To what extent should "the state" regulate the use of technology in employment matters?

In the final analysis, the many chapters in this volume document the introduction and very early-stage effects of information and communication technologies on employment. It is too soon to make any firm conclusions. The ability to raise good questions is the main contribution of this volume.

Table 1
The Evolution of Managerial Policies

General Regulations To Be Observed by Persons Employed by the Lawrence Manufacturing Company (Lowell, Massachusetts, 1833)	Modern Corporate Policies To Be Observed by Persons Employed by Large Employers in North America (2004)
1st. All persons in the employ of the Company, are required to attend assiduously to their various duties, or labor, during working hours; are expected to be fully competent, or to aspire to the upmost [sic] efficiency in the work or business they may engage to perform, and to evince on all occasions, in their deportment and conversation, a laudable regard for temperance, virtue, and their moral and social obligations; and in which the Agent will endeavor to set a proper example. No person can be dissolute, indolent, dishonest, or intemperate, or who habitually absent themselves from public worship, and violate the Sabbath, or who may be addicted to gambling of any kind.	1st. All employees must be engaged in company purposes when on company property and when using technology provided by the company; Neither the e-mail system or the Web should be used to transmit pornographic, profane or sexually explicit or otherwise offensive materials. No person can access pornography or other materials offensive to minorities or likely to create vicarious liability to the employer. The company shall circulate a formal policy in an endeavor to set a proper example and limit employer liability. All employees must read and abide by the policy as a condition of employment. While some tolerance may be shown by the employer for the playing of "Free Cell" and "Solitaire" and the accessing of "E-Bay" and exchange of innocuous pleasantries with friends, any interactions involving immorality and impropriety shall be grounds for discipline up to and including discharge from employment.
2d. All kinds of ardent spirit will be excluded from the Company's ground, except it be prescribed for medicine, or for washes, and external applications. Every kind of gambling and card-playing, is totally prohibited within the limits of the Company's ground and Board house.	
3d. Smoking cannot be permitted in the Mills, or other buildings, or yards, and should not be carelessly indulged in the Board Houses and streets . . .	2nd. Employees working in safety-sensitive positions or engaged in inter-state or international transport may be randomly tested for drug and alcohol use. Other employees may be tested to the extent that their employers establish cause.
(Source: Excerpted from William Cahn, *A Pictorial History of American Labor*. New York: Crown Publisher, 1972. p. 49; as cited in Thomas A. Kochan and Harry C. Katz, *Collective Bargaining and Industrial Relations*, Irwin, 1988, 2nd edition, p. 21)	3rd. Smoking cannot be permitted in the main buildings, stairwells, or cafeteria except in designated areas and then only as permitted by prevailing municipal, state or provincial laws.

Penalties for violations may depend on the
extent to which employees can establish
that they have addictions, dependencies,
disabilities, or another officially recognized status that is protected from discrimination under the prevailing human rights
laws.

(Source: Crafted by D. Taras based on
jurisprudence and company policies.)

References

Bodor, Jim. "Non-Strikers' Names Posted on Web Site." *Telegram & Gazette*, Worcester, MA, 5 April 2000, A1.
Cybersettle.com. "Fact Sheet." Corporate brochure. New York. Distributed 2001.
Diamond, W. M., and R. B. Freeman. "Will Unionism Prosper in CyberSpace? The Promise of the Internet for Employee Organisation." *British Journal of Industrial Relations* 40, 3 (2002.): 569–96.
Finnamore, Hugh. "Labour Reform Day: The Union Members' Revolt." *Financial Post*, 2 September 2000, D11.
Fiorito, Jack, Paul Jarley, and John T. Delaney. "Information Technology, Union Organizing and Union Effectiveness." *British Journal of Industrial Relations* 40, 4 (2002): 627–58.
Fiorito, Jack, and W. Bass. "The Use of Information Technology by National Unions: An Exploratory Analysis." *Industrial Relations* 41(2002): 34–47.
Lee, Eric. *The Labour Movement and the Internet: The New Internationalism*. London: Pluto Press, 1997.
Taylor, Robert. "Inside Track: Workers Unite on the Internet." *Financial Times*, 11 May 2001.
Teel, Gina. "Alberta Firms Keep Covert Tabs on Workers." *Calgary Herald*, 22 May 2000, A1, A2.

2

The School of Hard Cyber Knocks: NEA's Experience

Sam Pizzigati, Barbara Yentzer, and Ronald D. Henderson
National Education Association

I. Introduction

A quarter-century ago, "information technology" held little interest for most leaders and staff within the National Education Association. Leadership and staff essentially dismissed "high tech" as merely a set of tools, albeit expensive ones, for streamlining NEA's existing operations, from processing memberships to keeping financial records. Real trade unionists didn't pay much attention to what all those computer people were doing. Real trade unionists bargained and organized and lobbied and rallied.

Today, a generation later, NEA's top leaders and staff pay enormous attention to computer people. In fact, they've become computer people themselves, incorporating digital technology, everything from e-mail to PowerPoint, into their daily lives in ways that would have been unimaginable back in 1975.

But the impact of the Information Age on NEA has actually gone far beyond these changes in daily work habits. Association leaders and staffers are currently debating the Association's digital options with such urgency and earnestness that a casual observer might think that the survival of the union depended on the choices they make. That casual observer would not be mistaken. The technology choices the Association makes, many NEA leaders and staff have indeed come to believe, *will* determine NEA's future.

In the emerging new Information Age, these activists feel strongly, new technologies are transforming both how NEA members do their work and how they relate to the organizations that seek to meet their needs. These organizations either need to transform themselves to meet these new realities — and opportunities — or write themselves off.

The National Education Association is, of course, not unique. Every union today faces new Information Age dynamics. But NEA has been facing these dynamics for considerably longer than most of the rest of American labor. Schools and colleges, the workplaces of NEA members, were among the first institutions in American life to experience a massive influx of digital and cyber technology. Many NEA members, as a result, started using computers and going online, both at work and at home, before cyberspace became a mass phenomenon. This long experience with computer- and cyber-savvy members may make NEA, the nation's largest union, also the union well situated to reflect on labor's prospects and potential in the Information Age.

This reflection — about how unions ought to use information technology in general and cyberspace specifically — is seriously needed within the labor movement. A new generation, after all, is stepping into American workplaces, bringing with it Information Age expectations shaped at school and home. Trade unions already feel pressured by these new expectations. Many have rushed to "go online," and today hardly any union of any size or significance lacks a website. But rushing into cyber activity, before carefully thinking through an organizational strategy, can quickly distract a union from its core mission. Unions that race to ramp up online operations can find themselves eating up resources at shockingly rapid rates — and disappointing the very cyber-savvy members they seek to reach.

A carefully crafted cyber strategy, on the other hand, can help a union deepen and broaden contact with members and the public, increase the value members perceive in membership, and realize important organizational efficiencies.

Crafting a successful strategy, NEA has learned from the school of hard cyber knocks, demands thorough thinking in four key areas. In other words, we argue that there is a continuum from a rudimentary strategy to a well-developed Information Age.

- The ownership of an organization's cyber presence. In a developing cyber union, members visit a union's cyber presence when they want to know what the union thinks or is doing. Members consider the union's site something that belongs to the union. In a developed cyber union, individual members come to feel that the site created by the union is their site, because the site focus is on helping individual members both in their work and in their lives.
- The content an organization's presence presents. In a developing cyber union, the content presented on a union's website is developed by union staffers or leaders. This content is often largely repurposed from material originally prepared for print. In a developed cyber union, members themselves also generate content of value.
- The level of interactivity a presence promotes. In a developing cyber union, the union "interacts" with members by soliciting information from them. In a developed cyber union, the union both solicits information from members and enables members to exchange information and ideas with others.
- The impact of the cyber presence on an organization's ongoing business operations. In a developing cyber union, information technology is beginning to make some traditional union activities easier to do. In a developed cyber union, cyber work is actually transforming the union's traditional business practices.

Understanding how NEA came to appreciate these four points demands a much closer look at NEA's actual experience in cyberspace over the last dozen years.

II. One Organization's Odyssey: An NEA Case Study

NEA is a 145-year-old national organization, with 2.6 million members organized into over 13,000 local and 51 state affiliates. More than 70 percent of the nation's public school teachers are NEA members, and also included in the Association's membership ranks are over 300,000 education support personnel — from cafeteria workers to school bus drivers — as well as college faculty and staff.

In most states, NEA local affiliates do the same sort of work that any local union does. NEA locals bargain contracts, handle grievances, and conduct job actions of various sorts. But NEA members also work in communities where the labor movement literally has no presence at all. In these communities, education employees have no right to bargain and no contract to enforce. In short, about the only on-the-job reality that all NEA members share is an education-related employer. What work NEA members do, how well they are compensated for it, how their workplace operates, how members struggle to improve teaching and learning conditions — all these realities vary widely across the NEA membership.

Traditionally, NEA leaders and staff have worked to forge common bonds among members through a variety of communications strategies. All levels of the Association, for instance, publish regular periodicals for members. Some of these periodicals have, over the years, built large and appreciative member audiences. But all these publications, whatever their quality, share the limitations built into the print medium. Periodicals are effective vehicles for circulating information that has been gathered and processed, by editors, at a central location. Periodicals are top-down vehicles for communication: Information moves from one to many. What periodicals cannot do efficiently is help readers — the many — either communicate with each other or interact effectively with top leaders.

In the mid-1980s, a new communications medium began to emerge, with considerable potential for helping unions communicate in new ways to members. This medium, what we now commonly know as cyberspace, involved linking computers with other computers, typically via phone lines and devices called modems. By the late 1980s, thousands of NEA members had become "early adopters" of this new computer technology. Many of these members worked as the technology coordinators for their school districts or had joined local computer user clubs. This on- and off-the-job activity began to expose these NEA members to "bulletin board services" and other online communications tools. In short order, NEA staff and governance leaders started to take notice. NEA's era of online experimentation had begun.

III. Early Steps

The first initiative to emerge, beginning in the mid-1980s, was the NEA Bulletin Board Service, or the NEA BBS, as the effort was quickly dubbed. This service gave NEA members access to assorted documents as well as a forum for posting comments on message boards for all to see. For members, the service was free. All they needed to do to access the service was call a toll-free 800 number. Not many did. In absolute numbers, usage remained relatively low. The BBS basically attracted only the Association's "geek" element, those members who had become computer hobbyists either through job responsibilities or happenstance. In all, a small fraction of 1 percent of Association members ever dialed into the NEA BBS.

But those members who did dial in dialed in again and again, in the process racking up huge long-distance telephone charges for the Association. NEA's cost for maintaining the toll-free BBS access line quickly hit six figures on an annual basis. Clearly, as a cost-efficient Association strategy for sharing information, the toll-free BBS was a dead-end. The Association could never afford to underwrite, on any large scale, our members' direct, toll-free online access to their Association. By the early 1990s, the Association had regrouped for its next direction.

IV. Partnering with AOL

Our goals for this second stage were clear. We wanted to expand our online relationship with members past the BBS hobbyist base, and we wanted to stop hemorrhaging dollars. In those pre-World Wide Web days, we had only one realistic option for meeting these goals: partnering with a national computer online service. In 1992, we researched the available national online services, invited and compared proposals from these services, and ended up selecting a service that, at that time, boasted less than 100,000 subscribers nationwide.

The online service we selected, the fledgling America Online, was eager to work with NEA — and not surprisingly so. The Association offered America Online access to an audience that dwarfed AOL's own subscriber list. To gain that access, AOL agreed to give NEA members subscription discounts on the basic America Online service and to create a private cyberspace area open only to NEA members.

In early 1993, we began to "construct" this NEA member area, knowing next to nothing about what it takes to achieve online success. What we created, essentially, was a cyberspace "library," with cyber "bookshelves" full of documents that we felt would interest NEA members. We called our new private, member-only area NEA Online.

Problems surfaced almost immediately. The burden of posting content onto the cyber "bookshelves" we had created fell on NEA staffers with expertise in the particular content areas. These staff, for the most part, viewed NEA Online as an unwelcome add-on to their existing work. The predictable end result? The immense information architecture created for NEA Online remained largely static and incomplete, and users encountered the same information each time they logged on. Many second- and third-time visitors, understandably, never came back as fourth- and fifth-time visitors. Our online audience, as a result, never snowballed. New users would come on, perhaps find some information of value to them, then come back and find no additional new information of value. At that point, many would never return.

Many other NEA members never made it into NEA Online in the first place. As many as 40 percent of our members, we soon realized, lived in communities not yet accessible to America Online — or any other national online service — via a simple, free local phone call. To access NEA Online, these members had to first make a long-distance call, above and beyond the money they paid for their America Online subscription. NEA Online, in other words, placed some of our members in a situation where they would have to pay more than other members to receive the same service. This, needless to say, was an intolerable position politically for a national membership organization.

To governance leaders within the Association, hit with complaints from disadvantaged members, NEA Online didn't appear to be worth the aggravation it seemed to be creating. After two years from launch, only about 25,000 members had registered for the service, this despite a fairly extensive publicity effort within the Association, including massive giveaways of a customized NEA Online version of the America Online installation disk.

At the same time, maintaining a relationship with NEA became less of a priority for America Online executives. They had counted on NEA to help jumpstart their subscription rolls. NEA's help, it turned out, was not needed. AOL subscriber numbers began to soar, without any significant help from NEA. Over time, America Online reduced its staff time assigned to the NEA initiative, a move that only made the NEA Online site more difficult to maintain on a timely basis.

By 1995, after nearly three years of NEA Online experience, the organizational verdict was in. NEA Online was not going to become what had been hoped, a vast online area where NEA members, in organizationally significant numbers, would congregate, share, and learn together. Why did NEA Online fall so short of initial expectations? In one sense, the effort may have been premature. The society-wide "buzz" about the online world had not become loud enough for NEA Online promotions to grab member attention.

But part of our organizational failure to build member momentum behind NEA Online reflected our own imperfect understanding of the online medium. Most staff involved in creating NEA Online saw the online world as a limitless document library where members could find any information their hearts desired. This approach ignored one reality. Our members were not, by and large, interested in accessing documents. They were much more interested in connecting with their colleagues.

Fortunately, almost as a second thought, we had created within NEA Online some opportunities for members to interact, mainly through a series of online bulletin boards and chat rooms. Most users never found their way into these interactive areas. But some did, and, for these members, NEA Online actually became an appealing destination. Certain bulletin boards started flowing with interesting dialogues. Certain staff began to see they could use the online world to connect with members in ways that could facilitate the Association's traditional business operations. NEA lobbyists searching for NEA members to testify at congressional hearings, for instance, found they could post a message on an active bulletin board and generate a dozen quick leads.

Learnings like this, as valuable as they were, could not reverse NEA Online's downward trajectory. Above all else, our original premise behind partnering with America Online no longer made sense. We had assumed that, without discounted AOL subscriptions, our members would have trouble getting online. That proved not to be the case. In fact, early on, our Association members were beginning to get online through a wide variety of Internet connections, many through school-based Internet service providers. With all these alternate routes to the Internet, our private NEA Online area on AOL soon became organizationally obsolete, because members online who were not America Online subscribers could not enter it.

By 1995, the time had come for NEA's online odyssey to take another turn. Fortunately, by that same year, the cyber landscape had been transformed — by the newest Internet phenomenon, the World Wide Web. With the Web, any organization could create an online presence without having to negotiate for space with a national online service such as America Online. Indeed, by 1995, members and the public alike were beginning to expect national organizations to have their own distinct online presence, their own "dot-org" address. Every membership organization worth its dues seemed to have a web page. Where was yours?

In December 1995, after some six months of preparation, the first NEA website appeared. Unlike NEA Online, this new site was open to everyone, members and non-members alike. To some degree, this openness was forced upon us. Authenticating NEA members online, the necessary first step before we could create a member-only online area, was beyond our technical and budget means at the time.

V. Shifting to the World Wide Web

We approached this third phase of our cyber experience with no small degree of confidence. After several years of BBS and NEA Online trial and error, we felt we knew the basic cyber mistakes that needed to be avoided. In our initial web planning, we consciously aimed to *not* create:

- a site full of "brochureware"— content that simply regurgitated what was already available elsewhere in print;
- a site that mirrored our internal bureaucracy, with separate sections for each organizational department; or
- a site closed to visitor dialogue and give-and-take.

The assumption that guided our web page preparation was eminently reasonable: We believe that visitors would come to our Association online if we made our NEA website attractive and easy enough to use. We would try to keep the needs of our end users in mind and try to come up with imaginative, interactive content that would speak to these needs.

To some extent, we succeeded. Our initial website was attractive, friendly, and distinctly nonbureaucratic in tenor and tone. The site also carried some imaginative features that took advantage of the Web's interactive capacities. The site's "Thank a Teacher" section, for instance, invited web surfers to post salutes to the individual teachers who have meant the most to them over the course of their lives. This "Thank a Teacher" section soon generated fascinating dialogues that dramatized just how powerfully and positively teachers can impact students, providing, in the process, a morale-boosting experience for educators and an object lesson for the public.

This sort of interactive feature sought to address the on-the-job needs of NEA members and help build public confidence in public education, a key goal for NEA in this era of widespread attacks on public schools. Other aspects of the NEA website more directly impacted the internal workings of the union, nowhere more dramatically so than in the NEA web space devoted to the Association's most contentious internal issue, merger with NEA's historic rival, the American Federation of Teachers (AFL-CIO).

Negotiations between NEA and AFT had taken place in the 1970s, but broke down. Talks resumed in the mid-1990s and hit their stride in 1997. By February 1998, the framework of a unity agreement had been set, and both unions had scheduled votes on merger at their upcoming July 1998 conventions. Within NEA, a union proud of its democratic decision-making process, four months of discussion and debate now began. For the first time ever, this discussion and debate would include an online component.

All the key merger-related documents soon appeared online, in the NEA website, for direct member access. Also placed online was a special bulletin-board-style forum, open to all comers, where merger questions could be posed and opinions about merger debated. The opposition to merger was quick to sense this forum's value. Postings rapidly proliferated, most from critics of the merger agreement. Supporters of the merger agreement were slower on the uptake. They, in effect, let the opposition grab the momentum in an online debate, and that momentum helped give opponents increasing confidence. In the end, that confidence translated into a convention victory for the merger opposition. The impact of the online debate over merger did not, by itself, produce that victory, but the overwhelming anti-merger sentiment online did definitely prefigure the eventual convention vote.

Ironically, the same medium that advanced the anti-merger cause in the spring of 1998 later advanced the cause of cooperation between the two unions the following fall. In September, NEA and AFT jointly conducted a conference about teacher quality issues in Washington, DC. This on-site conference also became the two unions' first "virtual conference." Almost the entire conference proceedings were placed online, including audio and text transcripts of all the major speeches. Virtual registrants were even able to ask workshop leaders questions online. In all, hundreds more teachers attended the virtual than the on-site experience, and the online conference record remained online, as reference, for many months to come.

These experiments in interactivity all demonstrated, in one way or another, the potential of cyberspace to add value to traditional NEA activities. Still, by the year 2000, after over four years of experimentation, the NEA web presence had not reached anything close to a communications critical mass with NEA members. NEA members, polling showed, were indeed online, but they had not become regular visitors to NEA's web presence.

March 2000 telephone surveys made plain just how ubiquitous an activity web surfing had become among Association members. According to this survey data, 94 percent of NEA teacher members — 99 percent of those 35 years old or younger — were surfing the Web. Back in 1996, by comparison, only 35 percent of NEA teacher members had ever typed in a URL. Some 86 percent of NEA teacher members, the March

2000 data added, had Internet access from their school workplaces, and 70 percent of all NEA teacher members had Internet access from home. Equally striking was the access to the Web enjoyed by NEA's nonteaching members — bus drivers, school custodians, paraeducators. Of the Association's support-personnel members, 69 percent had Internet access from work and 55 percent from home.

By March 2000, in effect, the vast majority of NEA members had gained the capacity to go online and visit any website. By this same date, however, only a small percentage of NEA members had chosen to make the Association's website one of their regular cyber destinations. The March 2000 survey found that only 21 percent of NEA members had ever visited the NEA site, usually just once or twice. NEA state affiliate surveys, for their part, showed similar results. Association websites, at both the national and state levels, had not been able to garner significant member cyber traffic.

The obvious question: Why, after over four years of website operations, hadn't the Association been able to forge a tighter cyber link with members?

This question probably ought to be expanded. All the evidence we have seen, mostly anecdotal findings shared with us by other unions, suggests that no union has yet successfully linked effectively in cyberspace with members. So the question becomes, Why has the labor movement, in general, failed to make a membership cyber connection? We in NEA can only speak for our own circumstances, but we don't believe that our circumstances differ appreciably from the experience of other unions.

Our original web assumption may have been flawed. We assumed visitors would flock to our organizational site if the site were attractive enough. What we ignored is the new communications environment that now envelops our members. Cyberspace has become central to many people's individual lives, part of their regular daily routines. Going online to check e-mail is as much a part of life, for cyber-savvy members, as checking the day's mail from the Postal Service. In this new environment, members don't waste hours, or even many minutes, searching for new and attractive destinations. Instead, they frequent websites they consider helpful to them in their own individual lives, sites that save them time or money or aggravation.

A trade union cyberspace presence — indeed, any cyber presence created by a membership organization — unfortunately starts with a basic positional problem. Members will always naturally assume that a site created by their organization is about that organization, not about them as individuals. And most members of most organizations, even trade unions, lead lives that do not revolve around their relationship with the organization. Why should these members regularly visit the organization's site when their life's interests might revolve somewhere else?

In other words, any union that seeks to establish a membership cyber connection faces the same challenge: How does the union convince members that its organizational site is about meeting individual member needs, not about the organization?

The more we looked at our NEA cyber operations, the more we realized that we had not adequately thought through those operations from a member point of view. We realized, for instance, that we were not using cyberspace to make it particularly easy for members to interact with their union. Members could neither join the Association or pay their dues online. In the vast majority of situations, they could not go online and check what their local contract says. Nor could they go online and report a concern or ask a question to a local union staff — or get training from their Association online. They could not even go online and, simply and quickly, change their mailing address.

Clearly, NEA had not come to grips with what membership means in the Information Age. The Association had not adequately explored how new information technologies could make interactions with members more convenient for them and more efficient for the organization. At a time when our members could go online and do their banking or watch their kids in daycare, we were conducting our union's business as if telephones were the ultimate in information technology. This made no sense. Our business practices, as an organization, needed to be reviewed and overhauled. How we go about doing our union's work needed to change.

At about this same time, we were also realizing, as an organization, that much more needed to change than how we do our union work. What we needed to change, to thrive in the new century, was the very work we do.

This realization actually predated our march into cyberspace. In the early 1990s, national and state NEA leaders began to engage in a remarkable dialogue and debate on the future direction of the Association. Many of these leaders had spent their adult lives building NEA into a powerful and effective organization, a union that could do everything that modern American unions can do — from bargain good contracts to elect friendly candidates. In traditional union terms, NEA was succeeding admirably. Membership had soared, from 1.6 million in 1983 to 2 million in 1990 to 2.3 million halfway through the 1990s.

These numbers, as heartening as they were, masked a more sober reality. The grand enterprise that employed NEA members — public education — was reeling, squeezed by rising enrollments and inadequate budgets, attacked constantly by ideologically driven critics who challenged the very idea that education ought to be public. In state after state, NEA affiliates found themselves forced to mount one huge, expensive, and draining defensive campaign after another, against ballot initiatives and legislative drives that aimed, in one form or another, to privatize public schools. The promoters behind these privatization schemes presented themselves as champions of the quality education public schools could no longer provide. They seized on every evidence of public school failure as proof that public education no longer worked.

In this climate, NEA activists had begun to rethink the Association's priorities. Real security for the men and women NEA represented, some began to argue, could never be achieved as long as the enterprise of public education remained at risk. NEA's job one needed to be restoring public confidence in public education, and that meant that NEA, as a union, needed to be about helping members succeed with students. Bargaining and lobbying for better hours, wages, and working conditions were no longer enough. The union, as priority union business, also needed to focus on improving student achievement.

NEA President Bob Chase, elected to office in 1996, in the middle of this strategic reappraisal, began calling this new mindset the "New Unionism." Most fundamentally, this New Unionism meant a new relationship between the union and members. Over the last third of the 20th century, NEA members had looked to their Association for economic security and support when they found themselves in trouble on the job. The New Unionism meant building a union where members could both continue the struggle for security and work collaboratively to improve their own professional practice.

If the New Unionism succeeded, members would begin to look to their union to meet the full range of their needs, personal and professional, economic and pedagogic. New Unionism aimed, in sum, at improving both the lives of NEA members and the quality of the educational services they provide.

This was an ambitious agenda, but NEA had welcomed ambitious agendas before. Back in the late 1960s, for instance, the Association had undergone a similar period of tumultuous change. At that time, NEA was evolving from a traditional professional association into a union able to defend and advance its members' interests. In the early years of this evolution, the organization lacked the infrastructure necessary to offer members, at the local level, the support they needed to bargain good contracts and make sure these contracts were fairly enforced. NEA eventually met this structural challenge, by solidifying the links that joined the local, state, and national levels of the Association and creating a national network of field staff jointly funded by the Association's distinct geographic levels. This "UniServ" network, in a few years time, put over 1,200 trained field staffers in communities across the U.S. and helped create the infrastructure for NEA's success as a vital, grassroots union.

The UniServ network was ideally suited to give NEA local affiliates the support they needed to bargain for and defend local members. But New Unionism demanded more from the Association. New Unionism demanded that the Association become a force that could, day in and day out, help individual NEA members help students learn. No staff network would ever be large enough to give individual members this sort of support. If New Unionism were to become more than an inspirational slogan, NEA would have to develop a new infrastructure that would enable the Association to deliver on the New Unionism promise. The NEA would help members succeed in the classrooms of America, places where the Association has not traditionally maintained a direct presence.

A decade ago, the search for this new infrastructure might have left the Association befuddled and adrift. But, with the 1990s coming to a close, Association activists began to realize that the emerging New Unionism and the emerging new technologies of the Information Age might indeed be meant for each other. How could an organization outside the classroom help members inside the classroom? The new technologies could be the answer. The new technologies of cyberspace could help the Association help members succeed with students, in the same way that, a generation earlier, the creation of a national staff network had helped the union struggle successfully for economic security at the bargaining table. Through cyberspace, the Association could perhaps forge a direct, ongoing contact with members, and, through this direct link, members could gain, from their Association and from their colleagues, the wisdom and resources they needed to improve student achievement. Cyberspace, more and more Association leaders and staff came to believe, could potentially turbocharge the New Unionism and empower NEA members as practitioners of and advocates for quality education.

VI. Linking New Unionism with Cyberspace Initiatives

Could cyberspace actually assume such an ambitious role? The Association might be interested in linking with members, via cyberspace, to help improve learning, but would members be interested in linking with NEA for this purpose? Was it realistic to expect that members would look to NEA, in cyberspace, for serious, ongoing professional support? Or was the union doomed to be pigeonholed, in most members' eyes, as the place you go only if your supervisor comes after you?

In early 2000, cyber-oriented leaders and staff could point to some encouraging signs. NEA members might not be visiting the Association's website in high numbers, but some Association cyber initiatives had indeed struck an enthusiastic chord with members. One example was a weekly Association e-mail newsletter called Works4Me.

Each issue of Works4Me consists of one practical classroom tip for elementary teachers and one practical classroom tip for secondary teachers. Works4Me is free. To be added, automatically, to the Works4Me mailing list, any interested individual need only send in an e-mail to a prescribed address. By the end of 2000, over 30,000 educators had signed up to receive Works4Me. Many of these individuals were local NEA activists, who were forwarding each week's tips on to colleagues in their schools, which meant that the total weekly audience reading Works4Me was running comfortably well over 100,000. This service was clearly connecting with individual NEA members, who found it a useful addition to their regular routines.

Works4Me was an eye-opener for the Association, on several fronts. For one, the service's wide circulation demonstrated clearly that an audience did exist for professional help made possible by the Association. But it was how this service was provided that was most intriguing. Unions traditionally see information as something that is generated by the union and then distributed to members. Works4Me was built on an entirely different model. All the weekly Works4Me tips come from members themselves. Each week's edition ends with a note inviting readers to send in their favorite tip, and, each week, large numbers of members do just that. The tips sent in go to the service's three editors, who are rank-and-file NEA members. These individuals select the best tips and send them out in the next week's editions. The staff role in all this? NEA staffers recruit the member-editors, train them in the logistics of cyber communications, and are there to help should any problems arise.

In other words, what Works4Me demonstrates vividly is cyberspace's capacity to empower members as information providers. Communication within the union setting need not be top-down, from one to many. With cyberspace, the Association could nurture horizontal communications among members, a horizontal communications essential to the Association's effort to help members succeed with students. The "experts" about student achievement, after all, are not NEA leaders or staff. The experts in student achievement are scattered throughout the NEA membership, and the wisdom these experts have needs to be shared. Cyberspace-driven information technology can enable this critically important sharing.

The Works4Me experience also reinforced a lesson the Association first began to learn during the America Online experience. By forging a regular cyber connection with members, we could strengthen our traditional union advocacy work. Staffers around NEA slowly realized that tens of thousands of NEA members were reading each week's Works4Me edition. The Association had no other communications vehicle that reached as many people as often. Could the next week's Works4Me, staff began to ask, carry an announcement or pose a question related to their work? The Works4Me editors carefully began to append, on a regular basis, a particular announcement or question after each week's tips, taking care not to divert Works4Me from its specific, practical tip-sharing purpose. And members responded to these addenda, supplying information that staffers would not have been able to gather otherwise.

Ironically, the staffers who caught on quickest to the potential benefits from the Works4Me link were those involved with the most traditional of the Association's communications vehicles, the union's magazine, *NEA Today*. Writers and editors connected with *NEA Today* began building a mutually beneficial relationship with the world. A writer working on an *NEA Today* cover story on the Association's campaign to pass national legislation for school modernization, for instance, would ask the Works4Me editors to tag on a query inviting readers to explain how outdated facilities at their school were undermining learning. That query would, in a day, generate via e-mail a wide variety of shockingly vivid examples. The writer would then e-mail follow-up questions to the most promising leads. The resulting *NEA Today* cover story would use the information from these leads to place a member "face" on the school modernization problem. The same connection could also be used to involve members in the Association's school modernization advocacy campaign. The *NEA Today* cover story would urge readers to check out the Association web page, from where they could easily contact their member of Congress, via e-mail, before the upcoming school modernization vote.

These sorts of experiences seemed to multiply in the late 1990s, building, among leadership and staff, an openness to further cyber exploration. An exciting vision of the Association's future began to take shape in many activists' minds. Imagine, they began to wonder, what the Association could accomplish if NEA could forge, on a massive basis, a regular connection with our members. The union could truly become the vital advocacy force activists had always envisioned!

But first the Association had to forge a regular connection with members. And that meant addressing, in an ongoing fashion, what members need to succeed in their lives. If the Association's cyberspace presence could help make members' lives easier and better, NEA would be able to link with members as the Association had never been able to link with them before.

The cyber advocates among Association leaders and staff didn't, for a moment, underestimate the nature of the challenge before them. To become more relevant to members in the Information Age, the union didn't need another website makeover.

The union needed a makeover of the organization. NEA needed to create an Association that was truly member-centric, at all levels. The Association needed to be able to speak — and respond — to members as individuals, with individual interests and preferences. And, to succeed as a union, the Association needed, from this stew of individual interests and preferences, to inspire and enable the collective action that goes to the heart of why trade unions exist.

VII. Reaching Members as Individuals

Realizing this vision would require adopting a new cyber strategy. To meet members in cyberspace, the Association needed to become indispensable to members' daily lives. To become indispensable to members' daily lives, the Association had to speak to members as individuals. It was no longer enough just to publish a web page that treated all visitors the same. The Association needed somehow to recognize, with the union's web presence, that members have different individual interests. Some members are just starting their careers; some are nearing retirement. Some teach second grade; some are high school guidance counselors. Some are intensely interested in political action; some dedicate their free time to mentoring. If the union's cyber presence could speak to these varying interests — and help people succeed at what was most important to them — the union's cyber presence would become part of members' ongoing lives. And if the union's cyber site became part of member ongoing lives, the union would have a chance at gaining the active input and involvement so essential to building a strong, democratic Information Age union.

The Association faced one immediate obstacle: How could the Association individualize its cyber presence when the Association did not really know who its members are, as individuals?

NEA, like many other unions, depends on local volunteers to enroll new members. In theory, each new member completes a membership application designed to collect a variety of information items, including what sort of work the member does. In reality, local volunteers are always pressed for time. If they can get a new member to sign on the dotted line, they feel they've made an important contribution. Getting the other information from the new member — or keeping information about existing members up-to-date — simply does not rank high on any local volunteer's priority list. After all, at the local level, whether a new member teaches geometry or French is a distinction without a difference. Local unions have not traditionally dealt with members as geometry or French teachers — so why expend scarce volunteer hours collecting this information or trying to keep it up-to-date and accurate?

This reality helps explain why the information that eventually finds its way into the NEA membership database has, historically, been so incomplete. The Association knows little about most members beyond the proverbial name, rank, and serial number. The membership database carries each member's mailing address and precious little else.

In years gone by, this lack of up-to-date, accurate, complete information did not matter much — because knowing who was who within the membership would not have particularly advanced the Association's action agenda. Even if the Association knew the subgroups to which members belonged, for instance, the union had no vehicle for providing members of these subgroups with timely information. That all changed with cyberspace.

One example dramatizes the new opportunities cyberspace created. In 1999, right-wing forces in Kansas were able to assume control of the state school board and pass new policy that essentially drove the teaching of evolution out of the curriculum. This outrageous attack on the academic freedom of biology and other science teachers made its way tortuously through the policy-making process over several months. At several key intervals, a sustained protest by the teachers most directly affected might have helped produce a different outcome. But the NEA Kansas state affiliate could not eas-ily mobilize the teachers most directly affected because, in truth, the Association did not know who these members were. The union did not know most of the members who taught biology or other sciences — and did not have the e-mail addresses of those who had been identified as biology or science teachers. If, on the other hand, the Asso-ciation had been able to identify the Association members with the most direct stake in this struggle — and had been able to blitz these members with e-mail action alerts at exactly the right moment — the politics of the Kansas evolution battle might have played out quite differently. The inability to reach the right members at the right time, in short, limited the Association's advocacy options.

To take full advocacy advantage of the new Information Age environment, the Asso-ciation needs to know who members are and where to reach them in cyberspace. The union's traditional business processes for gaining information about members were clearly inadequate to the task. The Association could not expect volunteer activists at the local level to ask all their colleagues — new enrollees and continuing members — year in and year out, to complete detailed individual questionnaires. Nor could the Association afford the expense of mailing such questionnaires back and forth to indi-vidual members. The reality the union faced was simple: The Association would never learn more about who NEA members are unless these members gave the Association this information — directly. And why would members share personal information about themselves — and keep this information up-to-date and accurate? Clearly, the Asso-ciation could not expect members to supply information for information's sake. NEA members — members of any national organization — are too busy and too worried about online issues around confidentiality to provide information just because that infor-mation has been requested. Members of an organization will only share information about themselves if they feel they will receive some sort of value in return.

Could NEA, as a national organization, create this value in the online environment? The more cyber-experienced Association leaders and staff felt the Association could create this value, but not if the Association treated cyberspace work as merely a mar-ginal activity, performed by specialists largely divorced from the ebb and flow of Asso-ciation advocacy and interaction with members. The Association could only create value for members online if the union were reinvented for the Information Age.

VIII. Technology Report: Beginning of a Portal Strategy

This perspective began to emerge in 1999, as NEA's Information Technology Services program unit began to host a series of dialogues that involved staff and governance at both the state and national levels. These dialogues, the Association's IT staff hoped, would identify the Association's technology budget priorities for the first years of the 21st century. The dialogues did that and more, as became evident in the fall, when the NEA Information Technology staff released a massive new technology report designed to inform the planning of NEA's 2000–2002 budget cycle.

The preparation of this technology report involved stakeholders throughout the Association, with a special advisory committee made up of representative NEA state affiliate presidents, executive directors, business managers, and technology directors playing a key role in the report's formulation. These state affiliate representatives made it plain that nothing was more important to the organizational future of the Association than coming to grips, in a most serious way, with the impact of cyberspace.

Over the last decade, the technology plan report noted, cyberspace has expanded out from its original university base into mainstream America, and some NEA members have begun to incorporate cyberspace "into their everyday lives to an extent that would have been barely imaginable only a few years ago." These "cyber savvy" NEA members, the report added, "do not make up a majority of our Association membership — yet." But that day was clearly coming, in the not too distant future. Will NEA, the report asked, "be ready to meet the expectations of cyber-savvy members — and potential members?" And what will those expectations be? The report hazarded a forecast.

- Cyberspace is evolving so fast that envisioning the future is always a tricky business. But some points do seem certain. In the near future, most educators will routinely be using cyberspace to interact effortlessly with the institutions that impact their lives, institutions that range from the universities that prepare them for careers in education to the school districts that employ them.
- These NEA members – and prospective NEA members – will, naturally, expect to be able to do business with their Association equally as easily. They will expect, for instance, to be able to join the Association online. Or change their address. Or ask a question. Or order a service.
- Our current capacity to meet these expectations is extremely limited. Join the Association online? That's just not how we do business.

Other national enterprises, the report added, had begun to change the way they do business. Merrill Lynch and "stockbroker," for instance, used to be synonymous: "Now, under the pressure of new cyber realities, Merrill Lynch is reinventing itself as an online brokerage, with customers making their own trades." Unions are not businesses, but unions operate in the same new Information Age environment. "In the cyber age," the technology plan asserted, "irrelevance can quickly befall any organization that lingers too long in the past." Above all, the report noted, decision makers within the Association need to realize that the emerging cyber world is, to use the business expression, a "buyer's market."

- In the information-on-demand culture of cyberspace, organizations that try to conform individuals to the convenience of the organization will be considered — and dismissed — as truly clueless.
- In the new Information Age, successful national membership organizations will be those that establish one-on-one relationships with members, relationships that recognize the unique individuality of each member. These organizations will center their business practices, at every level, around member needs and predilections.

"By the end of the 2000–2002 budget period," the report concluded, "an Association member who logs online should find an Association page that's individually constructed to speak to that member."

This page, in subsequent discussions about the technology plan recommendations, quickly became known by the shorthand of "the portal." By January 2000, the NEA elected leaders who make up the Association's Budget Committee had written the construction of a portal into their proposed new financial plan for the Association. Over the rest of the winter and into the spring, this portal became a prime topic of discussion and debate at one national and state meeting and conference after another. In July, the nearly 10,000 delegates gathered in Chicago for NEA's annual national convention formally adopted the Association's new strategic plan and budget, with funding for creating a new portal front and center in this strategic document.

This portal is now under construction, with a rollout to members currently planned for the 2001–2002 school year. The portal construction process, like the deliberative process that led to the decision to undertake the portal initiative, is involving leaders, activists, and staff throughout the Association. We cannot report here exactly what the portal, when launched, will be. We can describe here the principles that are guiding the portal construction, principles that we believe may help other unions better understand and evolve their cyber futures.

IX. Building a Cyber Future

Any cyber initiative, from the most primitive to the most cutting-edge, raises certain basic questions that a thinking — and learning — organization ought to try to address directly. These questions, as we noted earlier, revolve around four major issue areas: the ownership of a cyber presence, the content presented, the level of interactivity, and the impact of a cyber presence on an organization's business operations.

In NEA's work to create a portal, we have tried to think through these four areas carefully. Our success, we believe, will depend directly on how well our portal planning takes into account these four issue areas. In each of these, a portal "raises the bar" for a membership organization, forcing hard choices — and offering huge rewards.

Ownership. Any union that expects members, in massive numbers, to regularly visit the union's website, we have come to believe, is a union that will be forever disappointed. Our members are all complex individuals, with multiple demands and interests that lay claim to their time. For the vast majority of union members, their union speaks to only one aspect of their lives. At certain times — a bargaining crisis, for instance — a member's union connection may become the single most important aspect of the union member's life. But for the average rank-and-file member, at the average moment in time, life goes on as if the union were not really there. Contemporary unions, in the vast majority of individual situations, are not central to the overall lives of their members. In this environment, to expect a union's website to become central to the average union member's online existence — to expect this average union member to visit the union site repeatedly — is a totally unrealistic expectation.

Can a union's cyber presence become central to the lives of that union's members? Within NEA, many of us have come to believe that a union can become central to its members' online lives — and, by extension, to their overall lives — if the union creates a site that belongs to members. Members will see a site as theirs if the site is individualized to them.

On a traditional website, individualization does not exist. All visitors share the same cyber experience. The publisher calls all the shots. The site belongs to the publisher, not the individual visitor. In contemporary cyberspace, the most thoughtful web publishers are now working at changing this dynamic. These publishers are building regular relationships with their target audiences by individualizing their sites, by creating sites that address individual needs and speak to individual interests.

Two technological advances are helping this individualization along. Within the ranks of the "digerati," these two technical approaches are known as *personalization* and *customization*.

A web page that has been *personalized* delivers to the visitor information that matches the individual attributes of the visitor. Personalization lies at the heart of the NEA portal-building strategy. The Association plans to offer all members the opportunity to create their own personal portal. To create this page, individual members will be asked to register online by completing a simple form. Based on the information provided on this form, NEA will be able to begin the personalize the Association-provided portal page, in ways that will be familiar to any web surfer who has created a personal portal page with a general interest portal provider.

Internet users who create a personal portal page through a dot-com like Yahoo, for instance, start that process by answering a few questions online. Yahoo uses the answers to these questions to create personal profiles of the individuals. These personal profiles then generate the *My Yahoo* personal portal page that individuals see as soon as they power up their web browser. Individuals who live in Los Angeles see on their *My Yahoo* page, each time they log onto the Internet, a Los Angeles weather update.

The NEA member portal will use this same personalization approach. Members will register and create a personal profile, a collection of key individual attributes ranging from the member's NEA local affiliate to the work the member does. A third-grade teacher from Los Angeles would see, on her personal portal page, information from the NEA local affiliate in Los Angeles, information from the NEA state affiliate in California, and information from NEA at the national level. And third-grade teachers in Los Angeles, on any given day, might receive totally different information than Los Angeles high school teachers. The Los Angeles local, for instance, might want to alert third-grade teachers to an upcoming, union-sponsored professional development opportunity for elementary teachers, an item of no interest to high school chemistry teachers. On other days, the Los Angeles local might want to share the same piece of information with all the local's members.

This personalization is essentially passive. Users simply identify who they are, and the personalization flows automatically from this identification. But individuals have more than attributes. They have preferences. To create a page that users come to see as their own, a website needs to also recognize these preferences. Customization is the technical approach that enables this recognition.

The NEA portal will offer members a wide variety of custom content offerings. That third-grade teacher from Los Angeles, for instance, might also have just become a mentor teacher. She may be working, as a mentor, with new teachers in her school building and feel a little unsure about her new mentoring responsibilities. Enter the portal's customization capacity. The third-grade teacher would be encouraged to look through all the different information services the portal offers and choose those services she wants to appear on the portal page she sees as soon as she logs on. This third-grade teacher might, for instance, want the portal's daily mentoring tip program to appear on her portal front page.

A veteran mentor teacher, on the other hand, might not be interested in seeing a mentoring tip on her individual portal home page. But this daily tip program would still be available to the veteran mentor. All the content offerings NEA provides will be accessible to members, whether or not they choose to feature the content on their individual portal home page. The portal home page will list a series of Association-provided information "channels" — each devoted to a different topic — and each channel will offer different information "programs," such as the daily tip service for mentor teachers. At any time, a member would be able to "drill down" from that member's individual portal front page to see any particular program.

In sum, the portal page that individual NEA members will see every day they go online will feature two prime categories of cyber "real estate."

- The portal will feature some content that has been personalized to match the personal attributes of the individual member.
- The portal will feature some content that has been customized, by the individual, to match the preferences of the individual member.

The rest of the portal page will be devoted to navigational markers — "channel" buttons, for instance — that will allow users to jump off their portal home page into a wide range of additional content.

This personalization, customization, and access to additional content will all combine to create a web presence that speaks to the needs and interests of the individual member. That member will "own" this portal site — and frequent the site regularly because the site will be central to that member's life. In the process, NEA will become more central to that member's life, because the Association will be providing the portal opportunity. What we have here, in other words, is not just an opportunity for the union to gain more "hits" on its web presence. We have an opportunity for the union to forge a new, closer relationship to its members, and the deeper this relationship goes, the greater the union's potential capacity for effective advocacy.

But all this presupposes that members will find, through the portal, an incredible universe of personalized, customizable content. Where will this content come from? Let's move our discussion, at this point, to the second major concern that faces any union that seeks to do sophisticated cyber business.

Content. "Content is king." So went the Web maxim popularized by various dotcoms in the heady early days of cyberspace. Content, indeed, does reign supreme, a lesson NEA has had to learn and relearn over the dozen years of our cyberspace experimenting. Cyberspace is not a forgiving medium. Users bring to the Internet expectations about timeliness and comprehensiveness that they do not bring to more traditional media. Woe be to the Internet publisher who does not meet these expectations.

In the past, NEA has fallen short on both the timing and scope of our content. We have not always been able to "refresh" the content we have presented in cyberspace on a fast enough cycle. Members have been frustrated at not finding the up-to-date information they seek. And information that members might reasonably expect to see from their union has not always been online to find.

Logical explanations for these deficiencies certainly do exist. Cyberspace has an endless appetite for content, and the Association's traditional sources of content generation — staff — are distinctly limited. At the national and state level, staff hours are often already double-booked. To expect staff to do their "regular" work and take on new cyberspace content responsibilities is to expect, in most situations, the impossible.

The portal vision NEA is now seeking to realize ups the content ante — enormously. The portal envisions an Association able to supply content that's relevant to members' ongoing professional lives as well as timely content about Association work that is targeted to member subgroups the Association has never sought to reach before. The Association has, for instance, traditionally talked to teachers as a rather undifferentiated mass, because the union had no vehicle for reaching distinct groups of teachers. With the portal, the Association will have a vehicle for reaching distinct groups. Will the Association be able to generate content for them?

In a standard union communication framework, this challenge cannot be met. As a union, NEA simply does not have the existing staff time or expertise necessary to generate all the content the portal envisions — or the resources to hire the additional staff that would be necessary to supply this content. NEA, in the future, will only be able to generate the content demanded by portal users if the Association redefines the communications role members are expected to play. Within NEA, as historically within all unions, members have always played a fundamentally passive communications role. They have been the receivers of information generated elsewhere. In the new Information Age, unions need to see members as sources, not just recipients, of information. Members need to become, to use the inelegant phrasing popularized by the Internet gurus, "content providers."

How realistic is this vision? NEA cyber-minded leadership and staff feel confident that members can become a prime source of the content the new Association portal will seek to offer. Our NEA experience with Works4Me has demonstrated that, with cyberspace, members can and will share wisdom with other members.

Where does the staff role fit into this information exchange? Staff become more the facilitators of information than the source. Staff identify members with expertise that ought to be shared. Staff set up the cyberspace logistics that make it possible for the sharing to take place. And staff nurture the information-providing membership source, offering troubleshooting guidance. New software technologies make information sharing easy to implement. With "content-management software," the cyberspace term of art for software systems that allow content to be entered and presented to appropriate individual end users, a member "content provider" anywhere in the country can upload content without any technical skills more demanding than the ability to type in a URL and fill out a simple form online.

With modern cyber software, in short, content creation can be decentralized and democratized. Members can be empowered. But first, of course, members need to be trusted. A top-down union, comfortable with command-and-control internal information-sharing processes, might be unnerved by this prospect. A top-down union, uncomfortable with anything but command-and-control, will likely never succeed in cyberspace.

Interactivity. The labor movement was born, generations ago, in cities and towns where workers lived side by side in the same communities. This experience of shared community helped forge the solidarity essential for unions to survive and thrive. Today, union members seldom share any community outside the workplace. After work, they scatter in a dozen different geographic directions. No shared experience reinforces and strengthens their workplace community.

Community is desperately important to the members of NEA — and isolation an ever-present threat. Within a school building, physical proximity can create opportunities for collaboration. A high school, for instance, might have 12 social studies teachers. They can create their own collaborative community. Sometimes, unfortunately, NEA members can find their community-building frustrated by the lack of physical proximity. Many high schools have only one Spanish teacher, and that Spanish teacher might be the only Spanish teacher in the entire school district. How does this Spanish teacher find like-minded collaborators?

We could multiply these examples endlessly. An NEA local affiliate activist is interested in bargaining professional development for middle-school teachers. Where's the community of like-minded activists where this activist can bounce ideas? A young teacher is the only first-year teacher in her building. Where can she share her experiences? A retired teacher has relocated to a new community. How can he link up with other retired educators?

Cyberspace can become the place where all these members find and build the communities that will enrich their lives and enhance the potential for collective action. Cyberspace carries no physical, geographic address, but cyberspace is a place nonetheless, where communities can take shape and grow, communities that can potentially help strengthen the bonds of solidarity that give life to vital trade unionism. To realize this community-building potential, the NEA member portal will feature a variety of sophisticated cyber tools that help members interact with each other.

Operations. Every union has developed, over the years, various processes and procedures for doing the union's business. These operations are based on relationships and realities that have held constant over generations. National unions, for instance, have always had a capacity to reach rank-and-file members directly. They can circulate periodicals to members. But this capacity has eroded over time, as unions, in the face of ever-rising postal rates, have had to cut back on how frequently they publish their newspapers, magazines, and newsletters. Unions at the national, state, and regional levels have had to depend more and more on "information hand-offs" to communicate to members. A national union distributes information to the union's state or regional level, the state or regional distributes that information to local leaders, local leaders distribute the information to local members. Or so the theory goes.

In reality, a certain amount of information "leaks" whenever one union administrative level pours it down to the next. Members, at the end of the information chain, routinely end up uninformed. The information never reaches their desk or mailbox. This failure to communicate is profoundly anti-democratic — how can members participate in their union if information about their union is not flowing frequently and freely — and equally destructive from an efficiency standpoint. A union's inability to reach members directly and quickly undermines the union's ability to do its basic business and serve as an effective advocate for its members.

A simple example — from NEA's legislative operation — can help drive this point home. Every union, at one point or another, lobbies legislative bodies on behalf of its members, and NEA is certainly no exception. NEA maintains a sizable legislative staff in Washington, DC, and devotes considerable organizational treasure to the effort both to elect friendly candidates and to influence legislative outcomes. In NEA's traditional information environment, this work is often difficult to complete effectively, particularly when time is at a premium, a commonplace occurrence in legislative battles.

Imagine a congressional committee suddenly two days away from making a decision that will adversely impact the work of bilingual teachers. One member of that committee is still on the fence. That member's vote will likely decide the outcome. The best way to influence this legislator? Expose this lawmaker to the expertise of bilingual teachers from the lawmaker's legislative district. Let this legislator know that people back home who know the issue care deeply about the upcoming vote. The challenge facing the NEA lobbyist working this issue: to identify bilingual teachers in the swing congressional district quickly and to mobilize them into immediate action. Time is short. The vote is just two days away.

The NEA lobbyist swings into action. NEA, at the national level, does not have any up-to-date listing of bilingual teachers. So the NEA lobbyist calls the NEA state affiliate for help. The state staffer doesn't know who teaches bilingual ed in the target congressional district either. The state calls the local field staffer, who also doesn't know the individual bilingual teachers by name. This staffer calls the presidents of the NEA locals in the target district, who, in turn, contact the Association reps — NEA's term of art for shop stewards — in individual school buildings. These reps do know who teaches bilingual education, but they don't particularly understand the issue at stake in the upcoming congressional committee vote. The bilingual teachers, if they are reached in time, likely receive a garbled message. The swing member of Congress never hears any groundswell of opinion from bilingual teachers. The Association has missed an advocacy opportunity.

In NEA's traditional information environment, lost opportunities like this one are standard operating procedure. Information simply cannot be delivered in a clear and timely fashion to the individual NEA members who need this information. Staff members, for their part, cannot complete their missions effectively and efficiently.

The NEA member portal will hurdle these traditional information obstacles. With a portal in place, NEA will be able to identify bilingual teachers in the Association's ranks because these teachers, to receive the portal's personalized and customized services for bilingual teachers, will have identified themselves as bilingual teachers. These bilingual teachers will be going online and using their portal on a regular, ongoing basis because the portal is central to their daily lives.

In a portal-powered world, the NEA lobbyist working the bilingual committee vote would simply compose an alert for the bilingual teachers in the swing congressional district. On the day before the vote, the bilingual teachers would see the alert when they logged online. The bilingual teachers would have the information when they need to have it. The stage will have been set for effective advocacy. In a portal-powered world, the NEA lobbyist working the bilingual committee vote would simply compose an alert for the bilingual teachers in the swing congressional district. On the day before the vote, the bilingual teachers would see the alert when they logged online. The bilingual teachers would have the information when they needed to have it. The stage will have been set for effective advocacy.

The portal would create similar opportunities for staffers throughout the Association. Staffers who plan the Association's annual convention, for instance, could use the portal to recruit members from the communities surrounding each year's convention city to serve on the volunteer host committee. Local field staff could survey members, in a timely fashion, about a new management proposal that has just hit the bargaining table. Researchers could share an update on Social Security benefits to members nearing retirement. In any number of ways, the Association will be able to use the new portal presence to link directly to members. If the Association succeeds in this endeavor, if indeed NEA can create an ongoing, regular relationship with members in cyberspace, the Association's standard business processes could then become more efficient, at every level of the union.

This new vision of our union is now percolating throughout the Association. Scores of meetings and briefings and discussions have been held, all across the nation, to help leaders and staff understand that the new portal is about changing the organization, not just changing how the organization operates in cyberspace. The organizational consensus for the change has been growing steadily, and somewhat surprisingly so. Leaders and staff have, by and large, been quick to recognize that the union must change to meet the demands of the new Information Age environment that envelops us all.

One force driving this growing consensus is the changing membership — and the changing expectations of members. An estimated 2 million new teachers will be hired over the next decade, a massive increase demanded by the combination of rising student enrollments and the retirements of hundreds of thousands of teachers hired at the crest of America's last student enrollment boom. These newcomers to the teaching profession hail from America's first online generation. They grew up with chatrooms, compared colleges and submitted college applications online, and dealt with their professors via e-mail. They will expect the organizations that seek their participation to be cyber-savvy.

Unions don't initiate technology in a vacuum. Business is reaching out to our members and competing with us for their attention. Over the past three years, these enterprises have invested literally hundreds of millions of dollars in cyberspace efforts to become central to teachers' daily lives. These businesses envision a day when teachers will function just the same as the rest of America's office professionals — that is, they will power up their computers each and every day and their work lives will largely revolve around information they share and receive through their computer screens. The business that locks up a significant "eyeball" share in this teacher market will, Wall Street analysts believe, have hit cyber paydirt.

This corporate rush to capture teacher eyeballs, many NEA activists have come to understand, represents a definite threat to the Association's ability to organize and involve an entire new generation of educators. How relevant would the Association be to educators, in the Information Age, if some business enterprise, not the Association, becomes central to members' online lives? If NEA does not move — and move quickly — to serve our members online, many NEA leaders now believe, then the Association would risk irrelevance and worse in the years ahead.

The bottom line? The imperative to meet a new generation of potential educators online, and apprehensions about what would happen if the Association let someone else do that meeting have combined to place cyberspace right at the center of NEA's strategic planning for the future.

X. The NEA Experience: How Useful for Other Unions?

No union today can afford to ignore the new digital realities of the Information Age. The world has indeed changed, and unions need to evolve to address these changes. Does every organization need to make the same sort of changes that NEA is planning to make? Should every union follow the NEA cyber route? Of course not. The decisions each union needs to make ought to be determined by the factors peculiar to that union's situation.

NEA found that its cyber future was rooted in four factors:

- The *ownership* an organization's members feel toward the organization's cyber presence.
- The *content* an organization's presence presents.
- The level of *interactivity* a presence promotes.
- The impact of the cyber presence on an organization's ongoing business operations.

These are the key elements underpinning NEA's current cyber presence. Other unions may find a different set of factors that need to be considered. All, it seems to us, would benefit by careful analysis and investigation of four key areas.

Reality. Trade unions need to scan their environment regularly. Where are the union's members in the Information Age — demographically, psychologically, technologically? How familiar with the online world have the union's members become? What competition for members' eyeballs does the union face?

Readiness. Launching an ambitious cyber initiative is one thing, sustaining it another. Has the union planned adequately to handle cyber success?

Resilience. Any significant cyber work creates organizational turmoil. How committed are union governance and staff to creating a clicks-and-mortar union? Is leadership willing to confront the static that upsetting traditional business practices will almost assuredly produce?

Resources. Serious cyber work requires serious new infrastructure. Are content managers, member support, site administration, and budget all lined up?

Unions that have examined their membership reality, that are ready and resilient, and that have allocated the resources necessary for ambitious cyber action are unions poised for cyber success. Unions that are not yet at these levels, we believe, have some serious — and necessary — catching up to do.

3

Challenges and Opportunities: Unions Confront the New Information Technologies

Robert E. Lucore*
International Brotherhood of Teamsters

I. Introduction

A new economic and industrial landscape is evolving under the influence of new information technologies. New technologies have always had a profound impact on workers and the institutional arrangements under which they work. Therefore, we can expect that the new information technologies will also have a profound impact on today's workers and their unions.

By new information technologies, I mean recent innovations in communications and computing technologies, such as computer networks (including the Internet), cellular phones, fax machines, and global satellites. Most of my focus will be on the Internet and closely related technologies.

I will proceed by outlining the relationship between the new information technologies, by discussing the impact on some specific industries or sectors of the economy, and by speculating on the potential for the labor movement to employ the new technologies to its advantage.

II. The New Technologies and the Economy

Before turning to the impact of the new information technologies on specific industries, let us speculate on some changes that may result in the economy at large. For convenience, I divide the discussion into three arenas: (1) the product market, (2) the labor market, and (3) the structure of firms.

In the product market, or the market for the economy's output, as the economy shifts from producing mostly tangible products to producing more products that are symbolic, informational, or artistic, we may need to change how we think of costs of production. Consider, for example, an intangible product such as a computer software program. It is likely to have very large average costs compared to its marginal costs. A software company may spend a fortune developing computer code, but can then reproduce the code to sell to consumers on CD-ROMs, which cost very little, or by making it available for download, which costs even less. Recorded music has similar characteristics. Even the manufacture of some tangible products, such as pharmaceuticals show continually declining marginal costs. (At one time, such industries were considered to be natural monopolies, but — sadly, in my view — that theory has become so unpopular that we are now seeing the deregulation of public utilities.)

Now, combine a situation of continually declining marginal costs with one where consumers are able to instantaneously compare prices. Internet shopping technology makes it possible for an individual to find out at the click of a mouse what other sellers are asking for the same item. This is a prescription for ruinous competition. Sellers will not be able to charge much above marginal cost, or they will lose their customers to another seller. But, they must find a way to charge some customers enough to cover their higher average costs, or they will be unable to stay in business. For some time, Internet business were able to deal with this by simply continuing to lose money, while raising more funds in the equities market. However, this would seem to have come to and end with the recent collapse of high-tech stock prices.

How is all of this relevant to unions? It is virtually impossible for a union to survive, or even gain a toehold in an industry where cutthroat competition prevails. Given the low union density overall in the U.S., it would be unlikely that unions could impose any standards on companies in such industries. I have argued elsewhere (Lucore, 2000) that the raison d'être of unions is to take wages and benefits out of competition, but this is hard to do unless firms have some degree of price-setting power.

However, experience shows that in such situations, some degree of monopoly power usually emerges. Microsoft is able to charge much more than the marginal cost for its products, because it has relentlessly either absorbed or wiped out most effective competition, and it has gained intellectual property rights that confer monopoly power. Sellers may also be able to use the ability of the Internet to track individual buying patterns in such a way that they can practice price discrimination, charging each customer what they are willing and able to pay, rather than merely covering marginal costs. Amazon.com was recently reported to be experimenting with charging different customers different prices for the same product (Krugman, 2000). This would make the economy of the new information technologies one in which union prospects were a bit brighter.

The signature characteristic of the new technologies is improved information. Improved information has the potential, if properly harnessed, to greatly improve the operation of the labor market. Numerous bulletin boards now exist where employers can post openings and search through potential candidate's resumes, while workers can seek new jobs or compare their current job to other openings. Many of these are private sector services, sometimes start-up dot-com companies, but often old-economy companies such as newspapers. However, the states and the federal government have also been quite active. The Employment and Training Administration of the U.S. Department of Labor has a project under way called America's Labor Market Information System (ALMIS) to set up an interactive infrastructure that makes available quality information on employment and training programs. A component of ALMIS is America's Job Bank, which is reported to have between 1.2 and 1.3 million job vacancies posted daily and over 400,000 resumes (see <www.lmi-net.org/about.htm> and <www.doleta.gov/individ.asp>). The stated goal of the ALMIS is to help labor markets to function more efficiently, presumably by lowering information costs to both employers and job seekers.

Organized labor has generally supported measures that would make labor market information, especially information about job openings, more widely available. Unions have even called for mandatory listings of job openings with the Employment Service (Friedman and McDonald-Pines, 1993; Lucore, 1999). Clearly more information would empower workers and decrease the degree of employer monopsony power. It is therefore laudable.

Ironically, improved labor market information for individuals could hurt unions. Workers with more information may be more likely to employ the exit strategy (quitting one job to take a better one), rather than the voice strategy (organizing a union to bargain with the employer), if they are unsatisfied with work. (For an explanation of the exit and voice mechanisms, see Freeman and Medoff, 1984). Unions have a long history of backing reforms that help workers while paradoxically making unions less necessary (Bennett and Taylor, 2001). My own view is that they do this out of a sense of social mission to improve the lives of workers. It makes little sense in terms of narrow economic calculus.

Some unions are trying to harness the tendency toward increased availability of information by becoming information providers. The Teamsters recently began providing easy links to job openings with union employers (<www.teamster.org/job-bank.htm>) which provides a way for Teamsters who are laid off by one employer to easily find another union job. It is also an online resource for non-Teamster job seekers who would like a job with Teamster representation. One can envision unions developing modern versions of old-fashioned hiring halls and referral systems.

Another labor market development occurs when new technologies enable work to be done from a wider variety of locations than ever before. Intellectual workers can now work at home, on the road, or in the office. Project teams can be set up that work on producing intellectual output on a 24-hour cycle, with U.S. workers passing along work to Asian colleagues who in turn pass it along to Africans and Europeans, as the globe turns. In such an environment, the use of temporary workers, independent contractors, and offshore employees is much more likely, and this makes the job of unions much more challenging. Furthermore, such trends are not just limited to intellectual output. Underpaid workers in countries without unions can be hired to sort documents or letters by remote control, or to answer customer service calls. In a brave new world, one can even conceive of cyberspace-enabled workers who are remote security guards, secretaries, or even child-care workers for older children who need only minimal supervision (Miller, 2000).

The new technologies are contributing to important changes in business practice and the structure of the firm. Business-to-business networks have allowed substantially reduced procurement costs, and have contributed to the fashionableness of outsourcing. Such innovations have contributed the popularity of focusing on core competencies rather than diversifying. The trend toward lean, flexible, and networked firms probably had more to do with management fads and pressures from Wall Street to increase profit margins than it did with new technologies. However, new innovations in communication and computation have certainly reinforced the tendency.

These developments in the structure of the firm have not been beneficial to unions. Established bargaining units have been broken up when work has been outsourced. Flexibility has come at the cost of stability for workers, which is a large part of what unions have traditionally offered. Furthermore, technology has made outsourcing possible on a more global scale, meaning that workers have to compete in a more global labor market, making it even more difficult to remove wages from competition.

Unions have confronted the challenge of new firm structures in a variety of ways. To name a few, unions have attempted to organize outsourced work, target new organizing to work that is not easily outsourced, bargain for protections against downsizing, achieve plant-closing legislation, and to include labor standards in trade agreements. However, to date these efforts have not stemmed the tide toward decreasing union density. The new technologies are certainly not the only cause of labor's difficulties. The forces of globalization, deregulation, privatization, and the continued vigor with which corporations are willing to oppose unions are all at least as important. But, the new technologies are interwoven with these other factors and do create challenges for labor. However, the trends made possible by the Internet and similar technological innovations are not all bad for unions, as discussed below.

III. Focus on Specific Industries

The Internet and similar technologies will have an uneven impact on organized labor, punishing unions in some sectors, while rewarding those in others. The mixed impact of the new information technologies can be seen in more concrete terms by narrowly focusing on specific industrial sectors. I have chosen the industries below as cases in point, mainly because I have knowledge of them as a union economist whose job is mostly to provide research in support of organizing and negotiating. I make no pretense that they provide a representative sample of the entire economy, but I do think they illustrate the changes taking place.

Manufacturing. The impact of the new information technologies on manufacturing sector unionism is apparent from much of the discussion above. The emerging importance of the Internet to the manufacturing supply chain is illustrated by the automobile industry's joint electronic supply platform called Covisint (Levy, 2000, p. 5). The major companies — General Motors, Ford, DiamlerChrysler, Renault, and Nissan — will be linked to online catalogs, bidding systems, outsourcing networks, and auctions.

Hailed as the worlds biggest commercial marketplace, with an estimated $200 billion in annual orders, Covisint will allow the major companies to put downward pressure on prices. This has the potential to reduce profit margins for suppliers, and thus increase their incentives to avoid unions or seek concessions in collective bargaining.

Communications technologies have made it much easier for manufacturing corporations to produce components in far-flung locations and have contributed to plant shutdowns in high-wage regions while production has shifted to low-wage regions. This is not new. The history of capitalism is replete with examples of employers seeking to reduce labor costs. But, it would seem to be encouraged by the new technologies. Similarly, the trend toward outsourcing cited above has had its biggest impact on unions in the manufacturing sector. Manufacturing unions in the U.S. will not have much luck pursuing new members who manufacture modems, semiconductors, or other components, as many of these newly created jobs are in places like China and Singapore. Because unionization is higher in manufacturing (14.8 percent of wage and salary workers) than in the private sector at large (9.0 percent), these trends do not portend well for unions (U.S. Department of Labor, 2001). However, the negative impact of these developments may moderate in future years. So many manufacturing jobs have already been transferred abroad that we may soon reach a point of diminishing returns for corporations seeking to boost profitability by relocating factories abroad.

Retail. One of the most publicly visible arenas affected by the Internet is the retail sector. Say "Internet" and many people think of Amazon.com or eBay. However, the long-run impact may be important for traditional retailers who move online. In a very short time, Wal-Mart, Costco, J.C. Penney, Target, and a huge number of traditional retailers have opened web sites. Catalog giants like Land's End and L.L. Bean also have a big Internet presence. Companies, such as Peapod, Webvan, and Home Runs, believe that they can make a profit taking grocery orders over the Internet and delivering directly from a warehouse to the home, thus bypassing the traditional supermarket.

If a large proportion of customers switch from buying in a physical store, to buying on the Internet, this could represent a challenge for unions such as the United Food and Commercial Workers (UFCW), who represent retail clerks and in-store workers, and the Teamsters who represent warehouse workers and truck drivers who deliver goods to retail outlets. Although only 5.2 percent of workers in the retail sector are represented by unions, this figure is much higher in certain regions and subsectors, such as the grocery industry, where over 20 percent are union members (U.S. Department of Labor, 2000; Hirsch and Macpherson, 2000, p. 52). Replacement of old stores by new virtual markets means the replacement of existing bargaining units. This presents the familiar and perennial challenge of "following-the-work" by organizing the new units.

It is very important to remember that retail dot-com companies do have an old-economy base that exists outside of cyberspace. They are selling real products produced by real workers, and those products are warehoused in real facilities. The workers at these facilities may already be union members and are certainly potential members.

Transportation. A recent article the *Journal of Labor Research* noted that the new organization brought about under the new information technologies is supported by advances in transportation infrastructure. The authors say that "systems such as UPS and Federal Express, which allow material goods to move across distance with almost the same facility as voice, image, and data," provide critical support for these new developments (Townsend et al., 2001, p. 277).

Clearly, the growth of the new technologies and the growth of transportation are linked. Firms that can offer rapid, or time-definite delivery, have grown along with the popularity of just-in-time inventory management. The expansion of communications technology has not seemed to dampen the need for business travel or the desire for leisure travel, as total passengers enplaned grew by more than 40 percent between 1991 and 1999 (author's calculations based on Air Transport Association, 2000).

The Bureau of Labor Statistics projects that the transportation sector will add 675,000 new jobs to the economy between 1998 and 2008 (Thomson, 1999, p. 41). This may be a conservative projection, especially if companies such as UPS experience unanticipated growth due to electronic commerce. Within the transportation sector, UPS is perhaps the best equipped to benefit from expansion of electronic commerce, and the Teamsters have added between 15,000 and 20,000 new members at UPS since the strike in 1997 by our estimates. As Forbes magazine put it "As power in the economy shifts from the movement of atoms to the movement of bits, the ultimate winner is the company that moves both: United Parcel Service (Barron, 2000, p. 78).

This should be good news for unions, as transportation is more highly unionized than the rest of the private sector, with a 26 percent density (U.S. Department of Labor, 2000). Furthermore, UPS totally dominates the small-parcel segment of the transportation sector, and virtually all of its blue-collar workers are unionized.

However, the picture for unions in this sector is not unambiguously rosy. The growth of fax and e-mail is a very real threat to the highly-unionized Postal Service. Federal Express remains largely nonunion (only its pilots are represented). It is also possible that new technology will eliminate jobs as package sorting machinery improves.

Newspaper Publishing. Even though newspaper publishing is not a major employment sector, it is worth examining simply because of the tremendous impact of the Internet on the industry. The newspaper industry has long been an interesting example of how new technologies bring about changes in industrial relations (Dertouzos and Quinn, 1985).

The cost lowering potential of the Internet is staggering in newspaper publishing. Electronic publishing could totally eliminate costs for ink, paper, printing, and delivery. Perhaps this overstates the potential, for the printed page may not disappear entirely (recall that not many years ago we were told that the office of the future would be paperless). Still, as readers shift from getting news in print to getting news online, costs will decrease substantially.

The Internet also provides an opportunity for newspaper publishers to reach out to a new audience. For years newspapers have faced declining readership. The Internet may provide an opportunity to increment their readership, with little increased cost. However, the ease with which information can be delivered online is also a threat, as a huge number of new entrants are providing online news. In response to this threat, the industry has moved aggressively to offer their product online. The Newspaper Association of America says that over 1,000 newspapers in the U.S. offer their product on the World Wide Web (Newspaper Association of America, 2000).

While newspaper companies will probably meet the challenges offered by the Internet quite effectively, the same is not true for many newspaper unions. The Teamsters union represents many newspaper truck drivers are part of the system for delivering the "old-fashioned" printed newspapers. Many so-called mailers, who work at sorting, stacking, and handling inserted material in the print editions are also Teamsters. To the extent that online media will replace print media there will be attrition in Teamster membership. Unions representing such workers are in a defensive posture, working to protect their members with seniority language and job-security provisions.

Technology has also made it easier for newspapers to acquire news from wire services or from other parts of the growing media conglomerates that often own newspapers. This is a threat to news reporter's jobs, and makes it more difficult for them to strike, because the "news hole" can be filled even in the absence of reporters.

The situation is summed up by the blunt observation of one industry official that "Technology is useless without eliminating people" (Winsbury, 1975, cited in Dertouzos and Quinn, 1985). Current workers will probably be fairly well sheltered from the winds of the new technology, where they have union representation. But, this will not be a growth area for unions.

Public Sector. Milton Friedman has remarked that one of the great virtues of the Internet is that it makes it more difficult to collect taxes (Friedman, 2000). Even before Internet commerce exploded, state and local governments were losing billions of dollars in revenues due to untaxed interstate catalog sales. The Internet expands the potential for tax loss.

Nevertheless, because 33 percent of state revenues come from sales taxes, it is a threat to the public sector that cannot be ignored (Goolsbee, 2001). Furthermore, since the government sector is the sector of highest union density, public sector unions would be well advised to pay attention to this threat.

Of the 17.9 million workers represented by unions, almost 8 million or about 45 percent work in the government sector. Forty-two percent of those working in the government sector are represented by unions (U.S. Department of Labor, 2000). So clearly any trend that threatens to shrink the government sector must also be seen as a threat to union membership.

Goolsbee (2001) has carefully summarized the implications of electronic commerce for tax collection. He estimates that by 2004, the estimated tax loss due to the Internet would be 2.6 percent of sales tax revenue. He points out that this is only about one tenth of the amount lost due to catalog sales. So it is likely that both free-market utopians and government-sector alarmists probably both overestimate the impact of electronic commerce on state tax revenues.

Governments may find a way to survive and even thrive in the new economy. They have certainly adopted the Internet as a way to deliver information to citizens and to make government more interactive. I see no reason to think that they will not be able to devise tax systems that can keep pace with technological changes. Over the long sweep of history, economic development has brought about an increasing role for government. And despite decades of anti-government rhetoric dominating U.S. politics, government, especially at the state and local level, employs a growing number of workers. The Bureau of Labor Statistics's 10-year projections show state and local governments adding over two million new jobs between 1998 and 2008, while the federal government is expected to decline by 136,000 (Thomson, 1999, p. 43).

IV. Unions Learn to Use the New Technologies

The use of information technologies by unions is far from new. Unions realized long ago that computers were essential to keeping track of membership and dues. As the number and complexity of agreements and corporate structures grew, unions increasingly used computer data bases to track contracts and employers (for examples dating back to the 1960s, see Ginsburg, 1968). This traditional use continues today. For example, Teamsters Research Department has a database of contract information for over 200,000 Teamster collective bargaining agreements (both expired and current), and we track nearly 40,000 separate employer-union relationships. Such a task would not be possible without modern information systems. Unions have also increasingly used computers for such mundane tasks as computing contract cost estimates or tracking and presenting information on employer finances.

Communications technologies have a long history in the labor movement. Eric Lee, citing the work of Tom Standage, points out that in the telegraph era hundreds of employees of American Telegraph Company met and held a union meeting by Morse code (Standage,1999; Lee, 2000, p. 57). Lee also quotes Karl Marx as saying that the ever expanding union of workers "is helped on by the improved means of communication that are created by modern industry, and the place the workers of different localities in contact with each other" (Marx cited in Lee, 2000, p. 57).

But what of Internet-like technologies? Lee (2000) traces the first labor computer network to the British Columbia Teachers Federation in 1981. However, the Teamsters can claim much earlier application of electronic networking to union affairs. Starting as a small pilot project in the late 1960s, the Teamster Information Terminal and Accounting Network (TITAN) was initially a way for local unions to tie into the International Union's mainframe to simplify dues accounting and post per capita information to the International. Over the years it grew to serve several functions: accounting system, membership database, and a system allowing locals to electronically generate paper mailings to the members. By the late 1970s it was also an electronic mail system allowing locals to instantly contact each other or the International or regional bodies. It became a major means by which requests for information or research were made by affiliates to the International. Today TITAN continues to be updated as a dedicated and secure Teamster electronic network (*International Teamster*, 1978, 1981).

But how are the new information technologies being used by unions now? What advantages do they confer? How can they help unions meet the many challenges they face? Below I will discuss some of the ways that unions and their members are adopting new technologies such as the Internet. To focus the discussion, we can categorize developments into five areas: (1) Information Gathering, (2) Communicating with

Members, (3) Presenting Labor's Public Image, (4) Building Solidarity, and (5) Making Unions More Democratic.

Information Gathering. I start with this relatively mundane sounding category because it is the one that has had the most substantial impact on my own work life. One of the primary functions of the research department in an international union's headquarters is to respond to requests for information from locals and other affiliated bodies. Generally these requests can be spit into two types: those who want sample contracts from other locals for purposes of helping them craft language or propose wages and those who want information on a company for purposes of organizing or negotiating.

Requests for contracts are technically not that difficult to fill. But electronic-database technology has enabled unions to track and cross reference contracts much more readily. For the most part we still rely on paper copies and filing cabinets to keep the actual contracts and use the computer database to cross reference these files. However, to a limited degree unions have begun to create electronic databases containing entire contracts that can be searched for specific language. We look forward to an era when we can search and analyze contact language, wage and benefit information, and the like. The Bureau of Labor Statistics also keeps a paper file of large contracts at their offices in Washington, DC. This is available for public use, but it would be valuable for union research staff, and I assume many human resource managers, if the Bureau were to make this information available for download online.

It is in researching companies that the Internet shows its greatest value to the union research department. Not too many years ago, we kept massive files of annual reports, proxy statements, and Security and Exchange Commission (SEC) filings. Huge amounts of staff time were devoted to making trips to the SEC or other agencies to copy documents. However, today, massive amounts of information on companies are available for free or at little cost over the Internet. This is not because unions asked for it, but because investors demanded it. Nevertheless we have benefitted greatly. The time saved in document storage and retrieval can now be better put to use in analysis or strategic thinking. Furthermore, many savvy union activists in the field have learned how to retrieve such information on their own, thus decentralizing information and decreasing the burden on the international headquarters. At the Teamsters, it is now common for our research department to offer workshops about doing company research via the Internet for members who attend conferences or education programs.

Communicating with Members. Communicating with members has long been difficult and expensive for unions. Printing and mailing costs are high enough to make anything much beyond a monthly or even quarterly magazine or newsletter prohibitive. The time lag in traditional publishing makes quick responses on fast developing issues impossible. The World Wide Web changes that. It is possible to electronically publish information at very high speed. Unions now routinely use e-mail and the web to update members and activists on progress during negotiations or on organizing issues. For example, during the 1997 Teamster negotiations and strike with UPS, the Teamsters' web site provided daily updates and downloadable leaflets for anyone to access.

While it is true that use of the Internet for union communications is limited by the extent of union member access to computers, the number of union members online is not small. A Peter Hart poll in 2000 showed that 60 percent of union members own a computer, and of these three-quarters are online (Bureau of National Affairs, 2000). Unions have successfully negotiated agreements where employers provide members with computers or inexpensive Internet access (Ramirez, 2000).

Members of AFL-CIO-affiliated unions are able to get discounted Internet access through workingfamilies.com, a project of the AFL-CIO and Internet startup firm iBelong (Greenhouse, 1999). Each union also has a portal on workingfamilies.com where members can get union news, find out about political or legislative issues, and even (in some cases) access information about their retirement accounts. With the advent of the Internet, union staff can now send information to millions of members, suggesting that they take a whole range of actions: anything from boycotting a product, to wearing a button on the job, to sending an e-mail to a politician.

The Internet also offers opportunities to provide members with a deeper education on labor issues, the economy, and techniques for bargaining and organizing. Although much of this potential remains untapped, some unions have taken some really promising steps. One of the most effective is the AFL-CIO's economic education web site (<www.aflcio.org/cse/>).

Presenting Labor's Public Image. In much the same way that new technology enables unions to more effectively communicate with their members, it also creates new opportunities for presenting labor's public image. For a long time the feeling among many unionists coincided with A.J. Leibling's famous quip that freedom of the press is limited to those who own one. But now the cost of publishing declined dramatically. Almost all international unions have web sites that are available to the public and thousands of locals also have sites. These sites are beginning to allow labor to present its public image unfiltered through the media. Most union activists would probably argue that the conventional media outlets have suspect class allegiances. They are, after all, increasingly owned by major multinational corporations. An even worse problem is that few reporters are really knowledgeable about labor issues. Union leaders can also be frustrated with the tendency for reporters to want to paint every issue in black and white, with good guys and bad guys, or as two-sided. Often issues have subtleties, gray areas, multiple facets, and points of agreement as well as conflict. Now the web provides a place where unions can present their version of the news, unfiltered and unedited.

Again, there is much untapped potential here. But already unions have seen great benefits from being able to put their ideas out on the web where anyone who wants to find out what the union thinks can do so. The web now plays a key role in getting news out to the public in almost any major contract campaign, organizing effort, political campaign, or legislative effort.

Building Solidarity. The Internet has greatly improved the ability of unionists to share information across unions and around the world. In countless chat rooms, on hundreds of bulletin boards and automated e-mail lists, unions and union members are meeting to discuss common issues. Sometimes these discussions take place as union-sponsored activities, perhaps more often they are started by one innovative member and take on a spontaneous life of their own. Often message boards that are originally intended for those seeking to chat about their stock-market investments have become places where employees (union or nonunion) seek to vent.

Such interaction has already started to build a kind of spontaneous solidarity and has the potential to do even more. Workers who might never meet each other can be drawn together across multiple time zones and across multiple unions. Take for example a major multinational employer such as General Electric. Some 14 unions in the U.S. represent workers at General Electric. Many more unions represent GE workers at other locations around the world, and there are others trying to organize against stiff company opposition. Only technologies such as the Internet could conceivably allow workers in all these locations to interact and support one another. As I write this, a web site for all GE workers around the globe is scheduled to go online soon (it will be accessible at <www.cbcunions.org> and several other domain names).

Working through the established international trade union secretariats, such as the International Transport Workers Federation (<www.itf.org.uk>), Union Network International (<www.union-network.org>) or Public Services International (<www.world-psi.org>), unions have been able to set up networks to coordinate actions in support of strikes or to publicize issues, such as truck driver fatigue or privatization, on an international basis. Outside of these formal bodies:

> . . . a loose international coalition now exists, drawing together individual labor Internet activists, local branches, national unions, international federations and various union support organizations. This network is based on new, open, horizontal channels of communication. Old hierarchical, official, vertical lines of communication are challenged by the fact that any union activist with a modem can discuss strategy and tactics with colleagues in five continents virtually instantaneously and access sources of information that would be the envy of most national union research departments only five or ten years ago (Davies, 1998).

Web sites such as Cyber Picket Line (<www.cf.ac.uk/socsi/union>), LabourStart (<www.LabourStart.org>) and LaborNet (<www.labornet.org>) have publicized workers' struggles worldwide, while maintaining a great degree of independence from any official union body. Dockworkers striking in Liverpool have been able to get their picket lines honored in the U.S. by means of the Internet. The International Federation of Chemical, Energy, Mining and General Workers Unions (ICEM) has used a worldwide e-mail protest campaign to support Americans on strike at Bridestone/Firestone. Company officials, overrun with pro-union e-mail, had to construct a parallel e-mail system. When seventeen South Korean unionists were arrested in 1999, protests from all over the world electronically mailed to the Korean President were thought to have had a major impact. The unionists were released within 48 hours (Davies, 1998; Lee, 2000).

Finally, the Internet has also promoted solidarity between labor and non-labor groups such as environmental activists. Protests such as that against the World Trade Organization in Seattle were in large part popularized by Internet activists.

Making Unions More Democratic. Several threads in the discussion above lead to the conclusion that the new information technologies are making unions more democratic. When members are able to gather more information, to communicate horizontally across official structures, and to publish their own information about labor happenings, the effect is to empower members.

In unions where the members directly elect their international officers, such as the Teamsters, a web-strategy is almost mandatory for every candidate. In the 1996 Teamster election both the incumbent, Ron Carey, and the challenger, James P. Hoffa, made extensive use of the Internet. As later scandals caused the overturn of the 1996 election, a hurricane of information and gossip swirled about labor-oriented Internet chat rooms. As this is written, another election is in its initial stages, and both Teamsters and non-Teamsters will be able to follow developments on many web sites, including those of the candidates (see <www.hoffa2001.com> and <www.leedham.org>) and at independent sites not sanctioned by either candidate or the union, such as <www.teamster.net>.

This phenomenon can make life quite difficult for incumbent union administrations. When their members are able to communicate with each other more than before, they must remain on their toes and be ready to answer unsubstantiated rumors and misinformation rapidly. I became personally aware of this when the Teamsters Airline Division and Teamsters Local 2000 reached a tentative agreement for the 10,000 Northwest Airlines flight attendants in 1999 after years of negotiating. I was involved in a great deal of the number crunching, comparing the new tentative agreement to the old agreement and to industry norms. My feeling, along with the Airline Division staff and the local leadership, was that it was a very good agreement. However, a small band of activists, using web and e-mail technology almost entirely, were able to whip up a storm of controversy that resulted in the rejection of the contract by the rank and file. This campaign against the contract had to reach out to 10,000 flight attendants, domiciled all over the country and across the globe. Teamster negotiators got the message and returned to the bargaining table. After another year of negotiations, a new tentative agreement was reached and passed by the membership. Several other airline unions have experienced similar Internet-led contract opposition.

Clearly, the new information technologies can be a source of disinformation as well as information; one needs only to cruise the many tabloid-like news web sites to see this first hand. Yet, democracy is a process. It is a process through which people learn over time. Members will learn, with experience, whom to trust in chat rooms and what web sites are reliable. And in those unions that are most democratic, the learning process will work better. When the direction of the union is driven by the will of the members, the members will gain better skills at steering. It is hoped that a virtuous interrelationship will develop, in which those unions that are most democratic and responsive to members will be best able to employ the new technologies, and those that employ the technologies will become more democratic.

VI. Concluding Remarks

History has a nice way of setting up natural experiments that can only later be evaluated by social scientists. How will the Internet affect unions? How important is it to the economic environment in which unions operate? Will unions adapt to the shifting employment patterns brought about by the new developments? Will unions be able to employ the new technologies in ways that reinvigorate the labor movement? The answers are as yet unknowable, but I have tried to offer some educated speculation on the possible trends. I have painted with some pretty broad brush strokes, and there are big parts of the canvas that need to still be covered. For example, I have said almost nothing about the unique problems facing the information technology work force or the challenges faced by unions who wish to organize them. I have not discussed workplace issues such as privacy and employee monitoring. I leave that to others who are more qualified to comment.

Note

*For identification purposes only, I am Senior Research Analyst with the International Brotherhood of Teamsters. The views presented here are mine only and do not necessarily represent the views of the Teamsters. I thank Daphne Taras for many helpful comments on an earlier draft. I alone am responsible for the remaining errors or omissions.

References

Air Transportation Association. *Traffic Summary 1960–1999; U.S. Scheduled Airlines.* June 2000, <http://www.air-transport.org/public/industry/24.asp>.

Barron, Kelley. "Logistics in Brown." *Forbes*, January 10, 2000.

Bennett, James T. and Jason E. Taylor. "Labor Unions: Victims of Their Own Success?" *Journal of Labor Research* 22 (Spring 2001): 261–73.

Bureau of National Affairs. "Sweeney Projects Union Growth in 2000 Comparable to Last Year." *Daily Labor Report*, August 30, 2000, p. A-1.

Davies, Steve. "Workers of the World Online." *People Management*, September 1998. <http://www.cf.ac.uk/ socsi/union/eng.htm>.

Dertouzos, James N. and Timothy H. Quinn. *Bargaining Responses to the Technology Revolution: The Case of the Newspaper Industry.* Santa Monica: Rand Corporation, 1985.

Freeman, Richard B. and James L.Medoff. *What Do Unions Do?* New York: Basic Books, 1984.

Friedman, Milton. *Milton's Paradise Gained. Interview on Uncommon Knowledge*, March 10, 2000. Transcript at <http://www.hoover.stanford.edu/Main/uncommon/winter00/421.html>.

Friedman, Sheldon and Jane McDonald-Pines. "In Search of a 'New Covenant' for America's Dislocated Workers." *North American Outlook* 4 (September 1993): 67–100.

Ginsburg, Woodrow L. "The Computer's Uses and Potential in Bargaining: A Trade Union View." In Abraham J. Siegel, ed. *The Impact of Computers on Collective Bargaining.* Cambridge, Mass.: M.I.T. Press, 1968, pp. 26–68.

Goolsbee, Austan. "The Implications of Electronic Commerce for Fiscal Policy (and Vice Versa)." *Journal of Economic Perspectives* 15 (Winter 2001): 13–23.

Greenhouse, Steven. "AFL-CIO Members to Get On-Line Access and Discounts." *New York Times*, October 11, 1999.

Hirsch, Barry T. and David A. Macpherson. *Union Membership and Earnings Data Book: Compilations from the Current Population Survey*. Washington, D.C.: Bureau of National Affairs, 2000.

Krugman, Paul. "What Price Fairness When Price Discrimination Comes to Cyberspace?" *Seattle Post-Intelligencer*, October 5, 2000.

Lee, Eric. "How the Internet Is Changing Unions." *Working USA* 4 (Fall 2000): 56–72.

Levy, Efriam. "Autos and Auto Parts." *Standard and Poor's Industry Surveys* 168 (December 28, 2000): 1–33.

Lucore, Robert E. "Guidelines for Worker-Centered Training," Unpublished presentation to the Council of Economic Advisors, December 1999.

_____."The Fictitious Commodity: A Union View of Labor's Antitrust Exemptions." *Journal of Labor Research* 21(Fall 2000): 563–70.

Miller, James. "Brain Arbritrage: The Next Internet Frontier." *Dismal Scientist*, September 12, 2000, <http://www.dismal.com/thoughts/th_jm_091200.asp>.

Newspaper Association of America. *Facts About Newspapers*. <http://www.naa.org/info/facts00/33.htm>, December 20, 2000.

Ramirez, Charles E. "DaimlerChrysler, GM Workers Get Online Deal." *Detroit News*, November 3, 2000.

Standage, Tom. *The Victorian Internet: The Remarkable Story of the Telegraph and the Nineteenth Century's On-Line Pioneers*. New York: Berkley Publishing Group, 1999.

Thomson, Allison. "Industry Output and Employment: Projection to 2008." *Monthly Labor Review* 122 (November 1999): 33–50.

"TITAN." *International Teamster* 75 (September 1978): 20–21.

"TITAN Increasing in Usefulness To IBT Affiliates." *International Teamster* 78 (February 1981): 9.

Townsend, Anthony M., Samuel M. DeMarie and Anthony R. Hendrickson. "Information Technology, Unions and the New Organization: Challenges and Opportunities for Union Survival." *Journal of Labor Research* 22 (Spring 2001): 275–86.

U.S. Department of Labor, Bureau of Labor Statistics. *Union Members in 2000*. USDL News 01-21, January 18, 2001.

Winsbury, Rex. *New Technology and the Press*. London: Acton Society Press Group, 1975.

4

E-Voice: How Information Technology is Shaping Life within Unions

*Charles R. Greer**
Texas Christian University

> *Some people will tell you that labour simply doesn't adopt new technologies. But that isn't true. There are always some crazy people hanging around the labour movement, sometimes in positions of power, who will push forward an idea whose time has come.*
>
> —Eric Lee, *The Labour Movement and the Internet: The New Internationalism*

I. Introduction

A 1997 survey revealed that 70 percent of national unions provided general information to their members through websites (Fiorito and Bass, in press). Also a book-length treatment on the labor movement and the Internet in 1997 made the following prediction: "What the future will bring is already pretty clear: *more* online discussion groups, *more* electronic publishing, *more* use of e-mail in internal and external trade union communication" (Lee, 1997, p. 102). Since these studies there have been more IT applications and website development. More recently researchers have observed that all national unions now have websites (Diamond and Freeman, 2000). Another recent study has called attention to the fervor with which unions are adopting IT (Fiorito and Bass, in press) and IT staff members at national unions have described their Internet applications as the wave of the future (Howard, 2001).

The rapid and widespread adoption of IT by unions poses an interesting question of how IT is changing life within unions. While the literature provides only limited information on such changes, it identifies areas of union activity to which the Internet and e-mail have been applied. These include (1) internal communication between union officers, staff, and members, particularly when they are geographically dispersed; (2) external communication, such as to inform the public about union issues potentially affecting the public, workers, and unions; (3) facilitation of bargaining activities, such as conducting research, collecting information about employer practices, tracking issues in negotiations, and informing members about employer practices; (4) contract administration, such as communicating grievances and tracking decisions of arbitrators; and (5) political action, such as informing potential voters about union views and those held by labor's friends and adversaries (Lee, 1997; Shostak, 1999).

In addition to effects on the way unions communicate, prepare for negotiation, administer contracts, and engage in political action, widespread IT applications also may produce social transformations of unions. Unions that have undergone such social transformations have been described in normative terms as cyberunions. It has been asserted that unions that have undergone such transformations through widespread applications of IT tend to place more emphasis on their members and attach great importance to union democracy (Shostak, 1999). More specifically, it has been asserted that unions transformed by IT will adopt participative practices based on IT. For example, they are expected to (1) conduct regular online surveys of their members in order to determine their needs and concerns, (2) use such surveys to ascertain members' preferences and priorities on issues, (3) use e-mail and websites to inform members on union developments and learn from their members, (4) use e-mail for meaningful and timely dialogs between officers and members, and (5) regularly update their IT infrastructures and encourage members to embrace IT (Shostak, 1999).

My purpose is to describe major effects of union applications of IT, to shed light on some of the literature's normative predictions about potential social transformations of unions, and to offer speculations on how IT may affect life within unions in the future. I draw on findings from a literature review, an intensive examination of a sample of several national and local union websites, a content analysis of 63 websites, and interviews of several IT professionals who develop and maintain such websites. I use the term IT to designate the entire range of technology in which information is analyzed, stored, disseminated, and communicated through the use of computer technology. However, my major focus is the subset of IT dealing with communication, specifically the Internet and e-mail.[1]

II. Conceptual Framework of the Union Affairs and IT Nexus

Union Democracy

I assess how IT affects the four measures of union democracy by examining IT's influence on accessibility of information to members, decentralized decision making, participation of members, and effectiveness or responsiveness of representation. While union democracy is a broad, elusive topic and the subject of substantial academic discourse (Estreicher, 2000; Jarley et al., 2000; Strauss, 1991, 2000), my discussion is limited to measures that appear to be influenced by IT. It is recognized that some of these measures of democracy, such as decentralized decision making and participation, are complex.

Accessibility of Information. Easy accessibility and distribution of information about union leadership and policies provided by the Internet have several impacts on union democracy. One is that power is redistributed in unions in which leaders have restricted information and centralized decision-making processes. Presumably, as union members become better informed, they acquire greater power. Another is that the speed and efficiencies of the Internet facilitate consultations between union leadership and members and generally enhance communication effectiveness (Diamond and Freeman, 2001). On the other hand, the information power of the Internet can potentially magnify the power of the union majority over individuals. For example, during the Boeing strike in the winter of 2000, union activists listed the names of scabs on websites (Fiorito and Bass, in press).

Decentralized Decision Making. IT use is strongly related to decentralized decision making in national unions, which entails greater coordination requirements. For example, with decentralized bargaining more information must be exchanged to provide a common front on issues, and IT is critical to such coordination (Fiorito, Jarley, and Delaney, 2000). Nonetheless, IT effects on decision making are probably moderated by the origin and culture of the union. For example, decision making in national unions having industrial union origins is highly centralized even though many such national unions and their locals are democratic. In contrast unions having craft origins typically have decentralized decision making even though the locals' autonomy may allow them to operate undemocratically (Belzer and Hurd, 1999).[2]

Participation of Members. The procedural view of union democracy relies on high levels of member participation, at least at the local level, with members expressing their views directly in the decision-making processes both within the union and in the workplace. IT now provides such direct access when unions solicit input or conduct online surveys through their websites or by e-mail. Such channels provide the means for participation although their existence does not guarantee democracy. For example, union constitutional provisions requiring regular elections and permitting members to run for office are important for democracy but are not sufficient. The personal costs of running for office may simply be too great for these provisions to have much impact on the degree of democracy. For union democracy to exist there must be responsive leadership, and members must be able to speak out without high personal cost (Strauss, 1991, 2000).

One outcome of the availability of Internet services and economical website hosting is that some of the personal costs have been lowered. Dissatisfied factions can maintain their own websites where they can voice their dissident views (Diamond and Freeman, 2000). Some sites even provide criticism of their national unions. For example, a website maintained by the British Columbia Carpenters Union has provided critical commentary about the lack of democracy within the United Brotherhood of Carpenters and Joiners of America (UBC) and asserted that the UBC general president was using dictatorial power. The site also criticized the UBC's disaffiliation from the AFL-CIO (British Columbia Carpenters Union website, 2001).

Effectiveness of Representation. Under the service or outcomes view of democracy, IT also can enhance union democracy if it helps unions accomplish members' objectives. This view is more indirect as it holds that there is democracy when the countervailing power of unions is used against that of employers to achieve members' objectives (Belzer and Hurd, 1999). Thus, to the extent that IT helps unions accomplish members' objectives, through better communication and greater efficiencies for example, there should be more democracy. Better communication also may reduce the potential for internal factionalism, which can destroy the ability of unions to negotiate favorable agreements with employers (Belzer and Hurd, 1999; Strauss, 1991).

E-Voice

Voice may be defined as "any attempt at all to change, rather than to escape from, an objectionable state of affairs, whether through individual or collective petition" (Hirschman, 1970, p. 30). When there is union representation, employees have a mechanism for voice; in the absence of unions, the only option is often exit or the threat of exit. Voice also is needed within unions, such as to make union leaders aware of a faction's desires. However, there also are costs associated with exercising voice within unions. When the costs are high, as when members have to attend meetings and rally dispersed members, there is less likelihood of participation.

E-voice has evolved in unions through website chat rooms, discussion boards, website surveys, or e-mail directly from the rank and file to the officers. Such e-voice provides an opportunity for members to air their views or dissent at low cost, if there is no retaliation, and should make unions more democratic. When unions do not provide such access, e-voice may occur, as noted earlier, when dissident groups express their views on their own websites. In addition, e-voice can have an impact in electronic balloting when members can vote from work or home with a few clicks on a mouse. Furthermore, with the Internet there is now potential for the town meeting form of union democracy in cyber space, which Strauss (1991) noted was not feasible in larger unions only a few years ago.

Institutional Aspects of IT Use

The literature has identified several structural factors related to IT use in unions. Size of national unions, which is expected to spread the fixed costs of IT over more members, has been found be positively related to such use. Rationalization or the operation of unions in a manner similar to businesses also is moderately associated with IT adoption. Rationalization is generally viewed as involving greater formalization, standardization, and specialization for efficiency gains (Fiorito, Jarley, and Delaney, 2000). Members' access to the Internet also has an obvious influence on the impact of IT in unions. Access is already fairly high as the proportion of union members who were on line in 2000 was 48 percent and is expected to reach 82 percent by 2005 (Diamond and Freeman, 2000). The importance of access is evident in the AFL-CIO's program to supply IBM PCs and Internet access at low cost to the members of its affiliates

(AFL-CIO website, 2001; Diamond and Freeman, 2000). Access also is important to employers such as American Airlines, which has spent $35 million on a similar program with the intention of enhancing communication with employees (Jones, 2001). Furthermore, access also has become a negotiation issue as the U.S. Postal Service and the American Postal Workers Union (APWU) have been negotiating on a similar package for postal service employees (APWU website, 2001).

The Internet also allows unions to represent isolated or dispersed members who they might not otherwise be able to serve (Diamond and Freeman, 2000). Airline pilots provide an example of dispersed members whose unions rely heavily on IT. The Allied Pilots Association (APA), which represents airline pilots who are spread throughout the U.S. and the world, can get information out almost immediately through e-mail to its 15,000 members (Howard, 2001). Moreover, the necessity of communicating with geographically isolated members appears to have prompted use of electronic networking by labor unions. One of the earliest applications of the Internet occurred in 1981 when the president of the British Columbia Teachers' Federation (BCTF) used electronic networking and dumb terminals to communicate with his executive committee members who were dispersed through the large, sparsely populated province (Lee, 1997). In addition, unions having substantial numbers of members who telecommute may be inclined toward greater utilization of the Internet. With telecommuting there is less of a sense of community among workers, and the necessity of commuting to a union meeting after work has hampered unions' abilities to communicate with their members. The Internet provides an avenue for restoring or even enhancing such a sense of community (Fiorito and Bass; in press).

Functions Performed with IT Applications

A recent study based on a 1997 survey of 75 U.S. national unions found nearly universal use of some IT and almost universal agreement that the technology has a positive impact on their efficiency. However, the study found large variations across unions in the extent to which different forms of IT were used. The study specifically examined the extent to which 17 forms of IT were used, including e-mail, electronic bulletin boards, providing websites for general campaigns, providing websites with general information, database applications, and word processing (Fiorito, Jarley, and Delaney, 2000). A composite measure for the extent of use of all forms of IT was significantly correlated in a positive direction with perceptual measures of both union effectiveness and organizing effectiveness (Fiorito, Jarley, Delaney, and Kolodinsky, 2000).

Membership Input. Internet surveys are being used to take the pulse of union members on issues. The Allied Pilots Association uses its website to survey its members about their contract preferences and has the advantage of saving the expense of manual tabulations of survey results (APA Website, 2001). The Internet has already been used to poll union members about the terms of new contracts. During the strike at Boeing in 2000 by the Society of Professional Engineering Employees (SPEEA), members who were out of state were able to vote on contract proposals and the union obtained votes from 70 percent of its membership (Diamond and Freemen, 2000).

Organizing. As noted, recent literature indicates that unions see great potential in the Internet as a tool for organizing new groups of employees. They see a major advantage in the constant availability of information on union websites about the positive benefits of union representation. Union websites also have an advantage of privacy as employees can obtain information online at home without their supervisors' knowledge (Ad Hoc Committee on Labor and the Web, 1999).

In addition, a recent empirical study has found that websites can have a modest effect on organizing effectiveness (Fiorito, Jarley, and Delaney, 2001). Furthermore, there is anecdotal evidence that the Internet has been used successfully to organize employees. For example, the Service Employees International Union (SEIU) Local #100 in Houston organized nurses through the use of e-mail and chat rooms (Diamond and Freeman, 2000). E-mail also has been instrumental in union organizing. Professional employees of the Immigration and Naturalization Service, who are geographically disbursed, recently voted to unionize largely as a result of communication efforts through e-mail (AFL-CIO Cyber Drives, 2001).

There are numerous examples of union efforts to use the Internet for organizing. For example, a prominent feature on the website of the Communication Workers of American (CWA) includes material on why workers should organize, how the process works, and legal protections for organizers. There is contact information for the CWA's organizing department and an e-mail form that workers can complete and return to start the process. The site also has a link to the AFL-CIO's Organizing Institute (CWA Website, 2001). The International Brotherhood of Teamsters (IBT) website has similar content with a large section devoted to organizing and a long list of successful organizing campaigns and press releases. It also outlines some of the benefits of being a member of the Teamsters, in addition to representation, such as low-cost legal and health insurance (IBT Website, 2001). Such websites provide employees with information about their organizing rights and can educate them about the actions their employers can and cannot engage in during organizing campaigns. This and other information about the organizing process is available online to employees who may be considering whether to contact a union. Such information may be critical in the initial phases of organizing.

Employment Services. Unions are using the Internet to help members or potential members find jobs and increase the quality of employment services. For example, many locals of the International Brotherhood of Electrical Workers (IBEW) post jobs on their job boards, and the national IBEW website devotes substantial space to employment services (Cantrell, 2001). The Communications Workers of America also has a large section of its website devoted to employment services as well as training. This section includes information on its new distance-learning programs, which are made possible by advances in IT. For example, the CWA is a distance-learning provider for the Cisco Networking Academy and is preparing to offer courses in UNIX and web design in the near future (CWA Website, 2001). Other unions such as the American Guild of Musical Artists (AGMA) and the Actors' Equity Association (AEA) also post job openings (AGMA Website, 2001; AEA Website, 2001). In addition, the Teamsters' website has numerous links to firms that are sources of jobs. For example, the Teamsters' site has 68 links to the employment sites of a wide variety of employers in a broad range of industries such as aerospace manufacturing, breweries, motion pictures and entertainment, transportation, and warehousing (IBT Website, 2001).

Secure Applications. Unions also use secure or members-only sections of their web-sites for obtaining input for negotiations, to provide negotiation support, and for administrative purposes. These areas sometimes provide chat rooms, discussion boards, or "challenge and response" options. Secure areas also provide more detailed information about ongoing negotiations than provided in the public areas of the sites. In addition, those of national unions sometimes provide membership information for use by local unions such as names and addresses of members, labels, contract documents, sample contracts, safety material, and manuals. Some also provide more discussion of legislation than in the public sections of the site, online training information, benefit access numbers, and bid sheets (Bittner, 2001; Cantrell, 2001; Howard, 2001; Super-fisky, 2001; Witiak, 2001). There is some indication that unions plan to expand the amount of information provided in their members-only sections. For example, some plan to provide more information for their locals such as listings, reports, and information on legislative action for specific states (Superfisky, 2001).

III. Examples of Union Website Applications

Key website features of six types of unions and several of their local affiliates are described in order to provide an overview of current Internet applications. These examples were chosen to provide a broad range of different types of unions. These include unions representing employees such as engineers and pilots, as well as more traditional members — plumbers and pipefitters. They also include large unions, such as the United Auto Workers (UAW) and International Brotherhood of Teamsters (IBT), which serve a broad range of industries and occupations. In addition, the examples include a union serving only public sector employees.

Engineering and Technical Employees. The Seattle Professional Engineering Employees Association (SPEEA) represents 24,500 engineers and technical employees at Boeing's various plants. SPEEA, which is Local 2001 of the AFL-CIO's International Federation of Professional and Technical Engineers (IFPTE), provides an example of the changing internal environment of unions (SPEEA, 2001). The SPEEA strike at Boeing in 2000 demonstrated how "connected" union members have become as a result of the Internet and the evolution of IT. The Internet became an integral component of the union's strike-management efforts with some media observers calling the strike the first Internet strike. During the strike the union's detailed proposals were posted on the union's website for all members to view. Hits on the site during the strike "were off the chart" with some members checking the site three or four times per day. In the union's view, the Internet had a huge impact on the union's success in the strike, as its communication role was a key factor in the union's ability to keep its members together. Furthermore, during the strike some union members provided e-voice through their websites, which had Internet addresses that were very similar to SPEEA's official site. These sites of SPEEA's technically savvy members provided a wide range of views, from radical to conservative, and a welcome sense of humor (Dugovich, 2001).

E-voice at SPEEA also occurs in normal day-to-day activities. For example, SPEEA's website has an electronic bulletin board and features for e-mailing representatives and union officials. It also posts the results of elections for delegates, promotes seminars on such topics as performance evaluations, has a feature for members to sign up on petitions to management on various union concerns, and has a section on layoffs. While the website was heavily used in the strike, SPEEA still mails out newsletters and finds that union members do not use the website as much as desired during normal times (Dugovich, 2001).

Another of Boeing's unions provides a similar example. The Southern California Professional Engineers Association (SCPEA), which is Local #90 of the Office and Professional Employees Union (OPEU), represents 5,000 engineers and technical workers at Boeing's plants in Southern California. During its negotiations in 2001 SCPEA provided detailed daily accounts of its bargaining sessions. In a section of the website in which the current negotiations were discussed, the union had an e-mail link requesting members to provide input to the negotiations committee as well as an open-ended survey form to be returned by fax asking members to tell the committee what they wanted in the negotiations (SCPEA, 2001).

Teamsters. The International Brotherhood of Teamsters, which has 1,400,700 members (Gifford, 2000) and represents a wide range of industries, has an elaborate website. A major portion of the IBT website is devoted to collective bargaining content. For example, the site presents information about union tactics, such as handbilling customers at stores where the IBT has disputes. It also reports on such issues as successful outcomes in representation elections and arbitration awards on master agreements as well as apprenticeship training programs for drivers. In addition, the IBT's site provides more detailed information broken out by its trade divisions — freight, newspapers, carhauling, warehouses, airlines, etc. A governmental affairs section deals with IBT's political activities and outlines its legislative agenda. It also has a well-developed feature that allows members to pass on their views on various issues to their congressional representatives. In addition, there is a large separate section that describes union election rules, results of protests over elections, electronic election protest forms, and a search engine for use in identifying information for election protests. The national IBT website also reveals the importance of efficiency as there are relatively few telephone numbers listed. The IBT's large membership could easily overwhelm the national headquarters if phone calls were made directly to the headquarters (IBT Website, 2001).

The IBT website also features a local union website of the month, such as Local #707 in Hempstead, New York. The website has substantial content of a tactical nature such as highlights of its negotiations with large firms. It has reported favorable court rulings in litigation and has issued a challenge to a company to bargain in good faith. It also reports the receipt of hotline calls alleging unfair actions, and recently the local's website announced its list of convention delegates (IBT Local #707 Website, 2001).

E-voice also is evident in dissident groups opposed to the way in which their unions are run. For example, a website is maintained by a group of Teamster dissidents called the Teamsters for a Democratic Union. The website reports news such as results of the election of reform candidates in local union elections; delegates that the locals will send to the IBT's convention; a court ruling that protects members' voting rights; changes that are needed in contracts with major employers such as United Parcel Service (UPS), and guilty pleas by two stockbrokers to federal racketeering charges involving the pension funds of an IBT local union (Teamsters for a Democratic Union Website, 2001).

The e-voice of dissident members has demonstrated its power to provoke the targets of criticism. A website maintained by dissident members of a different union and acts of retaliation to the site's content have been the subject of recent litigation. In *Konop v. Hawaiian Airlines, Inc.* (9th Circuit Court, January 8, 2001), Konop, a pilot for Hawaiian Airlines, operated a website on which he provided unfavorable information about his employer. He also criticized his union officials as well as the union itself and promoted representation by another union. Visitors to the website were required to register and obtain a password with the agreement that they would not reveal the contents of the website (Dannin, 2001). A vice president for the airline used the identity of other pilots to enter the website and obtained information which he passed on to the company's president who contacted Konop and threatened to sue Konop for defamation. The Ninth Circuit Court of Appeals found that the employer's entry to the website through false pretenses violated the Wiretap Act as well as several provisions of the Railway Labor Act (Dannin, 2001).

United Auto Workers. The website for the United Automobile, Aerospace, and Agricultural Implement Workers of America (UAW), which has 762,439 members at the international level (Gifford, 2000), has several major sections. For example, sections deal with organizing, political activism, safety, and the history and organization of the union. In addition there are descriptions of the UAW's departments, such as arbitration, consumer affairs, retired workers, health and safety, organizing, and information systems. The site also contains a large "buy American" section and an e-voice "contact us" feature, which has a long list of sources of information, numerous other contact points addressing a variety of issues, and a disclaimer that a response from the international level could take two months. In addition, the site provides a description of how the locals function and how local officials are elected. Like the IBT website, the UAW site reflects a need for efficiency. For example, only a few telephone numbers are listed on the entire UAW site such as for the organizing department and a Washington, D.C. switchboard for communicating input on governmental concerns (UAW Website, 2001).

One of the UAW's extensive lists of local links is to UAW Local #249, which represents Ford workers in Kansas City. The website for Local #249, which represents 5,500 workers, presents information on future meetings and important phone numbers and voice mail codes such as for legal issues, a hotline, the union hall, health service, and committee chairs. There also is a request for input for the local's monthly newsletter. Information is also included about upcoming officer elections, procedures, and dates of elections. In addition there is a section on political initiatives and a sample letter for the local representative to Congress and a senator (UAW Local #249 Website, 2001).

United Association of Plumbers and Pipefitters. The United Association of Journeymen and Apprentices of the Plumbing, Pipefitting, Sprinklerfitting Industry of the
United States and Canada (UA) has 299,136 members (Gifford, 2000). The national
union's website indicates that organizing is a priority and provides a list of 35 practices that employers cannot engage in while workers are attempting to organize. In
addition, there is a heavy focus on training with sections that address apprenticeships,
journeyman training, instructor training, certification, and training for union officers.
There also are course schedules for different regions for such specific topics as electrical and refrigerant controls and building automation systems. The section also has
a feature through which members can request specific types of training. In addition,
there are sections on safety, the union's administrative organization, a members-only
section, a section for children, and links to local unions. Like most sites the UA site
also has a section on political affairs, with a feature that enables members to conveniently e-mail their congressperson and senators about their political concerns (UA
Website, 2001).

UA Local #400, which represents plumbers in Green Bay, Wisconsin and surrounding areas, has a comprehensive website. The site places substantial emphasis on
training. For example, the site provides contact information for different apprenticeship programs in plumbing and steamfitting, as well as information about a welder certification program. In addition, there are sections covering benefits such as health
insurance, the 401(k) program, and the employee assistance program. The site also provides contact information for organizing, a list of the elected officers, and an extensive section on political action (UA Local #400 Website, 2001).

American Federation of Government Employees. The American Federation of Government Employees (AFGE), which has 191,171 members (Gifford, 2000), represents
federal government employees. Unsurprisingly, since the AFGE's members cannot
strike, a large proportion of the national union's website is devoted to political activism.
Examples include a legislative section, portions of a "what's new" section that deals
with political issues, and a large section outlining the union's opposition to the contracting out of work performed by government employees. AFGE members can enter
the website's members-only section to find out what they can to do to stop the government's contracting out and privatization efforts. In addition, there is a section on
organizing, which is a common feature of national union websites (AFGE Website,
2001).

Several of the website's features provide opportunities for e-voice. For example,
correspondence from members, including dissenting views, is presented in a letters-to-
the-editor section. The website also seeks input from women through a link to an AFL-
CIO site that contains a survey entitled "Ask a Working Woman." After responding to
the survey, respondents submit their input online. In addition, there is a service feature link to the AFL-CIO's website, which provides national and world news features,
weather forecasts, stock quotes, and online stock portfolio tracking and offers online
household bill payment services and credit cards (AFGE Website, 2001).

There also is an extensive list of links to AFGE locals with designations of award-
winning local union websites as well as for districts and councils. The website for

AFGE Local #1916 was the first place local and, as with the national AFGE website, contains a heavy emphasis on political activism. In addition, the website contains high-lights of a new contract, a complete copy of a new contract, a members-only section, and information for organizing including a membership form (AFGE Local #1916 Web-site, 2001).

Allied Pilots Association. The website of the Allied Pilots Association (APA), an independent union representing 11,500 American Airlines pilots, provides frequent, and at times almost daily, reports on union negotiation and contract administration activities (APA Website, 2001). In 2001 it devoted substantial attention to APA's nego-tiations with American Airlines over the acquisition of TWA airlines and even more detailed information on this issue in its members-only section (Howard, 2001). Exam-ples of other issues reported on the website include issues relating to Federal Aviation Administration (FAA) flight time regulations, such as the 16-hour maximum-duty day, routes flown, and results of elections for union officers. There also is an e-voice feature urging members to complete a website survey seeking their input on negotiation issues.

IV. Data and Measures for Analysis of Websites

Website Data. Data were obtained by examining the websites of AFL-CIO national or international unions affiliates linked to the AFL-CIO website.[3] Content from all 63 of the national affiliates having websites was collected during the period from Janu-ary to April 2001.[4] Membership data were obtained from the Directory of U.S. Labor Organizations (Gifford, 2000) or from websites when unavailable in the directory. The average size of unions in the sample was 240,682 members. Canadian members were included because the websites for these unions are accessible by all members. Of the total websites examined, 16 percent were those of unions whose primary jurisdictions included public sector employees. In addition, 12 IT professionals from different unions were interviewed by telephone about their unions' websites and future applications of Internet technology. Information from these interviews has been incorporated through-out this article.

Measures. The potential influence of union websites on democracy may be assessed through such measures as discussion boards, union solicitations of their memberships for input, control of content on websites, and presence of dissident publicity on the Internet (Diamond and Freeman, 2000; Jarley et al., 2000). Several measures of this nature were used to code website data. Website content was coded by a graduate assis-tant, with my assistance, according to the following: (1) indicators of democracy (con-tent devoted to office holders' issues, content devoted to members' issues, calls to members to run for office, and changes in officers and staff); (2) e-voice functions (solicitation of input on issues desired in new contracts, encouragement of members to make input on union governance, and chat rooms); (3) collective bargaining con-tent (new contracts signed, work stoppages, benefits, wage trends, and ongoing nego-tiations); (4) confidential information (members-only sections requiring sign-in); and (5) political activism (material on legislative initiatives or political support). Measures used in this exploratory content analysis are relatively coarse-grained with all items having dichotomous response categories for the presence of a feature or indicator (either yes or no) or the amount of content devoted to an issue (high or low).

V. Results of Content Analysis of Internet Effects

The results of the content analysis of websites are presented in Table 1. As indicated in the table the four coarse-grained measures of union democracy revealed more emphasis on members' issues than officers' issues. Only 16 percent had sites that were coded as having substantial content devoted to officers' issues while 70 percent of the sites were coded as having a high proportion of their content focusing on the interests of members. On the other hand, there was relatively little content devoted specifically to democratic governance as only 8 percent contained material encouraging members to run for office. However, as noted earlier in the examples of websites from six different types of unions, websites commonly include information on election processes. A somewhat larger proportion (22 percent) reported changes in officers or staff members.

A relatively low proportion of websites had functions devoted to e-voice. Only 14 percent solicited input from members about issues to be negotiated in new contracts. Similarly, I found that only 16 percent had features encouraging members to contribute input on union governance. Likewise, only 13 percent had chat room or discussion board functionality in unsecured areas. However, some unions place their chat rooms in secure or members-only sections in order to keep discussions confidential. Thus, there are more chat room features than indicated by this figure (Howard, 2001; Superfisky, 2001). Public sector unions may be more inclined to use chat room features or to place them in unsecured areas of their sites. Of the 10 public sector unions in the sample, 3 (30 percent) of the sites had chat rooms in public areas compared with 6 (11 percent) of the 53 sites for the other unions. While these specific features address democracy, reliance solely on these data would understate the impact of IT on union democracy because e-mail links to the top officers are a common feature of websites. Furthermore, our interviewees revealed that unions are receiving high volumes of e-mail from members providing input on their views.

I found that a great deal of website content is instrumental as it deals with processes or outcomes of collective bargaining. Substantial content is devoted to informing memberships about the results of negotiations or ongoing negotiations as 49 percent reported on new contracts, 48 percent reported on ongoing negotiations, and 44 percent described work stoppages. More than half (57 percent) reported information about benefits negotiated or provided by the union, and 22 percent reported information about wages or wage trends. Several of these website features tended to occur together. News of contracts signed was highly correlated with reports of information about benefits negotiated ($r = .85$, $p < .01$) and information about strikes ($r = .65$, $p < .01$). Similarly, reports about benefits were significantly correlated with information about strikes ($r = .58$, $p < .01$).[5] In addition, 24 percent of the sites had secure or members-only areas. This proportion may be understated as members-only sections are sometimes difficult to iden-

Table 1
Website Content of National Unions

	Percent of Sites with Feature
Content Indicating Democracy	
Substantial Content Devoted to Office Holders' Issues	16
Substantial Content Devoted to Members' Issues	70
Calls for Members to Run for Union Office	8
Change in Officers and Staff	22
E-Voice Functions	
Solicitation of Input on Desired Issues to Be Negotiated in New Contracts	14
Encouragement of Members to Use the Website to Make Input on Union Governance	16
Chat Rooms or Discussion Boards	13
Collective Bargaining Content	
New Contracts Signed	49
Ongoing Negotiations	48
Work Stoppages	44
Benefits Negotiated	57
Wage Trends	22
Confidential Information	
"Members-Only" Section	24
Political Activism Content	
Political Issues	84

Note: Several of these unions are internationals with Canadian members.

tify. As noted earlier, some websites use these secure areas for dissemination of information about on-going negotiations or for chat rooms that discuss employers or negotiations (Howard, 2001; Superfisky, 2001).

Finally, the most pervasive feature was information of a political nature with 84 percent of the sites presenting political information mostly about federal elective office holders and legislative initiatives. As indicated in the earlier examples, some of the political sections are very large, particularly for unions that rely heavily on political means such as unions representing governmental employees.

VI. Discussion

The results of the literature review, in-depth examinations of websites for six different types of unions, and content analysis of websites, indicate that IT is affecting life in unions in several import ways. Unions have embraced IT and see Internet and e-mail technologies as keys to their futures. In many unions IT has enabled members to participate more in the affairs of their unions, such as by providing input for upcoming negotiations and their views on union governance. The use of e-mail technology by rank-and-file members to communicate with top union officials has become commonplace. In addition, union members have access to more information through the Internet and e-mail. These developments provide preliminary evidence that IT provides e-voice. While the impact of e-voice on union democracy cannot be determined at this time, there is evidence that IT has lowered the cost of exercising voice. In addition, anecdotal evidence indicates that some dissident members are using independent websites to air their views about union affairs, such as a lack of democracy, and a few unions are using their websites to criticize the lack of democracy in their national organizations.

IT applications also provide unions with tactical advantages in organizing and in negotiations with employers. The Internet and e-mail provide important communication and coordination tools, which enable unions to better manage their efforts during strikes. Unions also see efficiencies in IT and have been able to serve geographically dispersed members as a result of IT applications. These efficiencies and the information dissemination advantages of IT also have enabled unions to provide more employment services to their members. Unions also are using websites and e-mail in attempts to enhance their political power. These IT applications disseminate a great deal of political information to members and the general public about issues that are helpful or harmful to unions. Nonetheless, because companies and other lobbying groups are attempting to obtain the same advantage through similar IT applications, it remains to be seen whether unions will achieve relative gains in political advantage. Nonetheless, because there has been widespread adoption of IT by unions for various purposes, including political lobbying, there is potential for greater impact in the future. The following section offers speculations about the future effects of IT.

VII. Speculations about Future IT Effects on Life in Unions

Results of the literature review, the survey of website content, the more intensive examination of selected websites, and telephone interviews of union IT staff members provide the basis for several speculations on how IT will affect life in unions in the future. These speculations fit into four categories: (1) leadership, (2) governance and structure, (3) service to members, and (4) collective bargaining and political action.

Leadership

Speculation 1. Emergence of Leaders with IT Knowledge. IT or Internet innovators in the local unions may gravitate toward leadership positions in the future. There is substantial innovation and skill reflected in some of the local union websites, and a number of innovations have filtered upward to the national union sites (Cantrell, 2001). In many locals members perform site development and maintenance work as a hobby. It is possible that members having IT or Internet expertise may gravitate toward leadership positions as more of the business of local unions involves IT. As conduits of information, such members may have control of content or access to websites, and their skills should become critical to locals as they become more reliant on IT applications. Such individuals possess knowledge power and can withhold IT knowledge on which their leaders and peers depend. Their ability to withhold their knowledge may provide them with the power to obtain leadership positions on their own terms, if they are so inclined. At this time it is unknown whether these individuals will have the desire to assume the political and negotiations responsibilities involved with higher leadership roles. On the other hand, it also is likely that other members who arise to leadership positions through traditional paths in the future will develop IT knowledge before reaching the top leadership positions. There also may be similar implications for ascendancy to leadership positions in national unions.[6]

Speculation 2. Allocation of More Resources to Cope with the Demands of IT. While e-mail provides tremendous opportunities for economical and rapid two-way communication with members, the volume of e-mail can become overwhelming in terms of the time required to respond. Where the work of union members involves constant use of computers, there is easy e-mail access and greater likelihood of increased e-mail volume. For example, SPEEA's members are engineers and technical workers who have access to e-mail at their workstations. Unsurprisingly, SPEEA leaders receive heavy amounts of e-mail from the membership to which they need to respond (Dugovich, 2001). Personal e-mail responses from union leaders should increase the quality of service to union members, and one IT professional stated that he took a great deal of pride in the fact that the national president of his union (IBEW) was online and that every rank-and-file member had access to the president (Cantrell, 2001). However, it is easy to envision a situation in which the sheer numbers of e-mails may overwhelm union leaders unless they are able to delegate the task of providing responses. Several IT professionals noted that their unions were having difficulty coping with the volumes of e-mail. Unions will need to allocate sufficient resources to process member input or they will be viewed as providing only a mock form of grassroots involvement.

Speculation 3. Potential for Strategic and Environmental Myopia. There may be another downside result other than the personal time or organizational resources required to simply respond to such matters as increased numbers of e-mails. The experience of corporate CEO's may be applicable. Peter Drucker has noted that the development of sophisticated information systems has had a downside for CEOs because the information provided by such systems causes them to focus more internally. As their focus shifts inward because of information availability, the CEOs' attention is distracted from the external environments in which their companies operate. In a sense Drucker says that these information systems have caused CEOs to become myopic and that there are serious dysfunctional consequences when the CEO becomes less focused on the external environment (Drucker, 1997). Greater volumes of information from members may tend to shift the focus of union leaders in a similar manner to internal affairs. With such a shift it is easy to envision a situation in which union leaders cut back on the time they devote to the external environment and environmental scanning.

Governance and Structure

Speculation 4. More Democracy. While the content analysis did not find widespread adoption of website features specifically designed to provide e-voice, several unions have focused heavily on voice. A number of websites provide sophisticated features directed unequivocally toward e-voice, such as online surveys that solicit input for ongoing negotiations. Furthermore, as noted earlier, a number of large unions provide their members with direct e-mail access to their presidents. In addition, as noted earlier, the AFL-CIO has encouraged greater membership input into the operations of its affiliates by supplying low-cost computers and Internet service, and the APWU has negotiated with the U.S. Postal Service over a similar package. Such programs should increase Internet access in union members' homes and should provide a stronger base for potential enhancement of participation.

An alternate view is that unions more inclined toward participation, such as those that traditionally have sought member input or that have accessible leaders, will use IT to provide greater participation or democracy while those without such inclinations will not use IT for such purposes. With this view, IT is not a driving force toward participation or democracy but is simply a reflection of the underling culture of the union. Future research should address the direction of causality in these potential relationships.

Speculation 5. More Efficient Staffing, Structures, and Processes. IT has been an enabling influence in the reengineering or process redesign of corporations. While the concept has usually failed to produce expected results and has been viewed as another management fad, there is some value in reengineering in more limited applications (Nadler and Tuschman, 1997). Reengineering typically combines the tasks of employees and reduces the number of "handoffs" in workflow, such as between individual workers and between organizational units. After reengineering, a single employee armed with a powerful information system is able to perform a broader range of activities, which previously would have been performed by several different specialists. In services work reengineering allows one customer service representative to provide "one stop shopping" (Hall et al., 1993; Stewart, 1993). While reengineering characteristically produces conflict from changing power relationships and job elimination, the driving force behind reengineering is often increased competition and the need for greater efficiencies (Hall et al., 1993; Hammer and Champy, 1993; Stewart, 1993).

Since unions are service organizations there may be some parallels with trends toward IT-empowered staff members who perform a broader range of activities. Unions also have needs for greater efficiencies as demonstrated by the long series of national union mergers. Furthermore, the experience of the IT innovator, the British Columbia Teachers' Federation, provides an example of the coordination functions of such technology and its impact on union positions. At the BCTF the network's direct linkage between its leadership, staff, and members eliminated the need for regional coordinators who previously performed information dissemination and coordination functions (Lee, 1997). It will be interesting to see whether IT innovations and needs for efficiency cause unions to adopt processes such as reengineering.

Service to Members

Speculation 6. Improved Perceptions of Unions. Websites with sophisticated design and graphics potentially provide richer forms of communication than traditional materials mailed to members' homes and can potentially reach a larger number of members than face-to-face meetings or personal phone calls. In addition to visual images, which conventional newsletters provide, they can combine audio and much greater variety of information that members or potential members can access according to their interests. The literature on information or media richness argues that decision makers tend to use richer media to convey more ambiguous or equivocal information. Face-to-face communication carries the most richness while numeric documents carry the least. Essentially, richer information has greater ability to change understanding in a given amount of time (Ngwenyama and Lee, 1997). This richer form of communication may have the potential to convey greater emotion about issues to union members. Richer Internet communication also may enhance union affiliation by increasing awareness of the activities in which the union is involved. In addition, it may increase union loyalty and satisfaction with the union through increased service quality and efficiencies, which the technology makes possible. On the other hand, because the standard for information richness will probably continue to increase at other websites, unions will most likely need to constantly improve the quality of their sites in order to retain members' interest.

Speculation 7. Improved Communication with Members. As noted earlier, at American Airlines, which has been plagued in recent years by a hostile labor relations climate, the CEO is trying to reverse his predecessor's "scorched earth" approach to labor relations. In this new IT approach the company has spent heavily to provide Internet access in employees' homes in hopes of establishing improved communication (Jones, 2001). If other employers pursue similar programs, unions may perceive potential risks of losing such competitions for the loyalties of their members. The AFL-CIO's program to provide computers in members' homes may be followed by even greater investments by unions in Internet and e-mail communication.

Collective Bargaining and Political Action

Speculation 8. Increased Political Activism and Public Awareness. As noted earlier, virtually all examples of websites include substantial material on political initiatives. Many of them have a convenient link by which members can express their views to elected officials. A legislator facing an upcoming vote can be overwhelmed with thousands of e-mail responses advocating the union's perspective on a bill. While union members may not be sufficiently interested to monitor their unions' websites on a frequent basis, as more members gain access to the Internet and e-mail at work or home, there is greater potential for strengthened political action by unions. One IT professional at a large union indicated that the union would expand its political action alerts and grass-roots political programs. It seems clear that union members will become more politically aware of legislative developments as a result of union websites and e-mail.

Speculation 9. Better Management of Members' Expectations in Negotiations. The review of websites indicated that several unions, particularly those involving professionals such as airline pilots and engineers, provide updates on negotiations almost daily. In addition to providing information to members, as noted earlier, a number of websites ask for input from their members through e-mail responses or online surveys, although the ease of communication makes it possible for members to swamp leaders with input. Timely updates through the Internet and e-mail may enable union negotiators to better manage the expectations of their constituents. To the extent that such updates enable union leaders to shape expectations, there is less likelihood of negotiation breakdowns resulting from a divergence between union leaders and members' expectations over attainable negotiation outcomes.

Speculation 10. Negotiating in Goldfish Bowls. Close monitoring of progress reports on websites or through e-mail may provide barriers to the use of integrative negotiation approaches because union negotiators may become more accountable to their members. Greater negotiator accountability may result from a sort of "audience effect" produced by frequent website or e-mail disclosures. Such increased accountability may cause negotiators to adopt more competitive approaches while they seek to avoid appearances of weakness implied by concessionary behavior (Lewicki et al., 1999). Furthermore, as union members learn about the details of negotiations without having in-depth knowledge of the other side's strengths, weaknesses, and the intangibles involved, there is some likelihood that they will arrive at inaccurate assessments of the performance of their own negotiating teams and apply misdirected pressure. In addition, it may be more difficult for union negotiators to downplay their inability to obtain individual issues in complicated negotiations. In the absence of close monitoring and when there are many issues, negotiators are sometimes able to allow an issue to fall by the wayside without having to admit that they failed to obtain agreement on the issue (Walton and Mckersie, 1965).

Notes

*   I acknowledge the research assistance of Joy Davis as well as the many helpful suggestions of Jack Fiorito, Florida State University, and Daphne Taras, University of Calgary. In addition I am indebted to Steve Inman, Sarah Thomas and Fran Eller, Texas Christian University, for their editorial work with the manuscript. I also thank Dorothy Leidner, Texas Christian University, and Ellen Dannin, California Western School of Law, for their suggestions of helpful literature.
1   Some researchers have referred to these IT components as informatics. Informatics has been described in the works of Karlgaard (1998) as "the marriage of telecommunication technologies, as exemplified by the Internet and the computer" (Shostak, 1999, p. 3). Others have referred to these components as communications technology (CT).

2   Decentralized decision making and greater autonomy at the local level are not necessarily associated with increased democracy as the relationship is complicated by the potential for corruption. In fact, the opposite may be true as illustrated by the corruption in some of the locals in the Teamsters' decentralized organization (Belzer and Hurd, 1999).
3   This is according to the list of links that was posted on the AFL-CIO's website as of April 6, 2001.
4   The Actors' Equity Association (AEA), the American Federation of Television and Ratio Artists (AFTRA), and the American Guild of Musical Artists (AGMA) are branches of the Associated Actors and Artists of America.
5   The strength of the correlations is limited because the variables are dichotomous.
6   It is interesting to speculate on the leadership implications of the personality types of union members having IT interests and skills. While Internet and website expertise are not the same as programming or systems analysis, there may be some similarities from a general technical orientation. Research on the personality traits of programmer analysts and systems analysts has provided information in terms of the well-known Myers-Briggs Type Indicator (MBTI). One study has found the ISTJ personality type to be most prevalent among such IT professionals. The ISTJ type indicates introversion, sensing, thinking, and judging traits. While 25 percent of the subjects in the study had this particular combination, only 6 percent of the general population has similar traits (Bush and Schkade, 1985; Keirsey and Bates, 1978). More specifically, the programmers and analysts were more introverted than extroverted; more likely to use their senses to gather information than to rely on intuition; more likely to evaluate information by thinking or rational analysis instead of how they feel about or value a situation, and more likely to judge or seek closure as opposed to perceiving or feeling comfortable with open or fluid situations (Keirsey and Bates, 1978). The mixture of these personality characteristics may be compatible with the requirements of effective union leadership, although their tendency toward introversion may require some adaptation. Furthermore, the dependability and honor ISTJ types place on their word may enable them to build trusting relationships with the employers with whom they negotiate.

References

Actors' Equity Association (AEA) Website: <www.actorsequity.org> (2001).
Ad Hoc Committee on Labor and the Web. "Why the Internet Matters to Organized Labor." <www.mindopen.com/laborweb> (1999).
Allied Pilots Association (APA) Website: <www.alliedpilots.org> (2001).
American Federation of Government Employees (AFGE) Website: <www.afge.org> (2001).
American Federation of Government Employees (AFGE) Local 1916 Website: <www.afge1916. org> (2001).
American Federation of Labor – Congress of Industrial Organizations (AFLCIO) Website: <workingfamilies.ibelong.com> (2001).
American Federation of Labor – Congress of Industrial Organizations. "Cyber Drives: Organizing, Bargaining and Mobilizing." <www.aflcio.org/articles/cyberdrives/> (2001).
American Guild of Musical Artists (AGMA) Website: <www.musicalartists.org> (2001).
American Postal Workers Union (APWU), <www.apwu.org/burrusupdates.htm> (2001).
Belzer, Michael H. and Richard Hurd. "Government Oversight, Union Democracy, and Labor Racketeering: Lessons from the Teamsters Experience." *Journal of Labor Research* 20 (Summer 1999): 343–65.
Bittner, Andrew. Information Systems, Fraternal Order of Police (FOP), telephone interview, April 25, 2001.
British Columbia Carpenters Union Website: <www.carpentersunionbc.com> (2001).
Bush, Chandler M. and Lawrence L. Schkade. "In Search of the Perfect Programmer: Which Personality Traits Point People toward Success in the DP Industry?" *Datamation* (March 15, 1985): 129–31.

Cantrell, Carl. Information Systems, International Brotherhood of Electrical Workers (IBEW), telephone interview, April 20, 2001.

Communications Workers of America (CWA) Website: <www.cwa-union.org/jobs/index.asp> (2001).

Dannin, Ellen. *Industrial Relations Research Association, IRRA National Newsletter, Law and Employment Law Section*<www.irra.uiuc.edu/newsletters/index.html#LELSNEWS> (January 2001).

Diamond, Wayne and Richard B. Freeman."From the Webbs to the Web: Unions and the Internet." Leverhulme Trust Research Programme Workshop, December 12, 2000.

Drucker, Peter F. "The Future Has Already Happened." *Harvard Business Review* 75 (September-October 1997): 20–24.

Dugovich, Bill. Communications Director, Society of Professional Engineering Employees in Aerospace, telephone interview, April 13, 2001.

Estreicher, Samuel. "Deregulating Union Democracy." *Journal of Labor Research* 21 (Spring 2000): 247–63.

Fiorito, Jack and William Bass. "Information Technology Use in National Unions: An Exploration." Industrial Relations (in press).

Fiorito, Jack, Paul Jarley, and John T. Delaney. "Information Technology, Union Organizing, and Union Effectiveness." unpublished manuscript (March 2001).

———. "The Adoption of Information Technology by U.S. National Unions." *Relations Industrielles* 25 (Summer 2000): 451–76.

———, and Robert W. Kolodinsky. "Unions and Information Technology: From Luddites to Cyberunions?" *Labor Studies Journal* 24 (Winter 2000): 3–34.

Frost, Ann C. "Union Involvement in Workplace Decision Making: Implications for Union Democracy." *Journal of Labor Research* 21 (Winter 2000): 265–86.

Gifford, Court, ed. *Directory of U.S. Labor Organizations*, 2000 Edition, Washington, D.C.: Bureau of National Affairs, 2000.

Hall, Gene, Jim Rosenthal, and Judy Wade. "How to Make Reengineering Really Work." *Harvard Business Review* 71 (November-December 1993): 119–31.

Hammer, Michael and James Champy. *Reengineering the Corporation.* New York: Harper Business, 1993.

Hirschman, Albert O. *Exit, Voice, and Loyalty: Responses to Decline in Firms, Organizations, and States.* Cambridge, Mass.: Harvard University Press, 1970.

Howard, Mark. Information Systems, Allied Pilots Association, telephone interview, April 20, 2001.

International Brotherhood of Teamsters Website: <www.teamster.com> (2001).

———, Local #707 Website: <www.ibt707.com> (2001).

Jarley, Paul, Jack Fiorito, and John T. Delaney. "National Union Governance: An Empirically-Grounded Systems Approach." Journal of Labor Research 21 (Spring 2000): 227–46.

Jones, Katherine. "American Flier." *Texas Monthly* 29 (March 2001): 74–78.

Karlgaard, Rich. "The Web Is Recession-Proof." *Wall Street Journal*, July 14, 1998.

Keirsey, David and Marilyn Bates. *Please Understand Me: Character and Temperament Types*, 5th ed. Del Mar, Calif.: Prometheus Nemesis Book Company, 1978.

Konop v. Hawaiian Airlines Inc., No. 99-55106, 9th Circuit Court, (January 8, 2001).

Lee, Eric. *The Labour Movement and the Internet: The New Intertnationalism.* London: Pluto Press, 1997.

Lewicki, Roy J., David M. Saunders, and John M. Minton. *Negotiations*, 3rd ed. Boston: McGraw-Hill, 1999.

Nadler, David A. and Michael L. Tushman. *Competing by Design: The Power of Organizational Architecture.* New York: Oxford University Press, 1997.

Ngwenyama, Ojelanki K. and Allen S. Lee. "Communication Richness in Electronic Mail: Critical Social Theory and the Contextuality of Meaning." *MIS Quarterly* 21 (June 1997): 145–67.

Shostak, Arthur B. *CyberUnion: Empowering Labor through Computer Technology.* Armonk, N.Y.: M.E. Sharp, 1999.

Southern California Professional Engineers Association (SCPEA) Website: <www.scpea.org/ nego2001/ index.htm> (2001).

Stewart, Thomas A. "Reengineering: The New Management Tool." *Fortune* (August 23, 1993): 41–48.

Strauss, George. "Union Democracy." In George Strauss, Daniel G. Gallagher, and Jack Fiorito, eds. The State of the Unions. Madison, Wisc.: Industrial Relations Research Association, 1991, pp. 201–206.

Strauss, George. "What's Happening Inside U.S. Unions: Democracy and Union Politics." *Journal of Labor Research* 21 (Spring 2000): 211–25.

Superfisky, Jim. Information Systems, Brotherhood of Maintenance of Way Employees, telephone interview, April 20, 2001.

Teamsters for a Democratic Union (TDU) Website: <www.tdu.org> (2001).

UBC Yes Website: <members.aol.com/bbaker4583/ubcyes.html> (2001).

United Association of Journeymen and Apprentices of the Plumbing, Pipefitting, Sprinklerfitting Industry of the United States and Canada (UA) Website: <www.ua.org> (2001).

United Association of Plumbers and Steamfitters (UA), Local #400 Website: <personalpages.tds.net/~ua400> (2001).

United Automobile, Aerospace, and Agricultural Implement Workers Union (UAW) Website: <www.uaw.org> (2001).

———, Local #249 Website: <www.local249.org> (2001).

Walton, Richard E. and Robert B. McKersie. *A Behavioral Theory of Labor Negotiations: An Analysis of a Social Interaction System.* New York: McGraw-Hill, 1965.

Witiak, Diane. Information Systems, American Federation of Government Employees, telephone interview, April 20, 2001.

5

Today's Unions as Tomorrow's CyberUnions: Labor's Newest Hope

Arthur B. Shostak
Drexel University

I. Introduction

Ongoing efforts by the AFL-CIO and its 66 affiliates to maximize their creative use of computer power may help slow, stem, and finally reverse Labor's decline in union density. Computerization makes possible certain distinctive reforms vital if Labor is to soon improve its renewal chances.

While emphatically not a "magic bullet" or an instantaneous cure, computerization makes possible wide-scale communications of dazzling speed and enormous outreach (national and international). It enables unprecedented accessibility of officeholders, and timely exchanges of views among them and members, and among the members themselves (via electronic bulletin boards and chat rooms, including some run unofficially). It makes mobilization for political action and strike support far more feasible. And it facilitates corporate campaigns that would otherwise overwhelm with complexity and data.

On the level of the local, computerization enables International Representatives and Business Agents to download into a laptop reams of relevant material (grievance and arbitration records, previous contracts, etc.). This enables them to do on the spot the high quality job expected by dues-payers influenced by the "Buck Rogers" high-tech world around them. As well, locals can create electronic listserves to link together the entire membership, appeal to prospective members, address subcultures differently, and in other overdue ways, build a new form of "electronic community," a 21st-century adaptation of yesteryear's solidarity.

Where labor militancy is concerned, intriguing new tools are available: Unions can encourage members to threaten to shut down or in other ways impede the use of their computers at work. Or they can create "picket lines" in cyberspace. Or urge boycotts of the products or services of targeted employers — and do this faster and with far wider coverage than was possible relying on old-fashioned mailings offering "Do Not Buy" lists. Contrariwise, concerning co-creating a high-performance workplace in partnership with a cooperative employer, Labor's use of computers can facilitate employee dialogue about overdue workplace boosts to productivity — complete with a union imprimatur.

Accordingly, although insufficient in and of itself to "rescue" Labor, computer power raises fresh hope that ensuing gains in efficiency and effectiveness may help attract many new members. It could help raise the level of support of existing members (always Labor's best organizers). And in 101 other significant ways, it could rapidly bolster Labor's urgent effort at recovery (http://workingfamilies.com/; http://afscme.org/ publications/puttc.htm).

II. Background

When in the early 1970s Labor first got involved with mainframe computers, they were used to handle the massive data-warehousing, data-mining, and record-keeping needs posed by dues and fringe-benefit matters. Word-processing desktop PCs followed, and in due course, certain especially progressive unions and locals began to employ the laptop and e-mail power of Internet and the World Wide Web.

Were this all there was to the computer use story it would reduce only to a minor tale of bureaucratic modernization, a necessary, but insufficient explanation for Labor's (continually more threatened) existence. While commonly overlooked, aspects of this tale are, in fact, much richer matters.

Computerization has begun to challenge the status quo in many critical aspects of modern unionism (and modern life alike). Components of trade unionism from A (accountability) to Z (Zeitgeist) are being substantially altered, especially matters of internal administration (the special concern of this essay) (Lee, 1997).

Symbolic here is the conversion of the *AFL-CIO News*, the bland, mind-dulling house organ that John Sweeney, new head of the Labor Federation, inherited in 1996. His aides quickly turned it into a bright, brassy, and "hip" publication now called *America @ Work*, in which nearly every issue has a page devoted to Internet sites and cyberspace tools worth union attention. This move showed recognition by the Sweeney forces of the need to present a new "face" for Labor, one that signals "being with it," via energizing, colorful, and morale-boosting messages.

Herein, I explore how computer uses are altering the internal operations of certain progressive International Unions and their best locals. More specifically, I discuss five related matters: (1) What are the major areas of advancement? (2) What are the major causes of concern? (3) What are the relevant types of computer-using (or non-using) unions and locals? (4) What defines a CyberUnion? And (5) what pending changes in computer options should Organized Labor take carefully into account?

Given an inexcusable neglect by scholars of this subject, and the related paucity of available data, only very tentative answers can be shared at this time, answers that hope-fully will earn testing and improvement in further discourse.[1]

III. Methodology

Drawing on 47 years of formal study of unionism here and abroad, and especially on my last 26 years of adjunct teaching at the AFL-CIO George Meany Center for Labor Studies in Silver Spring, Maryland, I have long tracked the complex pattern of union uses of computer power (Shostak, 1991).

Most recently, I attended LaborTech Conventions held in 1998 in San Francisco, 1999 in New York, and 2000 in Madison, Wisconsin, as these three-day events high-light progress and problems in an invaluable (and unofficial) way. (They are self-spon-sored by grass-roots activists, and only in 2000 did the AFL-CIO send several representatives). I have often interviewed key AFL-CIO and International Union com-puter specialists (webmasters, etc.), and I have attended several workshops given for unionists eager to gain computer skills. I was an invited guest at the inauguration in 2000 of the new Teamster Union website, and I have guided teams of my students in close studies of the 64 websites of the 66 AFL-CIO union affiliates (along with hun-dreds of local union sites and several overseas sites).

In 1999 I authored *CyberUnion: Empowering Labor through Computer Technol-ogy*, and I am busy now preparing a successor (manual-like) volume for publication in 2002 (Shostak, 1999). In 2000 I co-produced a 30-minute VHS film, "Labor Com-putes: Union People, Computer Power," made up of pithy interviews with Labor digerati types. Naturally, I participate in various Labor-oriented listserves, maintain one of my own (www.cyberunions.net), and "surf" both the literature and the Internet (with its estimated six billion pages) for relevant material.[2]

IV. Areas of Advancement

Four key aspects of internal affairs appear significantly changed by Labor's use of computer power. Just about every aspect of unionism has been impacted, but the four — alliance-building, communications, organizing, and staff development efforts — are at the forefront in demonstrating whether or not computer uses make a really conse-quential difference.

1. Alliance-building has always been a priority, with unions and locals alike seek-ing strategic ties to other bodies in Labor and to various Non-Governmental Organi-zations (NGOs).

Historically, however, this has generally meant burdensome file drawers stuffed to overflow with relevant clippings and correspondence, etc. Union officers had a moun-tain of "must call!" pink phone slips on a desktop spindle, and a pile of business cards from contacts only vaguely remembered. Much of the information quickly grew stale and useless.

Today, reliance on computers means electronic files that can save space, are timely, and can with reasonable effort be kept current — thanks to e-mail exchanges designed to update information. Phone calls can give way to real-time e-mail exchanges (complete with a "paper trail"). As well, a union or local can discretely access the website of a prospective allied organization and determine privately whether or not to reach out itself for a new alliance in a coordinated boycott, educational venture, lobbying effort, picket line, or the like.

2. Communications has historically featured a staid house organ, poorly attended meetings, many (commonly ignored) mailings, and some new and breathless use of faxes or even beeper messages. The material generally came from the top down to the rank and file, and was commonly innocuous or manipulative propaganda (and just as commonly undervalued by many recipients, staff, and rank and filers alike).

Today, at a click of a mouse millions of members of 64 of the AFL-CIO's 66 affiliates with a website can have their own unprecedented access to facts, figures, documents, archives, rules, regulations, photos, videos, etc. They can re-sort this material to suit their purposes and can request additional material — including streaming video subject matter and other fascinating forms of communications they are coming to expect from their International Unions

Shop Stewards, for example, can access elaborately kept proprietary profiles of active mediators and arbitrators (their biases, idiosyncrasies, standards, etc.), as well as data on labor law cases and precedents. Especially helpful are clues as to how best handle a grievance, arbitration, etc., in light of yesterday's major decisions, clues the computer can format as an electronic tutorial or rulebook.

Members can be briefed immediately about fast-breaking developments, and kept abreast almost in a real-time mode. E-mails now go out in a 24/7 (all day/every day) format, and a remarkable new "web" of tight communications never possible with mail, phone, or fax now binds members as never before.

Especially novel is the opportunity that computer-based communication has made possible for a vast upgrade in the very old effort to forge strong bonds among unions around the world. With an estimated 2,700 Labor Union websites online now, and more being added weekly, the opportunities for networking are enormous (Freeman and Thomas in Taylor, 2001).

To be sure, various federations have struggled with this for decades (the ICEM, with its 403 union affiliates in 113 countries; and many others), but making phone connections and airmail letters were always a hindrance. Now, e-mails flash back and forth almost in real time, aiding far-flung port boycotts, corporate campaigns, and other coordinated international activities, despite daunting time and space challenges.

Not to put too fine a point on it, but perhaps *the* most far-reaching change in Labor's communications involves the newly found ability of members to reach one another. Historically, a member could to do this only through the union's newspaper or magazine and then only if the editors agreed to do so. Today, grass-roots activists are busy on a 24/7 basis exchanging advice, views, and visions where their world of Labor is concerned. Caucuses of like-minded members link together in e-mail listserves or through a shared website. Solidarity is built, and the cause of union democracy can receive a strong boost.

(To be sure, resistance to this sea change in communications is also part of the Labor scene. Many staffers resent heightened expectations on them to respond almost immediately via e-mail to scores of e-mail queries that never stop coming in, even while their previous workload weighs heavy. Top officers often shift their e-mail response load to staffers with blithe indifference. As well, paltry raises in staff salaries utterly fail to assuage the pain.)

3. Organizing has previously been a neglected stepchild, receiving only about five percent of the annual budget and little respect from many stand-patters (often waiting out their retirement, or disinclined to assume the heartaches that came with having to service a lot of new members with unreasonable and untutored expectations).

Today, however, in response to the crisis posed by Labor's steady numerical decline, and the unrelenting pressure from the Sweeney Administration, many unions and locals are spending more money and effort than ever before — with computers strategic in the process.

Many leads are coming in cyberspace to union websites specifically designed to attract nonmembers reaching out for help. Organizers are immediately advised by webmasters via e-mail whom they are to rush to contact. The computer also draws a roadmap to the home of a prospective member, and provides an analysis of the company, industry, and labor market history involved in this specific case.

Especially intriguing is the possibility that unions might soon use the Internet to organize "minority" locals inside a workplace as yet unorganized. Incubators for unionism, these computer-based "locals" could collaborate via listserves with one another around the country, trading field-proven advice and lending precious morale support. These unofficial "locals" could make a case for formal unionization by proving useful to their surreptitious members and promoting solidarity — even as participants wait until the times are propitious for seeking an open card count or NLRB election (Freeman and Diamond in Taylor, 2001).

Another less-heralded aspect of this matter, organizing the *organized*, can also receive a major boost from Labor's use of computer power. Local unions in particular can use their website as a 24/7 "newspaper," rich in very current coverage of the activities of members. Photos of participants in a rally, a picket line, a union picnic, or a meeting can appear within a few hours of the event (or sooner!). Immediate news of births, deaths, retirements, etc., can be proudly carried, the sort of homey material that used to grow stale in a once-a-month prosaic union paper, but now can excite and please members who appreciate a bit of positive recognition.

Especially creative webmasters can use their site to offer members a swap service. Or a garage sale outlet. Or a recipe-exchange page. Or for other "down home" services valued by a membership that comes thereby to think first of the local's website when seeking valuable information. In this way new bonds can be forged between local officialdom and dues-payers, bonds that may yet help secure the highly rewarding volunteer services of rank-and-file organizers.

4. Staff development efforts, while not as poorly treated as was organizing, have also suffered from neglect and low priority. They were commonly under-funded, sporadic,

uneven, and poorly assessed. Inadequate backing meant meager results, with ensuing inefficiencies, uneven effectiveness, high staff turnover or burnout, low morale, and other costly consequences.

Today, however, Labor knows it can and must do better. Staff obsolescence threatens unacceptable chaos, especially where getting the staff up to speed in computer use capabilities is concerned. Accordingly, tutorials on line or through computer workshops are increasingly common, and are budgeted for as a necessity.

As if this wasn't enough, a new type of staffer has been added to the lineup: a Labor Union computer specialist. These talented (and often expensive) individuals help assure the adequacy of the union's computer system, offer staff training, prop up the computer work of key officers, prepare PowerPoint presentations, and in general, keep the organization "online" (Katz, 2000).

In all, then, four key aspects of internal administration — building alliances, getting the word out (and back), recruiting new members (and re-organizing old ones), and upgrading the human capital of the union's or local's staff — would seem to benefit considerably from computer use.

V. Areas of Concern

Five sources of anxiety standout, and restrain Labor's use of computer power. While some of this can be traced to the newness of applications, it is still unclear how much will respond to gains in experience and the passage of time.

1. Many in Labor worry about a potential erosion of face-to-face contact, arguably Labor's greatest asset in earning and holding onto members. Dues-payers like to feel recognized (and valued) by union officialdom, a feeling that impersonal e-mails may not convey. "Pressing the flesh" and "showing your face" are practices many in labor think indispensable, regardless of the time-and-energy-saving (cyberspace) alternatives championed by Labor's digerati.

2. Many in Labor worry about loudmouths and troublemakers monopolizing dialogue in nonmoderated chat rooms and bulletin boards. They fear that "crazy talk" will drive others away and undermine the entire medium. They also worry that thin-skinned officers will be hurt by outrageous posted criticism and insist on either strong censorship or a shutdown.

3. Many in Labor worry about a Generation Gap that separates older leaders from young "hot shot" types. The younger leaders are often impatient to get on with it, to rush the computerization process faster than the older (pre-computer) leaders are comfortable with — a rift that exacerbates the natural divide between the generations — and undermines solidarity.

4. Many in Labor worry about loss of confidentiality. They fear that hackers and others possibly in the pay of government — RICO "snoops," union busters, union-hating employers, or the dangerous like — will break into union data banks and files, much to the union's dismay.

   As well, when a Federal Court in April of 2000 ordered seizure and search of the home computers of 21 flight attendants suspected of coordinating via e-mail an illegal sick-out, a chill went through Organized Labor that has left its mark. Never before had a court given an employer the right to tap the equivalent of a home phone, search for incriminating data on 43 people (many more than the 21 attendants), and "invade" private homes. Although fought by Ralph Nader's Public Citizen's litigation group and other like organizations, the story stays alive in Labor's oral culture — and scares many computer users (Wieffering and Kennedy, 2000).

5. Finally, many in Labor worry about the overload that e-mails entail in work-lives already stretched to the limit. Union staffers complain of their inability to keep up with electronic messages rushing in and earmarked for rapid response, almost regardless of the situation of the receiver. Many grumble about an unreasonable speedup, made all the less bearable by the absence of any commensurate increase in salary.

All five anxieties — possible erosion in face-to-face relations, loss of control over the medium, generation rift, loss of confidentiality, and (unappreciated) work overload — *can* serve as a valuable alert: None needs prove a paralyzing self-fulfilling prophecy.

Remedies are available, such as special schooling (private, discrete, and exceedingly sensitive) in computer use for older union leaders. Password protection schemes (as used now by the AFL-CIO and various unions) (Levy, 2000). And, redistributed workloads, the hiring of additional aides, and overdue salary increases for those genuinely overloaded by computer inputs.

Above all, Labor must remember that "high tech" computerization works best when aiding such "high touch" efforts as "one-on-one" organizing, "shoe leather" vote-getting, "button hole" lobbying for labor law reform, and so on . . . the humanizing dimensions of unionism that constitute its unique "value added" dimension.

VI. Three Patterns of Computer Use: A Division of the House

Given the pattern above of gains and pains associated with current computer use by Labor, three models seem to dominate the scene.

The first, which I call *Cyber Naught*, involves minimum employ of computer potentialities. Cyber Naught unions and locals generally hesitate to go beyond staid reliance on electronic bookkeeping. They pretend little has changed around them, deny being under pressure to modernize, and essentially sleepwalk through time.

The second, *Cyber Drift*, has labor organizations move spastically first in this direction, and then that, unable to guide their own efforts. Crippled by unthinking adaptation of incompatible — if glitzy and trendy — equipment, Cyber Drift unions and locals disappoint unionists eager to believe that Labor has much to gain from computer use.

The third, *Cyber Gain*, wins accolades for its state-of-the-art accomplishments where computers are concerned. Ironically, however, its lasting significance may be to set the stage for the emergence soon of its necessary successor, CyberUnions, today only an alluring distant possibility. Unless and until Cyber Gain organizations are succeeded by the CyberUnion variety, Organized Labor will continue to sub-optimize possibilities, and remain far more vulnerable than is tenable.

1. *Ostrich Approach.* Where the internal operations of a union are concerned, Cyber Naught labor organizations seek to preserve and persist, rather than to update or innovate. They employ computers primarily to satisfy traditional business needs, as in accounting and bookkeeping (payroll data, etc.).

   Put starkly, Cyber Naught unions and locals use computers to get through the day and do so in a flat and uninspired way. Labor officials and members settle for inertia and quietism . . . much as if Toffler's 1970 classic, *Future Shock*, had not been written, complete with its urgings that the Labor Movement pioneer in the use of information technology breakthroughs (Toffler, 1970, pp. 452, 480-83.).

   The problem here appears rooted in conceptual inertia: Out-dated habits of mind have far too many Cyber Naught labor leaders preferring form to function, protocol to results, and rhetoric to risk-taking. They want a future like the past, only more so. They treat unionism as a passive and reactive institution, and they act as a deadening hand on change.

2. *Galloping Off in All Directions.* Cyber Drift unions or locals move aimlessly, like a cork bobbing on a turbulent sea, though with far less likelihood than a cork of staying afloat. Lacking an Information Technology officer, and available for "seduction" by a never-ending series of slick-talking vendors, these organizations are crippled by incompatible software, hardware, and infrastructure components. Hardly anything works together, and frustration runs rampant.

3. *Labor's Best Hope — for the Moment.* In contrast with Cyber Naught types, Cyber Gain unions and locals make much of computer possibilities. Their use of computers can be creative (though as I shall argue later, it still does not go far enough). Officers, staffers, and activists alike appreciate how much more can be done, and enjoy adapting gains made elsewhere in and outside of Labor.

However, before too glowing an impression is given, it should be noted that Cyber Gain unions and locals have many telling weaknesses. More specifically, where computer applications are concerned, these unions and locals often remain frozen in the first generation of Internet use. They are preoccupied with meeting only straightforward informational needs. Their website typically offers their logo and basic facts, a static display critics dismiss as "brochure ware" or "billboards."

Cyber Gain Unions fail to understand, or decline to value, the fact that second-generation applications are quite different: Known as transactional, they emphasize the dynamic participation of the parties, rather than accept passivity, as at present in far too many Cyber Gain organizations.

While the Cyber Gain model is clearly superior to the Cyber Naught and Cyber Drift options, it will not suffice. It rebuilds, but it does not adequately renew. By failing to take the full potential of computerization boldly into account, Cyber Gain organizations do not so much deal with the future as they streamline the past. Only a far more ambitious use of computers will do the job necessary if Labor is to survive and thrive.

VII. Getting to a Third Wave CyberUnion F-I-S-T Model

If Labor is to reinvent itself as rapidly, as thoroughly, and as meaningfully as appears necessary, far more than Cyber Gain unionism seems required.

Specifically, early 21st century unions might well experiment with an ambitious and creative alternative that incorporates futuristics, innovations, services, and labor traditions (F-I-S-T). Labor urgently needs the rewards possible from reliable forecasting. And the rewards that innovations, such as computer data mining, uniquely offer. And the rewards that computer-based services, such as volume discounts on PCs, can provide. And the rewards possible from the computer-aided modernization of traditions (as in the production of interactive software rich with labor history material).

Futuristics would have CyberUnions employ forecasting to help get clues to where relevant companies and industries are heading, why, and what Labor might do about it. Forecasts would scrutinize demographic changes in the labor force and help develop plans that get out ahead of these shifts. Forecasts would enable Labor to test the warring claims that beckon for support, as in the Global Warming or Energy embroilment. Above all, forecasts would enable Labor to better anticipate advisable training upgrades for members and continue thereby to distinguish dues-payers from less well-prepared competitors in the labor market.

Innovations would have CyberUnions gain a proud reputation for early adoption of cutting-edge items. Members would look to the organization for assessments and advice when considering testing a novel option themselves. Above all, innovations would mark the CyberUnion as forward-looking and self-confident; thereby, worth the support of all intent on making, rather than merely inheriting, a future.

Services refers to the ability of CyberUnions to use computer power to update and bolster 101 services of keen value to the membership. Typical would be arranging for the sale of PCs and laptops at great discount, thanks to volume buying (as demonstrated already in Sweden, Norway, and elsewhere). Another service might have a local facilitate car-pooling, using a listserve of members sorted by zip code, or arrange for swap meets in cyberspace, as managed (and policed) by a local.

Traditions refers to honoring the culture and lore of a union or local. Every effort might be made to create an oral and video record of the reminiscences of older members, complete with archival storage. The history of the organization might be recreated by actors and actresses, video-taped, and placed permanently on the website. Many relevant labor songs, anecdotes, and historic speeches might be added, along with streaming video celebrations of special days and events (positive and negative alike) in the organization's past.

Labor urgently needs the computer-aided rewards possible from reliable forecasting. From innovations, such as computer data mining and storage. From computer-based services, such as software dedicated to meeting Labor's instant-alert needs. And from the computer-aided celebration of traditions, culture, and lore, as in the production of CDs rich with labor history material. Together, these four items (F-I-S-T) just might help provide Labor achieve CyberUnion status . . . or, life after proud Cyber Gain achievements (Shostak, 1999).

Together, then, these four items (F-I-S-T) just might help provide Labor with the foresight, the dynamism, the appeal, and the heart necessary if is to build on its Cyber Gain strengths and reverse its long-term decline (Shostak, 1999).

Pivotal in the matter is the possible rise to power soon of Labor's digerati. When such activists envision the years ahead, they expect computers to soon secure unprecedented access of everyone in Labor to everyone else . . . officers to members, members to officers, unionists to nonunionists, and vice versa.

The digerati dream includes rapid polling of the membership. Galvanizing of rallies or e-mail protests. Spotlighting of models worth emulating, and wrongs for the righting. Libraries put at a unionist's beck and call, along with valuable arbitration, grievance, and mediation material. And open chat rooms and bulletin boards for unfettered telling and listening, for the creation of a High Tech electronic (virtual) "community" to bolster High Touch solidarity among real folk.

As if this was not enough, the vision of Labor's digerati includes a quantum increase soon in the collective intelligence and consciousness of "global village" unionists in a global International. Unprecedented cooperation across national borders. The first effective counter to transnational corporate behemoths. And, going out a year or two further, possibly even Intelligent Agent software housed in computer "wearables," empowering unionists as never before.

Guided by this growing cadre of computer-knowledgeable types, Labor can soon move more unions and locals into CyberUnion status. And thereby invigorate the membership. Draw in new members. Intimidate opponents. Intrigue vote-seekers. Meet the very high aspirations union "netizens" have for the Labor Movement. And in other valuable ways, significantly bolster Labor's chances of moving especially advanced unions and locals up to CyberUnion status early in the 21st century.

Forward thinking and visionary, these techno-savvy men and women have a hefty dose of indefatigable optimism. Unlike many of their peers, their expectations concerning the renewing of Organized Labor are almost without limits. As they learn more about the F-I-S-T model, and make it their own, their influence may soar.

VIII. What Should Labor Be Monitoring?

Expectations of changes in information technology are very exciting and underline the life-and-death importance of Labor staying abreast: Internet cognoscenti "are betting they will soon rekindle the mega-innovation of the Web's early days [a mere ten years ago] . . . a world of pervasive computing that lets people communicate more efficiently than ever" (Ante, 2001).

By the end of 2002 there may be more mobile devices than PCs accessing the Internet, so powerful appears the next "killer ap," the "teleputer" (otherwise known as an advanced wireless mobile phone). By 2007 as many as 59 percent of all Americans (up from 2 percent today) are expected to own a device that can access mobile data (pager, phone, Personal Digital Assistant) (Gunther, 2001).

Where stationary PCs are concerned, knowledgeable forecasters expect household penetration to plateau at about 73 percent by 2005, up from 57 percent in 2000, an expansion that underlines the increasing number of unionists able to use Labor websites and access Labor e-mail (Baker, 2001).

By 2007, then, a significant number of union influentials (officers and members) may wear a compact picture-phone and computer on their wrist, and dictate to it by voice and listen to its "voice" in turn. They may use it to access any type of information, anywhere, at anytime. To stay in touch with significant others all the time. To send and receive messages in all languages, as if their own. To surf the Internet and Web with the stressless help of "smart" software that provides useful information even before they ask for it.

If only half of this is realized in the next few years, the rest is likely to be very close behind, and the impact is likely to prove mind-boggling . . . for social movements like that of Organized Labor, and everything else.

Cyber Gain organizations, and their successor, CyberUnions, will need new hardware, software, and infrastructure resources to handle the challenges entailed in volume, language, and time zone matters. These and scores of related possibilities cannot be followed closely enough, or reacted to fast enough.

IX. Summary: Labor Union Prospects?

American Labor Unions five years from now are likely to be very different from their 2002 counterparts: Their hallmark will either be irrelevance, or they will draw handsomely on CyberUnion attributes (F-I-S-T). While computerization cannot "rescue" Labor, unless Organized Labor soon makes the most creative possible use of it, as with the F-I-S-T model, Labor probably cannot be rescued.

At least where four areas of advancement are concerned — alliance-building, communications, organizing (external/internal), and staff development — Labor would seem well on its way. Where five major anxieties are concerned — losing its personal touch, being battered by internal criticism, hurting its older leaders, suffering breaches of confidentiality, and work overload and speedup — Labor has several available remedies to employ and other reforms still to create.

Alert to advances that other organizations — businesses, NGOs, levels of government, schools, etc. — are busy making in their uses of computer power, Labor is not too proud to adapt and utilize their hard-earned gains. Little wonder that academics like Harvard's Professor Richard Freeman now contend "employee organizations will prosper in cyberspace because the Internet is the bridging technology between an increasingly heterogeneous work force and individualistic workers and the collective activity and solidarity that lie at the heart of trade unionism" (Freeman and Thomas in Taylor, 2001).

This much at least seems clear: With about three rewarding decades already spent learning how to better employ computer power, Organized Labor can be expected to explore creative possibilities here long into the future. Early in the 21st century, a new model of computer-based unionism — one celebrating the F-I-S-T model — may help Labor finally achieve the security and well-being that has eluded it from pre-Colonial years to date.

Notes

1   Typical of academic neglect here is the fact that only one page of the 127 pages in nine articles commissioned for the first part of this journal's two-part exploration of the future of private sector unionism even touched on this significant possibility (Townsend et al., 2001, p. 285).
2   I plan now to devote a sabbatical year (2002) to tracking in the field new uses unionists are making of IT in general, and computer power in particular. In this connection, I welcome leads to sites I should visit and people I should interview (shostaka@drexel.edu).

References

Ante, Spencer E. "In Search of the Net's Next Big Thing." *Business Week* (March 26, 2001): 140–41.
Baker, Stephen. "A Net Not Made in America." *Business Week* (March 26, 2001): 124.
Fiorito, Jack, Paul Jarley, John Thomas Delaney, and Robert W. Kolodinsky. "Unions and Information Technology: From Luddites to CyberUnions?" *Labor Studies Journal* 24 (Winter 2000): 3-34.
Freeman, Richard and Wayne Diamond, as quoted in Robert Taylor. "Trade Unions: Workers Unite on the Internet." *Financial Times*, May 11, 2001.
Gunther, Marc. "Wireless E-mail." *Fortune* (March 19, 2001): 76.
Katz, Jon. *Geeks.* New York: Villard, 2000.
Lee, Eric. *The Labor Movement and the Internet: The New Internationalism.* Chicago: Pluto Press, 1997.
Levy, Steven. *How the Code Rebels Beat the Government — Saving Privacy in the Digital Age.* New York: Viking, 2000.
Shostak, Arthur B. Robust *Unionism: Innovations in the Labor Movement.* Ithaca, N.Y.: ILR Press, 1991.
———. *The CyberUnion Handbook: Transforming Labor Through Computer Technology.* Armonk, N.Y.: M.E. Sharpe, 2002.
———. *CyberUnion: Empowering Labor through Computer Technology.* Armonk, N.Y.: M.E. Sharpe, 1999.
Toffler, Alvin. *Future Shock.* New York: Bantam, 1970.
Townsend, Anthony, Samuel M. Demarie, and Anthony R. Hendrickson. "Information Technology, Unions, and New Organization: Challenges and Opportunities for Union Survival." *Journal of Labor Research* 22 (Spring 2001): 275–86.
Wieffering, Eric and Tony Kennedy. "Search Raises Privacy Issues." *Minneapolis Star Tribune*, February 8, 2000.

6

Information Technology:
The Threat to Unions

Gary Chaison
Clark University

I. Introduction

We are at the early stages of a revolution in information technology that will occur in yet-to-be-imagined ways over the next few decades. At the same time, labor unions are at a crossroads in their history, and it is not yet clear whether the severe drop in membership and bargaining power is irreversible or if union revival will somehow occur. These two phenomena converge as the adoption of new information technologies, primarily the Internet and the Web, is commonly depicted as essential for union revival. The link seems obvious. If faster and more powerful ways of communicating enable companies to compete in a quickly changing and challenging environment, shouldn't they also make unions stronger and more efficient as organizations and workplace representatives?

We read reports of the *cyber-unions* that integrate information technology into their operations, the *cyber-organizers* who spread the word about unionism to previously inaccessible groups of workers, and the *cyber-strikes* during which unions use the Internet to mobilize workers (Lazarovici, 1999; Shostak, 1999a,b; Yager and Threlkeld, 1999). Unions are going on the Internet to "get the word out, organize the masses, and agitate the opposition" (Peter, 1997, p. 82), "overcome corporate disinformation in organizing," "orchestrate grass roots lobbying efforts" and "coordinate far-flung union activities" (Ad Hoc Committee on Labor and the Web, 2000, p. 1).

The Internet and the Web are presented as inherently beneficial to unions; we are warned only that they might be harmful if used incorrectly or if relied on too heavily (Shostak, 1999a,b). Overlooked in this enthusiasm, however, is the dark side of information technology — the ways that it will inevitably and seriously threaten unions as institutions and representatives. This threat will occur as the Internet and the Web transforms work and lessens workers' interest in unionizing; becomes a substitute for unions as a voice mechanism; and changes the relationship between unions and their members.

II. The First Threat: The Transformation of Work

Early information technology such as mainframe and desktop computing improved internal operations but created "islands of automation" in organizations, i.e., sections and operations with few linkages between them. Later technology connects rather than separates and, by doing so, reduces costs and increases productivity. Information is converted into electronic form (e.g., data storage and retrieval and searchable data bases) and distributed widely and quickly, e.g., the Internet, the Web, and e-mail, and their wireless communication (U.S. Congress, Office of Technology Assessment, 1995). Such technology will transform many types of work and greatly reduce the likelihood that those who do this work will become union members.

A fundamental dilemma of the labor movement is increasing private sector union membership under conditions in which "job growth is fastest in industries where unions are weakest while job losses are greatest in industries where unions are strongest" (Greenhouse, 1999b, p. 23). An AFL-CIO analysis found that from 1984 to 1997, the 30 fastest growing sectors in the economy, e.g., child care, finance, and retail trade, added 26 million jobs, but only 5 percent of the workers in those industries joined unions. Meanwhile, in the eight industries with the greatest job losses (e.g., autos and steel) about 80 percent of the 2.1 million jobs lost belonged to unionized workers (Greenhouse, 1999b). Net union growth can occur only if membership losses in declining industries are offset by organizing where there is growing employment though little union presence (Draezen, 2001a,b). This is highly unlikely because sales, clerical, technical, and professional positions are predominant in the growth industries (U.S. Department of Labor, 1999), and people in those positions will have their work radically changed by information technology.[1] The importance of this limitation to union growth is not widely understood and appreciated.

Presently, public attention is drawn to the most dramatic instances of collective bargaining over the impact of new information technology. For example, actors' compensation for working on ads on the Internet had to be resolved in the nearly six-month dispute of the Screen Actors Guild and the American Federation of Television and Radio Artists with the producers of commercials (Weinraub, 2000). A key issue in the strike of the Communications Workers and the Electrical Workers against Verizon was union access to organize the expanding work force at the company's wireless division (Greenhouse, 2000). The difficulties that unions face in such negotiations, however, pale in comparison to those of organizing workers whose jobs are transformed by information technology.

Under the Wagner Act model of labor relations, our system of worker representation is embedded in the assumptions of industrial pluralism — the notion that unions should act as counterweights to the power of employers and impose a system of self-governance at the workplace through the negotiation and enforcement of collective agreements (Stone, 1992). This explicitly assumes that employees anticipate a continuing relationship with their employer and that union representation occurs at the workplace (Osterman, 1999). The Internet defies these assumptions by creating a corps of workers with lowered physical and psychological attachments to their place of employment (Gardyn, 2000; Townsend et al., 2001; Voigt, 2001). Reich (2001, p. A25) sees an emerging work force of "tens of millions of temporary workers, part-timers, freelancers, e-lancers, independent contractors and free agents — already estimated to constitute one-tenth to one-third of America's civilian labor force." It is noteworthy, for example, that there are roughly 19 million persons who work from their homes (Wood, 2001) — a figure exceeding the membership of all unions.[2]

Union organizing also presumes distinct boundaries between workers who have legal protection to bargain and their supervisors and employers. But the Internet enables workers to have access to information and participate in decisions in a manner similar to their supervisors, e.g., scheduling production and controlling quality, and to avoid traditional employment relationships by working as contracting freelancers and temporaries.

Prescriptions for renewed union growth inevitably mention the need to reach an increasingly mobile and dispersed work force. One option is "range of services" unionism that provides workers with an array of approaches to representation ranging from traditional collective bargaining to labor-management consultation (Osterman, 1999). Another is labor-market-wide organizing, in contrast to the usual company-specific organizing. The hope of labor-market-wide organizing is to attract part-time and temporary workers who want to be covered by collective agreements (Wever, 1998). Unions might also combine the activities of bargaining agents and professional associations, becoming both workplace representatives and providers of services and representation to workers between jobs (Heckscher, 1988).

Unions will not have the field to themselves, however, if they try to organize and represent workers whose jobs have been reshaped by information technology. They can expect stiff competition from a variety of worker advocacy or workers' rights organizations.[3] For example, organizations for contract and consulting employees such as the Professional Association of Contract Employees (PACE) provide members with group benefits and assistance with record keeping and contracting (PACE, 2001). Others, like Working Today, promote the interests of freelancers, independent contractors, temporary and part-time workers, and people who work from home. It offers group-rate health insurance, legal aid, financial services, and discounts on travel, computers, and office supplies (Heckscher, 1998; Working Today, 2001).[4]

Unions will also have to compete against identity associations that are based on ethnic, gender, racial, or sexual-identity lines or based on professional identity, or on both, e.g., minority engineers.[5] These have been formed, for example, among groups of workers at high-technology firms who felt they were bypassed in management decision making but were reluctant to be represented in collective bargaining (Hyde, 1993).

Union alternatives are flourishing precisely because they are not unions and can custom-tailor services and modes of representation to fit the needs of their members.

Heckscher (1998, p. 14) concluded that it is among these associations "where a great deal of energy is. When people say that workers aren't organizing nowadays, one might properly reply that they *are* organizing — they just aren't organizing unions."

If sufficiently pressed, unions may respond by reviving the option of associate membership — a special category for members who are not represented in collective bargaining but rather join unions as individuals to receive group benefits, e.g., low-interest credit cards, health insurance, legal assistance, and advice about workplace rights. The AFL-CIO and several affiliated unions experimented with associate membership during the 1980s to reverse declining membership. They enrolled union supporters where certification elections were lost or never held because of insufficient employee support. But such stand-alone associate membership — membership as an end-in-itself and not intended to lead to collective bargaining coverage — was largely abandoned by the labor movement because of its focus on the individual member as a consumer of union services rather than as a beneficiary of collective representation. When associate membership is now offered, it is usually a special status for retired members or as a bridge to eventual bargaining (Chaison and Bigelow, forthcoming).[6] Even in the unlikely event that unions revive stand-alone associate membership, they will have to compete not only with other advocacy organizations but with employers as well.

III. The Second Threat: Voice Substitution[7]

Unions are often characterized as organizations through which workers can express their collective voice on work-related matters (Helfgott, 2000). Dissatisfied workers can exercise an exit option by leaving the organization or a voice option (either as individuals or members of a group) by discussing and negotiating their concerns with management.[8] Unions are essentially a mechanism for the expression of collective voice; through negotiations and contract enforcement, they bring the actual and the workers' desired conditions closer (Freeman and Medoff, 1984).

Employers can engage in voice substitution, i.e., provide voice mechanisms for their workers with the intent of decreasing the workers' interest in independent, collective voice through union representation.[9] Unions are now well aware of the ways that employee involvement programs (e.g., quality circles, production teams, joint-strategy committees) serve as management-controlled voice mechanisms. Wary of these programs, unions have sought to co-exist with them, control them, or organize where workers find them to be inadequate (Rundle, 1997; Taras, 1998). But unions are unprepared for the power and pervasiveness of intranets — the ultimate in voice substitution.

Intranets are internal company websites that use basic Internet technology such as browsers and servers.[10] They provide a fast, low-cost way to distribute information throughout a company and to its employees at home. Intranets are simpler than LANs (local area networks); rather than having to be specially connected to the LAN, all workers need are computers with modems and web browsers to connect to their company's intranet. Intranets are designed with "firewalls" that make them accessible only to the company's employees who have passwords. They are controlled by management, usually located in corporate communication or human resources departments, and operated by the company information systems department (Stevens, 1996; Industry Canada, 1998: Hapgood, 1999; "Benefit Function," 2000; "The Truth About Leveraging," 2000).

In their most rudimentary form, intranets deliver company newsletters and training materials. Some allow employees to enroll in benefit plans, order supplies, and take courses. But more powerful intranets offer personalized communication links (e.g., employees can have direct links to their supervisors and technical experts), video-conferencing, and forums for employees to present grievances to management for eventual resolution by company ombudsmen. These intranets have evolved from an information source to part of the work environment (Stellin, 2001).

Presently, about 90 percent of large companies have intranets (Stellin, 2001), and their power will be magnified as more workers gain access to the Internet at work, and through it, to their company's intranet. Thirty-seven percent of full-time workers and eighteen percent of part-time workers have Internet access at work ("Wired Workers," 2000). Internet use will spread even further as employers help their workers purchase computers and go online from home. Probably the most widely publicized program was Ford's offer of low-cost computers and Internet connections to its 300,000 employees. Internet access is through a portal that also offers direct links to Ford and the United Automobile Workers websites. Computer purchase and Internet access programs have also been offered by General Motors, Daimler-Chrysler, Delta Airlines, and Intel, among others ("Ford and Internet," 2000; Perlmutter, 2000).

In the near future, we can expect most employers to use their intranets to collect and resolve workers' grievances online and run discussion groups of workers, their supervisors, and human resource specialists. They will also use intranets to foster closer identification with the company and its goals.[11] Workers will access intranets anywhere and anytime as wireless connection becomes commonplace. Confronted with the ubiquitous employer intranet, unions will likely respond in kind by increasing their own presence on the Internet. As they do, they will unwittingly create the third threat of information technology.

IV. The Third Threat: A New Relationship between Unions and Their Members

Early union applications of information technology dealt mostly with administrative matters, e.g., communicating with members, simplifying office work, and producing newsletters, and collective bargaining, e.g., economic analysis and monitoring grievance activity. Union officers were contemplating a future of office networking and electronic mail linked to database and word-processing systems (Templer and Solomon, 1988). Later, they came to appreciate the power of the Internet (Fiorito, Jarley, and Delaney, 2000).

Half of all union members are online (Perlmutter, 2000), and nearly all unions have their own web pages for providing updates on negotiations and strikes, links to organizers, descriptions of benefit plans, reports of officers and committees, and notices of job openings on the union staff.[12] The AFL-CIO has a web page (www.aflcio.org) as do its component organizations, e.g., the Working for America Institute at www.workingforamerica.org and the Asian Pacific American Labor Alliance at www.apalanet.org. The federation also has an Internet portal, workingfamilies.com, available to members of affiliated unions and used for coordinating strikes and consumer boycotts, among other activities. It has an e-mail listserv (Labornet) with updated federation information and a chat room. Union factions and caucuses have their own pages, e.g., the Teamsters for Democratic Action at www.igc.org/tdu (Greenhouse, 1999a).

Unions enthusiastically develop web pages, seeing them as a quick and inexpensive way to strengthen organizing, labor education, membership mobilization during strikes, public relations, and political action — e.g., voter registration, issue advocacy, and candidate endorsement (Ad Hoc Committee on Labor and the Web, 2000; Fiorito, Jarley, and Delaney, 2000; Fiorito et al., 2000). A few academic observers have warned of the limitations of information technology. Shostak (1999b, p. 131) cautioned:

> It is a complex, demanding and often exasperating tool, only as reliable and effective as the humans in charge. Also, it is no solo star. It works best when it is part of a mix that includes militancy, labor law reform, and political action. It works best when aiding such "high touch" efforts as one-on-one organizing, "shoe leather" vote getting, and "buttonhole" lobbying for labor law reform. It works best when kept as an accessory and an aid, rather than allowed to become a confining and superordinate system.

Fiorito, Jarley, and Delaney (2000, p. 471) go a step further by suggesting that information technology might pose a Faustian bargain for unions — "the possibility that unions will 'lose their souls' as collective worker representation instruments by changing themselves into something else." But, they conclude that "at present, at least, that danger seems small" (p. 471), and a greater danger would be that unions do nothing to reverse their decline.

Such cautionary statements may not go far enough; the unions' unrestrained adoption of information technology can lead to a dependency that greatly reduces the chances of union revival. Proposals to revitalize the labor movement have a common theme: Unions must transform themselves into a social movement which struggles for social change by ameliorating the imbalance of power between worker and management and by securing greater rights for all workers, not just union members. To do this, unions should be controlled at the local level; otherwise they are simply "top-down" bureaucratic organizations that provide representation services in exchange for membership dues. By broadening their mission and increasing membership control, unions can credibly argue that the right to union representation should be promoted and protected by the state as nothing less than a fundamental civil right (Johnston, 1998; Mantsios, 1998; Nissen, 1999). Expressing such themes, Moberg (1999, p. 23) wrote: "Unions can't survive as institutions without dues-paying members, but unions will never flourish if they are seen as working only for their members — or, worst of all, only for their leaders." They must avoid "insurance unionism," that is offering only pay and job security without encouraging membership participation and without using their economic and political power to "make workers' rights the human rights and social justice issue of the decades ahead" (Moberg, 1999, p. 32).

A heavy reliance on the Internet can take unions on a sharp detour away from revival. Unions cannot be impersonal websites and social movements, online providers of services as well as communities of workers. As unions deepen their Internet presence to compete against employer-controlled intranets, they can begin to do through their web pages what they would otherwise do through personal contact with members. Union resources and effort can be shifted away from activities requiring personal contact such as meetings, rallies, and social activities and toward the faster and less expensive promotion of an Internet presence. The union web page can become the primary means to communicate with members. Organizing can simply mean developing a website to attract potential members, connect them with online organizers, and collect digital signatures on union authorization cards.

If unions become dependent on the Internet to communicate with members and provide services, the typical member would be attracted only to supportive participation — relatively passive activities that require little time and effort, for example reading the union's web page and discussing union issues with co-workers. Websites do not produce members' occasional participation, i.e., activities that occur intermittently but nonetheless entail substantial effort, such as making speeches at union meetings and taking part in bargaining. This participation leads to higher level activities such as running for or volunteering for union office (Chaison et al., 2001).

Furthermore, if unions distance themselves from their members by relying on the web, members will react by evaluating their union in terms of an exchange relationship. From a purely pragmatic perspective, a member will ask: Am I getting value from my dues, or could I do better without a union, with another union, or with an advocacy organization that serves as an alternative to the union? Their evaluations will not be made on the basis of whether the union promotes societal welfare and supporting it is the right thing to do (Chaison and Bigelow, forthcoming). Under these conditions, the possibility of reviving unions as a social movement with a broad agenda will be highly unlikely.

V. Conclusions

Although seldom recognized in the flurry of enthusiastic support, information technology has a dark side for unions. The Internet and the Web, with its power and convenience magnified by wireless communication, will reduce the relevancy of the traditional workplace-centered appeals of organizing unions. With greater physical distance and less psychological attachment to their employer and workplace, professional, clerical, technical, and sales workers will believe that collective bargaining does not fit their situations. Organizing these workers will require that unions not only have to broaden their mode of representation, perhaps even reviving associate membership, but also compete against advocacy and identity organizations. To make matters even worse, when unions try to organize any group of workers regardless of whether or not their jobs have been transformed by information technology, and when unions try to maintain their influence in already organized workplaces, they will have to compete against employer-controlled intranets.

Intranets add new power and sophistication to employers' union substitution strategies by linking workers to their supervisors and human resource specialists, and quickly disseminating company information and resolving grievances. Unions are in a bind here: If they attempt to respond to intranets with their own elaborate web pages, they risk reducing their chances of revival as a social movement and become little more than online providers of representation services.

Admittedly, any appraisal of the future impact of information technology must be speculative. But there is already enough evidence based on the present technology to see the contours of the threat to unions. Workers whose jobs have been reshaped by the Internet (e.g., sales representatives, professionals working on a contractual basis, home workers) are not approaching unions in large numbers and unions are not successfully recruiting them. The employers' use of intranets is already widespread and it has among its explicit objectives enhanced communication between workers and human resource departments and fostering a closer identification with the company. And union officers and staff are avid web enthusiasts with little if any appreciation of its potentially negative effects on the relations with members and revival. All signs point to serious, perhaps unsolvable, problems for unions.

Notes

1   A similar transformation will occur among clerical, profession, and technical positions in the public sector where employment and union membership have been growing.
2   The growth of telecommuting is described by Gardyn (2000) and Voight (2001). It is estimated that about 20 percent of all workers will working at home by 2005 (Gardyn, 2000).
3   Unions may also create or affiliate with advocacy organizations. For example, the Communications Workers of America has an affiliate, the Washington Alliance of Technology Workers (WashTech) that seeks to organize workers at Microsoft (Lazarovici, 1999).
4   Wheeler (2000) describes workers' rights organizations, as well as other types of organizations for worker representation and protection, in terms of goals, solidarity, perspective, costs, employer opposition, and government support.
5   For example, see Haeussler (2000) for a discussion of identity organizations among Hispanic workers at AT&T, Apple Computer, General Electric, Nike, and Xerox.
6   For example, the Communications Workers of America offers associate membership to employees of high-tech companies such as Microsoft and Cisco. The option includes benefit plans and skills training. The goal is the eventual organization of contract and temporary employees for collective bargaining (Flanigan, 2000).
7   This term for the role of the intranet was suggested by Joe Sarkis.
8   Workers can also exercise the exit option by being absent, partially withdrawing their labor, reducing their work effort, or sabotage (Helfgott, 2000).
9   For a study of the range of collective voice mechanisms in union and nonunion workplaces, see Benson (2000). The workplaces are in Australia but similar voice mechanisms are found in the U. S.
10 In contrast, extranets use the same technology to link companies to customers, suppliers, and shareholders.
11 For example, when information managers of large companies were asked in a survey what was the biggest impact of the intranet on their company, one third responded "an increased sense of community," roughly the same proportion that mentioned increased productivity (Kotwica, 1998).

12 For typical union websites, see the Service Employees at www.seiunet.org, the American Federation of Government Employees at www.afge.org, the Auto Workers at www.uaw.org, and the American Federation of State, County and Municipal Employees at www.afscme.org.

References

Ad Hoc Committee on Labor and the Web. "Why the Internet Matters to Organized Labor." December 11, 2000. <www.mindopen.com/laborweb>.

"Benefit Functions Top All Others on Company Intranet." *Managing HR Information Systems* (June 5, 2000): 2.

Benson, John. "Employee Voice in Union and Nonunion Australian Workplaces." *British Journal of Industrial Relations* 38 (September 2000): 453–59.

Chaison, Gary and Barbara Bigelow. *Unions and Legitimacy*. Ithaca, N.Y.: Cornell University Press, 2002.

Chaison, Gary N., Magnus Sverke, and Anders Sjöberg. "How Union Mergers Affect Membership Participation." *Journal of Labor Research* 22 (Spring 2001): 355–72.

Dreazen, Yochi J. "Percentage of U.S. Workers in a Union Sank to a Record Low of 13.5% Last Year." *Wall Street Journal*, January 19, 2001a.

———. "Slower Growth Threatens Labor Unions." *Wall Street Journal*, January 16, 2001b.

Flanigan, James. "Variety Spices Work As Internet Drives Change." *Los Angeles Times*, September 3, 2000.

Freeman, Richard B. and James L. Medoff. *What Do Unions Do?* New York: Basic Books, 1984.

Fiorito, Jack, Paul Jarley, and John Thomas Delaney. "The Adaptation of Information Technology by U.S. National Unions." *Relations Industrielles/Industrial Relations* 55 (Summer 2000): 451–76.

———, and Robert W. Kolodinsky. "Unions and Information Technology: From Luddites to Cyberunions." *Labor Studies Journal* 24 (Winter 2000): 3–34.

"Ford and the Internet." *Buffalo Evening News*, February 8, 2000.

Gardyn, Rebecca. "The New American Worker: Who's the Boss?" *American Demographics* 22 (September 2000): 52–56, 58.

Greenhouse, Steven. "AFL-CIO Members to Get Online Access and Discounts." *New York Times*, October 11 1999a.

———. "Union Leaders See Grim News in Labor Study." *New York Times*, October 13, 1999b.

———. "Phone Workers Fight for Place in Wireless Era." *New York Times*, July 31, 2000.

Haeussler, Aimee R. "A Common Purpose." September 12, 2000, <http://www.hispanicbusiness.com/community/hispanic_orgs.asp>.

Hapgood, Fred. "The Next Generation." *CIO Web Business Magazine* March 1, 1999. <http://www.cio.com/>.

Heckscher, Charles. "Taking Transformation Seriously." Paper presented at the Cornell University Conference on the Revival of the Labor Movement. October 16, 1998.

———. *The New Unionism*. New York: Basic Books, 1988.

Helfgott, Roy B. "The Effectiveness of Diversity Networks in Providing Collective Voice for Employees." In B.E. Kaufman and D.G. Taras, eds. *Nonunion Employee Representation: History, Contemporary Practice, and Policy*. Armonk, N.Y.: M.E. Sharpe, 2000, pp. 348–62.

Hyde, Alan. "Employee Caucus: A Key Institution in the Emerging System of Employment Law." *Chicago-Kent Law Review* 69 (1993): 149–93.

Industry Canada. "Intranets" December 12, 1998, <http://strategis.ic.gc.ca/SSG/>.

Johnston, Paul. "Social Movement Unionism: Labor as Citizenship Movement." Paper presented at the Cornell University Conference on the Revival of the American Labor Movement. October 16, 1998.

Kotwica, Kathleen. "Survey: Internet Implementation and Management." January 1998, <http://www.cio.com/>.

Lazarovici, Laureen. "Virtual Organizing" *America@Work* 4 (September 1999):8–11.

Mantsios, Gregory. *A New Labor Movement for the New Century*. New York: Monthly Review Press, 1998.

Moberg, David. "The U.S. Labor Movement Faces the Twenty-First Century." In Bruce Nissen, ed. *Which Direction for Organized Labor? Essays on Organizing, Outreach and Internal Transformations*. Detroit: Wayne State University Press, 1999. pp. 21–33.

Nissen, Bruce. Which Direction for Organized Labor? *Essays on Organizing, Outreach and Internal Transformation*. Detroit: Wayne State University Press, 1999.

Osterman, Paul. *Securing Prosperity: The American Labor Market: How It Has Changed and What to Do About It*. Princeton, N.J.: Princeton University Press, 1999.

Perlmutter, Rod. "Ford Computer Deal Signifies Union Trend." February 2, 2000, <http://www.mediacentral.com/>.

Peter, Kristyne. "Labor on the Internet." *Working USA* 8 (May-June 1997): 82–87.

PACE (Professional Association of Contract Employees), <http://www.pacepros.org/>.

"Pros and Cons of Providing Employees With Home P.C.s to Extend HRIS." *Managing HR Information Systems* (June 2000): 1.

Reich, Robert B. "Working, But Not 'Employed'." *New York Times*, January 9, 2001.

Rundle, James. "Winning Hearts and Minds in the Era of Employee-Involvement Programs." In K. Bronfenbrenner, S. Friedman, R.W. Hurd, R.A. Oswald, and R.L. Seeber, eds. *Organizing to Win: New Research on Union Strategies*. Ithaca, N.Y.: Cornell University Press, 1997, pp. 213–31.

Shostak Arthur B. *CyberUnion: Empowering Labor Through Computer Technology*. Armonk, N.Y.: M.E. Sharpe, 1999a.

———. "Organized Labor's Best Bet? CyberUnions!" *Working Today* 3 (November-December 1999b): 120–33.

Stellin, Susan. "Intranets Nurture Companies from the Inside." *New York Times*, January 29, 2001.

Stevens, Larry. "The Internet: Your Newest Training Tool." *Personnel Journal* 75 (July 1996): 6–7.

Stone, Katherine. "The Legacy of Industrial Pluralism: The Tension between Individual Employment Rights and the New Deal Collective Bargaining System." *University of Chicago Law Review* 59 (1992): 575–674.

Taras, Daphne Gottleib. "Nonunion Representation: Complement or Threat to Unions?" In Paula Voos, ed. *Proceedings of the Fiftieth Annual Meeting of the Industrial Relations Research Association*, Vol. 1. Madison, Wisc.: IRRA, 1998, pp. 281–90.

Templar, Andrew and Norman Solomon. "Unions and Technology: A Survey of Union Use of Information Technology." *Relations Industrielles/Industrial Relations* 43 (Spring 1988): 378–93.

Townsend, Anthony M., Samuel M. Demarie, and Anthony R. Hendrickson. "Information Technology, Unions, and the New Organization: Challenges and Opportunities for Union Survival." *Journal of Labor Research* 22 (Spring 2001): 275–86.

"The Truth About Leveraging HR Information Services." *HRfocus* (June 8, 2000): 11.

U. S. Congress. Office of Technology Assessment. *The Technological Reshaping of Metropolitan America*. Report OTA-ETI-643. Washington D.C.: U.S. Government Printing Office, 1995.

U. S. Department of Labor. Bureau of Labor Statistics. "BLS Releases New 1998-2008 Employment Projections." Press release USDL 99-339, November 20, 1999.

Voigt, Kevin. "For 'Extreme Telecommuters,' Remote Work Means Really Remote." *Wall Street Journal*, January 31, 2001.

Weinraub, Bernard. "Tentative Pact Is Reached in Actors' Strike." *New York Times*, October 24, 2000.

Wever, Kirsten S. "International Labor Revitalization: Enlarging the Playing Field." *Industrial Relations* 37 (July 1998): 399–407.

Wheeler, Hoyt N. "The Future of the Labor Movement in the USA." Paper presented at the Twelfth World Congress of the Internation Industrial Relations Association, Tokyo, Japan, May 30, 2000.

"Wired Workers: Who They Are, What They're Doing." *Pew Internet Life Report* (press release) September 3, 2000, <http://pewinternet.org/>.

Wood, Winston. "Work Week." *Wall Street Journal*, February 6, 2001.

Working Today, <http://www.workingtoday.org/>.

Yager, Daniel V. And Thomas S. Threlkeld. "Workplace Cyberspace — Going Where No Board Has Gone Before." *Employee Relations Law Journal* 25 (Autumn 1999): 53–70.

7

Workers as Cyborgs:
Labor and Networked Computers

Mark Poster
University of California – Irvine

I. From Worker to Cyborg

Information technologies are indeed changing the world. The introduction of the computer and now the linkage of computers to the global network of the Internet vastly alter the patterns of life that have become customary in modern society. Individuals are now connected to one another, to the events and places around the world with an effective, instantaneous apparatus of information machines. The location in space of the individual body no longer limits the possibilities for that person to engage in relations with others, to act as a consumer, to participate in cultural or political events, to connect with others having the same special interest. These changes also affect the domain of work.

In the relatively short span of a decade or two, the workplace has been transformed. Networked computers are ubiquitous in large corporations, medium and small size companies, mom-and-pop retail outlets, restaurants, even gas stations, in short, anywhere that humans work. From the clay tablets of the ancient world, to the introduction of double-entry bookkeeping in the Renaissance, the typewriter in the late nineteenth century, the cash register in the early twentieth century, and the copy machine in the 1950s, information machines have accompanied the activities of human labor. Without belittling the importance of these earlier technologies of writing, calculating, recording, and copying, it is fair to say that they pale in significance compared to the influence of networked computers. Earlier information machines might be regarded as tools to assist human workers; networked computing promises radically to displace humans from the activities of producing commodities. The keyboard writing, if I may paraphrase an old homily, is clearly on the screen. The current situation of labor then must be viewed in light of the grand transformation going on around us. And in this context we may well ask, What is the effect on workers of networked computing?

Before exploring in detail changes wrought by networked computing upon the domain of work, I wish to underline some important general features of what is at stake in this innovation. Human labor has entailed the application of muscle to the transformation of natural objects into usable goods. True enough, intelligence has always been at play in the process of work, finding the best and easiest method to produce the desired result. In addition animals and tools have for eons been employed to assist mankind. Yet information about work remained limited by its confinement to the brain. Of course, memory has helped. Collective traditions of village, town, and guild extend the memory capacities of the single brain and are passed on in the training practices for new generations. Devices for recording labor practices are another form of extended memory, but these have been very slow to find a place in the routines of work. As late as the eighteenth century, Diderot's *Encyclopedia* was an early compendium on craft labor practices, breaking with guild traditions that kept them secret. The application of scientific methods to labor practices — a further example of information functions applied to work — began with Frederick Taylor only in the early twentieth century.

Today computerized information is being applied to human and machine labor with breathtaking rapidity. What distinguishes this effort from recording methods in books or applying systematic methods is that the computer, a machine, takes pride of place over the worker as well as over the mechanical machine. Henceforth we must understand labor as a product still of humans and mechanical machines but even more as an accomplishment of information machines. These complex objects seriously upset the habits of mind we apply to the work world. Whether one conceives work in the capitalist model of costs of production or the Marxist one of the organic composition of labor, information machines disrupt our models of comprehending work. When computers are central to production it becomes difficult to measure costs and performances of either humans or machines. Information machines do not fit well into our frames of reference about work. Thus to add an information machine to a work place is quite different from adding another worker or another mechanical machine.

Networked computing not only introduces into work the ontological oddity of the information machine, it also changes the territorial and temporal specificity of labor. Networked computing deterritorializes labor, rendering irrelevant the location on Earth of the work being done. Similarly it retemporalizes labor by introducing a register of instantaneousness that is comprehensible as computer time but not as human or even machine time. Because computers process information almost at the speed of light, this temporality is inserted into the calmer, more recognizable pace of the Newtonian temporalities of humans and machines. Furthermore, information technology opens up to human inspection the microworld, with nanotechnology and other advanced procedures promising profoundly to transform entire regions of experience such as work, human reproduction, and medicine. In these ways, networked computing alters the cultural frame of labor, restructuring it in shapes that are not readily discernible.

Because networked computing inserts information machines into work and reorders the basic conditions of time and space, it also reconfigures the basic categories of mind and body, subject and object that we unconsciously deploy in understanding the meaning of labor.

II. Digression on Method

Information technology is an emergent phenomenon, one that is undergoing continuous and basic changes. If technologies like the automobile and even the airplane have achieved a level of stability, such is not the case with networked computing. Because of the fluidity of the phenomenon, methods of analysis that measure it, usually in quantitative forms, are deeply limited in the study of information technology. For example, through the 1990s studies measured the demography of online users, showing consistently that the population was affluent, young, white American males. All sorts of conclusions were drawn from these studies about the limitations of computer technology. By the end of the decade women surpassed men and non-Americans surpassed Americans as online users. The elderly, the less affluent, and minority groups increased as a percent of total users. What is more, the purposes of online use have changed drastically as the technology developed. The introduction of the graphic user interface of the world wide web in 1993 added to networked computing sounds and images, altering completely the nature of online applications. One must then be careful in drawing conclusions from statistical measures in the realm of information technology.

Even methods of extrapolation are risky. Not only is information technology disseminating ever more widely around the globe and doing so among different groups, it is also changing its fundamental character. As new applications are developed and as new technologies merge with older ones, the very character of networked computing changes.

III. The Class Struggle by E-mail

In more traditional work locations, disruptions are almost as intense as in cyberspace. At major high-tech corporations such as IBM and 3Com, with the introduction of e-mail back in the neolithic era of computing in the mid–1980s, management sought to modernize the practice of the suggestion box by replacing paper with electronic messaging. Without wasting time by moving the piece of paper with the proposal for change to the physically located suggestion box, the worker now simply sent an e-mail to management while seated at his or her workstation. At the forefront of the production of information machines, IBM and 3Com could certainly be proud of this innovation in working conditions. Yet with the aid of e-mail, workers took the occasion to embroider the idea of a suggestion box into a broad soapbox for critique. In their e-mails, workers at times reviewed management most often finding fault, much to their superiors' embarrassment. Unlike the suggestion box, the complaining e-mails were widely distributed throughout the workplace, becoming a bulletin board for publicly posting the foibles of the leaders of the firm. Commentators observed that not only did e-mail save time but "it encourages workers of all ranks to change the rigid, hierarchical nature of communication" (Kantrowitz, 1986).

Within a few years, management at IBM had learned its lesson. As a leader of the information technology sector, with computer messages surpassing phone calls within the company, it could not easily eliminate internal e-mail for workers. Instead it introduced software controls over its in-house conferences. By 1993, a system known as VOODOO (Virtual Organizer Optimizer Disk Organizer Optimizer) was introduced which automatically monitored e-mails for offensive language, controversial topics, and the like. The program even discouraged irony and sarcasm. VOODOO did not last long but controls are still in place over worker critiques of management (Scott, 1993). Thanks to the widespread dissemination of computers and e-mail software, the 1980s and early 1990s saw a contest between management and workers over free expression and control of electronic communications internal to the firm.

In a recent case workers invoke the National Labor Relations Act of 1935 in an effort to stop management from monitoring and censoring e-mail. The issue in many of these cases concerns again the right of workers to criticize management. Workers who were fired because of their carping e-mails have been reinstated or compensated as a consequence of rulings which invoke the National Labor Relations Act. This act insures that workers have the right to communicate among themselves and with these rulings by the NLRB, e-mail is recognized as a valid means of communication. The surveillance of workers' e-mail by software programs, as well as the electronic surveillance of work with techniques, for example, of counting keystrokes, remains outside the jurisdiction of these decisions (Yegyazarian, 2000).

If management appears to have gotten the upper hand by the end of this period, the struggle, if one may call it that, moved to another level with the birth of the World Wide Web in 1993. Now workers might have homepages on the Web outside the purview of management. Unhappy workers were henceforth able with impunity to vent their spleen for all the world to see. The scene of control shifted from management to Internet Service Providers. When disgruntled workers used the Web to engage in "cybersmearing," raising questions about the economic status of the firm which at times had repercussions on the stock market, pressure was placed on ISPs to monitor its users. Yahoo, for example, posted rules that prohibit messages that are "unlawful, harmful . . . defamatory, libelous . . . or otherwise objectionable" (Miller, 1999, p. A7). Such protests took a much wider turn when, in June 2000, a virus (known as the "I Love You" virus) that disabled computers of major corporations and nations was attributed to a resentful man from the Philippines whose dissertation was rejected by his advisory committee. Workers with modest programming skills were perceived as a threat to the world's most powerful institutions.

IV. Cultures of Work

When the conditions of labor are so drastically restructured by information technology, we can expect disorientation and disruptions at the phenomenological level.

And there are many of these. First, at locations most sensitive to these transformations, the breaks are greatest. In the labor of writing software programs we find entirely new patterns and cultures of work. The figure of the nerd and the hacker are basically new types of workers. In the development of the computer industry during the 1970s and 1980s a distinctive culture of work arose. Software programs were produced by highly educated workers who were trained in the new languages of machines. These workers were writers, after all, people who inscribed symbols except these symbols were designed to control information machines, that is, were designed to be read not by an educated public but by machines. One can say that programmers pioneered a new relation between humans and machines. They deployed cognitive abilities to communicate with inorganic objects. And they did so in a way that these objects would be empowered, so to speak, to perform tasks on information. Surely this is all very confusing.

Programmers were aware that they were participating in something new and even revolutionary. The ambience of Silicon Valley in Northern California resonated with the counter-culture and New Left movements of the 1960s and 1970s, interpreting their highly technical activity as a continuation of the anti-authoritarian spirit and Aquarian sensibility. During the anti-war movement in 1970, one such hacker professor at University of California, Irvine announced to the striking students with the gravity of Trotsky or Lenin speaking to the workers' councils in 1917 that a computer connection now linked UC Irvine with Stanford University and UC Los Angeles. We now had available, he intoned as if an oracle, a means of communication with northern California that was not controlled by the media and could not be monitored by the FBI. By dint of networked computers, the movement was now autonomous, he thought, with its own links between campuses. The completion of the revolutionary takeover was only a matter of time.

The style of work in this nascent industry resembled nothing of the Fordist industrial factory or the offices of corporate America. Writing code requires great concentration and intellectual stamina. Programmers wrote for long hours brooking no supervision. It was as if software companies employed a bevy of talented literary people. One cannot exert Taylorist disciplines over the likes of Ernest Hemingway (Ross, 1991). These workers had skills that were over the heads of management. In addition these workers were comparatively young. To this day, programming and computer skills vary inversely with age. The figure of the young millionaire who earned his/her money rather than inherited it was born in the computer industry in the 1980s and 1990s. A young Steve Jobs working in his garage is legend. Many basic features of the Internet were developed by graduate students in their twenties: MUDs, MOOs, Usenet, Internet Relay Chat, and the like. Teenagers with programming skills continue to threaten major corporations and even industries, such as Shawn Fanning at nineteen writing Napster, a program to facilitate sharing of music files, and Jon Johansen, a Norwegian, at 15 writing DeCSS, a program designed to defeat copy protection on DVDs. In addition young people have been responsible for introducing viruses that paralyze major computer networks of the government and the economy (Robert Morris, a graduate student at Cornell) or invade sensitive computer sites (Kevin Mitnick, arrested at age twenty-five by the FBI). With no experience of the corporate world of work, these youngsters with their programming skills wreaked havoc on the timeworn practices of capitalist modernity.

V. Informatics and Control

If the culture of programmers introduced transgressions into the workplace, so did the business organization of high-technology companies. The top down, pyramid authority structures of industrial capitalism, with their continuous deskilling of workers, is not suited to information technology companies. From the outset a much looser and perhaps more democratic structure arose in this industry. An early proponent of the democratization thesis concerning information technology is Shoshana Zuboff in her important book, *In the Age of the Smart Machine: The Future of Work and Power* (1988). Zuboff argues that the introduction of computers in the workplace and the general application of information technology makes possible more democratic communications. With workers having access to computers, the larger processes of the firm's activities can be made available at each desktop. Instead of a hierarchical organization in which each level knows only what is particular to it, the computerized firm becomes, at every stage of activity, open for all to see. Zuboff writes, "Shared universal transparency can create a sense of mutual participation in and responsibility for operational and behavioral events. Joint access to the behavioral text can mean opportunities for joint learning" (Zuboff, 1988, p. 361). When all departments, from purchasing to sales and customer service, have access to information about a work order — what Zuboff calls the "behavioral text" — a new degree of collective intelligence is brought to bear on economic operations. A process of dialogue might then open about the work order that would be impossible without computerization. The practice of negotiating and giving inputs from many points in the firm in turn might lead to a deeper sense of shared responsibility, again rendering obsolete the older structure of hierarchy.

Critics have been quick to point out problems with Zuboff's position. Stanley Aronowitz, for instance, argues against Zuboff's claim that informatics creates "a richer social text," claiming on the contrary that computer-mediated texts are "merely a kind of collective privatization, not a genuine democratic development" (Aronowitz and DiFazio, 1994, p. 102). This position, I believe, misses the point of Zuboff's contention. Information technology, she shows, changes in a fundamental way the very nature of work. In a stunning example from the paper industry, Zuboff describes the change in labor from an artisanal method in which workers touched, felt, and sensed the quality of paper at various stages of its formation, judging when the materials were ready for the next process to be applied, to an informaticized method in which workers monitored computer screens to insure proper quality of production. In the latter case, the worker becomes a symbol manipulator, working cognitively rather than sensually. Once the paper worker operates on information machines, she is extracted from physical location and may easily have knowledge of the entire process of production. Work becomes the use of language and any worker who has facility with aspects of the language in question has a degree of power.

Critics of Zuboff also complain that far from democratizing the workplace, information technology makes possible new degrees of control by management over the worker, affords new ways through which the least movement of the worker can be monitored, recorded, and analyzed for performance evaluation. The computer affords management the ultimate power of knowing everything about the worker's activity by yielding it an absolute panoptic gaze. At issue here is what Michel Foucault called a "technology of power," a system of control of a few over many by a combination of discourses and practices (Foucault, 1977). In the nineteenth century prison, Foucault surmised, a new form of power was constructed in which inmates could be monitored by a guard in a central tower without themselves being able to determine if the guard was on duty, was watching them or not. The purpose of this design, invented by Jeremy Bentham, was to instill into the prisoner the sense of constantly being watched. This internal authority, Bentham gauged, was the first step toward reform. Such a surveillance technique was supplemented by the development of the case file, thanks to the emerging field of criminology, in which records were kept on each convict. In addition, a fixed schedule of activities was introduced, also designed to discipline the criminal and introduce regularity into the life of the deviant. The regime of the panopticon thus brought to bear a system of power that would "correct" "abnormal" behavior. Foucault conjectured that the panopticon was disseminated throughout modern society — in hospitals, schools, factories, and the military — establishing a new form of social control he called "discipline."

There is little doubt that management has deployed panoptic methods in the course of the past century and a half and it is now becoming clear that the introduction of information technology furthers the spread of this type of control. In fact Zuboff is well aware of the phenomenon of the panopticon, devoting a chapter to "The Information Panopticon." But she notes that the

> rendering of panoptic power reflects an important evolution of the original concept. It rests on a new collectivism in which "the many" view themselves and each views "the other." Horizontal visibility is created even as vertical visibility is intensified. The model is less one of Big Brother than of a workplace in which each member is explicitly empowered as his or her fellow worker's keeper. Instead of a single omniscient overseer, this panopticon relies upon shared custodianship of data that reflect mutually enacted behavior. This new collectivism is an important antidote to the unilateral use of panoptic power, but it is not a trouble-free ideal. Horizontal transparency breeds new human dilemmas as well. . . (Zuboff, 1988, p. 351).

This analysis of the panopticon enhanced by information technology is not often noted by critics who simply observe that workers may, after the introduction of the computer into the firm, be monitored more effectively. They fail to see that workers also, in this system, take on the position of the observer and may watch management and other workers. It is most important in the discussion of information technology to take cognizance not only of the way the new machines alter existing positions of work but also the way they enable new kinds of workers and new organizational forms of work practices. Sensitivity to new patterns of exploitation must be accompanied, as in Marx's analysis of early industrial capitalism, by an awareness of new possibilities for democratization. Otherwise analysis is limited to what Nietzsche called resentiment, discursively effecting not liberatory change but paralysis and defensiveness.

VI. Digital Organizations

But then there is the "real" world, which means the Microsoft Corporation. If any company represents metonymically the information technology revolution it is not IBM but Microsoft. And a glimpse of the Redlands monster yields a picture that is not at all pretty. Readers of Douglas Coupland's *Microserfs*, portraying in intimate detail the daily life of Bill Gates' company, come away with a sad, disconsolate sense of lost opportunity (Coupland, 1995). Just as William Gibson's *Neuromancer* (1984), a punk science fiction novel, defined the Internet as "cyberspace" more compellingly than any computer scientist, social scientist, or humanist, so *Microserfs* depicted through a work of imagination the reality of labor in the greatest software company, indeed, as of 1999, the most highly capitalized corporation on the globe. Microsoft Corporation embodies the victory of old-style entrepreneurship over the more beneficent possibilities opened by the introduction of information technology. The commodities created by Microsoft, first DOS then Windows, then the rest of the applications (Word, Excel, Access, Internet Explorer, and so forth) have domesticated as much as possible information technology to preexisting forms of economic activity and organization.

Notwithstanding Microsoft and other firms that have adapted new technologies as much as possible to Taylorist business organization there are those who discern large opportunities for change in the domain of labor through the digitalization of information. Don Tapscott's *Digital Economy*, written for a popular audience with executives in mind, and Manuel Castells, *The Information Age*, a massive three-volume compendium written for an academic audience, both herald fundamental changes in the economy, both depict this change as a consequence of the introduction of digital information technology, and both insist on the salience of the network, one global in scope, as the basis for a new economic order. Tapscott points out that some 60 percent of the work force now manipulate symbols and 80 percent of new jobs are in this sector (Tapscott, 1996, p. 7). Less than 20 percent of workers are in the traditional primary and secondary sectors of agriculture, manufacturing, and mining. Castells adds a level of subtlety to these familiar figures by arguing that ". . . the shift from industrialism to informationalism is not the historical equivalent of the transition from agricultural to industrial economies, and cannot be equated to the emergence of a service economy." At issue is not a shift in job activities because workers still perform in agriculture and manufacturing. Instead the change is at another level. He writes, "What has changed is not the kind of activities humankind is engaged on, but its technological ability to use as a direct productive force what distinguishes our species as a biological oddity: its superior capacity to process symbols" (Castells, 1996, p. 92). For Castells, and this is most important in understanding the effect of information technology on labor, information technology means humanization. Labor now is directed more specifically than in the past on the unique feature of our species: the brain.

The significance of Castells observation is immense. Those who defend older forms of industrialism often do so on the claim that it is more humane, that computers somehow dehumanize work. The argument here is the reverse: any animal may exercise muscle but no other species approaches the human ability with language. The move from an industrial to an informational economy is one toward the human. By implication, the direction and control of the new economy would have to proceed on principles different from those of the past. When muscle was being shaped and organized by management a certain pattern of hierarchy was installed and might be considered appropriate, a top-down system with clear lines of authority and responsibility, in short, a disciplinary regime as Foucault suggested. But when symbolization is the key to economic success, both Castells and Tapscott argue, a less rigid system of control is required, one that allows for inputs from many points in the structure, one that permits and even fosters the unknown, the invention, the creative insight to emerge from any position of speech and command respect regardless of the status of the speaker.

But Castells makes a fundamental error in his assessment of the humanization of the new digital economy. Paradoxically he fails to account for information machines. The "superior capacity of humans to process symbols" is a judgment relative to other living species. It is highly suspect when applied to computers. The new economy is one not of humanization but of posthumanization, of the deep symbiosis of humans with machines. It is not, as the Luddites argue, a dehumanization: that might have been true of industrialism which organized production around the capacity of the mechanical machine. The digital economy, by contrast, organizes production around the partnership of humans with information machines. And it should be clear by now that two further tendencies are at play that Castells does not consider enough. First, the machines are becoming better and better at symbolization so that they will surpass human capacities in many areas of language use, if they have not done so already. Second, the humans are also likely to change with the advance of the genome project and the progressive understanding of DNA. We can no longer assume a world of fixed species with fixed traits, such as symbol processing, but must acknowledge that machines and humans are in the midst of a profound process of distinct but interrelated transformation.

The global network further complicates the position and character of labor. The combination of globalized production with world-wide communications removes spatial and temporal limitations that have characterized all previous economic systems. It is true that transportation methods have developed over thousands of years, enabling the trading of good across local boundaries. It is also true that the industrial revolution expanded considerably the transport system by allowing motorized movement. The addition of networked computing titled things up to a new level. Economic activities now could be coordinated regardless of location, with more workers commuting by modem, more processes administered by computer, and more transactions occurring over phone lines (Carnoy, Castells et al., 1993). With the increasing amount of production and trade across national borders more and more workers find themselves in competition with workers from other lands and working for firms based in other lands. The condition of work is now part of what Manuel Castells calls "the network society."

He claims that "Relationships between capital and labor (all kinds of capital, all kinds of labor) are organized around the network enterprise form of production. This network enterprise is also globalized at its core, through telecommunications and transportation networks. Thus, the work process is globally integrated, but labour tends to be locally fragmented" (Castells, 2000, p. 421). Labor then finds itself in a new economic context, one for which it is sorely unprepared.

Generally speaking the American labor movement responded to the network enterprise defensively. The North American Free Trade Agreement and the General Agreement on Tariffs and Trade, two trade agreement systems of the 1990s that recalibrated economies to the condition of globalization by removing obstacles to trade, were broadly opposed by the unions. Demonstrations in Seattle in early 2000 against meetings of the World Bank and World Trade Organization protesting against globalization included important participation by labor. The left generally hailed these protests as a sign that workers, ecologists, and many other groups had awakened to dangers of global capital. Before the demonstrations few Americans knew much about the World Trade Organization; afterwards the scene had been changed. A new awareness of the network society was thrust on the populace. But the import of the meetings and the protests are not at all clear. Did they in fact represent the rebirth of the workers' movement, or were they the last gasp of that movement as it developed in the context of the industrial revolution?

The inequities of global capitalism are beyond question. Within the United States the income gap is growing rapidly. As Don Tapscott, hardly a far left critic of capitalism, points out, "1% of American households own nearly 40% of the nation's wealth. The top 20% of American households . . . own 80% of the country's wealth. Wealth and income skewing is accelerating faster in the United States than in any other developed nation" (Tapscott, 1996, p. 285). Globally the situation is even worse. Estimates are that 85 percent of global wealth is consumed by 20 percent of population; the bottom 20 percent have 1.5 percent of world income. Although some Asian nations have vastly improved their economies since the 1970s, and although there are significant pockets of wealth in some Latin American countries, by and large, the North-South divide has grown deeper in terms of material conditions. Globalization and free trade, at least up to this point, appear to be benefitting primarily those already rich and harming those already poor. Proponents of globalization argue that a planet with free trade must increase the wealth of all nations while critics point to the unseemly facts of the present.

Yet the condition for the American worker wrought by the global network is itself globalized. Workers making shoes in Texas are in direct competition with workers making shoes in Bangkok. In fact they may be working for the same company. Yet the standards of living in the two places are vastly different as are the wages. The hard question to be faced is how to take the new circumstances into consideration. A policy of defensive resistance by American workers is likely doomed to failure. If we examine the preparedness of the labor movement to develop a far-sighted and effective response, we see serious problems. As Eric Lee points out, the labor unions as late as 2000 do not even have websites. There is little sharing of information across national boundaries;

almost no databases exist of union activity, working conditions, and the like. Lee proposes the development of "online global labor press, archive/discussion group/journal and early warning network on trade union rights." And even these elementary steps, he judges, are "premature" given the indifference and ignorance of the union movement about new information technologies (Lee, 1999, p. 242).

Even in these dire circumstances there are those who see the new global order as an opportunity rather than as a threat. Peter Waterman argues that capitalists pushing for global markets are inadvertently creating conditions for an international workers' movement. He calls for "new global solidarity" in the face of the march of the market (Waterman, 1999, p. 254). Workers globally are now de facto in conditions of collective production. Thrust upon them by the greed and dynamics of capitalism, workers of the world is now a phrase that resonates not simply has a noble ideal but as an empirical reality. For Waterman, looking backwards to Marx, the laws of motion of the capitalist mode of production are producing the global conditions for its overcoming. If he is right, the question remains how the workers are to become aware of these circumstances and how are they to build a political movement to attain that end. One thing is sure: the only way a movement can be constructed of workers on a global scale is through the Internet. Network computing alone affords workers of different lands the possibility of communicating, accumulating mutually relevant knowledge, and building a political movement. Given the slowness of at least the American labor movement to adapt the Internet to their purposes, the situation at present is bleak indeed.

If the deployment of information technology by the labor movement is a key in the response of labor to globalization, another condition that might also be understood as cultural is equally critical. Workers must see their identities as constructed through information technologies and in need of transformation from national to global configurations. Castells is cogently aware of the question of identity in relation to the network society. He contends,

> In a world of global flows of wealth, power, and images, the search for identity, collective and individual, ascribed or constructed, becomes the fundamental source of social meaning. . . . Identity is becoming the main, and sometimes the only, source of meaning in a historical period characterized by widespread destructuring of organizations, delegitimation of institutions, fading away of major social movements, and ephemeral cultural expressions. . . . It follows [that there exists] a fundamental split between abstract, universal instrumentalism, and historically rooted, particularistic identities. *Our societies are increasingly structured around a bipolar opposition between the Net and the Self* [Emphasis in original] (Castells, 1996, p. 3).

The difficult problem that Castells puts in abstract language is that workers need to abandon their national identities and find a new source of identity as points in the network.

VII. Software and You

This is a colossal conundrum. Cultural change of this sort is difficult, disorienting, and confusing. Information technology introduces a restructuring of cultural space, putting into proximity phenomena that hitherto remained separate, and a restructuring of culturally defined temporality, bringing into simultaneity events that previously appeared in a sequential or linear manner. Changing cultural configurations of time and space transform the individual's sense of self. Since the self is composed of relations with others that serve to orient the individual in the world, new linkages such as remote intimacy upset the stability and coherence of everyday life.

Social scientists are discovering the profundity of these changes in micro-studies of the workplace and information technology. Jackie Zalewski and Anteaus Rezba studied a hospital in the Midwest that introduced a software program for ordering supplies from the Internet. Previously workers from various departments of the hospital filed new requests with the purchasing department, which then procured them from vendors. This procedure led to face-to-face meetings between workers in purchasing and other sections of the hospital. Relationships developed over the years between purchasing agents and others so that if someone needed certain supplies more quickly than usual these special requests could be accommodated. Zalewski and Rezba note also that the earlier system was inefficient, one of the motivations for management to introduce the new software. They also point out that the older procedures were more difficult than the new ones for management to control.

Making purchases directly on the Web thus eliminated a network of personal contacts and relationships. To order equipment and supplies workers now interfaced silently with a software program. The new system was more efficient and also, Zalewski and Rezba point out, facilitated greater control of the workers by management. Theorizing from the perspectives of Marcel Mauss, Raymond Williams, and Harry Braverman, among others, the researchers embed their findings in a narrative of worsening labor conditions. Information technology, they argue, furthers the alienation of the worker. They write,

> In general, electronic communications are void of personal nuances characteristic of face-to-face communications. Specifically, they lack framing, such as "Hello. How are you today?" This is, in large part, a function of the standard format of electronics' applications and Accolade's mandate to use them as the primary form of communications between departments. As a result, electronic communications can be characterized as instrumental, their content generally relays a Departmental supply need. Because the electronic System has the unique capacity to direct and document the actions of workers in the supply chain, obligations formerly developed between workers through verbal communications are replaced, to a large degree, by "an obligation to the System" (Zalewski and Rezba, 2000, p. 11)

While the authors are careful to present their work impartially, a narrative of decline and dehumanization creeps into their analysis.

The same cast is given by more well-known students of the labor process. Stanley Aronowitz and William DiFazio's *The Jobless Future* (1994) studies the introduction of information technology among architects and engineers in both the public and private sector in mid-Atlantic states. After extensive interviews and analyses, conducted over several years, they conclude that "computerized engineers and architects lose professional status by becoming more tightly controlled by managers. . . . Our studies showed that the Panopticon is not easily dislodged, that even the most revolutionary technology can be recruited in the interest of reproducing power, in this case to further degrade the labor of engineers, and even to be used as an instrument of proletarianization" (Aronowitz and DiFazio, 1994, pp. 104, 131). Although some of the workers in the study prefer the new technology, the students of labor, sensitive as they are to workers' rights, present a narrative of decline and a logic of suspicion about the motives of managers.

Information technology may not always fit easily into the interests of the rulers of industry. Joan Greenbaum studied the introduction of information technology since the beginnings of the introduction of computers into the workplace. She indicates how early mainframes fit into management strategies in very different ways from desktop or micro-computers. The latter provide workers with more flexibility and independence, certainly not a deliberate goal of management. In the next phase, desktop computers were connected by Local Area Networks. Network software attempts to bring workers again under more centralized control, but at the same time it enables the dispersion of the workplace in space. Greenbaum (1998, p. 178) points out, "Network software, user-friendly interfaces and integrated application packages reflect the interests of organizations to bind divided office labor back together, and simultaneously spread the results of this labor out over geographically dispersed areas of separate out-sourced units." A new condition of spatial separation is made possible by networked computing. And this condition leads to unintended consequences with ambivalent implications. Linking dispersed workers precipitates new communications and new organizational possibilities. In Greenbaum's words, "The design concept of communication, like that of automation, may be running into conflict with the objectives of companies to compete in post-industrial capitalism, for it could be opening up possibilities for more bottom up communication and thus slowing down or interfering with management controlled objectives" (1998, p. 181). Here we have a more complicated perspective on the impact of information technology, one that points to the possibilities for new labor forms within networked computing.

VIII. Postmodern Perspectives

A review of some examples of labor studies concerning information technology indicates the need for vigilance concerning concepts and narrative structure. The story of networked computers in the workplace cannot be concluded at this moment. We are in the midst of a great transformation, to allude to the visionary writing of Karl Polanyi, whose outcome is far from certain. Information technology challenges us to expect the unexpected and search for concepts that allow the researcher to grasp the new as well as the old. At the theoretical level, Nick Dyer-Witheford provides a good instance of combining older theoretical perspectives with newer understandings of the possibilities for labor in the present conjuncture. He writes,

> At each point [in the circuit of capital] we will see how capital uses high technologies to enforce command, by imposing increased levels of workplace exploitation, expanding its subsumption of various social domains, deepening its penetration of the environment, intensifying market relations, and establishing an overarching, panoptic system of measurement,

surveillance, and control through digital networks. . . . . I argue that the development of new means of communication vital for the smooth flow of capital's circuit — fax, video, cable television, new broadcast technologies, and especially computer networks — also creates the opportunity for otherwise isolated and dispersed points of insurgency to connect and combine with one another (Dyer-Witheford, 1999, pp. 92-93).

To take advantage of the economies of computerization, Dyer-Witheford continues, capitalism is compelled to promote a cadre of highly trained and skilled workers, what he calls "a virtual proletariat," a work force strewn with new forms of resistance such as hacking. Far from a docile, disciplined, and controlled labor force, acts of non-compliance and outright resistance may be seen, he claimed, as increasing. *La perruque*, Michel de Certeau's term for informal, dilatory resistance, finds new avenues in the world of high technology (Certeau, 1984). Even traditional forms of labor protest are making their way into the high-technology sector, as in the strike by Verizon workers in August of 2000. Some 86,000 workers went out on strike surprising the information industry behemoth which relied on traditions of relative docility and booming economic success. Equally, however, phone-sex and Internet-sex workers in Germany protest their conditions and demand full parity with workers in more traditional sectors. And a judge in Kassel agreed with them (Reuters, 2000). Citing numerous examples of counter-movements and oppositions that take advantage of networked computing, Dyer-Witheford foresees networked computing as having the unintentional consequence of creating the conditions for major changes in labor struggles. He opines that "Somewhere between the ethereal activism of radio and computer networks, and the weary odysseys of proletarians trekking from San Salvador to Vancouver or from Manila to Kuwait City, a new global class composition is being born" (Dyer-Witheford, 1999, p. 147). Whether or not a "new global class composition is being born," the advance in Dyer-Witheford's analysis rests with his awareness of the changes in spatial and temporal configurations introduced by network computing.

Like Castells, Dyer-Witheford leaves relatively unexamined the cultural level of the question. The formation of new identities, in Castells' term, or new class composition, in Dyer-Witheford's more Marxist language, rests with mediation of the medium, as we return necessarily to Marshall McLuhan's categories. The self is being reconstructed in relation to information machines, machines that introduce a profound symbiosis with the human. While the emerging configuration of labor is necessarily, as Castells and Dyer-Witheford agree, a global one, it is also a posthuman one, uniting in depth technology with humans. The study of information technology and labor therefore must account for the assemblage of human and machine in new configurations of time and space, body and mind, subject and object, all of which, by the way, lie completely outside the intentions of managers and capitalists. In these new conditions, new forms of subjectivity must surely arise, those that are far more complex than the centered identities of the modern epoch. The mechanisms through which these multiple, dispersed, machine-linked subjectivities are constructed is a prime area for research and analysis in the domain of labor and information technology.

References

Aronowitz, S. and W. DiFazio. *The Jobless Future: Sci-Tech and the Dogma of Work.* Minneapolis: University of Minnesota Press, 1994.

Carnoy, M., M. Castells, et al. *The New Global Economy in the Information Age.* University Park: Penn State University Press, 1993.

Castells, M. *The Rise of the Network Society.* Cambridge, Mass.: Blackwell Publishers, 1996.

———. "Materials for an Exploratory Theory of the Network Society." In J. Hartley and R. Pearson, eds. *American Cultural Studies: A Reader.* New York: Oxford University Press, 2000, pp. 414–36.

Certeau, M. d. *The Practice of Everyday Life.* Berkeley: University of California Press, 1984.

Coupland, D. Microserfs. New York: HarperCollins, 1995.

Dyer-Witheford, N. *Cyber-Marx: Cycles and Circuits of Struggle in High-Technology Capitalism.* Urbana: University of Illinois Press, 1999.

Foucault, M. *Discipline and Punish: The Birth of the Prison.* New York: Pantheon Books, 1977.

Greenbaum, J. "From Chaplin to Dilbert: The Origins of Computer Concepts." In S. Aronowitz and J. Cutler, eds. *Post-Work: The Wages of Cybernation.* New York: Routledge, 1998, pp. 167–84.

Kantrowitz, B. "A New Way of Talking." *Newsweek*, March 17, 1986.

Lee, E. "Trade Unions, Computer Communications and the New World Order." In R. Munck and P. Waterman, eds. *Labour Worldwide in the Era of Globalization: Alternative Union Models in the New World Order.* New York: St. Martin's Press, 1999, pp. 229–44.

Miller, G. "Online Power Gives David a Little Leverage on Goliath." *Los Angeles Times*, February 1, 1999.

Reuters. "Germany Decides Online Sex Workers Have Rights." *New York Times*, August 11, 2000.

Ross, A. "Hacking Away at the Counterculture." In C. Penley and A. Ross, eds. *Technoculture.* Minneapolis: University of Minnesota Press, 1991, pp. 107–34.

Scott, J. "On-Line, and Maybe Out of Line Talking by Computer Has Changed the Way Workers Behave (and Misbehave)." *Los Angeles Times*, September 24, 1993.

Tapscott, D. *The Digital Economy: Promise and Peril in the Age of Networked Intelligence.* New York: McGraw-Hill, 1996.

Waterman, P. "The New Social Unionism: A New Union Model for a New World Order." In R. Munck and P. Waterman, eds. *Labour Worldwide in the Era of Globalization: Alternative Union Models in the New World Order.* New York: St. Martin's Press, 1999, pp. 247–63.

Yegyazarian, A. "Nosy Bosses Face Limits on E-Mail Spying — Workers Gain New Freedoms." *PC World* (September 2000): 62.

Zalewski, J. and A. Rezba. "'Where the Links Were Broken': Mandating Efficiency Through an Electronics Supply Chain." Unpublished manuscript, 2000, pp. 1–13.

Zuboff, S. *In the Age of the Smart Machine: The Future of Work and Power.* New York: Basic Books, 1988.

8

Solidarity.com? Class and Collective Action in the Electronic Village

Anthony M. Townsend
Iowa State University

I. Introduction

Information and communications technologies have evolved to where a significant portion of our lives is increasingly shaped less by physical reality and more by the reality of the media with which we interact (Poster, 1990, 1996). Where once a fairly local community informed our ideas about ourselves, our social status, and our relations with others, as citizens of the electronic village we are far less confined by the ideas in our local community. With Internet access, we have the widest diversity of information ever available. And unlike every preceding media, the Internet is absolutely egalitarian in that anyone can publish and be read by the entire electronic community. With access to this breadth of information, individuals can go far beyond the historically monolithic information sources (newspapers, television, radio, etc.) and discover both raw information as well as a tremendous diversity of interpretation of the meaning of events and ideas.

The Internet allows something else to happen too; unlike traditional media, which send their messages in one direction, an individual on the Internet can communicate back to the electronic community. In doing so, individuals can redefine themselves in a much greater context than ever before, as they interactively determine their positions in this diverse universe. Since individuals are no longer bounded by the physical and cultural realities of their neighborhoods, they may well abandon their old self-definitions, philosophical conventions, and class loyalties.

In addition to changes in the forces that influence an individual's social perspective, radical changes in the nature of work itself have changed the bases on which individuals assess their relations with others. The information revolution takes place during a radical transformation of the workplace; the post-industrial landscape offers few smokestack factories staffed by legions of union workers. Instead, contemporary workers are much more likely to work with their heads than their hands and are paid for performance more than by job category and seniority. Accordingly, union membership has declined precipitously as these structural changes have eliminated many of the traditional bulwarks of union strength.

In this study, I examine how changes in the community of work and moving out of the "neighborhood" changes individuals' fundamental assumptions about themselves and their social position, specifically in relation to their motivations for collective action. I argue that in a post-industrial economy and an information-rich context, class identification (and union support) becomes a phenomenon created more by the individual and less by economic and political structures. I then offer a theoretical framework to analyze this evolving phenomenon and examine the ramifications of this transformation on union relevance.

II. The Changing Community of Work

The Factory Town. In 1950, U.S. Steel operated factories employing thousands of men, all earning their wages in hard, backbreaking work. These men came to work together, lived in the factory town, and drank at the same bars. They knew each other, maybe not personally, but as members of the same community and as members of the same *class.* They knew too that there was a difference between themselves and "management." They could see management, in suits and starched white shirts, working with paper instead of with steel; they believed at a visceral level in a wide gulf between workers and managers. Union membership was a natural extension of this sociology, as these men clearly believed that their only means to higher wages and better working conditions was through collective action.

In the ecology of the factory town, union information was disseminated through hand billing, picketing, and mass meetings, and information was *controlled* because there were few, if any, independent sources of information available to workers. In the factory town, labor was also a restricted commodity, for the cost of bringing in workers from any distance added value to local labor. The final great union advantage in the factory-town union was its ability to enforce conformity to the collective will, either through social pressure or violence. In the factory town, a union was almost inevitable.

However, as factory towns declined in the 1960s and 1970s, unions were marginalized by a social ecology in which they were ill equipped to compete. The change from production to service industries, the economic transformation of the South, suburbanization, and the change in workers' roles within the organization, all represented radical departures from the historical environment of collective action. With the decline of the factory town, the clear sense of class that once spanned generations of workers declined as well.

The Post-Industrial Landscape. With the factory town becoming extinct, new forms of work emerged that are predicated on a fundamentally different economic ecology:

radically different organizational structures and worker capabilities are valued in comparison with those in the past. Based largely on information services, this new economy emphasizes *individual* productivity rather than *collective* productivity. Information services do not have an assembly line, a shop floor, or large congregations of workers, lunch bucket in hand, passing their counterparts during shift changes. Information services usually have the clean feel of an office for even the most menial jobs. In this context, the classic distinction between blue-collar and white-collar blurred into a continuum of ascending levels of managerial power.

The Rise of the e-Corporation. With the transition to a post-industrial economy well underway, a number of technological and economic factors converged in the mid-1980s to create even greater economic opportunity and a further imperative for change in how people work. Faster computers, new telecommunications technologies, and new information infrastructures created a revolution in the informational and communication resources in industrialized nations. Simplified information retrieval systems and affordable access to the Internet attracted a new breed of information consumer, while at the same time informationally empowering a new class of people.

Additionally, the globalization of trade forced businesses to rethink their operating strategies and to restructure to effectively compete with offshore competitors. Where large and monopolistic organizations had once dominated the economic landscape, smaller and nimbler organizations began to establish themselves as the preeminent organizational form. Gradually, even the most successful of the giant firms began to disassemble into smaller and more adaptive operating units, reducing layers of administrative control and moving decision-making authority into lower levels of the remaining hierarchy. Even low-level jobs began to require decision making, as line workers were taught to manage quality control; the traditional assembly line effectively became a thing of the past.

III. The Electronic Village

Beginning with radio and motion pictures, and then television, American politics, culture, and social mores have been shaped by broadcast[1] media. These media were expensive to operate, and in the case of radio and television, access was limited by government regulation. While it is beyond the scope of this paper to discuss the ideological bent of these media, I can reasonably assert that the narrow control of these media clearly restricted the range of views presented. Thus, the average person's ideas about class, politics, and even self-identity were largely informed by media information and local custom.

The Internet revolution changes the historical role of mass media with two radical new factors: (1) Mass access, in the sense that anyone (or any institution) that publishes on the web is equally accessible to any web user; and (2) Robust interactivity, in that people can communicate with each other in a variety of different ways and discuss, debate, and critique the ideas of others in an almost unrestricted forum.

Where traditional media were controlled only by relatively powerful institutions (both private and public), the Internet is accessible to virtually anyone; the cost of putting a message in the public domain (at the time of this writing) is only about $20.00 per month.[2] While there is no guarantee that people will actually access a given Internet site, the potential exists. Consider this analogy: In traditional media forms, publishing a book or a newspaper was expensive, and even if you paid to create one that reflected your views, there was little chance that bookstores and newsstands would stock your publication. On the Internet, your publication is "stocked" in every bookstore and newsstand in the world; whether individuals read it is up to their discretion.

Aside from merely providing access to publications, the Internet has another characteristic that increases the likelihood that potentially interested parties will find your web site; the "search engines" (e.g., Altavista, Yahoo, Excite) that locate web resources are absolutely egalitarian. These search engines catalogue the text of virtually every site on the web at any moment and allow the user to find Internet sites that appear to relate to topics of interest; a search for sites related to labor is just as likely to turn up National Right to Work as it is the AFL-CIO. They will also turn up hundreds of other sites, both institutional and individual, that have some discussion of "labor." In other words, virtually every web site is subject indexed with equal standing on the Internet.

The Internet's interactivity is important, because it allows users to participate in the broad community of ideas represented on the Internet. Whether it is one-on-one correspondence with a web-site author or participation in a chat room or user group, the ability to go beyond unilateral publication of one's ideas on a web site and to interactively participate in a community of ideas allows the development of a social relationship among members of the electronic community. While not all Internet users participate interactively, seeing the interaction of others is much akin to attending a meeting but not speaking oneself; the participant experiences the discussion and passively participates just as saliently as if the meeting were held at the union hall.

Taken together, this access and interactivity create a potentially powerful social community for the Internet user; what becomes vexing sociologically is that each individual creates his own sociology from a limitless menu of options. Because users determine what ideas they address and how they interpret these ideas, it becomes very difficult to assert what factors in the political and economic environment meaningfully shape any given participant's ideas and self-identity. Thus, the predictable forces that shaped peoples' ideas about themselves and their place in the order of things have become unpredictable; we cannot know what any individual has now been exposed to, nor what has affected his thinking. As the community of ideas has become unbounded, so too has the community of reference; in such a broad community, once simple distinctions — such as class — become enormously complex.

IV. Class in the Electronic Village

Among traditional theorists, socioeconomic class is viewed deterministically (Sowell, 1985); if one works non-managerially, then by definition one is a member of the working class (Lukacs, 1986; Marx and Engels, 1969). In this traditional view, it is less up to individuals to interpret their class membership than it is to *discover* the membership they already have. Taken in the context of the historical factory town, where a common factory job could span generations and where social and economic institutions were fairly common to all, this deterministic view makes sense. In essence, what traditional class theorists argue (albeit unintentionally) is that we are products of our environment; when a given environment is common to a number of us, we constitute a class. Thus, in the micro environment of the factory town, a dialectic class structure of workers and managers makes sense; if individuals are indeed the product of their environment, and their environment is bounded by the limits of the factory town, then class membership is almost inevitable.

Accepting this view that class is a function of environment, it is clear that as environments change, so too does class affiliation. As workers moved from the factory town to suburbs and as the economy transitioned away from manufacturing, it follows that the historical class affiliations that encouraged union membership and collective action have changed as well. Although there is some resistance to this logical extension of traditional theory,[3] I am assuming for the present discussion that an individual's relevant environment informs a considerable portion of his class affiliation. Thus, as the lines between manager and worker have blurred, the clear dialectic that set them in unionized opposition to each other has lost salience as well.

Although the traditional view of environmentally determined class provides the bases for an evolving delineation of class boundaries, it lacks the necessary analytic to effectively determine actionable class in the individually-constructed community of the electronic village. Because the Internet provides so many options of involvement and sources of information, information relevant to the formation of an individual's self-perception will vary from person to person. Sowell (1985) argues that externally identified class membership is unable to bring the individual to action; rather, it is the individual's *perception* of his or her environment and its meaning that creates a sense of belonging and a willingness to act in consort with others of a similar disposition.

One final point about class in the electronic village is that I believe that classes will become much smaller, more particularly defined, and much more numerous. Class has always constituted a level of aggregation that is negated by experience; although a "working class" should by definition include all those who labor for wages, distinctions on the basis of race, gender, and relative income have long been the basis of exclusion. My operational definition of class in the electronic village is that it is a group with common economic and social interests large enough to exert pressure for social and economic change. While this definition is far from perfect, it should provide a point of departure for further discussion on the constitution of class in the electronic village.

A Theoretical Framework. If one accepts my view that class is individually constructed in the electronic village, it is critical to have a theoretical framework to predict how individuals in the electronic village will constitute their perceptions as to which class(es) they belong. In addition to determining their sense of class affiliation, theory is also necessary to predict when they will be moved to participate in a collective action. Self-Categorization Theory (SCT), Social Identity Theory (SIT), and Relative Deprivation Theory (RDT) provide a starting point for thinking about how an individual develops his sense of class membership in a broad system of possibilities, and how class members are then motivated to participate in collective action.

SCT (Turner, 1984, 1999) posits that individuals create their social self-perceptions based on their set of experiences and those of the class with which they identify. SCT (like SIT and RDT) has been designed primarily to deal with individuals' development of their sense of social self in environments bounded by physical proximity to other class members. Yet it does provide a theoretical basis to examine how the individual will assert his or her social self-characterization in the electronic village. Although the individual in the electronic village has a relatively unbounded set of choices from which to form the in-group to which they believe they belong, they nonetheless must form some sense of a relevant in-group and then define themselves in conjunction with that group (Johnston and Hawthorne, 1990). In essence, SCT provides an individual-level model of the phenomenon of belongingness and social self-categorization. An electronically mediated reality does create one paradox, however: According to Hogg and McGarty (1990), SCT predicts that the final stage of individual social identity occurs as the individual differentiates himself from other in-group members. However, Postmes et al. (1999) argue that in-group others lose unique identities in conditions of the relative anonymity of computer interactions. Without others against which to assert their own identity, individuals have difficulty placing themselves in the group's social order. In addition to a diminished sense of the other's characteristics (against which to juxtapose their own), individuals in the electronic village also lose important traditional social codes that help guide their formation of group identification and individual social identity (Mouzelis, 1999; Feenberg, 1995). Thus, individuals in the electronic village have limitless affiliative choices, but must make those choices without the traditional social signposts to guide their decisions. I believe that SCT raises three important research questions about the formation of group and class identity in the electronic village:

1. *Do individuals feel identity with the group but not with other individuals?*
2. *Do the plethora of choices for group membership allow individuals to create more precise groups with which to affiliate?*
3. *Does the lack of traditional codes that influence determination of the individual's social self negatively affect his or her ability to form a coherent social identity?*

SIT (Tajfel, 1984) is concerned with the formation of the group or class members' belief about their in-group and about those in out-groups. In essence, SIT posits that within the context of the group, individuals develop categories of similarity among the in-group and categories of dissimilarity with "others." The formation of these commonalities reinforces the meaning of membership (we are the same in this way) and the meaning of exclusion of the "others." Social identification then leads the members of a group to behave in ways that are congruent with the group's identity and which support institutions and actions that embody the group's identity (Ashforth and Mael, 1989).

As noted earlier, the formation of these in- and out-group characteristics is made difficult by the loss of traditional in and out definitions; the historical "us" and "them" is rendered useless when the formation of new social coalitions may put "us's" and "them's" in the same class. Furthermore, in the breakdown of traditional categories, the new categories that determine social identity and class affiliation are as likely to be psychologically based as they are to be based on objective externalities, e.g., race, gender, economic status (Zaretsky, 1994). Moreover, because individuals select information on which they base their class affiliation and only provide back to the group information that they choose, it is entirely possible to have tightly constituted coalitions whose members might not feel any association with each other in traditional interactions. In the formation of electronic class, many of the social cues that might either attract or repel potential members are not available; in this environment, the formation of class will be predicated only on the most instrumental characteristics that distinguish a class from "other" groups. An example of this might be an electronically formed coalition to end school-busing; in traditional settings, the racial characteristics of opponents of busing might preclude persons of different races from working together on the issue, due to historical suspicions of the motives of the others' race. In an electronic community, racial information is not necessarily available, allowing potential members to bond on the core issue of busing.

Finally, because the individual participant selects his or her interactions with others in the electronic community, it is also possible that individuals may develop strong affiliations with class groups that might appear to be at variance with each other. In traditional class affiliations, members are subject to a variety of social controls that require them to remain in step with other class members; failure to conform results in punishment or exclusion from the group (Merton, 1957). In electronic class structures, however, since the individual class member constitutes his or her own identity and controls his interaction with the group, the ability of others in the group to enforce norms or monitor the behavior of members is lost. This has an important effect on the formation of group identity and norms. For groups to retain the interest and commitment of their members, they must remain focused on the core issues or categories that determine affiliation. Groups that allow superfluous categories or norms to evolve risk alienating and losing members much more than in traditional settings.

Because of the differences in the bases in which class may form in the electronic village, I believe that there are three questions that need to be considered regarding the formation of class identity:

1. *Does the lack of physical interaction inhibit or encourage multiple group and class memberships, particularly in relation to different kinds of issues, e.g., a class for work and a distinct and separate class for political concerns?*

2. *Do electronic classes differ significantly from traditional social coalitions in terms of the categories of differentiation?*

3. *Do electronic class groups have significantly more precise definitions of group meaning and goals than traditional coalitions?*

While SIT and SCT provide a framework for analyzing how electronic classes form, RDT provides a framework for understanding what motivates the individuals in these classes to engage in collective action. RDT (Crosby, 1976) asserts that class membership forms a referent set for individuals, and based on how they perceive their class (or classes) to be treated, the individuals constitute their beliefs about how the broader system works for or against them and others like them. RDT has been used frequently by researchers to explain the effects of race on individual psychology; in this area of research, they suggest that to the extent that individuals identify themselves with a particular minority group and feel that this particular group tends to be mistreated in some way, they then believe that they too will be similarly mistreated. If the sense of affiliation is strong and the individuals believe the mistreatment of their identity group is serious, they are more likely to act in concert with others in their referent group (Mummendey et al., 1999; Kelly and Kelly, 1994).

It takes little transformation of this simple model to apply it to the individual experience of the electronic village. The individual determines his class affiliations following SCT and SIT, then constructs a sense of the unique challenges and opportunities for change that relate to his class. The only change that I believe is necessary to apply traditional RDT to the experience of social identity in the electronic village is the assertion of multidimensional referent structures. Traditional RDT views the individual construction of social position unidimensionally: one is black or white, one is male or female, etc. Because the Internet allows a much broader range of possibilities, infinitely more precise delineations of the relevant referent group may be possible; the individual may not simply see himself as a black male, for instance, but as a black male earning between $60,000 and $75,000 annually, who believes in gun control, tough anti-crime measures, and interventionist foreign policy. Likewise, a person may self-affiliate with a variety of different class groups, and go through a process of evaluating the equity of common effects for each group. As noted earlier, in a smaller community of reference only the most apparent of distinctions form the bases of social comparison; lacking a critical mass of others of a more precise similarity, members of a racial, political, or gender group coalesce around whatever common characteristic denominates a group of referents that seem to experience some common problem.

Once class is determined, if the degree of perceived deprivation of the individual's referent class is severe, the individual is more likely to be moved to action to change the condition of his or her class. Following this theoretical framework, collective action occurs when a group of individuals who perceive common affiliations begin to act through similar means to effect some commonly desired change. Probably the best example of this sort of action predates the Internet explosion. In the early 1990s, talk radio began to proliferate across the country; in addition to being a new format, talk radio shows were often conservative in political orientation and provided the first mass voice of a conservative sentiment that many listeners had ever experienced. By providing this voice and participation to a group that co-identified on the basis of political conservatism, talk radio empowered an informal conservative collective that may have had a significant effect on the 1994 congressional elections. In much the same manner as the Internet, talk radio provided access to historically excluded political ideas and commentary, and through its interactivity, created a sense of a broad community of similar thinkers.

Assuming that the talk radio analogy accurately applies to the Internet, the Internet may enable significant collective political response to issues that may have been largely ignored by traditional media outlets. The Internet has already seen enormous collective voice in a wide-ranging negative response to the Communications Decency Act (Whitman et al., 1999).

There is one additional Internet effect on the determination of relative levels of deprivation: Just as the burgeoning amount of information informs the individual's sense of deprivation, it may also add a degree of context that moderates that same sense of deprivation. Because the individual sees so much information on the Internet, it is possible that he will also see information about how "others" are fairing that might not have been available in more traditional information venues. The "realities" that form an individual's opinion about how "his kind" are treated relative to others in the factory town are radically different from those in the electronic village. As an increasing number of individuals participate in the electronic village, many historic beliefs about any group's relative position may change as individuals experience a broader informational context.

I see a number of critical questions arising from the RDT interpretation of the antecedents of collective action:

1. *Does the greater availability of information lead to greater or more diminished feelings of relative deprivation for individuals, as they compare their class to other classes?*
2. *Do new electronic classes emerge and take political and economic action, following the talk radio example?*
3. *Does the time frame of collective action change and do collective activities become more concentrated on specific changes because of tighter group focus?*

V. Implications for Union Organization and Action

To their credit, many international unions have recognized the importance of the Internet and have created an active presence online.[4] And just as it has for many institutions, the Internet allows unions a widely available and uncensored communication channel to the world. In this respect, unions have more communications capacity than ever before.

Additionally, all of the other tools of the electronic village are available to union administrators, organizers, and members; technologies such as e-mail and information warehousing, which have proven to be powerful marketing tools, are easily accessed by unionists. In many respects, unions have more technical potential for communicating and analyzing workplace trends and worker sentiment than ever before, so does this mean that unions will regain membership lost over the past four decades?

The answer to this question depends on whether unions can find some way to exploit the new social structures of the electronic village to overcome the loss of traditional structures that once enhanced union organization and power. As noted earlier, the rise of the electronic village has occurred in a post-industrial landscape, increasingly devoid of the organizations that were so successfully unionized in the past. As organizations restructure into progressively smaller, more global entities (DeMarie and Hitt, 2000), the ability of any local group of workers to restrict an organization's labor resources is completely marginalized by teleworkers and offshore labor. Thus, one of the traditional bulwarks of union power, restriction of labor through strikes and threats of strikes, is lost. Although the structural trends that led to the loss of this power have been developing for decades, the rise of the electronic village accelerated their effects.

In my own analysis, the acceleration of the evolution of a structural landscape unfavorable to unions is one of two negative effects of the electronic village on union organization. The second effect is the loss of dialectic class structures, as broader communities of interest become available to increasing numbers of workers. Union organizers can do little to resurrect the smokestack industries of the past; what they may be able to do is create the *electronic factory town*.

Unions thrived in factory towns not just because of the smokestack cathedral in the town, but also because of the rich network of communication among the factory town's residents. The combination of the rich communication network, coupled with a clear identification of the common bases of relative deprivation, created an environment where collective action was viable, given enough perceived ill treatment. The Internet provides the electronic village with a similarly rich communication network and allows individuals to find their collective identity among their selected referents. The only real difference, as far as unions are concerned, is that their potential role is defined somewhat differently by each class group.

What Unions Can Do. The easiest way to define what a union ought to look like in the electronic landscape may be to identify a contemporary example whose activities translate easily into the electronic landscape. I believe that the National Education Association (NEA), along with its affiliated state organizations, is an excellent example of the bases of successful union operation in the electronic village.

The NEA has advanced the status of professional employees in a service environment. Although the members of this union may meet an hour a day in the break room, or over lunch, their primary job duties are carried out independently. The strength of the NEA lies in its ability to identify enough issues that have common meaning to its members to activate them politically, which gives the NEA tremendous influence politically, ostensibly for the benefit of its members.

Translating the success of the NEA into a form compatible with the vicissitudes of the electronic community will probably require some change. As noted earlier, retaining active coalitions requires the organizing entity to focus tightly on core commonalities and concerns. The NEA has evolved a very broad action agenda over the years, much of which can only loosely be rationalized as relating directly to core member concerns. To maintain or increase its political clout, the NEA will likely need to refocus on core concerns and carefully evaluate its tangential political positions. The challenge for any organizing entity in the electronic community is to minimize alienating or unimportant action items, while maximizing political clout on items of great concern. Since an individual is far less captive to a single organization, any deviation from broadly based core issues may drive members into more tightly focused organizations.

Conversely though, broadly focused organizations may compensate for some lost "traditional" membership by attracting nontraditional "members." Organizations such as the NEA may be more able to reach out to noneducators and gain their support more effectively in the electronic village. Because the primary mechanism of action for this type of organization is political, this noneducator support provides a critical basis of power. Using e-commerce technology, new unions may want to reward support by providing informational, financial, or even consumer services to associate members. The idea of associate member support is not new in the union movement; what is new is the ability to more effectively promote associate membership and meaningfully interact with associate members.

In time, unions may be effectively replaced (or may evolve into) small political coalitions that affiliate with a variety of class interests. Although a significant portion of the bases of member affiliation may proceed from some common economic role, the organization may be defined more by commonly held political and social beliefs than by specific workplace issues. In an organizational environment characterized by dynamic change, workplace issues may prove too mutable for meaningful group orientation. Instead, class action will focus more on public policy or licensure and issues related to the entire profession or trade.

VI. Conclusion

In detailing the evolution of the economic landscape from factory town to electronic village and in discussing how class and collective action may be analyzed in the context of the electronic village, my goal has been to provide a framework that researchers can use to develop meaningful studies of class and collective action in the electronic village.

As class de-aggregates to more meaningful levels of coalition and as the rise of e-business effectively extinguishes many familiar forms of organization, the role of unions will be permanently altered. Many social critics have long decried the "business unionism" that has characterized the American union movement as an immature form that has neglected the politics of class (Gulik and Bers, 1987). In the new economic landscape, unions may well evolve into predominantly political coalitions, or conversely, into craft and professional associations. In their political incarnation, these new class representatives will be political actors, albeit for significantly more narrow classes. In their professional and craft roles, the new unions will function to ensure higher wages and better employment by securing high competency standards as barriers to entry to a given craft or profession; doing this will ensure that those that move beyond the barriers will be perceived (and rewarded) in the marketplace as important human resources.

I believe that our evolution toward an ever-richer information context will forever change the way that we define ourselves, our class, and our view of others. I also believe that this information richness will create greater precision in class definition and will obviate the cumbersome affiliations based on race, gender, or national identity. I fervently hope that the greater availability of information will end coalitions formed on the basis of demagoguery; although the demagog has equal access to the Internet, I expect that the pervasive availability of diverse ideas and interpretations will allow people to form better affiliative choices.

Notes

1   I use the term "broadcast" inclusively here, referring to any media form that presents a fixed message to the receiver.
2   This represents the current monthly cost of an Internet Service Provider, which usually provides its clients with an Internet address (URL) and an e-mail address. For a slightly higher cost, an individual can register a unique address and domain name, which further encourages contact with one's publication. The annual cost of this higher-level type of Internet presence is less than $500.00 per year.
3   Critical theorists (Adorno, 1995; Horkheimer, 1995) argue that there is still a class dialectic between the power elite and the powerless. However, their analysis is confounded by differing definitions of who constitutes the power elite and the powerless.
4   See www.aflcio.org for a starting point.

References

Adorno, Theodor W. *Negative Dialectics*. New York: Continuum, 1995.
Ashforth, Blake E. and Fred Mael. "Social Identity Theory and the Organization." *Academy of Management Review* 14 (January 1989): 20-39.
Crosby, Faye. "A model of Egoistical Relative Deprivation." *Psychological Review* 83 (March 1976): 85-113.
Feenberg, Andrew. *Alternative Modernity: The Technical Turn in Philosophy and Social Theory*. Berkeley: University of California Press, 1995.
Gulik, Charles A. and Melvin K. Bers. "Insight and Illusion in Perlman's Theory of the Labor Movement." In Simeon Larson and Bruce Nissen, eds. *Theories of the Labor Movement*. Detroit: Wayne State University Press, 1987, pp. 174–85.
Hogg, Michael A. and Craig McGarty. "Self-Categorization and Social Identity." In Dominic Abrams and Michael A. Hogg, eds. *Social Identity Theory: Constructive and Critical Advances*. New York: Springer-Verlag, 1994, pp. 10–27.
Hogg, Michael A., Deborah J. Terry and Katherine M. White. "A Tale of Two Theories: A Critical Comparison of Identity Theory with Social Identity Theory." *Social Psychology Quarterly* 58 (December 1995): 255–69.
Horkheimer, Max. *Critical Theory: Selected Essays*. New York: Continuum, 1995.
Kelly, Caroline and John Kelly. "Who Gets Involved in Collective Action?: Social Psychological Determinants of Individual Participation in Trade Unions." *Human Relations* 47 (Spring 1994): 63–88.
Lukacs, Georg. *History and Class Consciousness: Studies in Marxist Dialectics*. Boston: MIT Press, 1986.
Marx, Karl and Friedrich Engels. *The Communist Manifesto*. New York: Washington Square Press, 1969.
Merton, Robert K. *Social Theory and Social Structure*. New York: Free Press, 1957.
Mouzelis, Nicos. "Exploring Post-Traditional Orders: Individual Reflexivity, 'Pure Relations'

and Duality of Structure." In Martin O'Brien, Sue Penna, and Colin Hay, eds. *Theorising Modernity: Reflexivity, Environment and Identity in Gidden's Social Theory*. New York: Addison, Wesley, Longman, 1999, pp. 83–97.

Mummendey, Amelie, Thomas Kessler, Andreas Klink, and Rosemarie Mielke. "Strategies to Cope with Negative Social Identity: Predictions by Social Identity Theory and Relative Deprivation Theory." *Journal of Personality and Social Psychology* 76 (February 1999): 229–45.

Poster, Mark. *The Mode of Information: Poststructuralism and Social Context*. Chicago: University of Chicago Press, 1990.

———. *The Second Media Age*. Cambridge: Blackwell, 1996.

Postmes, Tom, Russell Spears, and Martin Lea. "Social Identity, Normative Content, and 'Deindividuation' in Computer-Mediated Groups." In Naomi Elders, Russell Spears, and Bertjan Doosje, eds. *Social Identity: Context, Commitment, Content*. Malden, Mass.: Blackwell, 1999, pp. 1–5.

Sowell, Thomas. *Marxism: Philosophy and Economics*. New York: Quill/William Morrow, 1985.

Tajfel, Henri. "The Social Dimension." In Henri Tajfel, ed. *The Social Dimension: European Developments in Social Psychology*, Vol. 2. Cambridge: Cambridge University Press, 1984.

Turner, John C. "Social Identification and Psychological Group Formation." In Henri Tajfel, ed. *The Social Dimension: European Developments in Social Psychology*, Vol. 2. Cambridge: Cambridge University Press, 1984.

———. "Some Current Issues in Research on Social Identity and Self-Categorization Theories." In Naomi Elders, Russell Spears, and Bertjan Doosje, eds. *Social Identity: Context, Commitment, Content*. Malden, Mass.: Blackwell, 1999, pp. 1–5.

Whitman, Michael E., Anthony M. Townsend, and Robert Aalberts. "The Communications Decency Act Is Not As Dead As You Think." *Communications of the ACM* 42 (January 1999): 15–17.

Zaretsky, Eli. "Identity Theory, Identity Politics: Psychoanalysis, Marxism, Post-Structuralism." In Craig Calhoun, ed. *Social Theory and the Politics of Identity*. Cambridge: Blackwell, 1994, pp. 198–215.

9

How New Lawyers Use E-Voice to Drive Firm Compensation: The "Greedy Associates" Phenomenon*

Daphne G. Taras
University of Calgary

A. Gesser
New York, NY

I. Introduction

Recent developments surrounding the salaries of junior lawyers at large firms have demonstrated the potential of the Internet to strike at the core of the employment relationship at the upper echelons of the legal industry — a nonunion environment where hatchling lawyers traditionally have had little bargaining power. The development of the Internet website phenomenon known as " the Greedy Associates" (GA) has stripped away some of the patina of lawyer-firm feudal loyalty and revealed an industry-wide partner-associate economic tension. Originally a Yahoo! Club message board, GA started as a website where a small group of young attorneys exchanged information about employment opportunities and working conditions in Manhattan. Within a year, its scrutiny widened to include top law firms across the country, and by the beginning of 2000, it was attracting hundreds of visitors daily. Soon after, a commercial legal website, anxious to attract Internet traffic from top-earning attorneys, lured the GA away from Yahoo! with promises of superior web hosting and monthly cash prizes. Since that time, the GA has become a powerful force in the legal community and an example of how web-based organization offers an effective means by which similarly situated employees across an industry can exchange information about their compensation and develop strategies for getting more.

Until the economic boom of the mid-1990s, salaries of associates in America's top law firms had achieved relative stability. There were two or three top paying or "benchmark" firms in New York. Other law offices either matched the salaries paid by the benchmarks or they did not, creating a tiered structure for law firms based on compensation. On the GA Board, the top-tier firms are somewhat pejoratively referred to as "BIGLAW." Our focus is primarily on these firms and the lawyers who work there.

Every couple of years one of the benchmark firms would raise its salaries by several thousand dollars. Over the next several months, in reaction to that development, other top-tier firms would adjust their own compensation. Sometimes a lower tier firm would match the benchmark cluster, thereby moving into the top tier. The result was that there were always about 25 New York law firms paying the highest wage in the country. At the end of 1998 the salaries including bonuses for top tier firms were around $110,000, $120,000, and $135,000 for first-, second-, and third-year associates, respectively. Generally, prominent firms in other cities did not feel compelled to match the New York rates because it was widely acknowledged that the higher cost of living and the demand of longer workdays in New York were built into the compensation packages for Manhattan lawyers. While salary figures were periodically published in legal magazines, there existed no mechanism by which legal associates could confirm which firm was paying what on a weekly basis. There did, of course, exist a word-of-mouth network, but it was notoriously unreliable.

This orderly system was challenged by the development of the GA message board. First started in the fall of 1998, the GA club provided young lawyers with a forum to endlessly complain about everything from their treatment by nasty partners to their firm's cafeteria food, all under pseudonyms and with virtually no fear of reprisal. But most significantly, GA quickly became the means by which junior lawyers across the country anonymously exchanged information about their salaries, bonuses, and benefits.

We explore the emergence of the GA phenomenon and assess its effect on law firm culture, economics, and recruiting, with particular attention to large New York firms — the employers and the focus of the original GA. Of particular interest are questions involving the significance of the GA Board and its broader implications for white-collar employee-employer relationship. Is this the beginning of a new form of collective action? Can Internet message boards in some way act as a substitute for unions in industries that would never unionize? Is the goal of the GA to take wages out of competition, as unions do, or to return wages into competition for labor markets where individuals should have bargaining power? Is the Internet, as a basis for the exchange of employment-related information, fundamentally different from the traditional media?

To gather information for this article we interviewed dozens of knowledgeable informants: associates, partners, journalists, and legal recruiters. We spoke at length to the co-creator and webmaster of the original GA site. A research program of semi-structured interviews with the promise of confidentiality was conducted in New York in March 2001. We also monitored the GA site from its inception until November 2001.

II. Institutional Features of BIGLAW

The legal community is segmented by size, with the biggest firms developing their own internal labor market, compensation rates, and conditions of work (excellent discussions of this phenomenon are in Galanter and Palay, 1991; Nelson et al., 1992; Tolbert and Stern, 1991). BIGLAW firms often have more than 500 lawyers with offices in several different cities. For a variety of reasons, these firms are considered the most prestigious places to practice law, offering an opportunity to work for multinational corporate clients, on sophisticated high-profile cases, at the very top of the legal pay scale.

In the BIGLAW industry, partners and associates form an "occupational community" dominated by lawyers with common training, specialized knowledge, and distinct reward systems (Van Maanen and Barley, 1984). There are large recruiting networks, such as the National Association for Law Placement, that serve the needs of over 681,000 lawyers in the U.S. (a 1998 U.S. government estimate) and over 81,000 lawyers in Canada (2000 estimate from the Federation of Law Societies of Canada). The legal profession not only has its own bar associations and large legal directories, but it is also supported by a service sector including a newspaper industry and Internet dissemination network. For example, on a typical Monday in 2001, the daily broadsheet newspaper *New York Law Journal* (*NYLJ*) contains 55 pages organized into four sections. Smaller cities and counties are served by large weekly newspapers. In 2001, the *American Lawyer* magazine listed 740 legal recruiters offering a broad range of matchmaking services. With the advent of the World Wide Web came service providers such as Vault.com and FindLaw.com that contain copious information about the legal profession. Included on such sites are detailed law firm profiles that allow both clients and future lawyers to conduct their own research before choosing a firm.

The Associates. The group of lawyers who want to work for BIGLAW firms is partially self-selecting. First, law students operate in a distinct market (Ehrenberg, 1989). On top of that, it takes a certain type of highly ambitious and driven law student to knowingly walk into the pressurized environment that characterizes BIGLAW firms. In order to get an interview, it is best that the would-be associate have an excellent pedigree — top half of the class at a prestigious law school, law review, moot court, summer internships, foreign languages, good college, academic publications, government service, and a sharp-looking interview outfit are all common attributes of BIGLAW interviewees.

On their customized websites, large firms post information about the proportion of their associates who came from top schools, as well as other information about their associate screening process that signals upper echelon credentials to both future associates and to interested clients. The status of the associate pool is an important selling feature of large law firms. In turn, law firms wine and dine their prospective associates at sometimes enormous cost. Interviewees declined to discuss specific amounts, but a few thousand dollars per associate before they are even hired full time was not unusual.[1]

The Training. Most firms provide significant training for their summer associates, which often continues for their first year. After that, many associates told us that, at least at some firms, the extent to which associates continue to receive mentoring depends greatly on the partners to whom they have been assigned to work. As one mid-sized firm declared in its promotional literature to the National Association for Law Placement, "Each associate works with particular partners who are responsible for the associate's training and growth as an attorney; this is one of the most important responsibilities of our partners."

Partnership at BIGLAW. The structure of most top-tier New York law firms resembles the "Cravath" system, named for the benchmark firm Cravath, Swaine & Moore, which supposedly perfected it. At these firms, all associates hired in the same year earn the same pay. Because of this, associates never individually negotiate their salary, which increases by ten to twenty thousand dollars on January 1 of each year. The only other promotion is from associate to partner, which means switching from a fixed wage to a share in the firms' profits, and, generally, a substantial increase in pay. Cravath-type firms have approximately three times as many associates as partners, with few associates actually becoming partners, and partners take home between four and ten times what the associates earn.

Forty years ago, large law firms recruited talented law school graduates from prestigious law schools with the expectation that a partnership would be in the offing after a multi-year apprenticeship period. During their associate years, these lawyers were under the tutelage of experienced partners who paid their salaries and to whom they owed fidelity. In the 1950s and 1960s the norms were that "the firms will not pirate an employee from another law office, and they maintain a gentlemen's agreement to pay the same beginning salary" (Smigel, 1969, p. 57). Partners remained with the same firm throughout their professional careers.

By contrast, the Cravath structure involves a steep positive wage curve for those few associates who are able to achieve partnerships, normally after six to ten years at the firm. Some have characterized the BIGLAW advancement system as a winner-take-all job market, in which "potential contestants" vie for limited and exceedingly lucrative partnerships (Frank and Cook, 1995; Galanter and Palay, 1991). This is also referred to in the economic literature as a "promotion tournament" (Rosen, 1986; Ehrenberg and Bognanno, 1990; Ehrenberg and Smith, 1994, p. 389). Bok dismisses the tournament metaphor, claiming there is little risk of career failure among law graduates: "one can scarcely describe these professions as having a lottery in which few winners deserve ample rewards for having survived against great odds" (1993, pp. 12-13). But in terms of BIGLAW partnerships, the tournament metaphor does seem apt. Firms hire dozens of young lawyers each year with the expectation that only one or two of them will achieve a permanent spot after a lengthy and often grueling apprenticeship.

Earlier in the century it was possible to remain with the firm as a permanent associate, but in the course of the 1960s many firms adopted an "up or out" policy that meant the demise of this career opportunity. Currently, most of those associates who do not "make partner" at BIGLAW usually leave the firm shortly after being "passed over." The process for determining winners in this high-stakes career management game is in part based on who is willing to dedicate the most time to their work, thereby accumulating substantial "billable hours" for the partners to share in. Over the course of their road to partnership, associates must build relationships with several partners who will then "go to bat" for them come decision time. In an effort to secure these supporters, associates often feel unable to resist increasingly relentless and competing demands on their time.

By the fourth or fifth year, it usually becomes clearer which associates have a realistic chance of making the great leap forward. At that point, many of the "dead enders" begin to voluntarily exit the firm, taking on legal positions in smaller law firms, government, or corporations, or quitting the legal profession entirely and going into business, consulting, and quite often, screenwriting. However, these exiting lawyers retain the luster of their years of association with prominent firms, and most often are able to strike better deals with future employers as a result.

III. Associates Begin Thinking in the Short Term

In New York, this tournament to the top became an acute problem in the 1990s. One senior partner recalls that when he was an associate only 15 years previously, he was one of three partners gleaned from the 50 associates who had entered the firm with him. (Studies of top firms conducted in the 1950s showed that the average chance of achieving a partnership was between one in six and one in twelve: quoted in Galanter and Paley, 1991, p. 27). In 2001, this partner estimated the odds for the entering group as only one in a hundred. Under the Cravath model, it is the associates whose ranks expand and contract with the economy and availability of work. During the good times of the late 1990s, there was a tremendous amount of work for associates to do, but most firms did not proportionately expand their partnership opportunities. Instead, BIGLAW partners use associates as a buffer in order to provide them with greater financial security at all stages of the business cycle.

The result of this model is that during times of economic growth, BIGLAW firms frantically recruit associates in order to feed their expansion (Galanter and Paley, 1991). Such feverish recruiting ought to substantially increase the bargaining power of new lawyers, but until 1999 it did not. This is largely due to the absence of a communication vehicle for coveted applicants to raise the wage issue in light of the fixed starting salary and no negotiation culture at the benchmark firms. In the 1990s, as BIGLAW firms began hiring hundreds of associates while still only "making" four or five partners per year, associates began entering these megafirms without any expectation of "making partner." Rather than waiting for a payday that likely would never come, they turned their attention to what they could get right now.

While Ehrenhart and Smith (1994, p. 396) conclude that "[d]eferred compensation schemes and promotion tournaments obviously can *only* be used in the context of long-term attachment," here we have a situation in which the expectation of long-term job security had dwindled substantially. Hence there was considerable pressure to raise the entry-level wage of associates to compensate them for their risk. Furthermore, as the costs of top-shelf law degrees grew, students began taking on enormous educational debts (frequently in excess of U.S. $60,000), and many felt an urgent need to begin making significant payments soon after graduation. Many law students who had no interest in working at a large firm nonetheless felt compelled to accept BIGLAW offers because they needed the money. What developed was a culture of young lawyers who went to work for BIGLAW with the intention of staying only until their student loans were paid off. Not surprisingly, these associates had little loyalty to their temporary benefactors (a hypothesis tested and confirmed in Wallace, 1995, pp. 235, 247).

The Changing Economics of the Legal Practice. The change in the structure of law firms coincided with a change in the economics of BIGLAW legal practice. In the 1960s, many large corporations gave all their legal business to a single firm. These clients "typically received a bill once or twice a year, which they paid obediently, seldom fussing over the petty details of why the charges were what they were" (Bok, 1993, p. 46). From 1970 to 1988 the total number of lawyers tripled. There was a "litigation explosion" and increased competition among lawyers for institutional clients. More options for clients meant that they began scrutinizing their service and bills more carefully. As firms had to better demonstrate their comparative value, the bidding for well-known experienced counsel drove up partner compensation. Firms began taking the formerly rare step of poaching counsel from competing practices, by promising them even more lucrative compensation in exchange for switching teams.[2] In the 1980s, lawyers profited from the frantic pace of business change, presenting enormous bills to clients engaged in billion-dollar merger and acquisition transactions.

The creation of corporate giants through mergers and acquisitions in the business community coincided with the rise of the mega-law firm. By the 1990s, a group of industry giants emerged. For example, the largest New York firm, Skadden, Arps, Slate, Meagher & Flom, has 748 lawyers in its New York office, and the total of its many domestic and international offices is 1,610 lawyers (<www.skadden.com>). In the New York BIGLAW, a firm of 200 lawyers in total is considered only medium-sized. The largest 25 law firms in the U.S. (most of which have offices in multiple locations) employ almost 8,400 lawyers in their largest offices alone, an average of 336 lawyers in a single large location.

Bigger Means Richer. BIGLAW firms can handle large complex cases for institutional clients, which often means more money for everyone at those firms. The largest twenty firms increased their profits per partner by over 50 percent between 1985 and 1990. Small firms increased their profitability by a much lower amount, while solo practitioners suffered greatly (Bok, 1993, p. 48). The top ten New York law firms (measured by the generosity of partner compensation) paid each of their partners between $1 and $3.1 million dollars each in 1998 (*NYLJ*, February 28, 2000, posted on law.com July 5, 2000).

Among associates, this segmentation also is evident. In 2000, the nationwide median salary for first-year associates was $85,000. For small firms with less than 26 attorneys, the median was $60,000. In large firms of over 500 attorneys the median was $110,500. The nationwide median salary for all first-year associates increased by 21.4 percent from 1999 to 2000, but the increases in large firms exceeded 30 percent (*NYLJ*,

September 8, 2000). In an interview, one partner in a prominent mid-sized specialty law firm discussed the hope he had developed until the mid-1990s that his firm would be able to match salaries with larger firms and attract the cream of the crop of freshly minted attorneys. But even before the raises of 2000, he realized his firm could not keep up with BIGLAW. He made a strategic decision not to compete and stopped hiring people directly out of law school because they would be too expensive to train. "A firm needs big deals to do that; big cases, big deals, big clients. This is the grease that makes the associate pay spike work." Firms generally aim to generate three times an associate's salary through that associate's billings. He claims that firms bill first-year associates time at around $200 an hour. So if a firm were to pay a first-year associate $160,000 in total compensation, it would expect that person to work almost 2,500 billable hours to hit that 3:1 target. But his clients can't generate that magnitude of billings; the typical transaction at his firm involves a legal bill of between $5,000 and $10,000 — quite respectable by any standard, but not approaching the millions of dollars charged to a stable base of elite clients enjoyed by the BIGLAW group. Thus it is not just a segmentation of law firms by size that has occurred in the legal industry, but also a tiering of clients (Abbott, 1988, pp. 122-4).

Lawyers as Free-Agents. At one time partners were engaged in a long-term relationship with a single law firm, and could develop mentoring and training roles with new associates in a situation similar to the apprenticeship system in the crafts. Partners shared their clients with novice lawyers and expected to retain the best and brightest of the apprentices to form a cadre of staff with considerable expertise to service clients. But in a world in which partners achieved mobility, and the tacit agreement not to allow lateral movement from firm to firm broke down (Smith, 1989), the need and desire to sustain a mentoring relationship with trainees eroded quickly at many BIGLAW firms. As one interview respondent put it, "face time" decreased. At some firms, both partners and associates began thinking of themselves and behaving as free agents. Prospective lateral transfers are wined and dined: A recruiter in a mid-size firm estimated that the firm paid $40,000 in expenses per lateral recruit attained.

At firms where partner loyalty declined, a psychology developed among associates that they were underpaid early in their careers, and that the partners were overpaid — a sentiment which continues today. Associates gripe that it is one thing to live in a secure employment situation knowing that some day there will be adequate compensation for the lean years (as is the case in the medical profession, for example), but it is quite another situation to have limited long-term job prospects and know that associates are being churned through the legal profession to support the security of partners. Sensitive to these concerns, firms try to address this demotivation issue by offering lavish perquisites — paid weekend getaways, expensive meals, the use of car services, designer handbags and briefcases, the latest computer and communications gadgetry, and other symbols of success in the BIGLAW world. But some still see it as an unfair bargain — working long hours in exchange for lobster dinners — which contributes to their feeling of being aggrieved. There is no doubt that a machismo culture exists among BIGLAW associates such that working long hours is a symbol of an associate's worth to the firm and status as a lawyer. Since associates "see it as a sign of weakness to declare that this incredibly hard life isn't for me," they displace their anger onto their relationship with the partners and the firm itself.

According to the recollections of two respondents, conditions took a dramatic turn for the worse in 1991 following a market crash. Some firms could not honor their job promises to summer students. There was a great deal of resentment as most law firms scaled back on their excesses (e.g., "fantasy nights," where firms might give associates $1,000 to take a date or spouse anywhere for a weekend, were eliminated). Promises were broken as a few firms laid off associates. The 1990s began with a lesson that the legal world was becoming tougher on its job entrants, and by the late 1990s resentment for some had reached a fever pitch.

IV. Greedy Associates Emerges

By 1998, disgruntled associates at BIGLAW were primed to vent. The widespread availability of the Internet, which allowed anonymous messaging, made webpages an ideal vehicle for employee self-empowerment (or "voluntaristic action": Sciulli, 1986). Generic sites sprung up all over the U.S., including mybosssucks.com, Iquit.org, Workingwounded.com, Disgruntled.com, Bullybusters.org, and so on (Franklin, 2000), where people exchanged complaints about their jobs, bosses, salaries, and work environment. The legal profession's own contribution to this phenomenon was started as a Yahoo! club page called Greedy Associates in September 1998 by a user known as "nowhitenoise" (Snider, 1998). As the founder of the club, she had the power to delete messages from the bulletin board at any time. She remains employed in the New York legal profession but is in deep cover due to fear of employer reprisal.

The original GA board was quickly overrun by childish postings and became a playground for law students and paralegals to talk about politics, movies, and other subjects not related to employment. Occasionally, postings on the site were informative, accurate, and timely. For example, the site correctly reported confidential special bonuses for associates at Sullivan & Cromwell, White & Case, and Cahill Gordon. But by June 1999, the discourse on the GA page had degraded into endless name-calling between the members and pointless discussions about which law schools were better than others.[3] Associates desperately wanted immediate and effective information dissemination so they could know exactly what was happening in the world of BIGLAW compensation, without having to wade through hundreds of messages about whether Harvard was a better law school than Yale. The *NYLJ* took far too long to publish announcements about raises and bonuses, and usually only provided salary information for the benchmark firms. Some law firms were tight-lipped by inclination and would neither supply press releases nor release any information about salaries.

Unhappy with the deterioration of the GA page, one of the regularly posting GAs, who called himself CornholioEsquire (inspired by "Beavis and Butthead"), along with six other associates, started a rival Yahoo! club called "the Real GAs." As a club founder, CornholioEsquire was able to influence the content on the message board and exert better control over the message board's decorum. Soon after creating the Real GAs, Cornholio was approached through e-mail by an *NYLJ* reporter, Anna Snider, and through her, began a tacit campaign of cooperation with the legal media. By publicizing the defection of the Real GAs through telephone interviews with reporters (particularly Michael Goldhaber), Cornholio sparked a great deal of interest in the GA site, which resulting in increased traffic and more postings. Thereafter, a series of newspaper articles appeared, describing and popularizing the electronic insurrection. This was the key to disseminating information about the GA phenomenon itself.

Media attention led to proliferation of GA boards. Sites were created for different cities — Washington, D.C., Los Angeles, Boston, Chicago, and even Canada — as well as boards devoted to certain areas of practice like tax or intellectual property. All combined, the GA boards were soon generating thousands of hits on a regular basis, with a surge estimated by Cornholio to be as high as 25,000 hits in late 2000. The Real GAs site for New York received 34,700 actual postings and incalculable page hits between March 3, 2000, when it was launched and November 3, 2001, when our data collection ceased.

Associates posting on GA boards use pseudonyms intended as symbolic messages of distress or irreverence: Comma Chaser, no money no money no money, Litingrate, LadyGreediva, Want a life, and DebtSlave. Some lawyers disloyally parody BIGLAW firm names: Aching Grump (Akin, Gump, Strauss, Hauer & Feld), Davis Polked Me (Davis Polk & Wardwell), Skattitude (Skadden Arps), and OhSmelveny (O'Melveny & Myers). Also common on GA boards is the use of ancillary identity monikers called "sock puppets" (named after Lambchop from the children's television show). Sock puppets are secondary names and personalities created by an individual to so that one person can create the illusion of a conversation about a topic. They are generally used to get the ball rolling on a particular issue. By his own admission, Cornholio has used at least 30 sock puppets to help run the GA site initially.

Since Cornholio allowed himself to be "outed" in the legal media, sharing recognition as one of the 100 most influential American lawyers by *National Law Journal*, we can openly attribute much of the flavor of the site to Arthur Schwartz, aka Cornholio.[4] A 28-year-old New Yorker from a privileged family in which both mother and father are scientists and an uncle is a Nobel Prize winner, Schwartz did not take well to the system of apprenticeship in law firms. Cornholio was a self-described "miserable" first-year associate with a major law firm (Cadwalader), who switched to another firm (Thacher Proffitt & Wood), but was still unhappy with the situation of associates. He and a small group of six other founders, who remain anonymous because of fear of reprisal from their law firms, did not expect to profit directly from GA; rather, they hoped to benefit indirectly by inciting a wage war among firms. Cornholio allowed his real name to be known only after he made a decision to leave the practice of law and is now contemplating an MBA.

Early discussions on the GA boards revealed that many associates were unhappy with their compensation on an absolute scale and also in relative terms. Young lawyers saw themselves as underpaid as compared to their peers who were working as bankers and traders in the major brokerages, who were widely believed to be earning almost $1 million dollars a year during the market frenzy of the late 1990s. This was rankling indeed, as young lawyers believed themselves to have better credentials and a lengthier more comprehensive training period than their non-law Wall Street counterparts. "My girlfriend was earning eight times more than me," complained Cornholio, "and I was working longer hours and had these huge pressures too!"

Out of this sense of being undervalued while everything else was being overvalued, the Greedy Associates emerged. What was the aim of GA, we asked. "Money," Cornholio replied. But what about the long hours and difficult working conditions, we asked. "The GA Board is about getting more out of our short-term situation. We aren't trying to work less, we are trying to get more compensation," he explained. And what about your relationship with the partners, we asked. "F*** the partners — they f*** us."

An October 9, 2001 posting by Gator captures the prevailing sentiment of the Greedy Associates: ". . . we are not arguing whether greed is good (that's the assumption) we are simply arguing about where the money should land amongst the greedy. As a matter of objective fact, if you support silence and complacency about bonuses, you are supporting an increase in take-home for the partners, because that is where the money will go." Multo Madefactus weighed in: "I live in the land of the biggest and the bestest, and I want my money. Now, if I choose to donate my money to some charitable and worthy cause, my call. And that cause is not lining some partner's pocket." This sentiment explains some of the bitterness about the site we encountered when interviewing the partners.

It is not disputed that in a very short period of time, during the height of GA activity and attention, wages for associates at top law firms rose by fifty percent. What is less clear is the role the GA played in salary hikes that took place during a boom economy and a tight labor market, where law firms were competing with investment banks and Internet companies for top legal talent.

V. The Search for a Home

An important part of the GA story also involves its search for an institutional home among the various Internet possibilities. Clearly the GA Boards are rather a free-for-all, and without some supervision, there is considerable risk of deterioration in both purpose and tone. In March 2000, the Real GAs moved to a commercial website at www.infirmation.com run by the authors of *The Insider's Guide to Law Firms*. Infirmation would make money from placing ads into the GA site and from posting information about commercial products. Cornholio and his group of founders argued publicly that the move was necessary because the Yahoo! chat club site was experiencing technical problems, but the Infirmation deal also provided enticements including the promise to cover a month of law school debt for one randomly selected contributor each month. Some justifiably suspicious associates queried whether Infirmation had paid the GA founders for the move, but at the time Cornholio "declined to discuss whether money had changed hands" (Keyse Soze posting on Greedy LA Board, March 1, 2000). In our interview Cornholio confirmed that some sort of compensation tied to ad revenues and the number of page hits was offered, but it is subject to a confidentiality agreement.

Infirmation's competitor is Vault.com (of which Law.com and American Lawyer Media Inc., the parent company of *NYLJ*, have a minority equity interest). Rather than luring the GA Board to its site, Vault.com created firm-specific message boards as well as legal industry and law school chat rooms. There is no shortage of information these days about law firms.

Internet-based industries are subject to frequent shakeouts and change, and soon after acquiring the GA webpages, Infirmation was acquired by FindLaw, a legal resources company that began in 1995 out of a list of Internet resources for a law librarian workshop (Findlaw.com). The GAs are now a community message board offered through FindLaw, and the multiple GA message boards provide FindLaw with a strong marketing vehicle for other products and ads. FindLaw has two full-time employees who monitor the GA sites.[5]

VI. The 2000 Associate Salary Frenzy

The GA began at the height of Silicon Valley's economic power and during a stock market rally that created the sense that triple-digit returns on investment were merely normal. But it was only when these phenomena resulted in a salary boom for Silicon Valley lawyers that the GA began getting national attention and affecting the ways in which law firms operate.

In late December 1999, the GA discovered that the Silicon Valley firm of Gunderson Dettmer Stough Villeneuve Franklin & Hachigian was starting to pay $145,000 to first year associates.[6] At the time, the Gunderson move seemed like smart recruiting. The firm had done well with its dot-com clients and was looking to expand by attracting top talent. Offering $145,000 would not only lure sought-after law students to Silicon Valley, but it would also prompt a flood of resumes from relatively undercompensated New York attorneys who, at that time, earned no more than the benchmark $110,000 in their first year. What was unclear was whether Gunderson was an anomaly or the beginning of a trend, but the GAs began monitoring salary developments closely.[7]

In January 2000, three Silicon Valley law firms boosted their compensation for first-year-associates to $125,000, plus an undisclosed bonus. Those announcements were immediately posted on all the GA Boards. New York GAs began complaining that it was "shameful" that their salaries were trailing the California newcomers. Associates posted messages detailing the annual income of partners and associates at their own firms, and compared the numbers. Armed with that information, they relentlessly demanded more money.

Within a few weeks, the GA made a specific demand on its site: New York firms with San Francisco Bay Area offices must match the new benchmark salaries or risk mass defection. After listing the earnings for the California firms that were "showing the money," one associate wrote "If your firm's numbers are the same or better, you should ask yourself, 'Why can't my firm pay me that much?'" Another replied "Two words: Greedy & Cheap." The first associate wrote back "I am sorry. That answer is unacceptable. We were looking for 'no good reason at all, your next pay stub will reflect this raise.'"

Soon after, San Francisco's Brobeck, Phleger & Harrison, a firm with a New York branch office, announced that *all* its first-year associates would earn a base salary of $125,000, with the potential to earn $155,000 for billing 2,400 hours (a figure that could only be ethically derived from working over 80 hours per week). That set off a frenzy of postings on the GA site. The demands for equal pay intensified as did the threats of packing up and heading west. Some associates actually wrote songs about headhunters finding them jobs in Silicon Valley. One associate posted an impressively detailed argument as to why Cravath, the New York firm known to set the benchmark for associate salaries, should be paying $150,000 to first-year associates, considering its $2 million per partner annual profits.

Then in early February, the dam broke. Davis Polk and Wardwell, a top-tier New York firm with offices in Silicon Valley, announced a $25,000 raise for all its associates in all of its offices. In December, Davis Polk had been criticized on the GA webpage for its relatively meager boom-year bonus of $5,000. As the partners were well aware, being the first to move enhanced its image among the GAs, who unanimously applauded the decision.

With that, the GA went to work pressuring the rest of the nation's top firms to match or beat the new benchmark. Within days another top New York firm, Skadden Arps, announced it would begin paying first year associates $140,000. While it was unclear whether that was a further increase in the base-level salary, or an up-front payment of the normal December bonus, Skadden became the GAs' instant darling, and the URL for the firm's recruiting department was repeatedly posted on the GA site.

What happened to firms that wouldn't match? New York's Shearman & Sterling first announced that it was making a "local market place adjustment" in its San Francisco office only, bumping first-year pay from $100,000 to $125,000, not including bonuses. The reaction was less than favorable. According to a GA posting, several young lawyers responded by giving notice, and many more complained "in the most vivid of terms." A firm-wide meeting was scheduled as several dozen associates prepared a demand for a matching raise. There was even talk of a strike. "DebtSlave" wrote "I think most of NYC associates should have a sympathy work stoppage with them (it works for French truckers, after all) — it is outrageous. . . . [T]he only solution to restore order is a rapid apology and matching-or-better raise."[8]

The main GA Board posted an explicit table of its wage demands. Those firms that did not comply were vilified. Pictures were posted of senior partners at noncomplying firms, along with taunts such as "sleep much last night?" illustrating the GAs' new sense of empowerment. A list was compiled of those firms that had yet to announce raises. When a firm did send around an internal announcement regarding a raise, that memo was posted on the GA webpage within minutes. According to one associate, it took only nine minutes between the time that a rival law firm made its wage announcement and the network of associates throughout Manhattan firms sent the information to his pager — allowing him to inform a partner with whom he was traveling of the development and begin putting pressure on that partner to match the raise. As time wore on, those firms that did match the new benchmark not only got little applause, they were criticized for waiting so long, even when the raises were retroactive. Traditional top-tiered firms that did not announce raises were placed on a "Hall of Shame" list and heavily criticized.

Within two weeks of the Davis Polk announcement, ten New York firms and several firms in Boston, Washington, D.C., and California had either matched or bettered the offer — a process that used to take months, or even years, prior to the existence of the GA information machine.

Why did it matter what the GA was saying? One reason is that law firms had been steadily losing mid-level associates to their finance and high-tech clients, resulting in a shortage of associates with 4 to 7 years of experience. For those who remained, a change of scenery accompanied by a $25,000 raise seemed an attractive proposition. Once associates knew just how much more they could expect for jumping ship, their firms began taking their complaints very seriously. Second, and perhaps more important, is the fact that law students use the GA webpages to help decide which firms to interview with, and ultimately, to join. For students facing tens of thousands of dollars of debt, which firm pays the most relative to the cost of living is often a deciding factor. For top students, who have their choice between dozens of seemingly indistinguishable firms, any information that allows them to eliminate choices is welcome. Therefore, firms try to avoid being criticized on the GA webpages so as not to risk a difficult up-hill battle come interview season. This is probably one of the reasons why Shearman & Sterling quickly reversed its decision to raise salaries only for its Silicon Valley lawyers. After a week of sustained pounding on the GA boards for that decision, Shearman relented and gave the raise to all its associates in all of its offices. Perhaps to hold the line was too big a recruiting risk.

By May of 2000, most firms had matched the new benchmark of $125,000 for first-year associates and activity on the GA pages quieted down. But it picked up again in November 2000, with ruthless demands for year-end bonuses. In the end, most firms paid first-years an additional $40,000 in December, resulting in a 50 percent increase in salary over the course of a year.[9]

VII. Where's the Money Coming From?

Where did the money came from to cover the wage spike? There are three possibilities. First, to cover the increased salaries and bonuses, many firms upped their hourly rate for all attorneys and paralegals in the firm, although this is difficult to confirm. While associate salaries and partner profits are now openly broadcast in order to drive recruitment needs, firms are more proprietary about billing rates. Some high-end corporate law firms like Wachtell, Lipton, Rosen & Katz began charging flat amounts per financial deal — small amounts in proportion to the size of the deals, but multi-million dollar billings nevertheless. So the clients picked up at least some of the tab. Second, in some firms there is the probability that overall profitability declined as associate compensation began eating into the "economic rent" previously enjoyed. For them, the wage curve flattened somewhat as associates made more, and partners contributed a portion of their share. These firms could not pass the increases onto their clients, or chose not to do so, but could not afford not to match their competitor's salaries. A third source of funds came from the associates themselves, who worked longer and harder than ever before.

Many associates found themselves caught in a Faustian bargain. In return for absorbing a larger salary for associates, some firms upped their expectations for billable hours. In the 1980s the average associate billed 1,820 hours per year. This figure grew to 2,200 hours in BIGLAW within that decade. In the mid-1990s, those large law firms that tied bonuses to hours gave substantial bonuses to associates who billed 2,100 hours. By the late 1990s many firms began to move that target upwards, with some firms creating a cut-off for bonuses after 2,350 hours. Assuming a two-week vacation, this target translates to 57 billable hours per week. The widespread rule-of-thumb is that 70 percent of hours worked should be billable, meaning that it can take over 80 hours of work per week to generate enough hours to justify large bonuses. It was not surprising, therefore, that many of the associates interviewed for this study were not available to be interviewed until after 9:00 in the evening. Some of them were anxious to find a more dignified lifestyle in a smaller firm whose competitive advantage vis-à-vis BIGLAW is that they don't "squeeze out the extra 300 to 400 hours." But those firms may not be so easy to find anymore.

The wage increases at large firms have affected mid-sized firm economics and culture, where salaries have also risen, although not as dramatically. Said one managing partner: "Since this firm is paying more, associates now have to hit 2,000 hours. We never used to have that expectation. If you work 1,900 hours, even if your work is stellar, you won't get a bonus." While a few firms at the top such as Cravath, Swaine & Moore made their bonuses automatic, other firms made their performance standards stricter, tying extra compensation to hours actually billed. This meant that associates were far less likely to take on pro bono work (which many firms would have happily counted towards billable hours targets in the past).

As Cornholio made clear, shorter hours is not the aim of the GA; associates want a redistribution of income within law firms, with associates getting more and partners getting less. It is not surprising that partners might resist these demands at least in part because partners view their high compensation as a justified reward for having won the tournament themselves in earlier days. Partners don't see themselves as the lucky survivors of a tough battle, but as the winners of a contest in which talent, skill, and perseverance distinguished them from the pool of incoming associates. Many partners not only work just as hard as associates do, but they also possess intangible, but nevertheless real, attributes that some might characterize as "royal jelly."

VIII. The Firms Are Watching

A journalist interviewee speculates that there is probably one partner or recruiter in each firm who tracks firm hits on the GA site. This was confirmed in our law firm interviews. One respondent recruiter recalls "I was looking at the GA page to see what associates want in the way of perks and then I saw that one of our former associates posted something less positive than I thought it should be. I was shocked. I began checking the site religiously for a month, and then only as warranted. It was only minimally harmful, but I definitely saw a buzz among our summer law students as a result of the posting."

To a generation well-versed in computer-based communication, the immediacy effect of the GA sites is seductive. The information is candid, offered in the first-person, and usually accurate. Said one legal journalist, "The only thing that makes me wade through a lot of the drivel is the immediacy. Sometimes announcements are posted only five minutes after they are made, and we cannot possibly monitor all developments and match the speed of the GA Board." It was a "godsend" for journalists — with the bonus race underway, journalists were incorporated into the information dissemination campaign, receiving confidential phone calls and faxes. Tip lines became a feature of some news outlets. Traditionally the *NYLJ* surveys would have been the source for salary information. Now associates look to their own fast-breaking grapevine on the Internet and journalists gather information from various anonymous on-line sources. There is quite a bit of evidence from the *NYLJ* articles that the GA Board is a source of many colorful quotes. A posting by "erinacea" in an alternative "distressed partners" website grumbled, "I am kind of intrigued at the idea that journalists can get quotes without having to actually speak to any humans, and without knowing for sure whether the people they are quoting are really lawyers or are actually nonagenerian nuns from Norfolk or 13-year-old Star Wars fans. This is quite a trend in journalism [and now in industrial relations academe]" (quoted in Balestier and Snider, 1999).

Many partners openly lament the rise of the GA and the new mercenary aspect of the legal profession. Stricken senior partners we spoke to described their disgust at both the title and contents of the GA site. Some partners view themselves as lawyers who "love the law for its own beauty — love to be a lawyer — aren't in it for the money," but feel that their young apprentices do not share the same values or discretion.

An attempt by a small group of BIGLAW partners to launch a site called "distressedpartners.com" in order to "lead to constructive, if anonymous, dialogue between the generations," did not succeed. Perhaps the generational divide was simply too great. For example, one poster complained that "In our day the system was sink or swim. I am weary of listening to the bestial wail of those who are sinking. Show some initiative. If you want a partnership, get off your ass and grab it." In our interviews, a partner described his feelings at first visiting the GA website: "I was hurt, I was angry. I don't want to see associates thinking we're the enemy. The mentality has changed. Associates don't see themselves on the same team as partners. Partners hate giving the added compensation to these types of associates but feel compelled by the market to do so. There is a lot of bitterness against associates and it is a downward cycle that makes us more reluctant to mentor them. All this ugliness is facilitated by Internet technology." He says, "I want to work with associates who don't have the time or inclination to get on the GA page." A legal recruiter describes her firm's reaction to the GA site: "It is disgusting. New associates have a very inflated sense of normalcy. The salaries are insane. To get $140,000 without any great understanding of the practice of law is absurd. If our associates leave us because of getting a Coach briefcase at

Skadden [a competing firm], fine then, let them go. On the other hand, why don't we offer them Coach briefcases and keep them?" In a tight labor market, firms could complain about the GA phenomenon, but they couldn't afford to ignore it.

IX. The Downturn

The demands of the GA waned and their threats became less convincing with the precipitous fall of the stock markets. There is no telling what would have happened had Wall Street not been shaken early in 2001 (followed by the appalling terror attack on September 11, 2001). The salary "bubble" was not sustainable for a lot of firms. Most of our interviewees hesitate to say that the GA postings had a direct influence on wages, but they certainly were part of the "drumbeat" creating a more frenzied quality to the compensation explosion. But by the spring of 2001, the mood within law firms changed dramatically. In March, one major firm had made a wage increase announcement, and no firm matched. Partners felt that they were already paying top dollar and that no more would be forthcoming. Some large firms began laying off their associates. Admitted one partner, "We locked ourselves into a long-term compensation structure to deal with what now turns out to have been an ephemeral competitive phenomenon" (quoted in Stracher, 2001). One observer commented that "if the economy remains in the doldrums, partners are going to expect something from those salary increases. Law is a business, after all, and not a particularly genteel one. . . . Young lawyers, many of whom have known nothing but the boom, may soon experience the boot." Said one respondent, "I expect big layoffs in the large firms. I would be shocked if they cut their prices, those are likely to hold firm. They might cut their bonuses or discretionary funds, but the real cuts will be in associate jobs." Some smaller firms plan to became more competitive by stressing that they don't have full-scale firings if the economy takes a turn for the worse. Recruiters tell us that prospective summer students and associates are asking much more about job security matters in 2001 than they did in the past. While at a cockier time the Greedy LA Board's header was "Where criminal defense attorneys are giddy with glee," now the tone is more somber. The header on the GA Board was rewritten to reflect a barricade mentality and a warning: "Who will mistreat their associates and harm their recruiting efforts for years to come?"

We examined the GA sites again in the Fall of 2001. Although the sites were as strident as ever, the number of hits at many of the sites (with the exception of New York) was only a small fraction of the previous vitality. However, the New York board was in a frenzy. On October 9, an internal memo from the management committee of Davis Polk was posted in its entirety by a GA using the name Bach. Although the firm announced that it would not lay off lawyers or withdraw offers of employment, it declared there would be no year-end bonus for 2001. There were almost 100 postings within 30 hours, most of them dealing with the "Davisgate" issue. Commented one poster, "[Davis Polk] pissed on themselves at the height of recruiting season. Stick a fork in them, they're done." Associates at the firm were encouraged by their cohort elsewhere to quit and look for lateral moves. How much pressure Davis Polk really felt to change its decision during an economic downturn was a matter of some debate on the message board, and it remains to be seen whether the GA is able to make good the threat to ruin Davis Polk's recruiting or force a revision of policy. By November 3, 2001 no other BIGLAW firm had made a bonus announcement, and a few had gone through a round of associate lay-offs.

Meanwhile, adjustments have been made by the legal profession and legal media industry that make the GA sites less relevant. Salary and other information is posted on law firm websites quickly, and wage announcements are often sent to the media for immediate release. The FindLaw.com website provides reliable information on firms that can be sorted by location, salary, bonus amounts, hours, and so on. The website law.com offers an "Associate Pay Watch" scorecard and prompts "If you have an off-the-record tip about associate pay or law firm news, e-mail our firm reporter. . . . Your identity, like those of the anonymous sources who contributed to the stories listed below, will be kept strictly confidential." The information flow is faster, and the stakeholder institutions have become more fleet-footed at circumventing the need for GAs' covert activity. The vital role of the GA sites in reducing information search costs has greatly diminished. And the psychology of associates themselves has changed as the financial world entered a bleak period. The cockiness is gone with the decline in bargaining power. Associates, once on the offensive, are a more quiescent group today.

X. Discussion and Conclusions

How can we distinguish the GA phenomenon from unions? Unions' *raison d'etre* is employee representation through collective bargaining, supported by a permanent institutional structure of professional officers and business agents and a revenue base from dues. The GA sites are idiosyncratic, based on the voluntarism and self-interest of secret founders, and lack any sort of disciplined approach to negotiation. Both unions and the GAs have adversarial relationships with management. Rather than bargaining, however, the GAs engage in concerted and surreptitious sniping. Both gather and share information, but unions use it to advance the interests of the collective whereas the GAs are left to their own individual devices when dealing with their employers. The GA sites suffer from problems of possible disinformation being posted by partners and others in the firms, and there have at times been false postings. The sock-puppet issue not only masks identities but also distorts the communication flow such that it is difficult to distinguish real conversations from ersatz relationships.

Journalists log on looking for quotes, unable to distinguish between real associates and associate-wannabes, creating a low standard for journalistic sources. Greedy Associates has no standing in labor law, and has no recourse to labor boards or tribunals. It is particularly difficult since the move to Infirmation and then FindLaw to know what is the purpose of the GA sites. Although the founders didn't start it for money, it didn't take too long to discover that a GA site could be a powerful marketing tool. In less than three years, an empowerment movement launched by new lawyers was captured as a website sweetener by private industry, which may be more concerned with generating hits and traffic than with disseminating information or benefitting associates.

Because of the lack of a permanent institutional structure, the GA sites are not a substitute for unions. The natural progression of these types of websites may well be entropy and disorder if not "rescued" by a sponsoring business. However, the real lesson is about the power of the Internet to provide information, especially when driven by a cohort of employees who have extraordinarily strong self-efficacy and a sense of entitlement.

Is GA a form of collective bargaining at all? According to one thoughtful partner, "there is nothing collective about it. GAs look to get something from *you* to help *me*. They end up helping each other as a group, but their individual goals are similar to professional baseball players." Cornholio confirms this interpretation: "This isn't a union thing where we can use our power to disrupt the product. Rather, we know how much money the employer is making. If the firm's rates are going up astronomically, we want more. This has nothing to do with who I am working for (because my own partner/boss was great) but rather with how hard I was working and how much I contributed to making the machine run. F*** you, pay more." Whereas unions try to take wages out of the competition among firms, it is the intent of the GA board to introduce frenzied competition among firms on the basis of wages. Only workers with high individual bargaining power whose goal is maximizing compensation levels can benefit from the GA phenomenon.

Despite the massive hype, GA probably played only a minor role in the associate wage hike. We see evidence of similar wage effects among Internet engineers without the use of a GA-like vehicle (Campbell and Brown, 2001). Even Cornholio agrees that the GA story is directly tied to the economic upswing of the late 1990s. "It definitely would not have happened in a bad economy." But the GA postings serve as an expression of the sentiments of junior lawyers at large firms. Associates, despite their high salaries, seem to be overwhelmingly unhappy, seeing many firms churn young lawyers without offering much prospect of mentorship or life balance flexibility. The GA probably did have an effect on billing pressures, making quite overt what was once merely a quiet expectation of workaholism. Although they now receive more money, it is paradoxical that associates' conditions are even worse than before the development of the GA vehicle.

The GA message boards may be the beginning of a new area of Internet organization marked by effortless and instant dissemination of information between similarly situated employees.[10] Some GA posters mused that "at some level this thing is a union hall, not a chat room or a shopping center" (Infirmation.com/bboard message 9051). Presumably, what works for lawyers could also be used by other nonunion workers such as bank tellers, software designers and lab technicians, especially those who, like lawyers, find themselves in high demand. Like a "virtual" union hall, the GA phenomenon is a vehicle that reinforces the identities of those who exchange stories, know a certain jargon, share similar experiences, and simply hang out together, albeit anonymously and electronically. But it is not a union. It is something else, something worth watching carefully.

Notes

*   We are very grateful to Professor Sam Estreicher for his gracious assistance during the field-work in New York. Discussions with Paul Adler, Rick Chaykowski, Bruce Kaufman, Laurie Milton, and Allen Ponak helped refine our analysis.

1   This figure can be explained in part by the fact that BIGLAW firms offer summer jobs to law students not necessarily because of what they can offer during the summer, but primarily to court them to become associates the following year when they graduate from law school. In addition to their substantial salaries of $2,500/week, these "summer associates" often receive free lunches at top restaurants, expensive tickets to the theater and sporting events, along with various other lavish perks during their summer.

2   The phenomenon of partners leaving or switching firms was also noted in the big six accounting firms (Addams et al., 1977).

3   In order to join any Yahoo! club, one must agree not to transmit any content that is "unlawful, harmful, threatening, abusive, harassing, tortious, defamatory, vulgar, obscene, libelous, invasive of another's privacy, hateful, or racially, ethnically or otherwise objectionable." Obviously adherence to this policy depends on the webmaster and the initiative of complainants who approach Yahoo! for investigations. But, if the anonymity enjoyed by those posting on these message boards is truly protected, detection would be virtually impossible, and there is little stopping determined employees from engaging in such conduct. The legal ramifications of posting false and injurious messages is beyond the scope of this article.

4   Had he known the eventual popularity of the GA Board, Cornholio definitely would have chosen a more serious name for himself.

5   Cornholio says he is likely to replicate this adventure for business school graduates.

6   Almost two years later, Greedy Associate boards still applaud Bob Gunderson, asking that associates give "the saintly Mr. Gunderson a standing ovation," for starting the upward wage spiral.

7   A comparable breakaway leap was made in 1986 by Cravath, Swaine & Moore when the firm feared that outstanding law school graduates were taking jobs with consultants and investment houses, but this increase in salary did not set off the same wage tsunami as in the late 1990s (Bok, 1993, p. 147).

8   A few times there has been mention of an "e-union" on the various GA sites, but despite the bluster there is little evidence of coordinated action.

9   The GA Boards not only disseminated accurate wage information, they were also the source of inappropriate gossip and unsubstantiated rumors. In February 2000, a few people on the GA board began "remarking on the beauty of certain women lawyers" at a particular firm. When the women got e-mail from anonymous greedy admirers, some cried "E-stalker!" The firm quickly removed all mug shots, attractive and otherwise, from its Web site (Goldhaber, 1999). The following year, there were rumors on the GA webpage about mass layoffs at the law firm of Simpson Thacher. The rumor appears to have originated with a remark made by a partner to the effect that the firm would be doing better if it were leaner by, say, 70 associates. It seems that in the hypervigilant age of the GA, loose partner-lips and wishing aloud can cause unforeseen mischief. To avoid such problems, partners became more cautious about sharing information with associates that could harm the firm's reputation if posted on the internet.

10 The use of information technology to create this type of employee mobilization was not foreseen in a 1963 review of both union and nonunion professional and occupational associations by Strauss.

References

Abbott, Andrew. *The System of Professions: An Essay on the Division of Expert Labor.* Chicago: University of Chicago Press, 1988.

Addams, H. Lon, Brian Davis, Ronald M. Mano, and Vicki Nycum. "Why Are Partners and Managers Leaving the Big Six?" *Journal of Applied Business Research* 13 (Fall 1997): 75–81.

The American Lawyer. "Legal Recruiters Directory 2001." New York: American Lawyer Media, January 2001.

Balestier, Bruce and Anna Snider. "'Greedy Associates' Defectors Start New Sites." *New York Law Journal* (28 June 1999). <www.nylj.com/stories>.

Bok, Derek. *The Cost of Talent: How Executives and Professionals Are Paid and How It Affects America.* New York: Macmillan, Free Press, 1993.

Campbell, Benjamin and Clair Brown. "Engineers' Voice in the Internet Economy." *Proceedings of the 53rd Annual Meeting of the Industrial Relations Research Association*, 2001, pp. 144–52.

Ehrenberg, Ronald. "An Economic Analysis of the Market for Law School Students." *Journal of Legal Education* 39 (1989): 627–54.

——— and Michael L. Bognanno. "The Incentive Effects of Tournaments Revisited: Evidence from the European PGA Tour." *Industrial and Labor Relations Review* 43 (February 1990): 74–88.

Ehrenberg, Ronald and Robert S. Smith. *Modern Labor Economics: Theory and Public Policy.* New York: Harper Collins, 1994.

Frank, Robert H. and Philip J. Cook. *The Winner Take All Society.* New York: Martin Kessler Books and The Free Press, 1995.

Franklin, Stephen. "Upset Workers Take Their Case to Cyberspace." *Chicago Tribune*, February 11, 2000 (<chicagotribune.com>).

Galanter, Marc and Thomas Palay. *Tournament of Lawyers: The Transformation of the Big Law Firm.* Chicago: University of Chicago Press, 1991.

Goldhaber, Michael. "Greedy Movement Comes of Age." *National Law Journal* (May 10, 1999): A1 (<lawlibrary.ucdavid.edu/LAWLIB/Dec99/0519.html>).

Nelson, Robert L., David M. Trubek, and Rayman L. Solomon, eds. *Lawyers' Ideals/Lawyers' Practice: Transformations in the American Legal Profession.* Ithaca, N.Y.: Cornell University Press, 1992.

New York Law Journal. Available on law.com

Rosen, Sherwin. "Prizes and Incentives in Elimination Tournaments." *American Economic Review* 76 (September 1986): 701–15.

Sander, Richard and E. Douglas Williams. "Why Are There So Many Lawyers? Perspectives on a Turbulent Market." *Law and Social Inquiry* 14 (Summer 1989): 431–79.

Sciulli, David. "Voluntaristic Action As a Distinct Concept: Theoretical Foundations of Societal Constitutionalism." *American Sociological Review* 51 (December 1986): 743–66.

Smigel, Erwin. *The Wall Street Lawyer: Professional Organization Man?* Bloomington: Indiana University Press, 1969.

Smith, Larry. "National Study: Lateral Hiring Continues Unabated." *Lawyer Hiring and Training Report* 9 (1989): 6–8.

Snider, Anna. "Associates Trade Pay, Bonus Data on Web Sites." *New York Law Journal* (November 4, 1998) (<www.ljx.com/public/lawjobs/bonusweb.htm>).

Stracher, Cameron. "Let the Lawyer Layoffs Begin." *Manager's Journal* (May 2001): (<interactive.wsj.com/archive>).

Strauss, George. "Professionalism and Occupational Associations." *Industrial Relations* 2 (1963): 7–32.

Tolbert, Pamela S. and Robert N. Stern. "Organizations of Professionals: Governance Structures in Large Law Firms." *Research in the Sociology of Organizations* 8 (1991): 97–117.

Van Maanen, John and Stephen R. Barley. "Occupational Communities: Culture and Control in Organization." *Research in Organizational Behavior* 6 (1984): 287–365.

Wallace, Jean E. "Organizational and Professional Commitment in Professional and Nonprofessional Organizations." *Administrative Science Quarterly* 40 (1995): 228–55.

10

An Identity Perspective on the Propensity of High-Tech Talent to Unionize

Laurie P. Milton*
University of Calgary

I. Introduction

Research on why workers unionize emphasizes unfair treatment and dissatisfaction with terms and conditions of employment (e.g., DeCotiis and LeLouarn, 1981). "The hypothesis that dissatisfied workers are more likely to vote pro-union has received more empirical attention than any other hypothesis in trying to understand union voting behavior" (Barling et al., 1992, p. 48).

Yet, viewing unionization simply as a response to dissatisfaction and adversity masks the complex role unionization plays in worker identity and the effect of identity on the propensity of workers to unionize. The identity dimensions of unionization have been largely ignored by labor researchers, many of whom appear to concentrate on equity and on the conflict of interest between labor and management. To some extent research that connects union image to the likelihood that individuals will join unions (Barling et al., 1992; Clark, 2000 for reviews) is relevant to an identity perspective on unionization. However, this work needs to be integrated into an identity-oriented theory of unionization.

My paper lays the foundation for such a theory. Herein, I draw on theory and exploratory interviews to develop an identity-based explanation of the propensity of highly skilled technical workers to unionize. Highly skilled technical workers, hereinafter called high-tech workers, include systems analysts, hardware and software engineers, computer scientists and programmers, and webmasters. High-tech workers may be employed in a variety of companies that vary in the way they use technology. They may, for example, work in *pure play* high-tech companies such as Microsoft or Dell

151

that primarily or wholly sell technology or technological products; in e-commerce companies such as e-Bay or Amazon.com that rely on the World Wide Web (Web) as their primary marketing channel to sell non-technological products; in businesses such as Yahoo that sell digitized products or content over the Web, or in companies like Hallmark, Ford, or Wal-Mart that use computer technology to rationalize their supply chains and thereby develop a technology-based strategic distinctive competency. In all instances, the high-tech workers on whom I focus are the highly skilled technical people who design, build, and maintain computer-based technology that is strategically relevant to their companies, that is, technology that helps these companies build and sustain their competitive position.

II. The Nature of High-Tech Worker Employment

"Unions are rare in high-tech businesses and nonexistent in dot-coms" (Ewalt, 2001, p. 93). Less than 2 percent of high-tech workers in North America are unionized (U.S. Department of Labor, 2000), and none have voluntarily formed their own union or en masse joined an existing union. Although unions have indicated an interest in organizing high-tech workers (Trombley and Ohlson, 2000), so far they appear to have focused on service and contingent workers and to have been relatively unsuccessful. Etown.com, home of a rare .com company showdown between management and organized labor, closed its doors and laid off all 100 employees, citing lack of funding as the reason (Ewalt, 2001). Efforts of the Washington Alliance of Technical Workers' (WashTech) to organize temporary software workers at Seattle-based companies including Amazon.com, Boeing, and Microsoft have met with limited success. The group has amassed a core of volunteers and 1,000 electronic newsletter recipients (Fitzgerald, 1999). Other groups trying to organize in high-tech corridors are similarly challenged.

Technology-driven industry environments are fast-paced, turbulent, and complex (Chakravarthy, 1997). Until recently, they were also extremely optimistic. Research has found that to succeed in this industry environment, companies and workers need to be competent, flexible, and fast (Brown and Eisenhardt, 1998). The ability to learn and make strategic decisions quickly appears to differentiate the successful companies from the failures (Eisenhardt, 2000).

Adopting an equity perspective, one could argue that high-tech workers are not unionizing in this environment because they are central to technology-based industries, are caught up in its excitement, and are largely satisfied with their employment conditions, feeling that their payoff structure acceptably reflects their inputs. Until recently, the press was replete with stories of the high salaries, lucrative stock options, attractive benefits, and promises of speedy mobility to ever more interesting work based on achievement in the technology sector. Workers were described as completely absorbed in their work and professional communities and thus as oblivious to external considerations. News headlines heralding success such as: "Goodbye B-School" subtitled "Two years ago, Jonathan Seelig left business school to cofound Akamai Technologies. Today, the company is worth $20 billion" (*Harvard Business School*, 2000, p. 16) were commonplace in even the most prestigious business journals. To a large extent everyone both inside and external to the industry seemed highly optimistic. Programmers and other highly skilled tech workers were stock-optioned up and in general appeared to have had adequate base salaries to live comfortably until their pots of gold materialized.

To attract and retain their valued talent, many high-tech companies have created attractive work environments. Juice/coffee bars, basketball courts, dry cleaning service, daycare, exercise facilities, and even company sailboats are available to employees. Reports of systems analysts, engineers and scientists, programmers, and webmasters quarreling over remuneration do not open evening news broadcasts. Yet, time is at a premium in technology-based companies. High-tech workers often work long days and much overtime without pay; many have neither job security nor stock options (Fitzgerald, 1999). The question of whether and if so, when they will organize, perhaps through unions, has always been interesting but may be more relevant now that the capital market bubble has burst in the high-tech sector.

Since the technology capital market crash of May 2000, stock options have lost much of their value, and even the most highly skilled are being laid off. Whether this ultimately stimulates demand for more traditional forms of compensation and makes collective bargaining and unionization more attractive remains to be seen. I explore issues around that question. In the following section, I introduce my theoretical perspective on the propensity of high-tech workers to unionize. Thereafter, I ground this perspective empirically.

III. Conceptual Framework

The conceptual territory covered by the proposed framework examines the identity dimensions of unionization and the influence that union instrumentality and opportunity structure have on the ability and willingness of high-tech workers to unionize. The underlying argument is that high-tech workers will unionize when and only when doing so is consistent with their high-tech identities, when they perceive unions to be instrumental, and when their social structure supports unionization (Figure 1).

Identity Dimensions of Unionization. Evidence suggests that people try to create and sustain social and psychological environments that are consistent with their identities (Lecky, 1945; Secord and Backman, 1965) and experience anxiety when these identities are not supported (Zaharna, 1989). Overall, people will prefer and seek situations, evaluations, and relationships that are compatible with their self-definitions, even when these are negative (Swann, 1987). Psychologically, identity-supportive environments provide a sense of security; people feel that the world is predictable and consistent with how they see themselves. Pragmatically, supportive environments help stabilize behavior and create reliable interaction partners.

Like others, individual high-tech workers will have multiple identities or conceptions of themselves that typically have evaluative components (Gecas, 1982) and are emotionally-valenced. Identities may center on definitions of oneself in terms of attributes, that is, characteristics, attitudes, or abilities (Rosenberg, 1979) such as intelligent, hard-working, liberally-minded, technologically skilled, or creative; in terms of group

Figure 1
Factors That Affect Whether High-Tech Workers Will Unionize

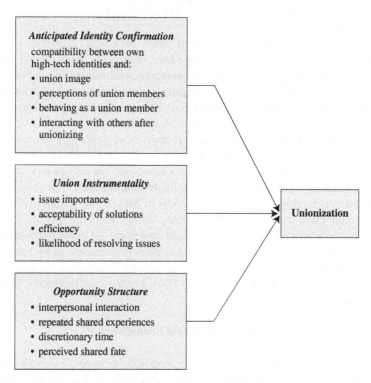

memberships or social identities (Tajfel and Turner, 1985) such as family member, programmer, or Canadian; or in terms of global self-esteem, that is, on their conceptions
of themselves as competent and likeable (Tafarodi and Swann, 1995). Not all identities are equally important to a person's self-definition and not all are active all of the
time. Individuals will be most concerned about supporting those identities that are central to their self-definition and those that are situationally relevant or working (Markus
and Kunda, 1986). Herein, I focus on identities that high-tech workers hold as central
to their conceptions of themselves as high-tech workers, that is, on the constellation
of attribute-, social-, and global self-esteem-based identities that together make up their
views of themselves as high-tech workers. In so doing, I assume these identities will
be relevant to high-tech workers at work and thus affect their behaviors in this arena
where they will also make decisions about unionization.

Consistent with image theory (Beach and Mitchell, 1990), I argue that when deciding whether to unionize, individuals will screen the idea to determine whether being
and acting as a union member is compatible with their conceptions of themselves as
high-tech workers.[1] Early in the unionization process, in a relatively automatic, intu-
itive fashion they will compare their definitions of themselves to their image of unions,
union members, and union activity, and think about how unionizing will affect the way

in which valued others perceive them as high-tech workers. Identity confirmation, a state they will be drawn to, occurs when an individual's mental, social, and physical environments support his or her identities or self-definitions (Milton, 1998). A person's high-tech identities will be confirmed within a union to the extent that they are validated and supported therein.

Inasmuch as high-tech workers see unions as an extension of their high-tech worker identities and as organizations where they would fit in and be able to sustain these identities, they will be predisposed to join. Inasmuch as they perceive their current and ideal high-tech worker identities as consistent with their would-be union member identities, the same would be true. Tom (1971) found that the greater the similarity between individual's self-definitions and his or her image of an organization, the more he or she preferred the organization. Dutton et al. (1994) extended this logic to argue that individuals identify with organizations that preserve their self-concepts. Other research has shown that individuals form mental images of their ideal selves, the selves they would like to be, and engage in activities that help them to become this person (Baumeister and Tice,1986). Although, past research has shown that workers who have negative images of unions are less likely to join them (Barling et al., 1992; Clark, 2000), beyond specifying an effect through behavioral intentions, the mechanisms underlying this tendency have not been fully specified.

High-tech workers may also compare their conceptions of themselves to their perceptions of union members to determine whether they have anything in common with union members and whether they would like to be affiliated with them. The homophily literature suggests that perceived similarity should increase interpersonal attraction (Bryne, 1971), mutual trust and reciprocity (Lincoln and Miller, 1979), and the likelihood that relationships will form. High-tech workers may perceive others who are similar to them as in-group members and thus be inclined to evaluate them favorably (Messick and Mackie, 1989) and cooperate (Brewer, 1981) or coalesce (Lau and Murnighan, 1998) and perhaps unionize with them.

High-tech workers may further screen opportunities to unionize by assessing whether they think that their would-be union colleagues would see them in terms of their high-tech worker identities as the high-tech workers see themselves. Interpersonal congruence, or congruence between how an individual defines him- or herself and how others define the individual, is the form of identity confirmation with the longest empirical history. Research has shown that individuals preferentially interact with others who see them as they see themselves (Swann et al., 1992). Moreover, interpersonal congruence has been positively associated with roommates choosing to remain roommates (Swann and Pelham, 2001) and with commitment and intimacy between marital partners (Swann et al., 1994). In a longitudinal study extending these observations to groups, Polzer et al. (2002) found interpersonal congruence to predict higher social integration and group identification and lower emotional conflict in MBA study groups. In a recent field study of emergency response and construction groups, Milton and Westphal (2001) found that social network ties based on interpersonal congruence were positively associated with cooperation. The fact that effects for interpersonal congruence held even in situations where lives literally depended on cooperation is noteworthy.

Moving beyond cognition and the behavioral effects of cognition, high-tech workers may ruminate on behavior directly and consider whether behaving as a union member would sustain their identities. Gramzow et al. (2001) found self-knowledge to guide expectancies for novel in-groups. Specifically, they found that perceivers were more likely to associate in-groups than out-groups with self-congruent behaviors. Self-knowledge and anticipated behavioral identity confirmation may also be important predictors of in-group selection. Disliking inconsistencies between attitudes and behaviors, cognitive dissonance theory argues that people try to align the two.

Being motivated to create and sustain social environments that are consistent with their definitions of themselves, high-tech workers are also unlikely to act in ways that increase discrepancies between their valued identities and how others define them. One of the cornerstones of the symbolic interactionist perspective on identity is that individuals come to understand who they are through the eyes of others, that is, through their reflections on how others appraise them (Mead, 1934; Shrauger and Schoeneman, 1979). Others have argued that people try to construct public selves that are congruent with the ideal selves discussed earlier (Baumeister and Tice, 1986). Whether high-tech workers believe that others will continue to see and treat them as they see themselves if they join a union may affect their decision to join. Social validation may help high-tech workers to feel comfortable in their high-tech roles and to enact these roles less self-consciously (Ashforth, 2001). By enacting their high-tech roles and related identities, high-tech workers signal these identities to others who are then encouraged to define them as credible high-tech workers. One recent study found that individuals whose identities were understood by team members had high levels of creativity and low levels of stress and absenteeism (Thatcher, 2001). In these ways they appear to benefit. High-tech workers may also consider whether, as union members, they would be able to maintain their reputation as credible high-tech professionals, and via this reputation access to the work and social environments that support their high-tech identities. Overall, people will tend to join groups, including unions, which validate their definitions of themselves and then find little need to compromise these.

Union Instrumentality. Successful unionization depends on attracting a sufficient number of people so as to represent an entire group. Small but sufficient issue-based coalitions are most frequent. Large multi-issue coalitions (such as unions) tend to be formed by adding one person at a time (de Swaan, 1975). Beyond being affected by identity concerns, individuals are likely to join unions (or other coalitions) when they believe there are compelling reasons to do so, that is, when they perceive issues to be important and likely to be effectively resolved in an efficient manner via unionization. The argument that individuals are motivated to act when they value the expected outcomes and believe these will be forthcoming has been argued conceptually and demonstrated empirically (Mitchell, 1983). The industrial relations literature examining union instrumentality (Beutell and Biggs, 1984) has recognized this.

Low union density rates among high-tech workers may in part reflect worker perceptions that they have fair employment deals and thus no issues worth tending. Alternatively, they may believe that unions do not address issues that concern them or that there are more efficient ways to resolve issues.

For several reasons, high-tech workers may not perceive themselves as having employment issues that warrant attention. First, technology workers whose skills are hotly pursued may perceive technology-based industry environments as exciting and full of opportunity. When companies deliver this opportunity and offer challenging assignments, workers may be motivated and relatively satisfied (Dessler, 1999). Working on interesting projects, they may become fully absorbed in their work and not notice what is going on around them (Csikszentmihalyi, 1990). A long line of research has found job satisfaction to be negatively related to unionization.[2] Second, to the extent that high-tech workers perceive larger payoffs in the future and are reasonably compensated in the present, they may be prepared to accept sub-optimal working conditions in the short term. Some may even be willing to tolerate terrible short-term working conditions because they are gaining skills and a reputation that enable them to move and gain payoffs elsewhere. Not intending to stay in the same job for long, they may not be concerned about making themselves comfortable. Third, from an identity perspective, some may believe that paying short-term dues is consistent with their upwardly mobile high-tech identities.

The dream of a brilliant future may introduce a fourth and much larger hurdle to unionization than would otherwise be encountered. Companies, as perceived sources of an ultimate financial or identity payoff, may benefit from workers willingly contributing beyond their job requirements and beyond what an independent third party may judge them to be rewarded for in the short term. High-tech workers experiencing the positive emotion associated with belief in a long-term payoff may be inclined to help out. Research has found that positive emotion is associated with higher levels of helping behavior and organizational citizenship (Isen and Baron, 1991). It follows that in positive, contribution-oriented environments, high-tech workers will be less likely to perceive issues regarding current working conditions as existing let alone worthy of attention. Thus, for several reasons unionization is undermined. High-tech workers may not perceive employment issues that others consider paramount to be worthy of attention.

In addition, high-tech workers may not believe that unions address issues that concern them, and, even if they do, they may not see unionization as the most effective way to resolve these. Coordinating efforts generally takes time and requires effort. When either individual or collective action is likely to successfully resolve issues, the former may be the most efficient. High-tech workers, who may be already working long hours and juggling priorities, are only likely to coalesce when they believe that collective efforts will be successful and they cannot achieve the same results more efficiently, perhaps by acting alone. Workers may feel that they already have voice within their organizations and that their employers will be responsive to their individual requests. High levels of worker participation, relatively flat organizations, and organization efforts to attract and retain high-tech talent may support these perceptions. Workers who already have a voice do not need to organize to achieve it.

High-tech workers may also prefer to work autonomously, and this may decrease the likelihood that they will coalesce with others. Although often carried out within a project-team structure, significant portions of systems work tend to be highly autonomous, even when workers are task or outcome interdependent. Individuals with strong preferences for autonomy are often attracted to situations where they can work alone (Birch and Veroff, 1966). Just as they may find working in groups to be constraining and frustrating (Wageman, 1995), workers may prefer to resolve employment issues by themselves and not see collective action as an alternative.

High-tech workers who are in demand may also be very committed to their work and professional groups but see their employers as fungible. Low continuance commitment and attractive employment alternatives may predispose them to change employers rather than lobby for change if they are dissatisfied with their employment conditions. Dissatisfaction is generally related to employee turnover (Tett and Myer, 1993) and may be a practical alternative when employment options are abundant (Capelli, 1999). Affective commitment to an employer and hence a predisposition to stay (Meyer et al., 1993) could develop when the employer provides interesting work and a place to develop professionally and when other employment conditions meet at least some minimal standard. Pressing issues that could lead to unionization are unlikely to exist in these circumstances. If serious issues arise and remain unresolved, the emotional tie to the employer may sever and result in turnover especially in strong employment markets. For each of these reasons high-tech workers may not unionize.

Opportunity Structure. The social structure of the technology sector also introduces pragmatic barriers to unionization. Even if workers feel aggrieved, their opportunity structure may not support collective action. Traditional face-to-face forms of union activity may prove particularly problematic.

Inasmuch as employees are moving from project to project, team to team, and company to company, their careers are without boundaries (Arthur and Rousseau, 1996; Capelli, 1999). Work assignments are often temporary and performance focused. Employers who want to retain their highly skilled and otherwise mobile talent often do so by offering workers large salaries, stock options, and a creative basket of perks and challenging meaningful work. Systems developers in some companies are required to sign agreements saying that they will not disclose the terms and conditions of their employment to others. Moreover, as noted previously, they often work long hours and measure their fit with organizations in terms of challenging assignments that completely absorb them and develop their technological skills. In this environment, conversations between employees may most often be work centered and not necessarily interpersonally rich.

Long hours at work also reduce employees' discretionary time and the time they have to congregate with co-workers and discuss working conditions or otherwise engage in political activity. Nondisclosure agreements contribute to information asymmetry between employees and employers and ensure that employees do not have the information needed to compare their situations and coalesce around issues. Within primarily work-centered conversations, co-workers do not necessarily develop the interpersonal relationships needed to create a psychologically safe environment (Edmonson, 1999) that could support collective action. Colleagues do not get to know one another well enough to align or coalesce on work issues.

Moving between assignments and companies and focusing mostly on work lessens the likelihood that they will develop the close interpersonal attachments often associated with long-term interaction and reciprocated interpersonal care and concern (McAllister, 1995). Consequently, they may find it difficult to develop relational trust. Mobility may also stymie work-related attachments between employees inasmuch as it reduces the opportunity for repeated cycles of exchange, risk-taking, and achievement, experiences that would strengthen the willingness of trusting parties to rely on each other and expand resources brought to the exchange (Rousseau et al., 1998).

IV. Method

My conceptual arguments herein are primarily based on theory and existing empirical research. They are, however, grounded in examples and comments drawn from eight exploratory interviews of high-tech workers in four companies and from my observations as a field researcher studying technology-based organizations. I asked programmers, systems engineers, and software engineers open-ended questions about whether they had ever thought of unionizing and why they and other high-tech workers would or would not do so. To probe the identity dimensions of their thinking, I asked them to describe themselves and other high-tech workers and, in separate questions, to describe union members and what being a union member would involve. Thereafter, I asked them to talk about whether these definitions affected the likelihood that they would join a union. To encourage concrete thinking, I asked several to imagine walking into a room where 100 union members were interacting and to describe the people, their conversations, and what they were doing. I then asked them to imagine leaving this room and walking down the hall into a room where 100 high-tech workers were interacting and to describe these individuals, their conversations, and their actions.

In the following sections, I share how interviewees described themselves and their work, integrate their comments to discuss why high-tech workers are not unionizing and why they sometimes do coalesce, and relate points of view to the conceptual framework articulated earlier. Implications for union activity are then explored.

V. How High-Tech Workers See Themselves, Their Work, and Their Industries

Consistent with the earlier overview of technology-based industries, interviewees described themselves and other high-tech workers as self-sufficient, creative, independent thinkers who are driven to excel. Moreover, they saw themselves and expected other competent high-tech "professionals" to embrace being flexible, adaptable, and agile in their technical skills and project assignments. They said that they expect change and turbulence and perceive themselves to cope well with this. Repeatedly referring to themselves as high achievers, they describe themselves and other technology professionals as having taken charge of their careers, and having re-invented themselves as free agents or *e-lancers*.

How interviewees defined themselves extended into how they defined their job role. Interviewees, for instance, expected to work long hours and to do whatever it takes to complete projects on time. Several argued that this is part of their professional role, and hence it is an identity issue. All described themselves as continually learning. Mostly, that is, within the limits of flesh and blood as discussed later, interviewees said they were attracted to continuous learning environments and challenging, complex, strategically relevant projects. They seemed to take pride in the fact that being involved in such projects reflected their technical skill and record of achievement. Every interviewee saw progression based on merit rather than seniority as essential to the success of technology-based companies and to their own success, and as central to their high-tech identity.

Each interviewee expected to work for several, if not many, companies over the course of his or her career. All described themselves and other competent high-tech workers as gravitating towards interesting work and opportunities to be exposed to cutting-edge technologies and to learn from projects. They said that they were drawn to organizations that encourage people to develop their skill base, experiment with new roles, and be flexible. It is a record of success on this learning curve that enables workers to move to more interesting and strategically important projects between and within fast-paced companies with shifting technologies.

In general, interviewees considered the terms and conditions of their employment to be fair and felt that it was up to them to negotiate new deals or to move if they did not like working at a given place. They also felt that over time their current efforts would payoff financially and via interesting work. Even now, in the high-tech economic downturn, those interviewed saw their skills as in demand and technology-based industries as exciting and full of opportunity. They perceived the current downturn to be temporary and argued that there was still a global shortage of competent high-tech professionals. Consistent with a free-agent mentality, several said very clearly that if they want to share in the upside of the industry, they fully expect to share in the downside. They perceived themselves to be an integral part of the companies that employed them, to be listened to, and in general to have voice. Overall, they felt valued for who they are.

The glow of these positive comments aside, I do not want to infer that systems developers and other high-tech workers were thrilled about every dimension of their employment situations. Two, in particular, talked about burnout within the profession; exhaustion from "having to" continually learn; concerns about being able to keep up the pace for a lifetime; pressures from having to achieve constantly in an ever-changing and often ambiguous environment; and unacceptable trade-offs between family and work lives. Three noted that high-tech workers tend to be very concerned with technology issues and with organizations maintaining their technological currency, noting that they are only as marketable as the technology they work on. Clearly, there are issues that concern very talented people in the high-tech sector, but these workers are not unionizing to address these.

VI. Why High-Tech Workers Aren't Unionizing

When asked about whether they had ever thought of joining a union, every high-tech worker interviewed responded with silence, and in several instances with pro-longed silence. To a person, they said that they had never thought, even once, of ever joining a union or engaging in collective action to improve their working conditions. When asked whether they would ever voluntarily do so, to a person, they said "no" and talked about the incongruence between their perceptions of unions and union members and their images of themselves as high-tech workers and about how union solutions to employment issues would be detrimental to themselves and to technology-driven industries. Several expressed concerns that others would interpret their willingness to unionize as a sign of professional weakness or unsuitability for the profession and industry. Consistent with the framework discussed earlier, themes of identity and union instrumentality ran consistently through their stories. Interviewees did not mention concerns about opportunity structure. Their perspectives on identity and union instrumentality are explored in the following two sections.

Identity Considerations. There was strong support suggesting that high-tech workers will not join unions when they perceive being and acting as a union member to be inconsistent with their high-tech identities. Overall, interviewees viewed unions negatively. More specifically, they saw the characteristics and approaches of unions to be incompatible with themselves and had a hard time imagining themselves as union members. They saw unions as anti-creative and opposed to the meritocracy system that anchors excellence in technology-based industries. Interviewees stated unequivocally that they and other high achievers did not want to be averaged down to a common level and that this is what unionizing involves.

Interviewees described unions as blue-collar, manufacturing-based organizations that are not involved in high-tech, new economy industries. Moreover, they perceived unions as fighting causes irrelevant or not central to technology-based industries and that may even prove detrimental to the skilled, technical professionals therein. Two interviewees described unions as conflict-oriented organizations that were always fighting rather than negotiating agreement. One expressed the sentiment that programmers and information technology contractors who joined a United Kingdom lobby group to defeat bill IR35, a bill to take away the self-employment status of contractors who only work for one client, might not have done so if the group had been called a union.

Interviewee descriptions of union members and of themselves and other high-tech workers had little or nothing in common. Unlike themselves, interviewees saw union members as inflexible and interested in preserving the status quo, as opposing change, and as unable to cope with the turbulence of technology-based companies. They commented further that individuals who cannot cope with change and turbulence are not suited to the "new" economy or technology professions. Unlike his creative, self-sufficient, e-lance self, one interviewee described union members as older, less educated, not very self-motivated, not likely to talk about their work, not energetic, having external loci of control, and opposed to technology — "as very different than programmers." Other interviewees shared his view. We could lament the stereotyping implications of these comments, but the point would remain that high-tech workers may see themselves as very different from union members and union members as belonging to an out-group.

Two interviewees also expressed concerns that joining a union would make them look bad, comparatively, as individuals. Not only would they be assumed to be weak, but also management might view them as troublemakers. One suggested that even if he agreed that more attention should be paid to seniority and current working conditions he would never publicly say so, let alone lobby for change or join a union. He felt that doing so would lead others to see him as "unable to cut it" and to discount him or not see him as a viable player in the profession. "After all," he said, "if you are competent, you will progress based on achievement." These comments support the theoretical argument made earlier that when deciding whether to unionize, high-tech workers will consider whether others will continue to support their high-tech identities if they do so.

Both the popular and academic press tell skilled high-tech people that they are valued. In many respects their current environments (at work and in general society) confirm their high-tech identities, while unionization does not. It appears that both high-tech workers themselves and others in their social world may construe involvement in collective action as a sign of weakness and unsuitability. In this respect unionized high-tech worker identities may be stigmatized identities that are avoided. Given people's tendencies to gravitate towards situations that are compatible with their identities and away from those that are incompatible, this suggests that they would be unlikely to unionize. In fact, it suggests that they would avoid doing so.

Union Instrumentality. Earlier I argued that high-tech workers will unionize only when they perceive unions to address issues that concern them and propose solutions that sustain their identities. I argued that for a number of reasons, high-tech workers might not perceive issues to be important. They may, for instance, believe that they have fair employment deals, believe that short-term inconveniences will pay off in the long run, or be absorbed in their work and inattentive to issues that would concern others. They may also believe that they can cut their own individual deals without having to invest in collective action. In addition, they may consider unions to focus on issues that are not relevant to them or to the technology sector or both. Interviewees substantiated each of these points. Unexpectedly, every interviewee also passionately argued that unions propose solutions that are not appropriate to the high-tech sector and that may even prove detrimental to the workers themselves. They felt that implementing union solutions would create conditions within which neither the industry nor tech workers could survive. In these ways, unions were seen as hostile to tech worker identities.

Interviewee comments support the argument that at least some high-tech workers do not notice or focus on employment issues that might concern others. When sharing his views about how to motivate and retain high-tech talent, the Vice President of Systems at one field-research site described his job as making the work so interesting and involving that his programmers, systems engineers, and software engineers didn't notice the evening marching by when they had been in since early morning. Interviewees described themselves and other high-tech workers as "caught up in solving puzzles" and "immersed in their work." Interviewees also described themselves as generally satisfied with their work and employment conditions and as feeling that they could negotiate any desired changes within their organizations. Several seemed to identify with their work and with their organizations indicating that they would be prepared to go above and beyond the call of duty to deliver results. Each of these comments suggests that they do not perceive themselves as having unresolved employment issues that warrant collective attention.

Interviewees focused primarily on three issues when expressing concerns about how "typical" union initiatives compromise workers and organization performance: seniority, remuneration and hours of work, and equality. Underpinning each were concerns about incongruence between union objectives and meritocracies.

In all cases, the first issue highlighted was seniority. Unions were seen as overly concerned with seniority issues that underscore lifelong employment in one organization or in a completely unionized profession where seniority transfers between organizations. Interviewees argued that seniority-based systems and the rigid job descriptions associated with them are suboptimal in learning-oriented meritocracies that rely on the most competent people doing the most advanced work. Institutionalizing these systems was also seen as incompatible with high-tech workers' perceptions of themselves as high achievers who advance based on accomplishment, continually learn, move between projects and across organizations, and enjoy challenging assignments. Some appeared to feel constrained by the prospect of unionization bringing in rules that would preclude movement between projects and companies. Basing advancement on seniority may prove additionally problematic in some technological companies where youth is correlated with their computer-skill base. Young, highly skilled programmers, systems engineers, and software engineers may feel especially disadvantaged and move.

The second issue highlighted was remuneration. Unions were described as being overly concerned with standardizing salaries and hours of work, and interviewees saw being placed on predetermined salary scales as undesirable. One individual described the high-tech industry as being based on going above and beyond the norm in pursuit of excellence. One commonly cited view in the organization behavior literature is that money is not a motivator or is, at best, a neutral factor in motivating workers (Pfeffer, 1998). It may, however, be a significant symbol of achievement and status and a signal that one's valued high-tech identities are recognized. High-tech workers who expect to be compensated according to their input may see unionized pay schemes that are divorced from, or not tied specifically, to individual performance, as undesirable. In commenting on seniority, remuneration, and hours of work, one interviewee talked about his perception of the typical union position that all workers are equal. He agreed that all people are equal, but argued that workers vary in their skills and ability to contribute to organizations and that this ought to be recognized. Comments seemed to focus on the perceived mentality of unionization, which once again, was construed as negative and not suited to the technology industry.

Overall, it appears that several issues, arguably foundations of historical collective action, are considered at least by some within the technology sector as hostile to the new economy. To say that unions are perceived as not addressing relevant issues would be one thing and certainly a block to mobilizing technology workers, but to say that union positions on key issues are undesirable and something to be avoided in the best interests of companies and workers alike introduces an altogether higher hurdle.

Three interviewees said that high-tech workers tend to be more concerned with technology and project issues than they perceive unions to be and, as noted earlier, two expressed concerns about burnout, pressures endemic in having to continually learn, and unacceptable trade-offs between work and family lives. Overall, however, high-tech interviewees did not perceive unions as addressing issues that concern them. And, perhaps more importantly, they perceived a traditional union mentality and basket of solutions as inconsistent with their identities and as detrimental to their interests.

VII. Why High-Tech Workers Sometimes Engage in Collective Action

Recent events in the United Kingdom and points made by interviewees suggest that high-tech workers are willing to engage in collective action, if not unionization, when important issues arise. Many programmers and other information-technology contractors recently joined forces with other contractors in the United Kingdom to lobby against IR35, a national bill taking away the self-employment status of contractors who work solely for one company. They and others formed the Professional Contractors Group in order to provide independent contractors with a voice in opposing the original IR35 proposals (<www.pcgroup.org.uk>, April 18, 2001). This group continues to exist as a professional trade organization, boasting over 10,000 members, to represent the interests of knowledge-based workers.

When asked whether there were issues that high-tech workers would organize around several interviewees stated that they would be more likely to coalesce over technology than more traditional employment-related issues. They may, for instance, lobby for a specific technology. In arguing that his company should upgrade to a new technology, the Vice President of Systems Development at one field-research site argued that unless this happened, the company would lose at least half of its programmers who would refuse to work on a dated systems platform being neither interested in doing so nor able to if they were to maintain their marketability outside of the company. The company did not upgrade and in less than one year lost one-third of its programmers and the Vice President. One of the systems engineers I interviewed relayed a parallel story where a company that refused to change to Java had an immediate programmer revolt and lost one-half of its programmers. Another interviewee described the opportunity to work on cutting-edge technology as the main reason he moved to his current employer and his company's willingness to invest in his training and certification as the main reason he would stay. He said that high-tech workers who do not continually educate themselves and work on state-of-the-art technology become trapped, and many employers who neither upgrade technologically nor help workers maintain their technological currency know this. Technological upgrading, clearly an issue for those involved in these stories, is not an issue that unions have historically addressed.

One interviewee divided programmers, systems analysts, and software and hardware engineers into two cohorts: those who joined the profession for the challenge and those who got into it because it was lucrative. He felt that members of the latter group might coalesce to protect what they joined for, that is, job security and remuneration, and perhaps also to lengthen the time that a programmer's skills are still considered valuable.

High-tech workers may coalesce to address issues that concern them, issues arguably connected to their conceptions of themselves as high-tech workers and to their ability to maintain their related identities and marketability. Herein, I focused on unionization — a strong form of collective action. High-tech workers may find other forms of job-related collective action to be more appealing, that is, more consistent with their identities and more in sync with issues that concern them. They may, for instance, be willing to join issue-based coalitions that disband when no longer needed or professional associations that represent them across companies and align more closely to their high-tech worker identities. They may also be responsive to forms of union activity other than those based on face-to-face communication, forms that more closely match their high-tech communication styles. They may, for example, be willing to share job-related information via interactive Web sites like the lawyers involved in GreedyAssociates.com (Taras, 2001). Or, they may engage in on-line lobbying as did those who tried albeit unsuccessfully to defeat bill IR35 in the United Kingdom but continue to exist as an association. With their skills, resources, communication channels and connectivity, high-tech workers are able to form issue-based networks and be very effective. Using technology intelligently, they may be more effective at this than most labor groups. In these and other ways, union activity in the technology sector may find its roots in issue-based, online coalitions or in repeated online communication and professional associations. The propensity of high-tech workers to engage in different forms of collective action warrants investigation.

VIII. Implications for Union Action in the High-Tech Sector

Although doing so has not been my focus, it is useful to consider what an identity-based perspective of unionization suggests for efforts to organize high-tech workers. Union density rates are declining despite recognition of the value of unions to workers and society alike (Century Foundation, 1999). As the manufacturing base of North American industry erodes and technological industries rise in prominence, the future of unionization may depend on the ability of unions to successfully address issues of the new economy in terms that appeal to high-tech worker identities.

Yet, speaking to high-tech workers about unionization may be akin to speaking a foreign language. Workers appear to have no experience base or schema of themselves as union members and appear to view unions as addressing irrelevant issues in ways that are hostile to their identities. Unions will need to demonstrate to high-tech workers how these workers can benefit from organizing and how doing so is consistent with their identities. Initially, they could focus on framing their images and issues in ways that are consistent with high-tech identities, addressing issues that concern high-tech workers and offering solutions that sustain high-tech identities, and using mobilization processes and technology-based communication media that are familiar to these workers.

Unions may benefit from reconstructing or rebranding their own images to make them more attractive to high-tech workers yet still appealing to existing union members and industry strongholds. By aligning their characteristics to broadly shared high-tech identities, unions may help workers across companies to focus on what they have in common and thereby increase the likelihood that these workers will join together and unionize. This approach would be sensitive both to identity concerns and to the fragmented nature of the high-tech sector where highly mobile employees are scattered in small groups among companies. By simultaneously focusing on what high-tech workers have in common with all other workers, unions may also bridge perceived differences between existing union members and high-tech workers.

To some extent benefits may also accrue from educating high-tech workers about unionization. Interviewees tended to think of unionization narrowly, focusing on manufacturing and blue-collar initiatives, arguably those most talked about in the mass media. Apprentice-based union models may transfer more meaningfully to the high-tech sector. Performance-based models common in sports and film may have even greater appeal, already offering basic protection to workers who may be seen as creative and high achieving in very mobile industries.

Unions may also benefit from reframing issues. Some argue that union density is decreasing because unions address issues that are no longer relevant. While this may be true of certain issues and some historically favored solutions, others may still be relevant and benefit from reframing. Unions may be presenting these latter issues in ways that are unpalatable or irrelevant to high-tech worker identities. Anticipated identity confirmation may be enhanced, for example, by reframing concerns about seniority in terms of learning and developing competencies rather than in terms of rewarding years on the job. As noted previously, this apprenticeship model found in craft unions may be compatible with both high-tech worker identities and the needs of technology-driven industries.

Cisco and Dell, arguably well-regarded high-tech employers, are renown for their internal training and development systems. In their efforts to organize elsewhere, unions could use specific companies as exemplars of particular employment practices. Anchoring to company exemplars would provide a signal to high-tech workers that their company and industry identities could be compatible with union identities.

Unions may also align their organizing processes with high-tech identities. They may find, for example, that processes that appeal to puzzle-solver and builder identities are more successful than adversarial approaches. Initial meetings designed as visioning exercises focused on the future may be consistent with high-tech worker conceptions of themselves as builders. Moreover, this approach would mirror processes used within many system design meetings, thereby making it possible for those involved to relate through a high-tech worker experience base. Research has found common visions and goals (Sherif, 1966) and positive emotion (Carnevale and Isen, 1986) to increase cooperation. Perhaps by building on these, unions would encourage the community-mindedness needed for successful unionization. They may also promote coop-

eration by using investiture rather than divestiture socialization programs. Valuing people for who they are and encouraging them to invest themselves in union activities
rather than encouraging them to assimilate would stimulate involvement (Fullagar et
al., 1994; Telford-Milton, 1996). Some would argue that this creates an individualistic group where people do not act in the best interests of the community. Evidence
discussed earlier suggests otherwise. Identity confirmation by way of bringing others
to see one as one sees oneself has been positively associated with attachment to a group
(Swann et al., 2000), and by way of congruence has been related to cooperation (Milton and Westphal, 2001). Group identification has been related to cooperation (Kramer,
1991) and prosocial behavior (O'Reilly and Chatman, 1986). These are pillars on which
community-minded union activity can be built. Thus, in various ways unions may
increase membership by creating and sustaining themselves as organizations that confirm the identities of sought after recruits and long-standing members alike.

Unions may benefit further by facilitating high-tech worker involvement in forms
of collective action other than unionization. At its simplest level, job-related collective action may involve two or more high-tech workers pooling resources to form an
issue-based coalition that disbands when the issue is addressed (Murnighan and Brass,
1991). As other issues arise, new coalitions may form and similarly disband. Membership may change as issues evolve. Issues may recur or correlated issues arise and
involve the same group of people. Repetitive interaction around issues may prompt
more membership stability, and albeit an informal but recognizable group lobbying for
better employment conditions may form. Over time, this group may institutionalize
its practices and roles in order to more effectively and efficiently represent its members. At some point, the group may unionize. Alternatively, an already active union
may convince workers that their interests are aligned with the union, and the workers
may join an already formed group. Herein, I focused on the propensity of high-tech
workers to unionize, presumably either by joining existing unions or forming new ones.
High-tech workers may be more inclined to join "softer" forms of collective action than
unionization, and unions may benefit by facilitating this engagement.

IX. Concluding Remarks

Overall, I suggest that high-tech workers will unionize when doing so confirms their
identities, when they believe that unions will successfully resolve important issues efficiently, and when their opportunity structure supports collective action. My intention
was to open up dialogue about how identity-based mechanisms affect the likelihood
that high-tech workers will form or join unions. I thus follow in the footsteps of others (Barling et al., 1992) who recognize the potential power of uniting behavioral science and industrial relations research.

It is important for union organizers to recognize identity concerns as both antecedents and barriers to unionization. When high-tech workers see unionization as consistent with their valued high-tech identities, they may try to overcome structural
barriers to unionization. They may, for example, organize events to get workers together
to share their views on employment issues. In these same circumstances, when workers

see unionization as inconsistent with their identities, they may not organize a meeting even if employment issues are pressing, and they believe these could be resolved through collective action. In these two situations, identity confirmation serves respectively as an enabler and as a barrier to collective action.

In arguing that high-tech workers need to organize to protect their autonomy, WashTech appears to recognize the importance of identity concerns and thereby attract people who do not see themselves as pro-union (Fitzgerald, 1999). Just as workers' images of unions may be influenced by early socialization experiences (Nicholson et al., 1981; Gallagher, 1999), they may be affected by anticipated identity confirmation.

I have focused on high-tech workers who include systems analysts, hardware and software engineers, computer scientists and programmers, and webmasters, arguably members of the new economy elite. The basic argument that workers will unionize when doing so confirms their identities, when they perceive unions to be instrumental, and when their social opportunity structure supports collective action should generalize to other occupational groups and across industries. Whether it does so begs empirical scrutiny. Workers in different industries and who belong to different occupational groups may focus on other issues. They may value different identities. Successful unions may be those that are intelligently pluralistic yet true to their core values and principles.

In all cases unionization reflects the identities of people. All forms of collective action are a form of social expression. Coalitions do not form solely to coordinate actions or collaborate; they form to affect a decision or resolve an issue for a group larger than themselves in circumstances where others not in the group are expected to oppose the group's stance (Murnighan and Brass, 1991). By joining a union, recruits implicitly or explicitly agree to define themselves as union members. Each step towards unionization implicates identity. Each requires personal investment. Identity-based hurdles and enablers affect individual decisions throughout the unionization process.

The economic downturn creates an interesting, naturally occurring experiment to test the robustness of my framework. On the one hand, some would argue that skilled workers are being redistributed in the economy rather than replaced. There continues to be a global shortage of programmers, systems engineers, and software engineers, and the demand for these workers is expected to continue to increase (U.S. Department of Labor, 2000). On the other hand, high-tech workers may weigh issues differently now than they did a year ago when the capital markets were buoyant, and some may be more drawn to collective action. Overall, however, I think this will only be true when they view such action as compatible with their identities.

Some may see their new fate as an indication that their previously valued high-tech identities are not so highly rated, and consequently they may be in a state of identity shock and experiencing disintegration anxiety (Zaharna, 1989). Consistent with attribution theory, others will likely focus on macro-environmental, rather than personalized, causes for their current situation (Kelly, 1972). People's core identities tend to remain relatively stable across situations and time (Markus and Kunda, 1986); they are not very malleable. And, in the current environment where so many high-tech workers are being laid off and seeking alternative employment, there is considerable evidence to cause workers to ascribe their change of fate to the business environment. Whether those affected feel aggrieved about and personally implicated in being laid off may depend more on the process used to let them go than on their ultimate dismissal (Brockner et al., 1994). When these processes threaten or denigrate worker identities, I expect workers to be particularly unhappy and interested in retribution.

To some extent the long hours of individualized work completed by high-tech workers within project team structures are a function of the nature of their work and organizational expectations. They are, however, also a product of how high-tech workers perceive their work and their professional role, perceptions linked intimately to their definitions of themselves. It has long been recognized that individuals will create and sustain a life that supports their identities. Managers in my other field studies say that one of the human resource issues that high-tech companies face and often do not anticipate is trying to get high-achieving technology workers to view the work week outside of a 24 × 7 grid in order to protect themselves from burnout. To the extent that workers' environments support their identities, it is unlikely that they will strive to change them. An outsider looking in at the long hours and sometimes deplorable tradeoffs of a systems developer's life may fail to see the logic of such effort when the personal price is clearly so high. But, the developers themselves may be satisfied with their work and their employer, intuitively feeling that their life at work is synchronized with their identities.

In the historically buoyant psychological and social environment of high technology, to have joined a union would have in many respects been tantamount to killing a dream, releasing valued identities, and letting hope slip away. It would have been a behavioral statement indicating that all was not well in the land of milk and honey. Is it really surprising that high-tech workers have tended not to unionize?

Notes

*   I appreciate the helpful comments of Nigel Goodwin, Cameron Telford, Sherry Thatcher, and Douglas Vickerson. Kim Wilson's suggestions and support as a research assistant are similarly acknowledged. To Daphne Taras, I express particular gratitude. Her encouragement as a colleague and pithy comments as an editor proved invaluable. Work on this paper was only possible because interviewees were so willing to participate. Efforts were supported in part by a Dean's Research Grant from the Faculty of Management, University of Calgary.
1   While image theory stresses consistency with principles, goals, and plans, I have stressed consistency with high tech identities.
2   This research is succinctly reviewed in Barling et al. (1992).

References

Arthur, Michael B. and Denise M. Rousseau, eds. *The Boundaryless Career: A New Employment Principle for a New Organizational Era.* New York: Oxford University Press, 1996.

Ashforth, Blake. "Role Transitions in Organizational Life: An Identity-Based Perspective." Mahwah, N.J.: Lawrence Erlbaum Associates, 2001.

Baumeister, Roy F. and Dianne M. Tice. "Four Selves, Two Motives, and a Substitute Process Self-regulation Model." In Roy F. Baumeister, ed. *Public Self and Private Self.* New York: Springer-Verlag, 1986, pp. 63–74.

Barling, Julian, Clive Fullagar, and E. Kevin Kelloway. *The Union and Its Members: A Psychological Approach.* New York: Oxford University Press, 1992.

Beach, Leroy R. and Terence R. Mitchell. "Image Theory: A Behavioral Theory of Image Making in Organizations." In Barry M. Staw and L. L. Cummings, eds. *Research in Organizational Behavior.* Greenwich, Conn.: JAI Press, 1990, pp. 1–41.

Beutell, Nicholas J. and David L. Biggs. "Behavioral Intentions to Join a Union: Instrumentality x Valence, Locus of Control and Strike Attitudes." *Psychological Reports* 55 (August 1984): 215–22.

Birch, David and Joseph Veroff. *Motivation: A Study of Action.* Monterey, Calif.: Brooks-Cole, 1996.

Brewer, Marilyn B. "Ethnocentrism and Its Role in Interpersonal Trust." In Marilyn B. Brewer and Barry E. Collins, eds. *Scientific Inquiry and the Social Sciences.* New York: Jossey-Bass, 1981, pp. 88–102.

Brockner, Joel, Mary Konovsky, Rochelle Cooper-Schneider, Robert Folger, Christopher Martin, and Robert J. Bies. "Interactive Effects of Procedural Justice and Outcome Negativity on Victims and Survivors of Job Loss." *Academy of Management Journal* 37 (April 1994): 397–409.

Brown, Shona L. and Kathleen M. Eisenhardt. *Competing on the Edge.* Boston, Mass.: Harvard Business School Press, 1998.

Bryne, Donn. *The Attraction Paradigm.* New York: Academic Press, 1971.

Capelli, Peter. *The New Deal at Work.* Boston, Mass.: Harvard Business School Press, 1999.

Carnevale, Peter J. D. and Alice M. Isen. "The Influence of Positive Affect and Visual Access on the Discovery of Integrative Solutions in Bilateral Negotiation." *Organizational Behavior and Human Decision Processes* 37 (February 1986): 1–13.

Century Foundation. *What's Next for Organized Labor?* New York: Century Foundation Press, 1999.

Chakravarthy, Bala. "A New Strategy for Coping with Turbulence." *Sloan Management Review* 38 (Winter 1997): 69–82.

Clark, Paul F. *Building More Effective Unions.* Ithaca, N.Y.: Cornell University Press, 2000.

Csikszentmihalyi, Mihaly. *Flow: The Psychology of Optimal Experience.* New York: Harper and Row, 1990.

DeCotiis, Thomas A. and Jean-Yves LeLouarn. "A Predictive Study of Voting Behavior in a Representation Election Using Union Instrumentality and Work Perceptions." *Organization Behavior and Human Performance* 27 (February 1981): 103–18.

Dessler, Gary. "How to Earn Your Employees' Commitment." *Academy of Management Executive* 13 (May 1999): 58–67.

de Swaan, Abram. *Coalition Theories and Cabinet Formations.* Amsterdam: Elsevier, 1975.

Dutton, Jane E., Janet M. Dukerich, and Celia V. Harquail. "Organizational Images and Member Identification." *Administrative Science Quarterly* 39 (June 1994): 239–63.

Edmonson, Amy. "Psychological Safety and Learning Behavior in Work Teams." *Administrative Science Quarterly* 44 (June 1999): 350–83.

Eisenhardt, Kathleen M. "Survival of the Swiftest." *Red Herring* (April 2000): 374–83.

Ewalt, David M. "IT Workers Look at the Union Label." *Informationweek* (March 19, 2001): 93.

Fitzgerald, Mark. "Guild Targets Microsoft." *Editor and Publisher* 5 (January 30,1999): 31–32, 61.

Fullagar, Clive, Paul Clark, Daniel Gallagher, and Michael E. Gordon. "A Model of the Antecedents of Early Union Commitment: The Role of Socialization Experiences and Steward Characteristics." *Journal of Organizational Behavior* 15 (November 1994): 517–33.

Gallagher, Daniel. "Youth and Labor Representation." In Julian Barling and Kevin Kelloway, eds. *Young Workers: Varieties of Experience.* Washington, D.C.: American Psychological Association, 1999, pp. 235–55.

Gecas, Viktor. "The Self-Concept." In R. H. Turner and J. G. Short, Jr., eds. *Annual Review of Sociology.* Palo Alto, Calif.: Annual Reviews, 1982, pp. 1–33.

Gramzow, Richard H., Lowell Gaertner, and Constantine Sedikides. "Memory for In-group and

Out-group Information in a Minimal Group Context: The Self As an Informational Base." *Journal of Personality and Social Psychology* 80 (February 2001): 188–203.

Harvard Business School. "Goodbye B-School." *Harvard Business Review* 78 (March/April 2000): 16–17.

<www. pcgroup. org. uk>. About the PCG. Retrieved April 18, 2001, from <www.pcgroup. org.uk>.

Isen, Alice M. and Robert A. Baron. "Positive Affect As a Factor in Organizational Behavior." In Barry M. Staw and L. L. Cummings, eds. *Research in Organization Behavior.* Greenwich, Conn.: JAI Press, 1991, pp. 1–53.

Kelley, Harold H. "Causal Schema and the Attribution Process." In Edward E. Jones, David E. Kanouse, Harold H. Kelley, Richard E, Nisbett, Stuart Valins, and Bernard Weiner, eds. *Attribution: Perceiving the Causes of Behavior.* Morristown, N.J.: General Learning Press, 1972, pp. 151–74.

Kramer, Roderick M. "Intergroup Relations and Organizational Dilemmas." In L. L. Cummings and Barry M. Staw, eds. *Research in Organizational Behavior.* Greenwich, Conn.: JAI Press, 1991, pp. 191–228.

Lau, Dora C. and J. Keith Murnighan. "Demographic Diversity and Faultlines: The Compositional Dynamics of Organizational Groups." *Academy of Management Review* 23 (April 1998): 325–40.

Lecky, Prescott. *Self-Consistency: A Theory of Personality.* New York: Island Press, 1945.

Lincoln, John R. and Jon Miller. "Work and Friendship Ties in Organizations: A Comparative Analysis of Relational Networks." *Administrative Science Quarterly* 24 (June 1979): 181–99.

Markus, Hazel and Ziva Kunda. "Stability and Malleability of the Self-Concept." *Journal of Personality and Social Psychology* 51 (October 1986): 858–66.

McAllister, Daniel J. "Affect- and Cognition-Based Trust As Foundations for Interpersonal Cooperation in Organizations." *Academy of Management Journal* 38 (February 1995): 24–59.

Mead, George H. *Mind, Self, and Society.* Chicago: University of Chicago Press. 1934.

Messick, David M. and Dianne M. Mackie. "Intergroup Relations." In Mark R. Rosenweig and Lyman W. Porter, eds. *Annual Review of Psychology* 40. Palo Alto, Calif.: Annual Reviews, 1989, pp. 45–81.

Meyer, John P., Natalie J. Allen, and Catherine A. Smith. "Commitment to Organizations and Occupations: Extension and Test of a Three-Component Conceptualization." *Journal of Applied Psychology* 78 (August 1993): 538–51.

Milton, Laurie P. "Managing Diversity to Improve the Bottom-Line: Confirming Identities to Enhance Work Group Dynamics and Performance." Doctoral dissertation, University of Texas at Austin. University Microfilms International, 50-09A (1998).

——— and James D. Westphal. "Identity Confirmation Networks and Cooperation in Work Groups." Paper presented at the Annual Meeting of the Academy of Management, Washington, D.C., August 2001.

Mitchell, Terence R. "Expectancy-value Models in Organizational Psychology." In *Norman Feather, ed. Expectancy, Incentive, and Action.* Hillsdale, N.J.: Lawrence Erlbaum Associates, 1983, pp. 293–314.

Murnighan, Keith J. and Daniel J. Brass. "Intraorganizational Coalitions." *Research on Negotiation in Organizations.* Vol. 3. Greenwich, Conn.: JAI Press, 1991, pp. 283–306.

Nicholson, Nigel, Gill Ursell, and Paul Blyton. *The Dynamics of White-Collar Unionism: A Study of Local Union Participation.* San Diego, Calif.: Academic Press, 1981.

O'Reilly, Charles A. and Jennifer Chatman. "Organizational Commitment and Psychological Attachment: The Effects of Compliance, Identification, and Internalization on Prosocial Behavior." *Journal of Applied Psychology* 71 (August 1986): 492–99.

Pfeffer, Jeffrey. "Six Dangerous Myths about Pay." *Harvard Business Review* 76 (May/June 1998): 109–19.

Polzer, Jeffrey T., Laurie P. Milton, and William B. Swann, Jr. "Capitalizing on Diversity: Interpersonal Congruence in Small Work Groups." *Administrative Sciences Quarterly* 47 (June 2002): 296–324.

Rosenberg, Morris. *Conceiving the Self.* New York: Basic Books, 1979.

Rousseau, Denise M., Sim B. Sitkin, Ronald S. Burt, and Colin Camerer. "Not So Different After All: A Cross-Discipline View of Trust." *Academy of Management Review* 23 (July 1998): 393–404.

Secord, Paul F. and Carl W. Backman. "An Interpersonal Approach to Personality." In Brendan A. Maher, ed. *Progress in Experimental Personality Research* 2. New York: Academic Press, 1965, pp. 91–125.

Sherif, Muzafer. Group Conflict and Cooperation. London: Routledge and Kegan, Paul, 1966.

Shrauger, J. Sidney and Thomas J. Schoeneman. "Symbolic Interactionist View of Self-Concept: Through the Looking Glass Darkly." *Psychological Bulletin* 86 (May 1979): 549–73.

Swann, William B., Jr. "Identity Negotiation: Where Two Roads Meet." *Journal of Personality and Social Psychology* 53 (December 1987): 1038–51.

———, Chris de la Ronde, and J. Gregory Hixon. "Authenticity and Positivity Strivings in Marriage and Courtship." *Journal of Personality and Social Psychology* 57 (May 1994): 782–91.

Swann, William B., Jr., Laurie P. Milton, and Jeffrey T. Polzer. "Should We Create a Niche or Fall in Line? Identity Negotiation and Small Group Effectiveness." *Journal of Personality and Social Psychology* 79 (August 2000): 238–50.

Swann, William B., Jr., Richard M. Wenzlaff, Douglas S. Krull, and Brett W. Pelham. "The Allure of Negative Feedback: Self-Verification Strivings among Depressed Persons." *Journal of Abnormal Psychology* 101 (May 1992): 293–306.

Swann, William B., Jr. and Brett W. Pelham. "Who Want Out When the Going Gets Good? Psychological Investment and Preference for Self-Verifying College Roommates." Working Paper, University of Texas at Austin, 2001.

Tafarodi, Romin W. and William B. Swann, Jr. "Self-Liking and Global Competence As Dimensions of Global Self-Esteem: Initial Validation of a Measure." *Journal of Personality Assessment* 65 (October 1995): 322–42.

Tajfel, Henri and J. C. Turner. "The Social Identity Theory of Intergroup Behavior." In Stephen Worchel and William G. Austin, eds. *Psychology of Intergroup Relations*, 2. Chicago: Nelson-Hall, 1985, pp. 7–24.

Taras, Daphne. "Network Building about Work: 'GreedyAssociates.com' and Law Firms' Wage Setting." Paper presented at Canadian Industrial Relations Association Annual Meeting, Quebec City, May 2001.

Telford (Milton), Laurie P. "Selves in Bunkers: Organizational Consequences of Failing to Verify Alternative Masculinities." In Cliff Cheng, ed. *Masculinities in Organizations*. Thousand Oaks, Calif.: Sage Publications, 1996, pp. 130–59.

Tett, Robert P. and John P. Meyer. "Job Satisfaction, Organizational Commitment, Turnover Intention, and Turnover: Path Analyses Based on Meta-analytic Findings." *Personnel Psychology* 46 (Summer 1993): 259–93.

Thatcher, Sherry M. B. "Do You Really Know Me? The Implications of Identity Fit for Diverse Work Teams." Working Paper (2001), University of Arizona, Tucson, AZ.

Tom, Victor R. "The Role of Personality and Organizational Images in the Recruiting Process." *Organization Behavior and Human Performance* 6 (September 1971): 573–92.

Trombley, Maria and Kathleen Ohlson. "Union Takes Aim at High-Tech Workers." *Computerworld* 33 (August 14, 2000): 1, 81.

U. S. Department of Labor. *Occupational Outlook Handbook 2000-01 Edition.* Washington, D.C.: Bureau of Labor Statistics, 2000 [<stats.bls.gov/oco/ocos042. htm>, April 18, 2001].

Wageman, Ruth. "Interdependence and Group Effectiveness." *Administrative Science Quarterly* 40 (March 1995): 145–80.

Zaharna, Rhonda S. "Self-Shock: The Double-Binding Challenge of Identity." *International Journal of Intercultural Relations* 13 (October 1989): 501–25.

11

The Use of Information Technology in a Strike

Vicki Barnett
Former *Calgary Herald* Journalist and Striker

I. Introduction

On November 8, 1999, 107 *Calgary Herald* newsroom employees went on strike. It was the first time since the daily newspaper's founding in 1883 that editorial workers had struck. In fact, the newsroom employees' decision to join a union 13 months earlier was itself an unprecedented development. Over several decades, while employees in newsrooms at most other urban Canadian dailies were organized, their counterparts in the fervently free-enterprise province of Alberta consistently declined to sign union cards.

Two days before their strike notice took effect, after most had gone home, they were locked out of the building, with no time to remove personal items from their desks. *The Herald*'s new, elaborate, computer-controlled security system, which required the scanning of a coded pass for entry through the doors, was reprogrammed to deny access to all nonmanagement newsroom employees except those who had informed the company in advance that they would cross the picket line.

The organized workers' fledgling Local 115A of the Communications, Energy and Paperworkers Union was fighting for a first contract. The strike was destined to be Calgary's last great labor confrontation of the 20th century.

The newspaper had been owned for almost all of that century by Southam, Inc., a family-owned chain. By the 1980s, however, the journalistic fervor that had driven the founders had been diluted after several generations, and the Southams began selling their majority interest in the company. Then, as part of a flurry of newspaper purchases in the 1990s by Conrad Black's Hollinger, Inc., Southam, Inc. found itself in the hands of a controversial, strong-willed owner. While sometimes professing that he liked journalism, Black had publicly expressed dislike of journalists and denounced many of them as being captive of feminist, environmental, and other "left-wing" causes. He also expected a higher return on investment than the Southams had demanded.

Herald editorial policy moved markedly to the right under Black's ownership, especially after the abrupt resignation of its publisher, Kevin Peterson.

It was also a policy of the newsroom to avoid getting too cozy with the advertising department. Soon after Black became the chain's proprietor, Peterson was replaced by Ken King, previously publisher of the *Calgary Sun* — a tabloid daily known for underpaying and overworking its journalists except for a favored few "stars," and a place used as a training ground for inexperienced journalists until they could land a job some place better, such as the broadsheet *Herald*.

King was a former ad salesman who believed there needed to be more co-operation between the *Herald*'s newsroom and its advertising department and was a champion of "alliances" between the paper and the city's businesses and business-led organizations.

The Southam/Hollinger grapevine spread the word that King had a political agenda, too. During the brief overlap of Peterson's and Black's reigns, the chain owner apparently was appalled that the *Herald* often took shots at the Progressive Conservative provincial government.

Many beats that had been vigorously covered in previous years at the newspaper — environment, social services, native-Indian affairs, women's issues, human rights — were now dabbled in sporadically by general-assignment reporters or abandoned altogether.

In 1997, 21 years after my arrival at the paper, I was the *Herald*'s environment reporter, a high-profile job in a province where wilderness was being lost at the rate of an acre an hour. But with the change of ownership and *Herald* management, I and other journalists experienced an enormous change in the way editorial copy was treated. My stories — which until recently had consistently appeared on front page or the city section front or were given prominent play in weekend papers, fundamentally unaltered — began to be severely edited and were dumped onto the back pages where they appeared as filler. I moved to the business department, which was enjoying a resurgence under the regime.

The new regime also adopted the mantra of FAB — "fairness, accuracy, and balance" — for news stories, which many employees considered to be an Orwellian-style phrase eschewing those very qualities. FAB meant that public attacks by critics on business or government by environmentalists, or the results of academic research unfavorable to somebody the *Herald* liked, would often be subordinated in the news story to statements of denial.

One day around this time, a long-time senior editor known for embracing whatever convictions the current publisher held let it be known his vision of the newsroom was that one-third of the staff would be permanent, one-third freelance, and one-third contract workers. The message he wanted disseminated was clear: it was time for many journalists to consider other options because life was going to be tougher at the *Her-*

ald. There would also, he said, be no severance packages like those paid out in response
for voluntary resignations a few years earlier.

In the newsroom, frustrations had traditionally been vented through something called
the "newsroom group." It had been set up — by management — during the 1970s. This
loosely organized group with no membership cards met about half a dozen times a year
to hear employees' grievances and solicit opinions on ways to improve the news-gath-
ering system. Annually, it would take a poll among employees on their expected wage
increase and then submit the request to management, which had no obligation to act
on that or any other request. The newsroom group was an important safety valve.

Joan Crockatt, the recently installed managing editor, walked by the glass-fronted
newsroom conference room early one afternoon in early 1999 and saw the assembled
newsroom group in action, with its typical attendance of fewer than 25 percent of editorial employees. Unaware of the group's history, including the fact it was a child of
management, Crockatt immediately announced that it couldn't meet anymore without
permission. The newsroom group never met again, and attention throughout the newsroom quietly turned to the possibility of more formal representation for employees.

Organizing began by cautious word-of-mouth, as it has always done throughout
the history of trade unions, but now there was a difference. It was the first time a core
of editorial workers at a large Canadian Daily began their organizing drive by setting
up an e-mail system. Only a trusted few used it at first, obviously restricting it to their
home e-mails but as the circle grew, so did the communication by home computer. In
October of that year, the newsroom voted 82 percent in favor of unionizing.

The CEP's organizing of the *Herald* newsroom cost Ken King his Southam career.
His replacement was Dan Gaynor, mostly an unknown quantity except for his tough
dealings with union journalists at the Southam paper in St. Catharines, Ontario, during a brief strike.

Few union members believed that picket signs would even be ordered, let alone carried. Reluctant to go on strike in a politically conservative province, the new union
local's negotiating position was a modest two percent wage increase in the first year
of the agreement, effective July 1, 1999. It also wanted the *Herald*'s employee manual enshrined in a collective agreement. During almost a year of exhaustive negotiations, the company rejected most of the key union demands other than a grievance
procedure. Most significantly, Gaynor wouldn't hear of a seniority clause such as all
the other Southam papers had.

When the strike began, the CEP members, most of them in a union for the first
time in their lives, anticipated being on the picket line only a few days because
Hollinger — heavily in debt because of newspaper acquisitions around the world,
including Chicago, London, and Jerusalem — had settled promptly with its more mil-
itant Ottawa and Vancouver news staffs.

The union had completely misread the situation in Calgary. Black's prime cost in
running newspapers was labor, and his long-term goal was to strike fear into the hearts
of employees with union cards. As it turned out, he was willing to spend millions of
dollars in the new battle site in Calgary to try to break the national union. Alberta is a
province with labor laws so weak that they have been criticized by the United Nations'

International Labour Organization, and it has a government unwilling to enforce even those tepid laws.

For most of the *Herald* strike, the CEP members walked alongside those from the GCIU, a union representing workers in the distribution center, who won a first contract just a few weeks before the CEP strike collapsed.

The CEP strike was to last eight months, with CEP employees voting June 30, 2000 to return to work. The vast majority, however, took a severance package, either immediately or after returning to the *Herald* for a short period. By Thanksgiving, only a dozen of the newsroom's former strikers were still on the job.

II. Picket Line Resources

The nature of the strike and strikers led to extensive use of technology during the prolonged event. In a province with a relatively low rate of unionization and no union newspapers, there were few role models to show strikers how to proceed traditionally.

On the picket line were a number of reporters and editors who were highly computer literate, and photographers who knew how to use digital cameras and sophisticated computer programs. Almost to a person, they were critical thinkers with an enormous thirst for knowledge. For this group, information was crucial.

A strike Web site, www.heraldunion.com, was established early in the dispute as an inexpensive tool for communicating with strikers, 75 percent of whom had Internet access at home. As well, there was that e-mail network, expanded by negotiating committee member Brian Brennan to give strikers daily — and sometimes hourly — updates on strike developments.

At the same time, the company was using extremely sophisticated technology to pick up every word that people said on the picket line in front of the *Herald* building in northeast Calgary. Rumors that microphones could capture virtually everything that was said were proven true later in the strike when videotapes and sound recordings of strikers were played by the company at an Alberta Labor Board hearing.

Afterwards, the union set up, at the start of each day's picketing, a "boom box" portable stereo just outside the company property, aimed at the security trailer window, where the main microphone perched. The pickets brought their CD collections of raucous rock music. Jimi Hendrix was a favorite.

Even so, verbal communication among strikers was kept to a minimum during most hours of the day on the line. Knowing there could be undetected mikes at locations well away from the boom box, strikers generally stuck to small talk or any non-work-related subject that implied cheery morale, while some mischief makers among them would try to disseminate false intelligence, such as naming some especially disliked picket-line crosser as a secret union informer.

But the snooping aspect, combined with the ineffectiveness of picketing a newspaper located in an industrial area away from most of the public, plus the apparent lack of legal solutions and the strikers' mounting frustration, caused them to turn to what they knew best — the battle for public opinion by distributing information, using the latest technology.

III. The Web Site

Joy Langan, the CEP organizer and national representative who was on site in Calgary during the strike, said a union web page delivering strike information wasn't a novel phenomenon, but Local 115A took it to a new level. The web site cost very little, was colorful and visually sophisticated, and linked Internet browsers to other unions, newspapers, journalists' groups, and advocacy organizations across the country. It was so effective that other locals have indicated they will do the same during labor disputes in the future, said Langan.

The union local's web site, with its reproduction of the *Herald*'s copyrighted logo, appeared to be one of the biggest irritants to the employer, judging by subsequent lawsuits and an injunction sought by the company. As the strike dragged on for two months, it was taken over by Grant McKenzie — whose pre-strike job was laying out the *Herald*'s entertainment pages — who then turned it into a vital public relations tool for the union. With his design skills, stories by experienced writers, and pictures by professional photographers, the web site was attractive and freshly updated. McKenzie was excused from picket-line duty so he could devote all his time to the site.

Backing the high-tech web site was one of the most traditional of methods to sway public opinions — leafletting. By the time the strike was over, *Herald* strikers had dropped photocopied leaflets at virtually every household in Calgary, a city with a population of 800,000. The back page of the leaflet urged Calgarians to visit the web site for ongoing information.

Once again, computers and their sophisticated printers were a great improvement on traditional leaflet-making by nonprofit groups. These leaflets, actually three pieces of 8 1/2 × 11-inch paper folded in half into booklet format, contained an outside page explaining the strike and the issues involved, and inside pages that changed periodically to reflect strike developments and the season. The material was timely and highly readable because it was written by journalists on home computers, then e-mailed to the union office. A single-page mail-out early in the strike done via Canada Post, which went to every city household, also touted the web site.

While the site was initially designed for strike supporters, it took on an unanticipated importance in countering negative coverage — and lack of coverage — of the strike. It was no surprise to strikers that the *Herald* did not give favorable coverage to the conflict, but the extent of negative coverage in the *National Post*, a newspaper also owned by Conrad Black, was shocking. Journalists understand that opinion pieces such as editorials, comments, and commentary pages will contain strongly worded arguments, but they also expect some semblance of objectivity in news stories. Both sides of an issue should always be represented. Sometimes, in extremely controversial coverage, that duty is taken to great lengths. For instance, when I was writing stories about environmentalists versus developers during my years on the environment beat, I would often measure with a ruler the column inches given to each side's arguments — not just to be fair, but to counter the arguments of "unfair bias" that reporters often receive when covering such stories.

An old adage bantered about newsrooms is that you should never get into a fight with somebody who buys his ink by the barrel. With the advent of electronic communications, there are at least alternatives for those who can't afford to buy ink by the barrel and newsprint by the ton. The union web site allowed strikers to publish their own opinions, photos, and stories, and counter some of the newspapers' negative coverage or lack of coverage.

The only pro-union coverage in the *Post* was penned by Jim Stanford, a Canadian Auto Workers columnist, and former *National Post* columnist and token left-wing voice. Aware that a Canadian Labor Congress (CLC) boycott of the *Post* was pending because of the strike, Stanford in his final column responded to a news story by *Edmonton Journal* reporter Ric Dolphin that ran under the headline "Picketing the Velvet Coffin." (The "velvet coffin" was a cynical phrase used by *Herald* journalists in the 1970s to refer to the fact that the then-paternalistic, family-run enterprise continued to employ drunks and other long-time employees past the time of usefulness, and was perpetuated as a form of black humor by journalists who felt trapped in long-time careers.) Dolphin decided it referred to a "tired, dull and politically irrelevant paper . . ." run by spoiled journalists with access to a fitness center and subsidized daycare and healthy $60,000-a-year salaries (Yearwood, 2001, p. 55). Dolphin's story included only perfunctory quotes from strike leaders who, in fact, weren't even contacted for his articles.

Strike leader Andy Marshall said that he was appalled by the unfairness and inaccuracy of the Dolphin story. Former *Herald* publisher Kevin Peterson said that he received calls from other *Post* reporters concerned about the piece because of its inaccuracies. Two of four reporters working at the *Post* in Calgary had previously worked at the *Herald*. Sean Myers, a *Herald* reporter who returned to work after a month on strike, described the Dolphin story as "a blatant attempt to provoke the union people," and noted that people inside the building were shaking their heads and saying, "Oh, wow" (Yearwood, 2001, p. 55).

The headline on an article that ran in the *National Post* December 18, 1999 announced, "Boycott of *Post* Doomed, Black Says: Council of Canadians, CLC Behind Move." The unbalanced article went into great detail on Black's opinions about the strike, but devoted only one paragraph to a response from an unidentified spokesperson for the Council and Canadian Labour Congress and to the reason for the boycott.

In another story on February 2, 2000, headlined "Hollinger to Sue MP for Defamation," Black explained why he was suing a New Democratic Party politician and blamed the NDP member's anger on his failure to settle the *Herald* strike. Then five gratuitous paragraphs were devoted to a Black attack on the union's goals.

On March 3, 2000, the *Post* ran a story that initially appeared in the *Herald*, headlined, "*Herald* Improved Since Strike: Black," repeating the pattern of having lengthy quotes from Black while devoting little space to the union's response. When Calgary's Catholic Bishop Frederick Henry criticized Black in the *Catholic Register*, a *Post* reporter gave the press baron a chance to retaliate in an April 4, 2000 article and cited the advantages of working at the *Herald*.

(Taking on the head of the Catholic Church in Calgary, who was openly backed by other church leaders, wasn't Black's wisest move, because it ensured that strikers appeared to have the high ground morally. The web site and "e-mail tree" reported every development.)

As well as trying to counter some of Black's negative comments, the strikers' web site and e-mails also played up his more outrageous ones such as strikers being "gangrenous limbs" that needed to be cut off. Electronic communications were also used to report on numerous items that never made Black's papers — dropping circulation, comments by prominent Calgarians urging a settlement to the strike, and comments from people who complained that after they cancelled the *Herald*, it kept appearing on their doorsteps.

The inches devoted to each side in a story are only one measure of objectivity and independent journalism. Just as important, and often more important, is whether the story is covered at all.

It was obvious to anyone reading Canada's two national newspapers that the *Globe and Mail*, then owned by the rival Thomson newspaper chain, devoted far more resources and space to the strike than did the *National Post*. The *Post* ran 23 articles and nine opinion pieces on the strike, compared with 40 news stories and 12 opinion pieces in the *Globe*.

Although it is easy to dismiss the *Globe* as having an anti-*Post* agenda, since it was engaged in a fierce circulation struggle with the *Post*, there are two arguments that can be used to counter that contention. The strike was more than just a local union dispute. It raised at least three critical issues — weak labor laws and even weaker enforcement of those laws in Alberta, concentration of ownership in the news media, and the continuing failure of the news media to adequately cover itself. (While Canada is generally considered more to the political left than the United States, its government can be amazingly tolerant of business excess. At the time of the *Herald* strike, approximately 75 percent of the country's dailies were owned by two corporations — Black's and Thomson's.)

There was one more factor that made it essential for the union to have a web site. The *Calgary Sun*, Calgary's other daily, devoted almost no coverage to the strike, and refused to accept ads from the union. Its flyer unit wouldn't deliver any printed material from the union. The *Sun* also refused to hire striking *Herald* journalists. With its notorious attitude toward pay scales and working conditions, the *Sun* had good reason not to assist any group of journalists in achieving a first contract, even if they were the enemy's headache.

With the broadcast media, the evidence of lack of journalistic objectivity was also in the lack of coverage. While the heavily unionized and publicly funded Canadian Broadcasting Corporation (CBC) conducted several interviews on the strike, other media outlets — with a few exceptions — covered only the spectacular highlights, such as angry confrontations between strikers and police at rallies or strikers yelling at strikebreakers crossing the picket line.

Was covering the highlights typical of the type of coverage generally given by local news media? Perhaps, but on two separate occasions, a reporter working for a Calgary television station and another working for a local radio station ruefully acknowledged to me and to other strikers that it was difficult to sell the story at the morning story meetings where it is decided what should be put on the air each day.

Although *Herald* strikers may have thought they were treated in a biased manner during the strike, they were at least professional communicators who managed to establish their own web site to counter to some extent unfavorable publicity and to present their points of view. A year-earlier local strike by relatively uneducated immigrant workers against a Calgary furniture-manufacturing company that had ended with the union being smashed had received almost no publicity, despite the workers' extremely poor pay and working conditions. Media owners, not surprisingly, are never fond of unions being presented in a favorable light. That group of furniture employees didn't have the advantage of in-house expertise on developing and maintaining a web site.

Peter Debarais, an ethics professor in Ryerson University's School of Journalism, said, "When a newspaper is writing about itself, its own business activities or its own labor activities, it, in principle, has an obligation to be as fair and accurate as possible. In practice, that almost never happens."

The use of high-tech means of communication such as web sites has implications for more than the *Herald* strikers. The use of web sites with credible content can do much to promote the views of groups that have traditionally been under-represented in coverage by the traditional media, including labor, environment, and peace groups, anti-poverty campaigners and others who are too often dismissed in newspaper editorials as "whiners."

This becomes even more important with corporate concentration in the news media, an issue that was first targeted by a Canadian Royal Commission in the late 1960s. Black's Hollinger company sold the *Herald*, almost all of its other Canadian newspapers, and 50 percent of the *Post* to Izzy Asper's CanWest Global Communications in the third quarter of 2000. Asper's media empire includes Global Television stations across the country, including one in Calgary.

The well-designed, informative web site in such a lengthy strike was extremely important. Among the most high-impact photographs that the web site contained was a picture of enormous stacks of undelivered, unwanted newspapers being readied for recycling. (The photo was shot surreptitiously by a noneditorial employee sympathetic to the strikers and e-mailed to the union web page.) Because advertising rates are based on circulation, the union hoped advertisers would question whether they were getting their money's worth. Another photo, shot at a public rally on the picket line, showed striker Terry Inigo-Jones facing down a *Herald*-hired security guard wearing a black balaclava to protect his identity.

Other content included an independent survey commissioned by the union in late 1999 showing *Herald* circulation had fallen between 20 and 25 percent (a figure that was denied by Conrad Black).

The web site included photos of replacement workers and employees who crossed the picket line, with a profiled "scab of the week," often someone who came from another newspaper. These attracted attention from employees at other newspapers and no doubt touched off spirited debate about those among them who had headed for Calgary to take advantage of this opportunity. Such easily obtained information by anybody with access to the Internet guaranteed there would be hard feelings about this battle, widely felt across the land, long after it ended.

Another target of the union web site was a particular reporter who crossed the picket line after promising to support the strike. He was known as an active freelancer in addition to his *Herald* work. Using an Internet search engine, a union member tracked the reporter's byline in various publications and discovered some of the work appearing under his name was remarkably similar to published stories written by somebody else. An example, which ran in a Canadian medical magazine, was posted on the web site alongside a near-identical story published previously, which was another person's work. Then the medical magazine's management was notified of the display. That reporter no longer freelances to the medical magazine.

The union, to boost strikers' morale and let neutral parties know this wasn't a local dispute, also posted on the site major examples of support, either verbal or in cash, from organizations and individuals willing to be identified. It also had a link to the web site of union workers at Conrad Black's *Jerusalem Post*, who were going through hard times of their own. Links like this helped to convey the message that the *Herald* strikers weren't alone.

While the web site ran throughout the strike, two portions were dropped. Initially, it was set up to accept letters of support, which came from as far away as Australia, Brazil, Britain, Germany, Ireland, Israel, Singapore, Switzerland, and the United States. But the letters section was abandoned when writers who crossed the picket line began submitting anti-union, pro-company letters.

A chat room was also established and abandoned. When the son of GCIU president John webster wrote anonymously to the chat room to describe how difficult things were in his household during the strike, and urge the *Herald* to negotiate, entertainment writer Blair S. Watson, who crossed the picket line daily, responded with an attack on John Webster. He had apparently hacked into the web site to discover who the writer was, but McKenzie "hacked back" to discover Watson's identity. The chat room was shut down because it had been designed to boost strikers' morale, but had turned venomous.

Although the union local didn't initially count visits to the web site, by the end of the strike the site was receiving more than 100,000 hits a month. It won the British-based International Labour Federation's web-Site-of-the-Month Award.

But one of the biggest measures of its success may have been the attacks it prompted by those affiliated with the *Herald*. To get into the web site, the viewer logged on to a rolled-up *Calgary Herald* with a circle and diagonal bar through it, indicating people shouldn't buy the paper. The *Herald* tried to get an injunction against use of its logo, an issue that was never settled before the strike ended.

Three lawsuits were launched against the site over the "scab of the week" feature, one because the union got a little sloppy and mistakenly identified a journalist from another newspaper as a replacement worker based on a quick sighting. Another lawsuit was launched because of the site's link to *Frank Magazine*, a publication known to be outrageous and willing to run unsubstantiated and speculative stories. The lawsuit was launched because *Frank* predicted the demise of one picket-line crosser's career, the kind of statement that can land a publication in legal hot water in Canada where freedom of speech has little protection under the Constitution and defamation laws are strictly interpreted by the courts.

McKenzie was not able to confirm rumors that the *Herald* had hired a hacker to try to get into the web site and shut it down.

At the end of the strike, the company threatened legal action if the site stayed up. Everything except the -30- used at the end of newspaper articles to signify the end of the story was removed. The content remains on a disc given to the union.

IV. E-mail

Bargaining committee member Brian Brennan ran the e-mail network of private addresses after the union local was formed in October, 1998. Like the web site, it began as a way of distributing union news. As soon as people signed a union card, they could receive e-mails.

It was an effective way of distributing information almost instantaneously to people who were intensely interested. The company could do nothing about it because company phone lines and e-mails weren't being used. People who didn't have private e-mail addresses were assigned e-mail "buddies" who would pass along, by telephone, information received.

The e-mails were used to communicate picket-line duty times, bargaining updates, and most commonly, support that came from other organizations and individuals in the form of checks and letters. When any one of the union representatives was interviewed by the media, it was promoted via e-mail. E-mails were also used for intelligence gathering, such as when anyone saw unused *Herald*s being taken to the recyclers, or any evidence of company slip-ups, such as factual errors or union bashing, in the newspapers. (All the strikers cancelled their free *Herald* subscriptions, but the union kept one copy at strike headquarters, an office established near the *Herald* for picketing convenience.)

When it soon became apparent that the company's strategy was to wear the strikers down by showing no interest in returning to the bargaining table, the union's e-mail was like a daily blood transfusion and became increasingly important as the strike dragged on and strikers became exhausted and at times discouraged. The e-mails provided a tremendous morale booster because of the support pouring in, the upbeat and sometimes irreverent shots at the *Herald*, and the enumeration of even the smallest union victory.

In fact, the e-mails became so critical that several journalists who had previously not had a home computer purchased one. Others obtained Internet hook-ups so they could read e-mails. It was their key link to a new world with new friends and allies.

The emotional connection provided through this form of technology was intense. When members of the "Club of 93" that remained on the picket line at the end of strike returned to work, they were removed from the e-mail list. Some subsequently quit the *Herald*, including one woman who then asked to be reconnected because "we walked a picket line together at −20 degrees Celsius." Explained Brian Brennan, who was responsible for distributing e-mails, "It's like people who have cancer or given birth. You had to have been there to understand what it was we went through."

E-mails were also used to pass along to strikers any information on temporary work that might alleviate their financial burden. Strikers made adjustments to living on welfare-level strike pay, but one of the hardest aspects of the strike was the uncertainty of how and when it would end, as the company seemed to have no interest in settling.

E-mails ensured that strikers didn't have to go through the emotional roller-coaster and uncertainty alone. The e-mails communicated social events such as an evening in a local bar, a children's Christmas party at a local union hall, or a potluck dinner.

Thousands of pieces of information were distributed to strikers via e-mails. Strikebreakers were identified and their backgrounds given. Members of other unions who had been down the strike road before communicated advice and support. Each week, strikers were urged to boycott a company still advertising in the *Herald*, and to write the company to protest.

Brennan, a senior journalist and former *Herald* theater reviewer, used humor, anger, and irreverence to communicate. In the spring of 2001, he had on his computer 120,000 e-mails messages that he had sent, and the vast majority of them were communications dispatched to Local 115A members between October, 1998 when the local began and the end of the strike.

The *Herald* also used e-mails as a morale booster for replacement workers, sending out messages to cheer them up and saying they were fighting for "job freedom." It was demoralizing for replacement workers to cross the picket line every day, and newsroom e-mails were used to cheer them up. Replacement workers were told they were courageous for taking a stand for "freedom."

On the union side, there were 20 to 30 e-mails sent each week. The strike started with 107 newsroom workers on the picket line. Today, many ex-strikers who left the *Herald* for other jobs still receive e-mails disseminating information on career possibilities, social gatherings, and news about new books written by former strikers from Brennan.

V. The "Cyber Picket Line"

Among the most innovative uses of technology during the strike was the "cyber picket line." CEP Local 2000 of Vancouver, British Columbia maintained the electronic picket line to support *Herald* strikers.

A daily printed sheet of news drafted by computer, called The Last Word, was put out for strikers by strikers. That handout and other information was sent to Karen Jolly of Local 2000 in Vancouver. Every day, news of the strike was e-mailed to a list of 200 to 300 people. That list grew to thousands by the end of the strike, according to the CEP's Langan. For a while, communications provider Telus blocked the e-mails because of the size of the list. Langan said she was unaware of any other strikers using a cyber picket line.

The e-mail list was used to disseminate critical information about Conrad Black and the strike around the world and to collect an expanding array of supportive messages from people in countries such as Argentina, Australia, China, France, Ireland, New Zealand, Peru, and South Africa.

The cyber picket line, besides giving people, nationally and internationally, updates on the strike, electronically published a "hit of the week." People on the electronic list would be asked to send an e-mail letter to Conrad Black, Alberta Premier Ralph Klein, Labor Minister Cliff Dunford, or people who crossed the picket line, such as high-profile columnist Catherine Ford.

As with most electronic communications, it's difficult to measure the exact impact. But Langan said that several hundred people responded. She acknowledged that the innovative cyber picket line would have had a greater impact if it had come out of Calgary instead of Vancouver. "But it worked very well, and it will be refined and used again in the future," she said.

Other e-mails on the cyber picket line called for a boycott of the *National Post*, and companies such as Shopper's Drug Mart that continued to advertise in the *Herald*. Langan said a dozen different national advertisers, who continued to advertise in the *Herald*, were subjected to leafleting campaigns in Vancouver, in the heavily unionized province of British Columbia. Union supporters would stand outside the store and distribute leaflets urging shoppers not to buy from the retail outlet. (A committee of *Herald* strikers also conducted a campaign against a different advertiser each week, monitoring ads in the *Herald* and urging others via electronic means and The Last Word to write letters or e-mails to the company, and to boycott it.)

Local 2000 gathered a list of journalists and photojournalists who were strike-breakers at the *Herald*, and sent it electronically to the union leaders of every unionized newspaper in the country, which includes almost every major daily except the *Edmonton Journal*. Since the strike, the CEP had reported that a *Herald* business reporter who crossed the picket line was almost hired at the *Globe and Mail* before being rejected because they didn't want trouble in the newsroom, while another person brought in as a *Herald* replacement worker was rejected by the *Winnipeg Free Press* for the same reason.

VI. Friends of the *Herald*

Another group of mostly Calgarians was established that also relied heavily on e-mail and Internet news. Its goal was to encourage a settlement in the *Herald* strike and express concerns about the declining quality of journalism in Calgary. Because of protests from television and radio stations, that was later changed to "print journalism," which was widely understood to be the *Herald*. (The tabloid *Sun*, with its daily Sunshine Girl and Sunshine Boy and relatively small staff, had not changed for better or worse since the strike, and is considered by many to be as much entertainment as journalism. The *Sun*, for example, generally has a business department with a business editor/writer and perhaps one other reporter, while the *Herald* maintained a business department of an editor, full-time columnist, numerous freelance columnists, and six to eight reporters.)

At its peak, Friends of the *Herald* consisted of 117 liberal-leaning residents of Calgary, Vancouver, and Ottawa. Its e-mail list was accessed by password, as many participants wanted to remain relatively anonymous. Several academics from the University of Calgary were involved, as were prominent Calgarians who did speak up, such as Wayne Stewart, a well-known local businessman.

Robert Bragg, a member of the group, said Friends of the *Herald* gave concerned people an option for action because there were few other initiatives or alternatives available. The group met once a week at a local United Church, but members kept in touch and were kept informed largely via e-mail, established through the Yahoo groups.

The organization was primarily a lobby group involved in electronic petitioning and communicating. It lobbied *Herald* Publisher Dan Gaynor to reach a settlement, and encouraged the provincial government to pressure the *Herald* to settle.

The most successful lobbying involved Calgary City Council, which in January, 2000 passed a motion urging both sides to sit down and negotiate. The result was one short, unsuccessful negotiating session in which the company stuck by all its previous stands and rejected any discussion of seniority.

Friends of the *Herald* also organized a conference on the news media and democracy that involved about 20 prominent Calgarians from various sectors of the community urging a settlement and emphasizing the need for quality journalism. The organization was in the process of petitioning the federal government for a review of media ownership when the strike was called off.

Through its actions and electronic communications, the organization helped raise the profile of the strike and corporate concentration in the news media in Canada.

VII. Cellphones and Other Electronic Devices

Cellphones became a major weapon for orchestrating strikers' campaigns. They were used to communicate among people leafleting neighborhoods or advertisers and between strike headquarters and the picket line. The most mundane use was in maintaining regular delivery of leaflets to picketers when they ran out of literature to distribute to cars crossing the picket line. Under Alberta law, it was possible to slow traffic entering the *Herald* building only if the drivers were being leafletted. Cellphones provided security and flexibility. They ensured nobody had to be tied to a desk waiting for a phone call.

When Langan was locked up in a police van after being arrested for refusing to stop sitting in front of vans loaded with newspapers leaving the building, she used her cellphone from inside the van to stay in touch with strikers. "High-tech communications kept us close," she concluded.

Both sides also used video cameras to record alleged misbehavior by the company's security force or strikers that could be used when making arguments before the Alberta Labour Board. Langan said that the union started to use videotape after the company would "conveniently lose" videotape unfavorable to its security forces when presenting a case to the Labour Board.

She said there has never been a strike that was so well-documented photographically. Highly skilled photographers using both digital and film cameras caught every essential scene of the strike, providing images for the web site, and in one case evidence that a bloodied member of another union supporting *Herald* picketers at a rally outside the *Herald* building had been struck by a police officer. The photographs have been sent to the University of Calgary for archiving.

Computers, of course, were essential component of the strike. Stories written for the web site, leaflets or The Last Word were written at home and e-mailed to the union office.

Among the most unusual technological items used in the strike were Globo lights, large stage lights employed for dramatic effect on the *Herald* building. The building features the names of the *Calgary Herald* and *National Post* set in large letters on its building because both papers are printed on the premises. The building sits atop a hill near the intersection of two of Calgary's busiest thoroughfares, and can be seen by incoming planes flying overhead en route to Calgary International Airport.

The strikers "cancelled" the *Post* and *Herald* names by covering them with a lighted symbol of a circle with a diagonal line through it, the universal sign for "do not" or "forbidden." To achieve the effect, which provided a good visual for local television crews, a stencil was put over the Globo lights.

VIII. Conclusion

Exhausted by almost eight months of striking, the CEP members urged their union officers to take a radical proposal to the *Herald*: forget the seniority clause, which the company had maintained was the main stumbling block. Many union members believed that the *Herald* and Conrad Black didn't care about seniority and had picked it as an issue in full confidence that it was the one item no union would drop. But since nothing else was working, despite evidence the *Herald* was suffering severe circulation and corporate-image losses, it was time to call the employer's bluff. The company seemed to be taken by surprise at the CEP's abandoning of the cherished principle when union and company representatives met in front of an official of the Alberta government. But within a few days, Gaynor was saying publicly there were other issues in the way, not just seniority. Despite the innovative use of electronic communications during the strike, there was no hope of obtaining a settlement if the *Herald* wasn't forced to negotiate with the union. The provincial government, however, failed to enforce provisions of its weak labor laws that required "bargaining in good faith."

But the employer was finally getting into the mood to settle, although not by way of a collective agreement. In June 2000, strikers were given the choice of returning to work without their union or taking severance packages. Two-thirds of the strikers voted to take the money and find new careers. The remaining third could individually make a choice, to take the money or go back to work without union protection, albeit with a written promise from the company that their salaries wouldn't be cut. There was no guarantee they'd get precisely their old jobs back. The strike was lost.

The offer of packages came at the end of June, and the deal was sealed in July, 2000. About 20 employees decided to return to work, although several subsequently left. I was put on an evening shift, even though I am a mother who had always prior to the strike worked a day shift. Shannon Duncan Wells, a photographer, found that the *Herald* had created a special shift just for her, starting at midnight. When she quit and took the package, the shift was abandoned. Copy editor Bob McLennan also returned to work and left, citing unpleasant working conditions. In all cases, wages earned while the returning striker made up his or her mind were deducted from the severance package, meaning that they had worked for nothing. This, too, was communicated to ex-strikers via e-mail, vindicating their decision not to return to work.

Among city reporters, none returned. Editorial board member and columnist (and single mother) Naomi Lakritz returned, and took legal action against the *Herald* when she discovered she would no longer have either of her previous duties. Under the terms of the settlement, she can't discuss the outcome, but she is currently writing editorials and a column on the editorial pages of the paper.

Kevin Peterson, who left his position as *Herald* publisher and took a package after Conrad Black's Hollinger, Inc. bought the newspaper, claims both sides won. The *Herald* succeeded in getting rid of most of its senior newsroom staff members, thereby making room for new lower-paid staff, while the employees in turn got severance packages. While Peterson is popular with many strikers, his viewpoint underestimates the emotional and financial impact of an eight-month strike on strikers. It also ignores the fact that many of the strikers were not long-service employees, nor aging baby boomers — just young people who believed principles are worth fighting for.

It's extremely difficult to determine precisely how big an impact the strike had on the *Herald*, which continues to deny there was much negative effect at all. The battle for public opinion was a heated one, and thousands of people cancelled newspaper subscriptions.

Did the strikers win the battle for public opinion through high-tech communications, media coverage, and low-tech leafleting? The evidence is largely anecdotal. Many Calgarians still mention to ex-strikers that they have not renewed their subscriptions, ignoring the *Herald* or picking up the paper occasionally from newspaper boxes. An untold number resubscribed during the *Herald*'s aggressive post-strike circulation blitz, and thousands of others never considered cancelling their paper at all.

Quality in the newspaper is another factor that's difficult to measure. But there is absolutely no doubt that the *Herald* lost its long-time aspiration — which it had likely achieved in the decade before the strike — of being Western Canada's best newspaper. The senior reporters at the newspaper have been replaced by mostly junior or intermediate reporters who had little or no big-city experience, and the lack of depth in the newspaper has prompted cancellations of subscriptions from people who kept getting the *Herald* when it was in a union battle.

The failure of almost all strikers to return may have been one of the biggest surprises for the company, although it conducted often-unpleasant back-to-work interviews with all returning strikers and gave some of them second-rate jobs.

The *Herald* is in a rapidly growing city. One key measure of a newspaper's success is market penetration — the percentage of citizens who read the paper. The *Her-*

ald has undoubtedly suffered in this area, but that trend was under way before the strike. It no longer published stories boasting about its circulation numbers, although that was routine prior to the strike.

In the interview conducted with employees returning to work, Editor Peter Menzies mentioned to me that he was aware there were now 93 negative ambassadors in the community (former strikers). While the strikers lost, it was no valiant victory for the *Herald*. It will take the paper a decade to recover. Whether or not the strikers won the battle for public opinion with their web site or e-mail lists, the strike did see the *Herald* falter in one crucial area: the *Herald* ruined its "brand," the concept of total image for which such companies as Coca Cola and Microsoft spend hundreds of millions of dollars on advertising and public relations. Confidential *Herald* surveys conducted under former publisher Peterson but shared with staff, consistently showed the newspapers rated an A when it came to integrity. While several readers each month would question the accuracy of a story, or challenge an opinion piece, the newspaper's motives overall were recognized as being good.

When Conrad Black sent in publisher Dan Gaynor from St. Catharines, Ontario where he was best known for trying to break another fledgling union, he seemed unaware of the *Herald*'s credibility and good-will. With the *Herald* being put out by former strike-breakers and former replacement workers, many of whom had no previous links with the community, it's unlikely that the newspaper will quickly regain credibility with union readers such as nurses, teachers, and blue-collar workers. It is undeniable that electronic communications had an enormous impact on the strikers themselves. Unable to communicate on the picket line because of the company's electronic eavesdropping, they were still able to communicate openly and frequently through the web site and e-mail.

High-tech communications maintained solidarity in an unprecedented way. Strikers who were discouraged or thinking of returning to work were immediately identified from their communications or comments on the picket line and given support by other strikers. Information that leaked from within the building was communicated rapidly to all strikers via e-mail. Every development became the subject of an e-mail if it was intended for strikers' consumption only or a web story if a broader public was to be informed.

Could more have been done with electronic communications? Absolutely. In the last months of the strike, some strikers talked about putting out a cyber-newspaper on the web as an alternative to the *Herald*. By then, however, most strikers were too tired to become involved in such an initiative. Because of the strike's length, most newsroom strikers were freelancing and a few had found full-time employment.

The lack of a competing newspaper was a fatal problem for the union. It's not sufficient to call for a boycott without offering an alternative. Local business people, for instance, must have local business news about their competitors and their industry. National coverage is only part of the news equation for them, so the Toronto-based *Globe and Mail* couldn't replace the *Herald*.

Moreover, advertisers didn't have an alternative. To reach Calgary consumers in large numbers, they needed the *Herald* — whether for upscale products such as luxury cars, or for food, clothing, and real estate.

After the strike, a new business tabloid called the *Business Edge* was started by ex-strikers, with Rob Driscoll and publisher and Terry Inigo Jones as editor. Ex-strikers handle circulation and some ad sales — and they write virtually all of the content. The first issue appeared in November 2000, and by Spring 2001, it had expanded to a second city, Edmonton.

It has been proven that the expertise existed among the strikers to set up their own cyber-newspaper, or a traditionally printed one. Many strikers complained that picketing the *Herald* was mostly a waste of time. While they acknowledged the need for token pickets to deter unionized drivers and supporters from crossing the line, to ensure the *Herald* incurred large security costs, and to remind those inside the building that they were crossing a picket line, the strikers' presence day in and day out during the strike's early months did not, in the end, appear to be worth the effort.

Strikers' time was better served in e-mail campaigns and other high-tech initiatives designed to win over public opinion — especially when the battle was against a news baron operating internationally.

Although the CEP's Langan said the use of technology in the strike was groundbreaking, the union could have relied on it even more. When there is no legal solution available to force a company to sign a first contract with a union, the battles to hurt the corporation financially through reduced advertising dollars and circulation are the only ones that count.

Reference

Yearwood, Emily. "Conflict of Self-Interest." *Ryerson Review of Journalism* 13 (Spring 2001): 50–57.

12

Privacy, Technology, and Conflict: Emerging Issues and Action in Workplace Privacy

Anthony M. Townsend
Iowa State University

James T. Bennett
George Mason University

I. Introduction

Individual privacy rights in the public arena have received considerable attention over the past several months, beginning with a congressional inquiry into the rectitude of a variety of "red-light cameras" and moving quickly to concerns about the use of face- recognition software by municipalities concerned with potential criminal activity in public venues. Beyond the municipalities that had instituted these systems (and their allied corporate providers), there were relatively few supporters of these intrusive technologies. However, following a series of terrorist attacks (and near attacks) in the Fall of 2001, many Americans began to view some of the more intrusive measures (such as facial-recognition systems) as a necessary evil in pursuit of safety and national security.

While the events of the fall of 2001 may have moderated the public's disquietude about governmental surveillance, there is little indication that these events have changed public attitudes about more personal aspects of their privacy — particularly when that privacy is threatened not by the needs of national security, but rather by the profit motive of the organizations that employ them. The continuing efforts on the part of corporations to observe and control more employee behaviors have led to an increasingly adversarial atmosphere between employees and their organizations, with growing numbers of employees expressing concern about the level of privacy accorded them by their employer (Minehan, 1999; Arbetter, 1994). Because of the remarkable level of intrusion that has become possible — and which some firms have fully operationalized — some remediation, either by statute or through employee action in the workplace, will eventually begin to establish a more livable equilibrium between legitimate organizational interests in employee activities and employee expectations regarding an acceptable level of individual privacy.

II. Privacy and Technology Issues

Organizational technology-based privacy concerns center around three issues: first, concerns about individual privacy rights vis-à-vis telecommunications and information technologies; second, concerns about work place monitoring (including both intrusive performance monitoring as well as behavioral monitoring); and third, concerns regarding the security of individuals' personal information that has been collected by the company. While each of these issues may appear to be disparate in nature, they are united by a common theme — they are all empowered by revolutions in information technologies that have allowed organizations to collect information on their workers on a far broader scope and more detailed scale than was possible even a decade earlier. Although organizations have always sought to monitor performance and restrict unproductive employee behaviors, monitoring and information-gathering technologies have made it possible for organizations to observe and record the most minute details of an employee's organizational life — even when the employee is not physically present at the workplace. Thus, what was once a moderately irritating supervisory intrusion on an employee's workday — the boss looking over his or her shoulder — has become a paranoia-inducing organizational omniscience of every aspect of an employee's life.

Privacy and the Use of Telecommunications and Information Technologies. As an increasing number of employees at all organizational levels become active participants in a firm's telecommunications/information technology matrix, more employees will be exposed to the vicissitudes of corporate policies regarding system use. Organizations can — and, indeed, should — develop comprehensive organizational policies that address the use of telecommunications and information systems under their control (Whitman et al., 1999). Sound organizational policy protects the firm from a range of legal problems associated with system misuse or abuse (Townsend et al., 2000; Whitman et al., 1999; Aalberts et al., 1997). Under ideal circumstances, organizations create policy that encourages appropriate system use — toward the goal of enhancing firm productivity — while simultaneously discouraging inappropriate or illegal uses of the system that might expose the firm to significant financial liability.

While the firm's goal of effecting a maximally productive working environment drives its design of telecommunications and information systems, employees experience a very different orientation toward the system. Unlike other tools and machinery *within* the work environment, information and telecommunication technologies actually *become* the work environment, serving not only as the primary tools through which an employee accomplishes his or her work, but also serving as a primary mediator of employees' interactions with coworkers and clients. As such, information and telecommunications systems are both tool and context — defining both the nature of the work and the social environment in which it occurs.

This added role of the information/telecommunications system — of creating the work context and enabling the social processes of the workplace — differentiates the information/telecommunications system from previous workplace technologies and creates additional workplace issues in the process. Paramount among this new set of issues is that of how employees will use these systems. Given that the information/ telecommunications system has the potential for personal as well as organizational use (to a far greater degree than any other organizational tool), one of the most critical issues that must be addressed is how much personal use is to be permitted, what constitutes personal use, and most importantly, what level of privacy is afforded to both personal and professional uses of the system.

The issues surrounding privacy within the telecommunications and information system are not particularly new; employees and employers have long jostled over employees' use of the telephone in the workplace. From the employers' perspective, the telephone is a work tool that enhances employee productivity. Although the employee certainly understands that use, he or she also sees the telephone as a necessary connection to the private world outside the office. Recognizing employees' needs to monitor family and other personal matters, most employers allow limited use of the telephone for personal business, usually restricting issues such as calling area, duration, and frequency of personal communications.

What is "new" in the evolving organizational landscape, however, is the increased assimilation of so much of an employee's private life activity into systems that are supplied on the desktop. While the telephone (along with company mail) were systems that employees might use to conduct personal business, employee access to the web introduces a remarkable new range of potential personal uses that may legitimately interfere with productivity, or even expose the employer to legal action and financial liability (Townsend et al., 2000; Whitman et al., 1999).

In addition to providing new opportunities for personal use by employees, computer-based communications systems also create remarkably more robust means to monitor the content of employee communication. Unlike the telephone (or the mail), which required a deliberate intervention on the part of the employer to monitor the content of employee communication (i.e., through wiretaps or other forms of call-monitoring), computer-based communications (either through conventional e-mail or through web-based formats) necessarily archive all of the content of employees' communications — all of the communications of every employee will reside somewhere in the computer network and can be retrieved at will. In addition to archiving the content of employees' active communications (such as e-mail), the employer's computer also monitors — by default — all of the information that employees retrieve using their web access. What is particularly insidious about this, from the employee's perspective, is that so many of the transactions that take place across the web would have gone unnoticed if the employee had initiated those transactions in the workplace a decade earlier.

Before the introduction of the web, particularly into the workplace, an employee might take some personal time during the workday to pay bills, to catch up with friends by phone or by writing a letter or note, or to peruse a catalogue or two. Now that so many of these activities are web-enabled, the same set of employee activities leaves behind an indelible and highly detailed trail for the employer to follow.

At the crux of the information- and telecommunications-use issue is the relative difference as to who possesses an employee's personal communications. Prior to the advent of e-mail and the World Wide Web, most employee communications existed only transiently within the reasonable domain of the employer. An employee making a phone call, for instance, might well be using the employer's equipment and his or her communication might pass through the employer's possession (via the company's telephone system), but absent some intrusive and deliberate effort on the part of the employer (i.e., a wiretap), there was no permanent record of the content of the communication. For the employee who used work time to write out checks for bills or to look through merchandise catalogs, there was (absent direct supervisory observation) no record of any of these activities whatsoever. Now, the same activities generate a permanent set of records that are necessarily within the employer's possession. No deliberate intrusion into the communications system is necessary, nor is any direct supervisory observation; by using e-mail and web-based technologies, the employee self-generates his or her own monitoring reports.

Under current law, particularly at the federal level, employees have relatively few privacy rights when they use their employer's communications systems. Most federal law regarding the privacy rights of employees using their employer's information system is subsumed under the Electronic Communications Privacy Act of 1986, which specifically excludes employer-operated systems from the Act's privacy protections:

> Any telephone or telegraph instrument, equipment or facility, or any component thereof, (i) furnished to the subscriber or user by a provider of wire or electronic communications service in the ordinary course of its business and being used by the subscriber or user in the ordinary course of its business or furnished by such subscriber or user for connection to the facilities of such service in use in the ordinary course of its business . . . (18 USC §2510(5)(a)).

Finkin (1995) notes that this exemption is apparently being actively exploited by employers; as early as 1993, over 20 percent of organizations responding to a privacy questionnaire indicated that they engaged in searches of employees computer files, voice mail, and e-mail. Yamada (1998, p. 7) underscores the ubiquity of employers' invasions of employee privacy:

> Recent studies confirm that electronic surveillance of employees is popular and growing. According to a 1997 survey by the American Management Association, "[n]early two-thirds of employers record employee voice mail, e-mail, or phone calls, review computer files or videotape workers." Up to a quarter of those employers who do engage in electronic surveillance do not inform their employees. According to the survey, the most popular forms of surveillance are the following: recording phone numbers and monitoring length of calls (37%); videotaping employees at work (16%); storing and reviewing employees' e-mail (15%); storing and reviewing computer files (14%). A 1996 ACLU study on privacy in the

workplace reported that between 1990 and 1996, the number of workers subject to electronic monitoring increased from approximately 8 million to at least 20 million, and more likely, 40 million.

Clearly, employers have become substantially more intrusive regarding activities that employees might reasonably consider private. Although the justification for these intrusions may be genuinely based on a concern for firm performance, they nonetheless have created an atmosphere in which employees feel that they must pursue greater privacy protections.

Privacy and Technology-Based Work Monitoring. Although employees have no doubt always been chafed by unwelcome supervisory attention, the amount of supervisory attention was bounded by the supervisor's ability to be physically present to observe an employee's activities. Even the most intrusive of supervisory environments retained a fairly human scale and constituted an acceptable extension of the social interaction of employment.

New communications and information technologies now make it possible to observe, archive, and analyze an employees' work activities at a high level of detail. In addition to the communications archive discussed in the previous section, employees' access to files, keyboarding activity, and machine operations can be monitored with absolute precision in great detail, even at remote locations (Connolly, 2001). Long-haul trucking companies can, for instance, use GPS systems and vehicle monitoring systems to track truck drivers' speed, fuel use, route location, and even gear-shifting patterns, on a real-time basis as the truck moves across the country. The same kind of systems can be used to track outside salespeople and service workers. Even within the physical confines of a firm, elaborate locating systems, coupled with video monitoring equipment, can track and record employee movements.

The introduction of these systems have at their genesis the usually laudatory goals of promoting workplace safety, security, and enhancing productivity by reducing shirking. Unfortunately, many employees believe that these systems betray a level of mistrust on the part of their employers. They begin to see themselves as the inmates of a technological panoptikon. While there are some limits on the kinds of behavior that an employer can monitor — it must generally be work-related — the employees' perception that they are under increasing levels of observation is not delusional; firms really are spending more money on security and employee monitoring (Daniel, 1995).

Privacy and Personal Information. As is the case with telecommunications-use privacy and privacy issues that arise as a function of workplace monitoring, employee concerns with the firm's use of their personal information are not particularly new. Rather, what is different are the new ways that personal information is used and the level of detail of that information, both thanks to the introduction of technologies that can collect, archive, analyze, and transmit huge amounts of information. Personal information that was once relatively confined to a single physical organizational location — the personnel file — is now accessible through a much broader range of locations as the information is collected and stored electronically.

In addition to the wider potential access to personal information, there is a wider distribution of personal information beyond the company's boundaries, as information is shared with insurance companies, benefit providers, and with outsource support service providers, e.g., payroll service companies and human resources providers. The concern about such matters is twofold: First, employees are increasingly and justifiably worried about the sheer volume of information being compiled by the modern employer; and second, they are concerned that this enormous volume of information may be intentionally or unintentionally disseminated to parties who will misuse it.

Concern about the security of readily accessible, detailed, personal information is justified. Personnel files that may have once languished with the human resources department are now active organizational documents, many of which can be accessed by a variety of organizational and extra-organizational personnel. As a growing number of employers outsource a variety of support services, such as payroll, human resources, employee assistance program administration, etc., a larger pool of users necessarily have access to employee records.

III. Responding to Privacy Concerns

The increasing level of concern regarding this particular set of privacy issues has engendered responses from three different constituencies: statutory and legal responses, from state and federal legislatures, as well as from state and federal courts; organizational responses, wherein the firm itself addresses the privacy concerns; and, finally, employee-based responses, where employee organizations (such as unions) work to assure that employee privacy expectations are met. Each of these constituencies respond to privacy issues based on their own interests and the boundaries of their authority; taken together, they form the evolving legal and policy context in which employee privacy concerns are played out.

The Statutory/Legal Response. Both the courts and the legislature have historically addressed the issue of individual privacy and have been actively involved in defining privacy rights in an era of rapidly changing technologies. The passage of the Electronic Communications Privacy Act signals a significant intervention by the federal government into a rapidly evolving technological arena that had few specific guidelines as to what constituted reasonable privacy. While the government's response in this Act (and in subsequent amendments) has certainly been far-reaching, the government deliberately deferred to the right of a business organization to set its own privacy standards with regard to a significant body of information germane to the operation of the firm (Finkin, 1995; Decker, 1989). As noted earlier, the Act specifically excludes company-operated systems from its coverage, and the courts have generally held that employers have broad discretion to monitor employee communications that take place over employer-operated systems.

The government has pursued employee privacy interests in other matters; numerous bills regarding both employee and customer privacy are currently being considered by Congress (Radcliffe, 2001). Of particular note is the proposed Notice of Electronic Monitoring Act, which is expected to enjoy wide bipartisan support. Although the proposed Act will not restrict an employer's right to monitor, it will require that the monitoring be conducted under explicit conditions (Principe, 2001).

Although there is certainly an active legislative agenda directed toward privacy, most of the employment-law impact of these statutory initiatives is consequential to a broader main purpose. Most current statutory initiatives are directed toward the financial services and health care industries and only affect employee privacy in areas regarding financial and medical information (Sweat, 2001; Hall, 2001). Nonetheless, these types of initiatives begin to draw a set of boundaries around what a firm can do with employee information and help to focus attention on the privacy challenge. One of the most pressing statutory initiatives in this area is the Health Insurance Portability and Accountability Act (HIPAA), which will effectively require employers to abide by health care privacy protections. Although the Act is designed to regulate insurers and health services providers, employers will fall under the Act's jurisdiction because they contract for health services for their employees (Elswick, 2001). Since information systems that contain employee benefit information often have a variety of other associated employee data as well, the Act will require significant improvement to employers' overall personnel data security.

There is an additional imperative to statutorily resolve many workplace privacy issues that arises from actions taken by the European Union; the EU has passed extensive workplace privacy protection regulations requiring employers to disclose the full nature of their monitoring activities as well as describe its relevance to firm performance (Minehan, 1999; Henley et al., 1999). Even though the U.S. may not directly attempt statutory compliance with the EU directives, U.S.-based multinationals will be forced to comply with the EU regulations if they exchange employee information with EU-based operations.

The Organizational Response. While legislators (and the courts) stake out the statutory landscape of workplace privacy, organizations themselves have developed an active agenda to respond to variety of privacy concerns, some of which affect employee privacy. Although it may be argued that there is an ethical imperative for organizations to address employee privacy concerns (Lock et al., 1998), as Yamada (1998) has noted, the majority of firms have adopted a fairly intrusive posture with regard to all forms of monitoring. Where employers have begun to take an affirmative position with regard to privacy rights, and to employee privacy rights specifically, is in areas of information acquisition and distribution. Fueled in equal parts by consumer concerns and by the increasing threat of state and federal regulation, organizations have created "chief privacy officer" positions to demonstrate their commitment to protecting their customers' privacy (Hopper, 2000). Although the creation of these positions is clearly a response to customer concerns, the increasing awareness of the importance of maintaining the security of private information that follows from customer-oriented policies should have a salutary effect on the protection of employees' information as well.

Even though organizations may be loathe to relinquish their rights to monitor employees' on-the-job activities and compile detailed personal information about their employees, there are likely competitive incentives to limit these behaviors. Among professional employees in particular, many firms are finding that it is becoming more difficult to attract and retain well-qualified individuals. All else equal, many prospective employees will opt for firms that provide some assurances that their employees will not be intrusively monitored, that the firm will not compile unnecessary amounts of personal information, and that personal information will be held with the greatest possible security. Connolly (2001) recommends that firms at a minimum adopt a set of policies that delineate clearly how monitoring will be conducted. By making the process explicit, a firm defines appropriate system uses and work behaviors and provides employees with a clear set of expectations about their working environment (Whitman et al., 1998).

Privacy and Collective Action. Given the reluctance of firms to relinquish their right to monitor almost all aspects of employee activities, and given too the reluctance of the legislature to restrict that right, the most promising avenue for the establishment of privacy rights in the workplace will probably come from employee pressure. Employee privacy protections may well evolve as a key collective bargaining issue over the next decade, as larger numbers of employees are affected by privacy intrusions.

Interestingly, unions have (on occasion) been on the "wrong" side of the privacy challenge; unions have sought access to employee information that is considerably broader than what was needed to perform collective bargaining activity (Susser, 1986), and have even attempted to negotiate away fundamental employee rights to be free from excessive monitoring (Hatch and Hall, 2001). In the latter case, a Teamsters local negotiated an agreement that specifically allowed an employer to use surveillance in employee restrooms, which was a violation of state law. The Ninth Circuit Court of Appeals ruled that since the monitoring was impermissible under California law, the union could not negotiate a contract that permitted these illegal activities (Hatch and Hall, 2001).

In spite of these early missteps, according to Susser (1988) unions have begun to pursue employee privacy protections, particularly through legislative initiatives. Although Susser (1988) does provide some evidence of union initiatives to protect workplace privacy, our own review of the AFL-CIO's website (<www.aflcio.org>) indicates relatively little interest in workplace privacy issues, with the notable exception of a significant interest in protecting employees from intrusive drug testing and the privacy of medical information held by the company. Although the AFL-CIO website does not offer much discussion of personal privacy issues (beyond drug testing), a recent publication of the AFL-CIO, "Workers Rights in America" (AFL-CIO, 2001), underscores the emerging importance of personal privacy in the workplace. The publication presents the results of a large survey of working people and notes:

> While more than eight in 10 workers say the right to personal privacy at work is key, even larger proportions label specific employer privacy incursions as "unacceptable." Ninety-three percent say listening in on an employee's personal phone calls without the employee's knowledge is unacceptable, and 84 percent feel the same way about an employer using video cameras and tape recorders to monitor employees without their knowledge (AFL-CIO, 2001, p. 14).

Engaging workplace privacy issues, particularly with regard to job-site monitoring and telecommunications/information-system monitoring, presents a new set of challenges to labor organizations and may explain why they appear to have been slow to respond to these issues. As Grodin (1991) notes, there are relatively few constitutional protections that accrue to the workplace; thus broader societal protections of speech and against unreasonable search and seizure do not necessarily translate into workplace rights, and thus require either specific legislative prohibition or coverage within the collective bargaining agreement to become defensible.

Given the high regard that respondents placed on personal privacy in the workplace, there is little doubt that union leaders will recognize the importance of this issue both as a tenet of ongoing contract negotiations and as a potential rallying point for future union organizing efforts. If personal privacy protection is as salient an issue as this survey indicates, it may well become as critical an organizing issue as workplace justice has been in the past.

Although privacy issues provide a fecund opportunity for union intervention, some protections will be harder won than others. As has been the case with drug testing, employers are pressured to conduct the testing not only to increase productivity, but also to indemnify themselves from liability for actions taken by employees who are working while under the influence of drugs or alcohol. Employer monitoring of employee e-mail, for instance, not only ensures that employees are engaging in productive activities in the workplace, but it also helps indemnify the employer from illegal uses of the e-mail system by employees (Townsend et al., 2000; Aalberts et al., 1997). According to Townsend et al. (2000), employers are virtually required by federal statute to ensure that employees use telecommunications systems appropriately. Thus, the burden of this statutory requirement will make it difficult for unions to effectively negotiate contracts that completely eliminate a variety of employers' monitoring activities.

Given the employers' interest both in maintaining productivity and compliance with statutory obligations to ensure appropriate system use and employee safety, unions may be most effective in pursuing the following types of initiatives within the context of collective bargaining:

- *Creating Clear Privacy Boundaries:* Currently, employers can (within the limits of state and federal law) monitor employee communications and workplace activities with little or no notification. Unions could be effective in negotiating contractual specifications of what types of monitoring are permissible and how such monitoring will be effected. While employers may not willingly embrace the limitations imposed by these types of contract provisions, they do allow the employer to conduct the monitoring activities essential to effective operations. From the employees' perspective, the creation of clear boundaries allows them to work in an environment where monitoring and observation are bounded and predictable.

- *Establishing Privacy Procedures and Guidelines:* In addition to creating contractual determinations as to the types of employee activities that can be monitored, unions can work to develop contractual guidelines on how the monitoring will take place. There is a difference between e-mail being monitored for impermissible content by the IT staff, and employee e-mail being monitored by supervisory staff. Who does the monitoring, as well how the information gathered in monitoring activities is used, is a reasonable subject of negotiation between the parties. Unions should be looking to impose clear contractual guidelines as to who has access to employee e-mail and other information systems data, as well as how information gathered during monitoring is used in disciplinary procedures.

- *Protecting Personal Information:* The AFL-CIO survey underscores the fact that employees, like consumers, are very concerned about the security of their personal information. While employers certainly need to maintain a fairly extensive base of information about their employees, there is clearly an opportunity for unions to develop security guidelines to determine how employees' personal information is to be used and protected. Although there is increasing statutory protection afforded to employee records, contractual negotiations can more specifically detail who within the organization will have access to personal data and under what conditions; this may be particularly important to employees whose information may be shared with outsourced service providers (i.e., payroll services, insurers, etc.).

IV. Conclusion

Growing employee awareness of the degree to which their personal privacy is compromised in the workplace, particularly with regard to information/telecommunication-system use and work monitoring, has created an organizational and political climate that may yield significant restrictions on employee monitoring and on how employers maintain and distribute employees' personal information. While both federal and state governments have generally deferred to the right of the employer-as-owner to set conditions of employment that may include intrusions into employee privacy (Grodin, 1991), a number of statutory restrictions have been promulgated or proposed that will significantly expand employee privacy rights in the workplace. Additionally, it is probable that unions will aggressively assert employee privacy rights within the context of collective bargaining, potentially using employee dissatisfaction with privacy intrusions as a basis for organizing nonunion firms.

Given the inevitability of increasing protection of employee privacy, either through statute or negotiation, proactive firms should pursue privacy policies for their employees as aggressively as they have for their customers. Just as many firms avoided organization by developing effective progressive discipline systems (which obviated a key issue for union organizers), firms that develop comprehensive and attractive employee privacy policies will promote greater worker satisfaction and will effectively remove the privacy issue from any organizing initiative. Additionally, by developing attractive privacy policies, firms will be better able to attract and retain better-quality workers in a competitive labor market.

References

Aalberts, Robert J., Anthony M. Townsend, Michael E. Whitman, and L.H. Seidman. "A Proposed Model Policy for Managing Telecommunications-Related Sexual Harassment in the Workplace." *Labor Law Journal* 48 (1997): 616–26.

AFL-CIO. *Workers Rights in America: What Worker Think about Their Jobs and Employers.* Washington, D.C.: AFL-CIO, September, 2001.

Arbetter, Lisa. "Privacy Perspective." *Security Management* 38 (August 1994): 14.

Connolly, P.J. "Activity Monitors Raise Ethical and Legal Questions Regarding Employee Privacy." *Infoworld* 13 (February 12, 2001): 57.

Daniel, Teresa A. "Electronic and Voice Mail Monitoring of Employees: A Practical Approach." *Employment Relations Today* 22 (Summer 1995): 1–9.

Decker, Kurt H. *A Manager's Guide to Employee Privacy: Laws, Policies, and Procedures.* New York: Wiley, 1989.

Elswick, Jill. "Privacy Rules Leave Employers in the Dark." *Employee Benefit News* 15 (September 1, 2001): 1–2.

Finkin, Mathew W. *Privacy in Employment Law.* Washington, D.C.: Bureau of National Affairs, 1995.

Grodin, Joseph R. "Constitutional Values in the Private Sector Workplace." *Industrial Relations Law Journal* 13 (Winter 1991): 1–36.

Hall, Mark. "The Politics of Privacy." *ComputerWorld* 35 (August 13, 2001): 32–33.

Hatch, Diane D. and James E. Hall. "Court Now Says Privacy Claims Are Not Preempted." *Workforce* 79 (September, 2001): 90.

Henley, Jon, John Hooper, Ian Traynor, and Stephen Bate. "Who's Reading Over Your Shoulder?" *The Guardian*, January 25, 1999, p. 10.

Hopper, D. Ian. "Corporations Hiring Chief Privacy Officers." *Fairfax (Va.) Journal*, July 12, 2000.

Lock, Karen, Sue Conger, and Effy Oz. "Ownership, Privacy, and Monitoring in the Workplace: A Debate on Technology and Ethics." *Journal of Business Ethics* 17 (April 1998): 653–62.

Minehan, Maureen. "Debate on Workplace Privacy to Likely Intensify." *HRMagazine* 44 (January 1999): 142.

Principe, Loretta W. "Federal Law on Employee Privacy Will Likely Open the Litigation Floodgates." *Infoworld* 13 (March 23, 2001): 64.

Radcliff, Deborah. "Privacy: The Liability Link." *Computerworld* 35 (August 27, 2001): 33–34.

Susser, Peter A. "Union Access to Company Information." *Personnel Administrator* 31 (April 1986): 32–36.

———. "Modern Office Technology and Employee Relations." *Employment Relations Today* 15 (Spring 1988): 9–18.

Sweat, Jeff. "Privacy." *InformationWeek*, August 20, 2001, pp. 30–35.

Townsend, Anthony M., Robert J. Aalberts, and Michael E. Whitman. "Employer Liability under the Communications Decency Act: Developing an Effective Policy Response." *Employee Responsibilities and Rights Journal* 12 (March 2000): 39–46.

Whitman, Michael E., Anthony M. Townsend, and Robert J. Aalberts. "Considerations for an Effective Telecommunications-Use Policy." *Communications of the ACM* 42 (June 1999): 101–108.

Whitman, Michael E., Anthony M. Townsend, and Robert J. Aalberts. "The Communications Decency Act Is Not As Dead As You Think." *Communications of the ACM* 42 (January 1999): 15–17.

Yamada, David C. "Voices from the Cubicle: Protecting and Encouraging Private Employee Speech in the Post-Industrial Workplace." *Berkeley Journal of Employment and Labor Law* 19 (Summer 1998): 1–59.

13

Privacy and Profitability in the Technological Workplace

*Dennis R. Nolan**
University of South Carolina

I. Introduction

The labor law and human resources literature of the 1990s was replete with warnings that employers used modern technology to keep an eye on their employees. Computers monitored work performance, we were told; software programs tracked Internet usage; supervisors read employees' e-mail; and soon "smart badges" would reveal our exact location at every instant. These efforts even touched employees' lives away from work, as some employers searched the contents of computers they provided to telecommuting workers. Many of these articles and books adopted distinctly unscholarly tones of high dudgeon and alarm (Lee, 1994; Gantt, 1995).

The warnings were true, but they no longer surprise anyone. By now every sensible employee knows or should know that employers do or at least may use all the tools of modern technology to supervise and direct them. Indeed, smart employers go out of their way to tell employees about company policies on monitoring and on use of communications systems precisely in the hope that doing so will improve productivity and prevent problems. Nor is it any longer surprising that the law provides little protection for employees. Despite some initial uncertainty, despite volumes of academic criticism, federal and state courts soon reached a strong consensus that constitutions, statutes, and the common law provide few remedies for those subject to employer inquiry and observation. Legislatures have not, for the most part, changed those rules.

Where do those developments leave the commentator on workplace privacy? Simply repeating the old formulas would be pointless overkill. Even the recommendations for new judicial or legislative rules have a tired familiarity. Perhaps it is time to take a step back for the sake of perspective, to recount just what employers do, why they say they do it, and to compare their objectives with their methods. Because many of the asserted reasons relate to the law, it will also be necessary to outline how little the law requires or forbids and how much it permits. But the law, we shall see, is really a fairly minor player in this pursuit. Policies — business policies and personnel policies and even political policies — are far more important.

Those matters — employers' practices, the explanations for those practices, and the controlling legal requirements and prohibitions — comprise the heart of this exploration. The following three sections cover each in turn. The final substantive section tries to distill lessons from the evidence. It addresses the oft-asked question, What Then Must Be Done?

II. What Do Employers Do?

Observation of employees is nothing new. Supervisors have always monitored their subordinates to make sure they worked steadily and well. All that has changed with the advent of the computer are the techniques and effectiveness of the observations. (I am primarily concerned herein with electronic monitoring; video and audio recording represent older and less controversial technologies, ones whose major issues were long ago resolved.) The new methods include monitoring work performance by means of software programs that record computer use, customer service contacts, and the like; limiting and monitoring employees' use of e-mail systems; limiting and monitoring employees' Internet use; and examining the stored contents of employees' computers. A recent survey by the American Management Association (AMA, 2002) provides a convenient look at the prevalence of these modern practices.[1]

Averages aside, individual employers' policies on privacy and on use of electronic technology resources vary widely in detail and theme. Some provide lengthy rules that emphasize restrictions on employee activity (e.g., Archdiocese of Baltimore, 2002; Florida State University, 2002). Florida State's Information Technology policy, for instance, prints out to nine pages, most of which are devoted to detailed lists of requirements and prohibitions. The brief section on "Privacy and Security" first states that the University cannot guarantee that it will retain all critical data. The only other paragraph under that heading paradoxically provides that "unauthorized access" to computer files, "either by direct examination or by automated searching," will not be permitted "unless there is reasonable cause and access is approved by the director" of the facility supporting the system — unauthorized access, in other words, is prohibited unless it is authorized.

Other employers have briefer policies that give more weight to employees' privacy. A good example is the University of Southern California (2002), which bluntly states that it will not interfere with communications merely because they offend some viewers:

Section 3. Responsibilities and Privacy
3.1 . . . The university cannot and will not attempt to protect individuals from material that may be offensive to them, except in cases of violation of the law, university policy, or standards, and in these cases only where technically feasible. Individuals making use of elec-

tronic communications are warned that they may willingly or unwillingly receive or discover material they find offensive. The university will not establish additional standards, beyond those that are legally relevant, for discussion or language in electronic communication, including all forms a [sic] digital media. . . .

The University of Michigan's policy is similar: "Censorship is incompatible with the goals of an institution of higher education. Research and instruction take many forms. Therefore, information accessible on the network may not be restricted through censorship" (University of Michigan, 1997).

Still other employers, for example my own University of South Carolina, say little one way or another. South Carolina's computer policies (University of South Carolina, 1995, 2002) deal primarily with access and security issues; while they warn that sending obscene messages is illegal under state law, the focus is on the proper procedure for reacting when one receives such a message. They say nothing about monitoring or content restrictions.

Computerized Monitoring of Work Performance. Use of computers to monitor employee performance is a natural extension of earlier methods for tracking employees' work. Consider a simple assembly line. As far back as Henry Ford's time and probably before, supervisors stayed near employees and watched their work. Piecework systems made precise recording more important, so workers themselves often completed the necessary records or made appropriate notes on tickets attached to work orders. New machines enabled employers to scan such records into computer data bases. From there it is just a short step to having employees enter the information into computers themselves, so that their effort and results could be tracked automatically. The differences between traditional monitoring by supervisors and modern monitoring by computers is thus one of style, not of kind. To be sure, computers don't nod as often as supervisors do, but it would be hard to argue that employees had a right to inefficient supervision.

Relatively few employees today work on traditional assembly lines. Many more work at computer terminals, handle telephone calls, make deliveries, or sell hamburgers or televisions in retail operations. Continuous monitoring in those cases is simple. Software programs can record and analyze the number of keystrokes, the percentage of time the computer is used, the number and duration of calls received, the time of each delivery, and the value of sales. Supervisors, who may not even be within sight, can track employees' performance by the minute. Software programs can even alert employees about their performance compared to stated expectations or to their co-workers' activities.

A decade ago, this seemed vaguely Orwellian. Some writers even warned about the developing "electronic sweatshop" in which employers would constantly raise demands based on their ability to determine what the most efficient employees could do (Boehmer, 1992; Lee, 1994). Today computer monitoring is standard practice in many industries, including telecommunications, insurance, and marketing and customer care departments of retailers and service providers. According to the AMA survey, 43 percent of employers record telephone statistics (time spent and numbers called) while nearly 19 percent record computer use (time logged on, keystroke counts and the like). No doubt many employees work harder or more consistently today than they did with less supervision, but their additional work has not yet produced the predicted "sweatshop."

One new development, however, is that these modern monitoring practices even touch professionals who have long been exempt from close scrutiny. Managed-care providers, for example, require detailed records of doctors' consultations with patients, tests ordered, prescriptions written, and so on. Lawyers routinely and carefully track time spent on the telephone or on Westlaw for each client, both for internal purposes and to provide accurate records for client billing. All such records are either entered directly into a computer or are promptly transcribed. All can be analyzed by computer for later review by employers or others. Comparable monitoring methods affect other professions as well. Not only is computerized monitoring more efficient than older styles of supervision, it is also more far-reaching.

Limiting and Monitoring E-Mail. E-mail is now a universal method of business communication, more common in many workplaces than telephones were just a few years ago. Like telephones, e-mail systems are subject to abuse by employees. Someone who formerly called a friend or family member to chat for a few minutes during the work day may now just exchange e-mails. And as with telephones, employers have tried to monitor and control e-mail use. E-mail monitoring ranges from innocuous to absurd, with some rational activity in between.

Sophisticated e-mail systems automatically store incoming and outgoing messages, so mere recording of transmissions is not a serious privacy issue. In fact, it can even be a convenient way for senders and receivers alike to retrieve needed communications. Privacy concerns arise only if someone else reviews one's stored e-mail messages. The AMA survey reports that nearly 47 percent of employers did so in 2001, more than double the 1998 percentage. Given the enormous volume of e-mail messages, however, employer review must either be sporadic, narrowly targeted, or restricted to a small sampling.

As with telephones, employers have found personal use of e-mail almost impossible to control. Most have resigned themselves to allowing some personal e-mail use, just as they permit some personal telephone calls. Florida State University, for example, recognizes that "Occasional, incidental personal use of IT resources is permitted" subject to certain limits. Some, though, still try to prohibit all nonbusiness use of the employer's e-mail system. The Archdiocese of Baltimore limits "personal use of the Internet Facilities and equipment to that which is incidental to the User's official assignments and job responsibilities."[2]

When e-mail was new, an absolute prohibition on personal use might have seemed feasible; now it certainly does not. Separating business and personal messages is no easy task. When communicating with co-workers, suppliers, and customers, employees often mix personal topics with professional ones; indeed, they may not perceive any bright line separating the categories. Routine employer review of e-mails might not disclose which is which, and anything more than routine review would require more managerial time and effort than the risks of lost work time would justify. Moreover, a blunt prohibitory approach or widespread monitoring could easily create morale problems and would certainly pose difficult enforcement decisions (Mignin et al., 2002).

More limited employer use of stored e-mails — for example, as part of an investigation into alleged fraud or harassment — makes more sense on both sides. For employers, it is far less costly than routine review, and far more likely to produce useful results. For employees, it means that few of their messages will ever be seen by a manager.

As an alternative or as a supplement to active monitoring of e-mail, some employers use filters that detect and delete messages containing "improper" words, or else alert and warn employees when such words are detected. When used simply as a caution to employees, such computer "flags" might make sense. An occasional alert might deter employees from using insulting or offensive language. Deterrence is one major reason why many employers put "splash screens" on office computers that restate some computer policies every time an employee boots up.

Some of these programs, however, are simply silly. One recent newspaper report described software used at a North Carolina high-tech company. This "cyber-censor" blocks e-mails containing offensive words. "Instead of the whole message, the sender receives a list of the swear words it contains, along with an explanation (e.g., 'dirty word' or 'sexual discrimination') of why they are offensive" (*Independent Weekly*, 2002, p. 3). Like most other computer filters, this one had some strange quirks that caused it to ignore some offensive language while flagging some perfectly harmless terms.[3] Rosen (2000, pp. 57-58) reports that George Washington University's law school, where he teaches, mistakenly installed an e-mail censorship system on computers in the library. "Students who typed the word 'drugs' on their university e-mail accounts . . . were automatically logged off the network with a stern warning."

The inaccuracy of e-mail and Internet screening programs is legendary. Every reader subject to screening could probably supply comparable examples. One has to wonder whether the benefits are sufficient to outweigh the inconvenience caused by the errors, even leaving aside the harm to an employer's image caused by clumsy screening.

Even when employers themselves do not read employees' e-mail messages, others might. In several recent instances, journalists and litigants have used state open-records laws to gain access to messages that senders never thought would go beyond their intended recipient. After a University of North Carolina at Wilmington professor, using his university computer, criticized a student's attacks on America's foreign policy on the Middle East, the student accused him of defaming and intimidating her. She sought copies of the professor's e-mail messages. University administrators reviewed his correspondence to determine if any were "public records." They decided none was, so they released only a log rather than the complete messages. Even so, the professor's correspondence was viewed by unanticipated people, and the prying student learned at least the addressees and times of the messages. A case in Tennessee was even more intrusive. A local newspaper obtained and published e-mail messages between the University of Tennessee's former president and a subordinate with whom he apparently had an affair. Some of the messages were so intimate that one blushes to read them, not that questions of taste would limit a modern newspaper.

Both of these cases are described in Foster (2002). The title of her article, "Your E-Mail Message to a Colleague Could Be Tomorrow's Headline," aptly sums up the current situation for local government employees. Private sector workers are not so exposed to the scrutiny of outsiders, but even their communications are reachable in the course of litigation or other investigations.

Limiting and Monitoring Internet Usage. Widespread employee access to the Internet is a newer phenomenon. As a result, employer monitoring was late in arriving. By 2001, however, over 62 percent of the AMA respondents monitored their employees' Internet use, up from 54 percent the previous year. The software programs available for Internet monitoring are simple and revealing. They can bar access to certain sites, alert employees that the accessed site is prohibited or questionable under the employer's policy, or create a record for later investigation by the employer's information technology staff. One program informs employees that their attempt to access a certain site has been reported to the company's computer help desk. An employee with a legitimate explanation for the attempted access could then contact the help desk for permission. Those without a legitimate reason could be warned or disciplined. Net Tracker, a program sold by Computer Age Co., provides daily reports identifying every employee who accessed improper sites. If an employer wishes to investigate further, it can produce a detailed list of every site the employee visited and the time spent at each. With very little effort, the employer can even print out the very pages viewed by the employee. As evidence in litigation or arbitration, the results can be devastating.

The primary target of this monitoring, intentionally or otherwise, seems to be the employee who accesses pornographic web sites. Virtually all of the reported court and arbitration cases involved such activities. Spending work time shopping, gambling, planning a personal trip, playing solitaire, and reading lawyer jokes online is just as costly to an employer as viewing pornography, but the published cases seldom show discipline for those activities. Only sex sites, it seems, draw serious discipline. Perhaps it is just easier for employers and monitoring software to identify sexually oriented web sites as being distinctly unrelated to work. Their names alone tell a story. More likely, as the next section suggests, employers' concerns extend beyond lost time to questions of morality, and morality is far more often concerned with sex than with shopping.

Internet filters are at least as problematic as e-mail filters: both are over-inclusive and under-inclusive. A filter imposed by the Loudon County, Virginia public library was so broad that it blocked access to harmless sites run by Zero Population Growth and the American Association of University Women (Rosen, 2000, p. 85). A Virginia law restricted state employees, even university professors, from accessing or storing sexually explicit material on state-owned computers. Although a federal district court struck down the ban as a violation of the First Amendment, an appellate court ultimately found the ban constitutional (*Urofsky v. Gilmore*, 2000). Similar restrictions have been upheld elsewhere (e.g., *Loving v. Boren*, 1997). As even high school students have demonstrated to their librarians, technologically skilled users have little difficulty evading filters. Still, their very existence may deter some misuse.

Examining Employees' Computer Files. Reviewing employees' computer files is much less common than the other forms of surveillance. Just over a third of the AMA respondents reported doing so in 2001, although the practice had nearly doubled since 1998. This may be surprising, given that individual computers are almost as "sticky" as e-mail systems. Many people still believe that deleting a file means that no one will ever see it again. They can be unpleasantly surprised to learn that almost nothing short of reformatting one's hard drive will truly eliminate a file. Widely available computer tools can locate and restore most supposedly deleted files.

Why then is review of stored files so much less common than other forms of monitoring? For one thing, reviewing hard drives is much more labor intensive than using an automatic filter on Internet usage. Employees may have thousands of files on their computers. File names may not obviously indicate contents, and there are simple ways to hide files from superficial monitoring. Unless one has a specific objective in mind and knows how to find the desired information, the chance of finding evidence of improper computer use would seldom be great enough to justify the effort — the game simply wouldn't be worth the candle. Moreover, even though employees' stored files on the employer's computer are legally no more private than their e-mail or Internet records, employees and employers alike might well regard hard-drive searches as more intrusive.

III. Why Do They Do It?

Employers offer — or writers offer on their behalf — several reasons for these sorts of investigations and restrictions. In addition, there seem to be a few plausible but dubious or even illegal unadmitted explanations. The "public" reasons center on profitability concerns, worries about loss of confidential information or compromising computer security, and fear of liability for employees' misuse of computers and communications systems (Mignin et al., 2002, p. 15). The "private" reasons include curiosity, morality, and union avoidance.

Profitability. Employers' profitability concerns involve the costs of the equipment and systems used by employees for non-work purposes and the time they lose from their duties. Equipment costs are impossible to estimate but likely to be extremely small. Once an employer has purchased a computer and necessary peripherals for an employee, employee misuse will not easily contribute to the equipment's depreciation. Cars and trucks rapidly deteriorate with use; computers normally don't. Obsolescence is a far more common reason than overuse for having to replace electronic equipment.

System costs from employee misuse are surely greater than equipment costs. Even so, the marginal cost of each additional e-mail message or Internet visit is trivial, far less than the cost of one personal long-distance telephone call. Only if large numbers of employees frequently used a large amount of bandwidth would the system costs of e-mail or Internet misuse be substantial (Kesan, 2002, pp. 314-15).

The real cost of such misuse comes from wasted time (Kesan, 2002, p. 314). While there are no hard figures available, the loss of work time while employees send personal messages or conduct personal business online must far exceed the minutes spent in the pre-computer age around the proverbial water cooler. One recent report indicated that half of all online shopping takes place at work (Mignin et al., 2002, p. 23). Another survey found that nearly a quarter of the online communications at responding companies was not work related. The most commonly visited web sites were those dealing with news, sex, investments, entertainment, and sports (Kovach et al., 2000, p. 295, citing Garofalo, 1998). It is therefore especially interesting that the reported cases do not show discharge or serious discipline simply for wasting time on non-work messages or sites. It may be that lesser actions such as counselings, which are not typically litigated or arbitrated, keep the problem to tolerable levels. Combine wasting time with sex, however, and employers react more strongly.

Security. An oft-cited justification for monitoring and system restrictions is the fear that employees will intentionally or inadvertently disclose confidential information, download or spread computer viruses, or otherwise compromise computer security. The explanation is plausible, at least until one tries to match it up to the means used. Unless managers consistently, thoroughly, and simultaneously review their employees' e-mails and Internet usage, monitoring could not prevent security problems. Screening programs do not distinguish between confidential and nonconfidential information. Viruses can and usually do arrive on any download, even those that sound innocuous. Virus scans are more effective and less intrusive "inoculations" than are a supervisor's eyes. Carefully restricting access to an employer's own confidential files or computer programs will do far more good than trying to read e-mails or block specific web sites. To put it in other words, the chosen tool is not likely to complete the task.

Fear of Legal Liability for Employee Misconduct. Three types of employee misuse of electronic communications systems and computers threaten employers with potential liability. First, employees may use these systems for their personal financial gain. The problem is most common in financial services businesses like investment companies and banks. Second, employees might use the employer's facilities to violate intellectual property laws by copying or distributing protected material such as software programs, movies, and music. Third and perhaps most importantly, employee misconduct might contribute to sex or race discrimination, particularly by fostering a "hostile work environment." These risks would exist even without computers, but the technological workplace exacerbates the problems by making violations so easy. A stockbroker, for instance, could shift a client's funds with a few clicks; there is no need even to forge a check. Copying videos or songs is now simpler than photocopying a text book used to be. Offensive jokes and cartoons that used to be passed hand to hand can now show up in a company-wide message.

Again, however, the literature of actual cases shows few disciplines for financial or copyright abuse. There have been no cases comparable to the litigation brought a few years ago by textbook publishers against a major photocopying concern that helped professors create course materials without the burden of getting copyright permissions. Even within the hostile work environment category, sexually oriented e-mails and downloadings prompt discipline and litigation far more often than, say, racist communications. It is not clear why this should be so. Perhaps sexual activity, a primal force, is more pervasive than racism, or perhaps women are more likely than racial minorities to perceive and challenge a hostile work environment. Perhaps employees complain to employers more readily about the former than about the latter. More likely, sexual materials, particularly graphic materials, are of wider interest and thus are distributed more widely; if so, they naturally would draw more managerial attention.

Curiosity and Morality. Employers are not likely to admit to less "business-like" explanations for monitoring or restricting employee e-mail and Internet use. After reviewing the cases and the literature, however, it is hard to escape the conclusion that some employers are simply curious, voyeuristic, or moralistic about their employees' conduct. The monitoring methods they use are so ill-suited to achieving other objectives that one has to be suspicious of their real motives.

The predominance of discipline for sex-related communications enhances that suspicion. More people use employer-provided e-mail and Internet service for other sorts of personal purposes, yet only those whose usage somehow involves sex seem to get fired. Fear of liability for creating a hostile working environment does not completely explain that disproportion. Most of the reported discharge cases involve either a single individual's Internet usage or communications between consenting adults, not complaints by unintended viewers. The chance that sensitive employees may inadvertently see such private communications may partially explain employers' concentration on these offenses but, at least in light of the minimal risks discussed in the next section, their responses look like overkill. Most of the reported arbitration cases mention violation of an Internet policy as the reason for discipline, not vicarious liability.

Suppose instead that some employers simply want to know what employees are up to. That would explain routine monitoring even when there are few practical risks of liability. In the same way, if some employers think that employees exchanging dirty jokes and looking at *Penthouse* Playmates is immoral, while keeping in touch with old friends or buying DVDs is not, both their methods and their reactions to discoveries make sense. They may logically punish the one but not the other.

But the search for a single explanation is unfairly reductionist. No doubt most employers act out of a host of motives, some real, some exaggerated, some questionable, and some quite unconscious. Curiosity and morality may simply be among the questionable or unconscious kinds. Even so, they could enhance employers' eagerness to adopt and enforce policies dictated by other, more legitimate considerations.

Union Avoidance. No smart employer will ever admit to using its communications policies to interfere with employees' rights to unionize. Nevertheless, as Malin and Perritt (2000) have shown, some do just that. Restrictive policies can be overt (as by prohibiting messages about unions or working conditions) or more subtle (for example, by prohibiting all non-work messages with the specific intent of preventing union-related ones). Monitoring for union-related messages or web sites or for other communications that would fall under the National Labor Relations Act's protection of "concerted activities for . . . mutual aid or protection" (Section 7) would also violate the law.

The touchstones for NLRA Section 7 analysis are intent and unequal treatment. Any rules adopted specifically to inhibit collective activity would run afoul of that section; so would facially neutral rules that are enforced unequally. While less clear, it is at least arguable that e-mail communications on the employee's non-work time are entitled to

212 Information Technology and the World of Work

the same protection as face-to-face communications, at least unless the employer can demonstrate a valid business reason for restricting e-mail communications more strictly than other forms of speech. If so, that would mean that under the NLRA, the employer could not lawfully prohibit communications during employees' free time. Because there is usually no measurable marginal cost to an individual message sent and received on the employees' own time, articulating a legitimate justification for a total ban would be difficult.

Thus an employer concerned solely about costs and efficiency might lawfully permit only business-related e-mail and Internet use during working hours. Permitting some nonbusiness uses during work time while prohibiting employee complaints about working conditions, in contrast, would certainly violate Section 7. Restricting e-mails during non-work hours with no demonstrable efficiency reason might also be illegal.

IV. What Does the Law Require, Forbid, and Permit Employers to Do?

Because employers primarily cite legal rules as the main justification for monitoring and restricting their employees' electronic communications, some discussion of the law is essential. It is not necessary or desirable here to parse all the statutes and cases. Others, notably Finkin (1995, 2002), have already done so well and at great length. Rather, a brief summary of the most significant points should suffice. In general, the law puts very few obligations on employers but allows them wide freedom. Accordingly, employers can largely choose how much or how little supervision of employee communications they will employ.

Legal Requirements. No law specifically obliges employers to evaluate employees' work by means of a computer, inspect their files, or monitor their e-mail or Internet activities. Many legal rules, however, place the employer at risk because of employee misconduct. Four clear examples include liability for employees' tortious activity, for their violations of copyright, trademark, and trade secret laws, for supervisory discrimination, and for employee-created work environments that are hostile to women, racial minorities, or other protected groups.[4]

(1) Under the doctrine of *respondeat superior*, employers can be liable for harms caused by an employee's wrongful act if the act occurred within the employee's "scope of employment" (an amorphous term to which courts have given broad meaning) and if the employer knew or should have known of the wrongful act (Ishman, 2000, p. 125). If a brokerage employee manipulates stock prices by spreading false rumors and the employer has reason to know about the activity, the employer might be liable to those defrauded, as Merrill Lynch seems to be learning as this is written. If a bank employee misappropriates a client's funds and the bank should have known about the thefts, the bank itself might be liable.
(2) If employees infringe copyrights or trademarks, the employer could be vicariously liable even without actual knowledge if it had the right to supervise the employees and had a direct financial interest in the infringing activities. The liability would be even clearer if it knew of, induced, or contributed to the infringing conduct (Ibid., p. 135).
(3) Direct workplace discrimination does not require a computer. Supervisors can refuse to hire or deny a promotion often without a word; they can trade benefits for sexual favors without a keyboard. Nevertheless, e-mail correspondence can provide both plaintiffs and employers with evidence of misconduct. Monitoring e-mails might therefore be one way for employers to detect and cure problems before they rise to the level of a lawsuit.

(4) Employers' greatest vicarious liability worry today stems from the possibility that employees may create a "hostile work environment" that would amount to a form of sex or race discrimination. The relevant statutes, most importantly Title VII of the Civil Rights Act of 1964, were reactions to commonly understood forms of discrimination, such as refusal to hire or promote people because of their sex and race. They did not expressly address sexual harassment. In *Meritor Savings Bank, FSB v. Vinson* (1986), the Supreme Court first held that sexual harassment could also violate Title VII. Its rationale was that some harassment creates a work environment that limits women's employment opportunities just as severely as the older forms of discrimination. The Court suggested that employers could reduce their exposure by establishing procedures for preventing or redressing such harassment. Among the types of once-tolerated conduct that could contribute to a hostile work environment are unwanted physical contact, sexual propositions, innuendo, foul language, gender-related jokes, and the display of obscene material.

Not every offensive act or word constitutes actionable harassment. In the usual legal formulation, the conduct must be "sufficiently severe or pervasive to alter the conditions of the victim's employment and create an abusive working environment," *Meritor Savings Bank, FSB v. Vinson*, 477 U.S. 57, 67 (1986); see also *Harris v. Forklift Systems, Inc.*, 510 U.S. 17, 21 (1993). Isolated or minor incidents may become evidence of a discriminatory environment but usually will not by themselves prove its existence (Finkin, 2002, p. 147).[5] The courts have not yet turned the anti-discrimination laws into a generalized code of workplace civility. Nevertheless, e-mail messages and other forms of communication, especially when combined with other evidence, can become sufficiently severe as to expose the employer to liability. For example, in *Blakey v. Continental Airlines* (N.J., 2000), the court held that an employer could be liable for a hostile work environment arising from allegedly defamatory statements on the employer's electronic bulletin board.

In two 1998 cases, *Burlington Industries v. Ellerth* and *Faragher v. City of Boca Raton*, the Supreme Court refined the law about an employer's potential responsibility for sexual harassment. It held that an employer is automatically liable for a supervisor's harassment that produces tangible job consequences, but that it might escape liability for harassment without such consequences if it promulgates and enforces a suitable sexual harassment policy and if the victim failed to use the policy to correct the errant behavior. Prudent employers reacted to these cases by prohibiting and punishing communications and conduct that might offend members of protected groups. That obviously includes overtly harassing communications but some employers now ban even relatively harmless speech and activity. Some (Rosen, 2000, pp. 81-82) would say that they have even overreacted to the point of "prohibiting far more speech than the law actually forbids."

These developments in sex discrimination law, along with extensions to the law of race discrimination, directly relate to the present topic. Employers understandably fear that offensive e-mails might later be evidence of a hostile work environment, or that unintended employees might inadvertently view offensive Internet sites accessed by less sensitive employees. To prevent some offenses and to establish their bona fides under *Ellerth and Faragher*, many employers have adopted or strengthened their prohibitions against sex-related messages and Internet use. The same developments and responses also help to explain why those forms of computer abuse draw more stringent punishments than other forms that simply waste work time.

In sum, risks of legal liability, particularly for harassment by supervisors or co-workers, give employers a strong incentive to prevent, discover, and correct employee misconduct, whether or not that misconduct involves computers. As plausible as this explanation for strict control of communications systems might seem at first glance, the solutions do not always match up to the actual risks. Leaving harassment issues aside for a moment, the other potential risks do not require general screening programs. Banks and brokerages might need to monitor their electronic communications with customers just as they randomly monitor telephone calls to insure quality of service. Implementing a screening program to detect arguably offensive words does not contribute measurably to that objective, and customer protection has little or nothing to do with the question of Internet access. Copyright infringement and comparable offenses are a little different because they could involve both Internet and e-mail use, and also stored computer files.

Once again, though, generalized screening programs seem more intrusive than necessary. Random monitoring or, in the case of video and music downloads, a narrow screening system for those uses would address the plausible risks while not otherwise encroaching on employees' privacy. A better explanation is needed to justify the side effects that accompany the communications restrictions adopted by so many employers.

To return to the knotty issue of sexual and racial harassment, the cure here also seems stronger than necessary to address the disease. Harassment does not occur when an individual acts alone, for example by downloading information no one else sees. Nor does it occur when consenting adults exchange such information. In both situations, the offense, if any, is of the same magnitude as conducting one's shopping online or spending too much time in idle chatter — that is to say, it involves a possible misuse of time or facilities but not potentially serious financial liability.

The reason for greater employer concern over offensive messages or files is that they might be seen by nonconsenting others. An employee who passes by the desk of someone looking at a pornographic picture, another who borrows a computer and finds offensive documents, a third who accidentally receives a racist e-mail intended for someone else: These are the possible victims. To become victims with a real cause of action against the employer, the workplace conduct they find offensive must be more than sporadic; only "severe or pervasive" comments, pictures, or actions will create a truly hostile work environment. Though small, the risk to employers is real. Occasional misdeeds of these sorts could, cumulatively, create sufficient evidence to convince a judge or jury that the employer maintained a hostile work environment. For employers, then, the unmistakable message of the law is that they should prohibit and punish all communications and conduct that might offend other employees. One method they use is to monitor and limit electronic communications on employer-provided equipment and systems. As one recent article (Adams et al., 2000, p. 35) put it,

The fact is that because of these concerns and the increasing efforts of the plaintiffs' bar to sue employers based upon allegations of employee misconduct of one sort or another, the obligation of employers to "police" (probably not too strong of a word) the conduct of employees and life in the workplace has never been greater. The role of the employer has become more paternalistic than ever. In this context, it is not unreasonable to expect employers to use any and all available technologies to monitor employees' conduct.

To protect themselves from liability, then, employers need explicit and effective anti-harassment rules. It is not so clear they need general bans on particular words in messages or on access to particular Internet sites, let alone bans on all non-work electronic communications or continuous or frequent monitoring of employee communications. Employers could instead wait until they learn of a possible offense and then address the specific case to make sure it does not recur. Alternatively, and more safely, they could emphasize prohibitions against computer misuse, then engage in more limited screening or monitoring, and enforce the prohibitions with progressive discipline. Instead, employers are increasingly adopting far broader rules and enforcing those rules by firing offenders.

Why do employers do more than the minimum required to avoid legal liability, even when that "more" involves spying on all employees or restricting otherwise lawful activities? The answer lies in the relative exposure to liability. The chance of losing a hostile work environment suit, or even of having to defend against a meritless suit, is more than minimal. As the next section shows, the law does not protect employees' interests in the privacy of their electronic communications at work, so there is almost no risk of paying damages to the employees subject to strict employer monitoring and control. Absent a legal counterweight to sexual or racial harassment suits, it is safer for employers to err on the side of intrusion and restriction than on the side of toleration: to do the former is almost costless; to do the latter could be expensive.[6] By prohibiting certain words altogether, employers might prevent the rare case where those words would reach and offend a protected employee; by prohibiting employees from accessing web sites with sexual content, they might prevent the even rarer case in which inadvertent viewings would poison the work environment; by dismissing an employee who commits one breach, they remove a possible repeat offender and might deter others from such conduct.

Legal Prohibitions and Permissions. The basic legal *requirements* are relatively clear though a bit fuzzy at the edges. Determining what employers must not do is more difficult. Several distinctions complicate this portion of the analysis. First, governmental employers are subject to constitutional restraints while private employers (with the exception of those in the few states whose constitutions do not require "state action" to trigger constitutional rights) are not. Second, the degree to which states value employee privacy against employer interests varies widely across jurisdictions. Third, the sources of privacy protection (constitutions, statutes, and common law causes of action) also differ in some respects.

Notwithstanding those complications, one element pervades almost all privacy protections. This common touchstone dates back at least to *Katz v. United States*, a 1967

Supreme Court opinion. In a concurring opinion, Justice Harlan asserted that privacy rights exist under the Fourth Amendment only when (a) a person has a subjective expectation of privacy that (b) society is prepared to accept as reasonable. In the phrase that is now universally used, a plaintiff must demonstrate a "reasonable expectation of privacy." If a person does not expect a particular mode of communication to be private, or if society does not regard that person's subjective expectation of privacy as reasonable, there is no cause of action. That is largely true for statutory and common law suits as well as for constitutional claims. The concept has also influenced the shape of legislative protections: Legislatures tend not to protect employees or others in matters over which they do not expect privacy or in matters over which society does not believe they should have privacy.

The primary application of the reasonable expectation of privacy concept to workplace privacy occurred twenty years later in another Supreme Court decision, *O'Connor v. Ortega* (1987). In 1981, officials at Napa State Hospital searched the office of Dr. Magno Ortega, a psychiatrist at the hospital, as part of an investigation of alleged misconduct (some of the allegations involved sexual harassment). While conducting the search, they opened his locked desk drawers and went through his private file cabinets, seizing some clearly personal and irrelevant items as well as some public and relevant ones. Dr. Ortega sued under federal and state law. By a 5 to 4 vote, the Supreme Court allowed his case to proceed to trial, holding that the constitutionality of a work-related office search depended on a standard of reasonableness.

That much was a victory for the plaintiff, but the Court's opinion, written by Justice O'Connor but representing the views of only four justices, sharply limited the ability of employees to prevail in such cases. While granting that Dr. Ortega had a reasonable expectation of privacy in his desk and file cabinets and that public employers had to act reasonably in both the inception and the scope of office searches, Justice O'Connor warned that particular office practices, procedures, or regulations may reduce otherwise legitimate privacy expectations. For example, some offices are so open to the public or co-workers that no expectation of privacy would be reasonable. Those determinations, she wrote, must be made on a case-by-case basis.

More importantly, Justice O'Connor wrote that whether a given search was reasonable, even when the employee legitimately expected the site to be private, required balancing the employee's expectation against the employer's need for supervision, control, and efficient operation of the workplace. If those employer interests are strong enough, she indicated, no warrant would be required either for investigatory or work-related but noninvestigatory searches of otherwise private spaces. Because the facts of this case were not clear enough to justify summary judgment, the Court remanded the case to trial.

In the end, nine long years after the Supreme Court's opinion, Dr. Ortega won a verdict of several hundred thousand dollars when a jury found that the hospital's search was unreasonable. On appeal (*Ortega v. O'Connor*, 1998), the Ninth Circuit Court of Appeals emphasized the importance of privacy even at work. Referring to the "stale and unsubstantiated charges of sexual harassment" made against Dr. Ortega, the court wrote:

. . . we reject the proposition that government employers are allowed to search their employees' private offices . . . and seize their purely personal belongings on the basis of the type of charges involved here. . . . Nor, equally important, may such a search be conducted in the absence of specific reason to suspect that particular evidence of misconduct exists and will be found as a result of the search. . . . A charge that a person has engaged in what may be offensive sexual conduct on one or more occasions does not make his or her entire personal and family existence fair game for indiscriminate and unrestrained governmental intrusion and examination. In any event, any search of private areas for evidence of such activities must at a minimum be based on a specific reason to suspect that particular evidence exists and that it will be found in the place to be searched; moreover, such a search must be carefully limited in scope, not only because of an historic respect for fundamental privacy but because of the need to insure that the search will not be "excessively intrusive."[7]

By then, however, the Supreme Court's plurality opinion had been widely accepted as establishing two key points. First, public-sector employees have no claims against their employers for office searches if they had no reasonable expectation of privacy. As the Supreme Court emphasized, particular office practices, procedures, or regulations may undercut an employee's expectation of privacy. Perversely, perhaps, that holding gave employers a strong incentive to prevent or destroy expectations of privacy — by establishing rules denying privacy, by requiring employees to consent to searches, and by frequently exercising their search rights. *United States v. Simons* (4th Cir., 2000), for example, held that a federal agency's Internet policy reserved the right to inspect and monitor employees' use of the Internet. Even though the policy did not refer specifically to inspection of office computers, the Court of Appeals held that it was sufficient to deny the employee any reasonable expectation of privacy in his downloaded files. "This policy placed employees on notice that they could not reasonably expect that their Internet activity would be private. Therefore, regardless of whether Simons subjectively believed that the files he transferred from the Internet were private, such a belief was not objectively reasonable after FBIS notified him that it would be overseeing his Internet use."[8] *A fortiori*, if the employee has no reason to believe that his or her e-mail messages or Internet records are private, the employer has no liability for examining them.

O'Connor's second point was that even if employees had a reasonable expectation of privacy, the employer's business interests could outweigh their privacy interests. These interests could include insuring employee performance, preventing violations of the law, or investigating suspected wrongdoing. Whether a given business interest supersedes a given privacy interest naturally has to be decided on a case-by-case basis.

Later decisions extended those points from alleged constitutional violations by government employers to alleged statutory or common law violations by private employers, and from searches of desks to screening of e-mail and examinations of computer files. A few examples illustrate the progression.

Several courts have addressed the first part of the *O'Connor* approach, the question of whether an employee has a reasonable expectation of privacy when using an employer-provided communications system. Almost uniformly they have ruled against the plaintiffs on that point. In *Bohach v. City of Reno* (D. Nev., 1996), for example, a police department examined the contents of messages the plaintiffs had sent to one another over the department's computerized paging system. Based on the contents of those messages, the department initiated an internal affairs investigation.

The plaintiffs sued to stop the investigation, alleging violation of their constitutional rights and of federal wiretapping laws. The court assumed that they had a subjective expectation of privacy, if only because they would not otherwise have sent the damaging messages, but concluded that their belief was not reasonable. When the system was installed, users were informed that messages would be logged and that certain types of messages were prohibited. Moreover, anyone with access to a department computer could scan all the messages. As a result, said the court, the plaintiffs could not reasonably have expected full privacy in their communications. In reaching its conclusion, the court quoted one law review commentator who generally favored employee privacy rights (Lee, 1994, p. 148, n.2) to the effect that employees' interests in e-mail privacy would probably "fail the 'expectation of privacy' test since most users probably realize that a system administrator could have access" to their e-mail.

Suits against private sector employers for invasion of employees' claimed e-mail privacy have met the same fate. Decades ago, employers who wanted to retain the right to inspect employees' lockers learned that they could defeat any expectation of privacy simply by telling employees that lockers were provided by the employer for their business-related uses and were subject to inspection. The contemporary equivalent is an electronic communications policy telling employees that information transmitted or stored on the employers' systems belongs to the employer and may be reviewed.

In *Garrity v. John Hancock Mutual Life Insurance Co.* (D. Mass., 2002), the employer's computer policy sent a similar message, bluntly stating that the company "reserves the right to access all E-Mail files." The two plaintiffs sent and received sexually explicit messages. When one of those messages reached a third employee who was not amused, Hancock investigated, discovered the offensive messages, and fired the plaintiffs. They sued for invasion of privacy, among other things, alleging that the company led them to believe that they could keep their messages private by using passwords and personal e-mail folders. The federal district court rejected their claim: simply by sending the messages to another person, the court held, the plaintiffs lost any expectation that the messages would remain private.[9]

To the same effect are earlier cases relied on by the *Garrity* court, *Smyth v. Pillsbury Co.* (E.D. Pa., 1996) ("[P]laintiff voluntarily communicated the alleged unprofessional comments over the company e-mail system. We find no privacy interests in such communications.") and *McLaren v. Microsoft Corp.* (Tex. App.-Dallas, 1999) (because messages stored in personal folders were first transmitted over a network accessible by third persons, even the use of a password did not manifest a reasonable expectation of privacy). The *Smyth* case is particularly instructive. Smyth asserted that Pillsbury "repeatedly assured its employees . . . that all e-mail communications would remain confidential and privileged" and that "e-mail communications could not be intercepted and used by defendant against its employees as grounds for termination or reprimand." According to the court, Smyth lost his expectation of privacy when he voluntarily sent his comments to his supervisor: "unlike urinalysis and personal property searches, we do not find a reasonable expectation of privacy in e-mail communications voluntarily made by an employee to his supervisor over the company e-mail system notwithstanding any assurances that such communications would not be intercepted by management." To put it more simply, even if an employer tells its employees that their e-mails are private, believing that statement may not be reasonable. Even if the employee's expectation were reasonable, said the court, a reasonable person would not "consider the defendant's interception of these communications to be a substantial and highly offensive invasion of his privacy."

Courts have likewise ruled against plaintiffs on the second portion of the *O'Connor* approach, finding that an employer's business interests could trump even a reasonable expectation of privacy. As *Garrity* noted, federal and state laws oblige employers to maintain a harassment-free workplace. "Therefore, once defendant received a complaint about the plaintiffs' sexually explicit e-mails, it was required by law to commence an investigation." Similarly, *McLaren* concluded that even if the employees had an expectation of privacy, "a reasonable person would not consider Microsoft's interception of these communications to be a highly offensive invasion. . . . [T]he company's interest in preventing inappropriate and unprofessional comments, or even illegal activity, over its e-mail system would outweigh McLaren's claimed privacy interest in those communications."

Thus the law in this field is relatively clear: In normal circumstances, employees do not have a reasonable expectation that their communications using an employer-provided system are private, but even if they did, the employer's interests in preventing, detecting, and punishing misconduct would supersede their privacy claims. The absence of any constitutional or common law prohibition on employer access to such communications suggests a corollary principle, that employers may monitor and restrict their employees' e-mails, Internet use, and computer files.

Statutory Issues. Nor do communications privacy statutes provide employees with much protection. At first glance, one might assume that statutory bans on wiretapping and the like would keep employers from reading private e-mails. On closer analysis, the laws contain gaping exceptions for just these circumstances.

The primary federal law in this area is the Electronic Communications Privacy Act of 1986, or ECPA, an amendment to the earlier federal Wiretap Law (which itself is Title III of the grandly-named Omnibus Crime Control and Safe Streets Act of 1968). ECPA's Title I broadly prohibits interception of electronic (and other) communications; Title II prohibits accessing stored electronic communications. Each of these contains exceptions that free employers to engage in virtually all the workplace monitoring they could want (Kesan, 2002, pp. 296–98; Adams et al., 2000, pp. 38–40).

Three exceptions in the earliest and broadest law, the federal Wiretap Law, are carried forward into ECPA's Title I, the "consent exception," the "provider exception," and the "business use exception."

- First, an employer is freed of liability if the employee consents to the interception. While an employee might impliedly consent to monitoring, knowledge of possible monitoring without more will not suffice. Thus a prudent employer who wants to eliminate any risk of a violation should implement a comprehensive and clear policy and require employees to agree to it.

• Second, the Wiretap Law exempts interceptions by a service provider that are made within the normal course of employment and for the purpose of rendering its services or to protect its rights or property. (An employer who provides e-mail and Internet access is apparently a provider for this purpose.[10]) Those purposes would include monitoring to ensure quality service and to prevent theft; they would probably also include monitoring to prevent other violations of the law such as harassment.

• Third, the Wiretap Law's business-use exemption excludes from the definition of a covered "device" certain standard equipment. Courts interpreting the business use exception have applied both a "content approach" that focuses on whether the intercepted communications are personal or business-related (only the latter may be monitored) and a "context approach" that focuses instead on whether the employer had a sufficiently weighty and legitimate business purpose for its monitoring.

In addition to these Title I exceptions, Title II has its own "provider" and "user" exceptions. Employers with their own communications systems are "providers" for purposes of Title II (*Bohach v. City of Reno*). The "user" exception is roughly analogous to the other Title's "consent" exception.

Putting these exceptions together, it is evident that ECPA does not generally bar employers from contemporaneously intercepting their employees' electronic communications or from accessing stored communications. The law protects employees only from third parties, not from those who provide the communications services in question. The most recent legislative action in this field, the Communications Decency Act of 1996 (a portion of the broader Telecommunications Act of 1996), added a new provision expressly protecting from liability "any 'provider or user of an interactive computer service' who restricts 'access to or (the) availability of' indecent material or helps others gain the technical means to do so" (Krattenmaker, 1996, pp. 147–48). Thus federal law not only permits employer monitoring of electronic communications, it positively encourages some such monitoring.

Many states have adopted their own electronic communications privacy laws but because most of these track ECPA's language, they allow employers the same freedom granted by federal law. A few states have stricter provisions or require employers to notify employees about potential monitoring, but these laws have significant limitations. Some address only tape recording or telephone interception and thus do not apply to electronic communications. Others contain exceptions that negate any promise of additional protection for employee privacy. Connecticut's law, for instance, generally requires notification to employees but exempts monitoring "when the employer has reasonable grounds to believe that an employee is creating a hostile work environment or is violating the law or the employer's legal rights" (Kesan, 2002, p. 301).[11]

Conclusion. Every branch of the law — constitutional, common, and statutory; federal and state — allows employers wide discretion to monitor, restrict, and inspect their employees' electronic communications and files. At the same time, several branches of the law, particularly federal financial regulations, intellectual property doctrines, and anti-discrimination laws, impose at least some risk of liability on employers for their employees' misuse of the employers' communications systems. Given the state of the law, it would be a strange employer indeed that opted to protect employee privacy rather than to invade it. The primary motivation behind employers' monitoring and restricting their employees' use of electronic communications is profitability. When profitability conflicts with privacy, the former will prevail to the extent permitted by law. As one recent study phrased it, "The profits inherent in increased worker productivity and less employer liability provide strong incentives for the employer to disregard employee privacy interests" (Kovach et al., 2000).

V. What Then Must Be Done?

Policy recommendations have taken two wildy irreconcilable positions. Almost without exception, those concerned with management interests have urged employers to adopt extremely restrictive and intrusive electronic communications policies. E-mail and Internet facilities, they urge, should be restricted to work-related purposes; employers should routinely screen employee communications, bar messages containing improper words, and prohibit access to inappropriate web sites. Employees who violate those restrictions should be fired or at least severely disciplined.

Many of the cases mentioned above reflect equally strict policies. A good example of what cautious management attorneys are recommending to their business clients appears in an article by two labor lawyers from one of the country's largest law firms, Jones Day (Towns and Girard, 1998, pp. 24–27). The authors make twelve recommendations to employers:

1. Integrate e-mail and other policies.
2. Limit use of technology to business purposes only.
3. Reserve right to review and monitor.
4. Notify employees that passwords do not ensure privacy.
5. Include notice and consent language.
6. Do not engage in privileged communications via e-mail.
7. Strictly define appropriate Internet use.
8. Prescribe penalties for failure to follow Internet policies.
9. Enforce policies in a nondiscriminatory fashion.
10. Consider whether blanket rules are too broad.
11. Protect employees from inadvertent violations of copyright laws.
12. Develop a comprehensive records retention policy.

Note that almost all of these recommendations involve restrictions and their enforcement. The only one that recognizes a possible limit on employers is number 10. The authors' explication of that recommendation makes it clear that their concern is with rules that might run afoul of the National Labor Relations Act, not with employees' privacy. The authors' explication of recommendation 7 illustrates the point: ". . . an employer's policy may provide that employees may access the Internet only through the employer's approved Internet access procedures. In addition, an employer may wish to restrict or prohibit subscribing to public mail forums, ListServs, discusssion groups, and the like."[12] Most advisors also recommend that employers adopt filtering and blocking software and that they investigate all flagged messages and accesses.

Restrictive policies like these might seem to solve management's problems with Internet and e-mail abuse, but restrictive rules carry substantial costs. Tight limitations could easily inhibit beneficial communications. Even the best filters are clumsy and often inaccurate. Heavy-handed rules indicate a lack of trust and might well hurt morale and team spirit. Enforcement would require managerial time and resources, and would necessitate difficult decisions. Does the employer really want to discipline its best sales person because of a few offensive e-mails that got into the wrong hands? Will it dismiss the CEO for accessing "unapproved" web sites? Should the employee who completes all assigned tasks quickly and well be punished for using spare minutes corresponding with friends? And if the employer does not apply its rules equally to all, how can it avoid allegations of discrimination brought by those it chooses to discipline? Furthermore, the discovery process in any subsequent suit could turn up information about others that the employer really would not want revealed.

Those questions assume that employers realistically can control their employees' electronic communications. In fact, the job may be impossible. E-mail in particular is so widespread among workers with access to a computer that trying to limit its use to business purposes is like trying to stuff the proverbial cat back into the bag. Employers are likely to be no more successful than they have been with counterpart rules governing telephone use.

Those in the opposite camp argue that employers should have extremely limited rights to monitor employee communications. Having lost their arguments in the courts, privacy advocates have lobbied for federal and state legislation. Their major effort occurred in 1993 with the proposed Privacy for Consumers and Worker Act (PCWA). While phrased as an effort to limit improper monitoring and reduce some of the ECPA exceptions used by employers, the effect of the bill would have been to make most routine monitoring impractical — in other words, to reverse the impact of the statutory exceptions and court decisions described above. In the face of immediate and heated opposition from employers (and even from the Clinton Administration's Department of Labor), the PCWA died in committee. A more modest bill, the Notice of Electronic Monitoring Act (NEMA), was introduced in 2000. Unlike the restrictive PCWA, NEMA would allow any monitoring provided the employer notified affected employees ahead of time. Even the notice requirements are complicated, however, and violations would be punished by heavy fines.[13] NEMA has made no more progress than the PCWA.

In addition to court and legislative efforts, some commentators have appealed directly to employers to change their emphasis. At the end of his chapter on privacy at work, Jeffrey Rosen (2000, pp. 89–90) makes this earnest if somewhat utopian plea:

> There is no reason for us to accept the passive view that all e-mail messages sent over a university or corporate network must be considered public rather than private. We should try instead to carve out backstage areas where people can joke, let down their hair, and form intimate relationships free from official scrutiny. Some studies suggest that 40 percent of e-

mail correspondence is unrelated to work; rather than trying in vain to exert managerial control over a medium that lends itself naturally to informal, and even irresponsible, communication, companies and universities might instead set aside e-mail accounts and areas of their networks as private places where speech and communications cannot be invaded unless there is cause to suspect individual users of serious misconduct.

As Rosen goes on to recognize, "this effort to distinguish between public and private speech in the workplace is something that current law refuses to allow." There's the rub: Given the potential liability on employers who do not restrict some types of communications, asking them to create specifically "private places" in which employees can "let down their hair, and form intimate relationships" is simply unrealistic.

As is so often the case, there is a lot of room for alternative positions between these extremes. Employers are not going to give up their rights to monitor employee performance, to insist on productivity during working hours, and to prevent and correct abuses of communications technology. They might, though, tailor their policies to accomplish their objectives with as little harm to other interests as possible. Moreover, employees themselves can do a lot to prevent intrusion on their privacy.

The starting place is the recognition that the law does not, and probably will not and should not, treat employees' communications at work or on an employer's communications systems as if they were private speech in their own homes. With that understanding, employees should limit the amount of personal business they do at work, use cell phones and pay phones and personal computers when feasible rather than using the employer's systems, and advise others not to send potentially offensive messages (and avoid distributing any that do arrive). Technologically adept employees should consider encrypting any personal messages whose disclosure could prove embarrassing, using anonymous remailers, and using "cloak" sites when browsing the web (Nichols, 2001, pp. 1602–03; Rodriguez, 1998, pp. 1470–72). Abstinence may not be the only guarantee of electronic privacy at work, but it surely is effective.

Employers, on the other hand, can balance profitability and privacy by adopting only as much restraint and monitoring as is essential for accomplishing managerial objectives. By balancing employee and employer interests and thereby minimizing overt intrusions, employers should enhance morale while keeping costs low. As one thoughtful commentator put it (Kesan, 2002, p. 331), monitoring "should be narrowly tailored to satisfy business-related, administrative, or legal needs, and any review of personal e-mail ought to be limited to ensure protection of personal information." Education should be a major component of any sensible computer policy. Once employees know the employer's expectations, the reasons for them, and the methods the employer will use to accomplish them, there should be few abuses. Just learning that messages cannot really be deleted and that supervisors can easily review Internet usage would go a long way toward deterring misconduct. Where some controls are necessary, blocking filters are more effective and less disturbing than human monitoring. It is hardly necessary to add that any policy should be clear, precise, written, well publicized, and consistently but reasonably enforced (Adams et al., 2000, pp. 44–45).

VI. Conclusion

New communications technology inevitably creates new problems of privacy; think of the introduction of telephones (when party lines were common), faxes (which can lie in a room accessible by many people before reaching the addressee), and cell phones (which allow bystanders to hear one side of seemingly confidential communications). Computer monitoring of performance, e-mails, and Internet access are no different in this regard. Each development requires adjustments.

Old wine in new bottles, perhaps. What seems to drive the differing responses to the new bottles is that the newest forms of communication present an illusion of privacy. Everyone soon understood the limits to privacy presented by telephones, faxes, and cell phones. When new, however, e-mail and Internet access seemed more protected. We can see bystanders who might hear our telephone conversations and read our faxes, but those who monitor the new technology might never be seen. They might not even be human. It would be easy indeed, in those early days of the new technology, to conclude that there were no monitors. One beneficial by-product of the attention given to recent cases, and of employers' recent efforts to publicize their electronic communications policies, is that fewer employees should harbor any illusions.

Many of the adjustments to the new technology reduce the scope of individual privacy. To some degree that is inevitable. If so, employers and employees alike can and should act to minimize the intrusions, employees by avoiding questionable use of employer-provided equipment and systems, and employers by adopting reasonable rather than draconian computer and communications policies. The temptation is great for employers to overreach; avoiding that temptation may well be a bigger challenge than the possibility of employee misconduct.

Notes

*   I thank Holly Newell of the University of South Carolina Law School Class of 2004 for her diligent research on and editorial assistance with this article.
1   The AMA's membership consists of the nation's largest employers, employing a quarter of the nation's work force. Moreover, larger companies are the most likely to use new technology and new managerial techniques. The survey's results therefore likely show the direction in which other employers are moving. Because most employers do not publish their policies for outsiders, learning the details of their rules can be difficult. The examples cited in this article come from quotations in court cases and from publicly available policies, chiefly from universities.
2   Note the apparent inconsistency: personal use is limited to that which is "incidental to" — that is, somehow associated with — official duties. Personal use is allowed, in other words, only when it is not truly personal. This sort of self-contradiction is all too common among the computer policies I have reviewed.
3   The screening system described in that article sounds much like a program called Assentor. According to Jeffrey Rosen (2000, p. 57), Assentor "screens every incoming and outgoing e-mail for evidence of racism or sexism or body parts. After assigning each e-mail an offensiveness score, the program forwards messages with high scores to a supervisor for review."
4   Ishman (2000) provides a thorough analysis of the law of vicarious liability in the technological age. See also Settle-Vinson (1998).

5   See, e.g., *Harley v. McCoach*, 928 F.Supp. 533 (E.D. Pa., 1996) (one offensive reference in an e-mail did not constitute a racially hostile environment); *Owens v. Morgan Stanley & Co.*, 1997 WL 403454 (S.D.N.Y., 1997) (same); *Schwenn v. Anheuser-Busch, Inc.*, 1998 WL 166845 (N.D.N.Y., 1998) (noting that other hostile work environment cases involved conduct extending over several years, the court held that sexually harassing e-mail over three weeks did not amount to a hostile work environment under New York law).

6   The state of discrimination law creates a difficult issue that is beyond the scope of this essay. The government could not constitutionally ban most forms of speech and communication simply because women or minorities would find them offensive. Nevertheless, Congress and state legislatures have made employers liable for tolerating such constitutionally-protected activity. As a result, employers are forced to restrict their employees in ways the Government could not do directly; the anti-discrimination laws thus provide an indirect route around the First Amendment. See Rosen (2000), particularly chapters 2 and 3.

7   *Ortega v. O'Connor*, 146 F.3d 1149, 1163-64 (9th Cir. 1998), quoting the Supreme Court's *O'Connor* decision, 480 U.S. at 726.

8   To the same effect is *United States v. Reilly*, 2002 WL 1163572 (S.D.N.Y., 2002). U.S. Department of Labor policies warned employees that "By using Government office equipment, executive branch employees imply their consent to disclosing the contents of any files or information maintained or passed through Government office equipment." Every time the defendant turned on his computer, he received this message: "Users have no right to privacy while using any government owned or leased information technology system, which includes workstations, . . . software such as word processors, Internet browsers, electronic mail etc." Against that background, the court held, Reilly could not demonstrate that he had a reasonable expectation of privacy in diskettes beside his office computer.

9   See also *Muick v. Glenayre Electronics* (7th Cir., 2002) (where the employer announced that it could inspect the laptops it supplied to employees, Muick had no right of privacy in his computer). Even without an express policy restricting computer use, employees should know some things they shouldn't do. *Autoliv ASP, Inc. v. Department of Workforce Services*, (Utah Court of Appeals, 2001) (sending explicit e-mails on a company computer network "violated a universal standard of behavior").

10 See *Bohach v. City of Reno*, 932 F.Supp. 1232 (D. Nev., 1996) (police department was a "provider" of electronic communications services).

11 For more detailed discussion of state regulations, see Settle-Vinson (1998, pp. 67–70) and Adams et al. (2000, pp. 40–41).

12 For examples of comparable policy recommendations to employers, see Hubbartt (1998, pp. 147–48) Ishman (2000, pp. 157–60), Kesan (2002, pp. 330–32), and Mignin et al. (2002, pp. 17–21).

13 Many of the articles in the References discuss these developments. See particularly Kesan (2002, pp. 299–300), Frayer (2002, pp. 868–71) and Rodriguez (1998, pp. 1464–65).

References

Adams, Hall III, Suzanne M. Scheuing, and Stacey A. Feeley. "E-mail Monitoring in the Workplace: The Good, the Bad and the Ugly." *Defense Counsel Journal* 67 (January 2000): 32–46.

Allen, Anita L. "The Wanted Gaze: Accountability for Interpersonal Conduct at Work." *Georgetown Law Journal* 89 (June 2001): 2013–28.

American Management Association. 2001 AMA Survey, Workplace Monitoring & Surveillance, <http://www.amanet.org/research/pdfs/ems_short2001.pdf>, last visited June 3, 2002.

Archdiocese of Baltimore. Computer Use & Internet Policy. <http://www.archbalt.org/technology/info/policy.pdf>, last visited July 2, 2002.

Autoliv ASP, Inc. v. Department of Workforce Services, 29 P.3d 7 (Utah App. 2001).

Baum, Kevin J. "Comment: E-mail in the Workplace and the Right of Privacy." *Villanova Law Review* 42 (3, 1997): 1011–42.

Beeson, Jared D. "Cyberprivacy on the Corporate Intranet: Does the Law Allow Private-Sector Employers to Read Their Employees' E-mail?" *University of Hawaii Law Review* 20 (Summer/Fall 1998): 165–219.

Blakey v. Continental Airlines, 164 N.J. 38, 751 A.2d 538 (N.J., 2000).

Boehmer, Robert G. "Artificial Monitoring and Surveillance of Employees: The Fine Line Dividing the Prudently Managed Enterprise from the Modern Sweatshop." *DePaul Law Review* 41 (Spring 1992): 739–819.

Bohach v. City of Reno, 932 F.Supp. 1232 (D. Nev., 1996).

Burlington Industries v. Ellerth, 524 U.S. 742 (1998).

Faragher v. City of Boca Raton, 524 U.S. 775 (1998).

Finkin, Matthew. *Privacy in Employment Law*. Washington, D.C.: Bureau of National Affairs 1995 and *2002 Cumulative Supplement*.

Florida State University. OP-H-6, Use of University Information Technology Resources, <http://www.vpfa.fsu.edu/policies/bmanual/itpolicy.html>, last visited July 2, 2002.

Foster, Andrea L. "Your E-Mail Message to a Colleague Could Be Tomorrow's Headline." *Chronicle of Higher Education*, June 21, 2002.

Frayer, Charles E. "Employee Privacy and Internet Monitoring: Balancing Workers' Rights and Dignity with Legitimate Management Interests." *Business Lawyer* 57 (February 2002): 857–74.

Gantt, Larry O. Natt II. "An Affront to Human Dignity: Electronic Mail Monitoring in the Private Sector Workplace." *Harvard Journal of Law and Technology* 8 (Spring 1995): 345–425.

Garofalo, Beverly. "Sharing a Middle Ground with Big Brother." *Connecticut Law Tribune*, May 18, 1998: pp. 1–6.

Garrity v. John Hancock Mutual Life Ins. Co., 18 IER Cases 981, 2002 WL 974676 (D.Mass., 2002).

Harley v. McCoach, 928 F.Supp. 533 (E.D. Pa., 1996).

Hubbartt, William S. *The New Battle Over Workplace Privacy*. New York: AMACOM, 1998.

Independent Weekly. "Cyber-cussing." May 15–21, 2002.

Ishman, Mark. "Computer Crimes and the Respondeat Superior Doctrine: Employers Beware." *Boston University Journal of Science and Technology Law* 6 (June 1, 2000): 115–62.

Katz v. United States, 389 U.S. 347 (1967).

Kesan, Jay P. "Cyber-Working or Cyber-Shirking?: A First Principles Examination of Electronic Privacy in the Workplace." *Florida Law Review* 54 (April 2002): 289–332.

Kovach, Kenneth A., Jennifer Jordan, Karen Tansey, and Eve Framinan. "The Balance between Employee Privacy and Employer Interests." *Business and Society Review* 105 (Summer 2000): 289–98.

Krattenmaker, Thomas G. "The Telecommunications Act of 1996." *Connecticut Law Review* 29 (Fall 1996): 123–74.

Lee, Laurie Thomas. "Watch Your E-Mail! Employee E-Mail Monitoring and Privacy Law in the Age of the 'Electronic Sweatshop'." *John Marshall Law Review* 28 (Fall 1994): 139–77.

Loving v. Boren, 956 F.Supp. 953 (W.D. Okla., 1997), affirmed on other grounds, 133 F.3d 771 (10th Cir., 1998).

Malin, Martin H. and Henry H. Perritt, Jr. "The National Labor Relations Act in Cyberspace: Union Organizing in Electronic Workplaces." *University of Kansas Law Review* 49 (November 2000): 1–64.

McLaren v. Microsoft Corp., 1999 WL 339015 (Tex.App.-Dallas, 1999).

Meritor Savings Bank, FSB v. Vinson, 477 U.S. 57 (1986).

Mignin, Robert J., Bart A. Lazar, and Josh M. Friedman. "Privacy Issues in the Workplace: A Post-September 11 Perspective." *Employee Relations Law Journal* 28 (Summer 2002): 7–23.

Muick v. Glenayre Electronics, 280 F.3d 741 (7th Cir., 2002).

Nichols, Donald H. "Window Peeping in the Workplace: A Look into Employee Privacy in a Technological Era." *William Mitchell Law Review* 27 (3, 2001): 1587–1608.

O'Connor v. Ortega, 480 U.S. 709 (1987).

Ortega v. O'Connor, 146 F.3d 1149 (9th Cir., 1998).

Owens v. Morgan Stanley & Co., 1997 WL 403454 (S.D.N.Y., 1997).

Rodriguez, Alexander I. "Comment: All Bark, No Byte: Employee E-Mail Privacy Rights in the Private Sector Workplace." *Emory Law Journal* 47 (Fall 1998): 1439–73.

Rosen, Jeffrey. *The Unwanted Gaze: The Destruction of Privacy in America*. New York: Random House, 2000.

Schwenn v. Anheuser-Busch, Inc., 1998 WL 166845 (N.D.N.Y., 1998)

Settle-Vinson, Mia G. "Employer Liability for Messages Sent by Employees Via E-mail and Voice Mail Systems." *Thurgood Marshall Law Review* 25 (Fall 1998): 55–74.

Smyth v. Pillsbury Co., 914 F.Supp. 97 (E.D. Pa., 1996).

Towns, Douglas M. and Jeana Girard. "Superhighway or Superheadache? E-Mail and the Internet in the Workplace." *Employee Relations Law Journal* 24 (Winter 1998): 5–29.

United States v. Angevine, 281 F.3d 1130 (10th Cir., 2002).

United States v. Reilly, 2002 WL 1163572 (S.D.N.Y., 2002).

United States v. Simons, 206 F.3d 392 (4th Cir., 2000).

University of Michigan. Standard Practice Guide 601.16, Policy and Guidelines Regarding Electronic Access to Potentially Offensive Material, July 10, 1997, <http://www.umich.edu/~policies/offensive-material-60116.html>, last visited July 2, 2002.

University of South Carolina. IT 2.15, Harassing or Obscene Telephone Calls or Electronic Messages, March 6, 2002, <http://www.sc.edu/policies/it215.html>, and ACAF 7.01, Computer and Network Access and Use, February 1, 1995, <http://www.sc.edu/policies/acaf701.html>, last visited July 2, 2002.

University of Southern California. General Policies Regarding the Electronic Communication Infrastructure at the University of Southern California, <http://www.usc.edu/isd/policies/general/#response>, last visited, July 2, 2002.

Urofsky v. Allen, 995 F.Supp. 634 (E.D. Va., 1998), reversed sub nom. Urofsky v. Gilmore, 216 F.3d 401 (2000) (en banc), cert. denied, 531 U.S. 1070 (2001).

Wilborn, S. Elizabeth. "Revisiting the Public/Private Distinction: Employee Monitoring in the Workplace." *Georgia Law Review* 32 (Spring 1998): 825–87.

14

Employee E-Mail and Internet Use: Canadian Legal Issues

David J. Corry and *Kim E. Nutz*
Gowling Lafleur Henderson LLP- Calgary

I. Introduction

The introduction of the Internet, e-mail, and other forms of electronic communication has revolutionized the workplace and given rise to new and improved business practices, including widespread access to information and instant communication among suppliers, customers, and employees. Management encourages employees to make full use of these new electronic tools to further the company's business objectives. However, increasing use of electronic communication has spawned new forms of employee misconduct.

As management responds to employee abuse of electronic communications, the tension between management rights and employee privacy rights is heightened. Management wants to be free to fully monitor electronic communications to ensure that they are used for legitimate business purposes in the company's best interests. Employees seek to safeguard their privacy and want the freedom to use these new electronic tools for personal and business purposes. This ongoing struggle — between privacy and management rights — underlies the legal issues arising from employee e-mail and Internet use in Canada.

In Canada, as in the U.S., job rights for unionized employees are protected by a "just cause" standard. However, nonunion employees can be dismissed without cause provided that reasonable notice of dismissal is given. Employers who do not provide reasonable notice of dismissal are liable for damages for wrongful dismissal. Various statutes govern the minimum notice periods, and common law has created precedents of notice periods substantially in excess of statutory minimums. (This statutory regime somewhat differs from the U.S. employment-at-will doctrine.)

Employers are concerned that their employees are spending a considerable amount of time on the Internet "surfing," and sending e-mail regarding subjects that are totally unrelated to their job duties during work hours. A recent Angus Reid poll (*Globe and Mail*, July 6, 2000), stated that Canadian employees spend 800 million hours per year surfing the Internet for personal reasons (Leone, 2000). Given the change in the traditional workday — the basic 9–5 job is becoming less and less common — it is important for employers to recognize that it is impossible to expect an employee to be doing business-related work 100 percent of the time they are on the employer's premises. Still, employers should be cognizant of the problems that exist when access to websites, such as Ebay and Playboy, begin to reduce the employee's productive time. This downturn in workplace productivity along with the employer's potential liability have resulted in increasing use of corporate Internet policies and employee monitoring.

In addition to harming productivity, employee access to the Internet creates more opportunities for employees to engage in virtually unprotected speech that could create liability for the employees and their employers.

Most worrisome is the possibility that computers are used to download pornography or materials offensive to minorities which may then be distributed around the office in electronic attachments or printed and viewed by groups of employees. Such conduct could in turn lead to harassment complaints by employees. The widespread and rapid distribution of offensive or discriminatory material can poison a work environment and may also give rise to criminal charges.

For these reasons, many employers have begun monitoring employees' use of e-mail and the Internet which raises issues related to the employees' right to privacy and about the new privacy legislation that has taken effect in Canada in 2001. E-mail and the Internet have revolutionized workplace practices. However, it has also given rise to new legal issues which pit management's rights against the employee's rights to privacy. Herein, we review the development of these legal issues in Canada.

II. Legal Issues Arising in Employment

Harassment in the Workplace. Employers have an obligation to provide an environment free from discrimination and harassment. If inappropriate or illegal material is being circulated in the workplace via company e-mail, that obligation may have been violated. The circulation of inappropriate material can therefore lead to the conclusion that the employer has condoned the creation of a hostile work environment resulting in discriminatory attitudes and a hostile workplace.

In Canada, employers can be held both personally and vicariously liable under human rights legislation for the discriminatory actions of their employees. An employer aware that its employees are sending or receiving offensive material in any form or are visiting sexually explicit web sites from office computers accessible or visible to other employees leaves itself open to discrimination claims by employees offended by such behavior. Consequently, employers should be aware that they may then find themselves liable for charges of sexual, racial, or gender harassment if they fail to adequately protect themselves when an employee uses the office Internet to download and distribute offensive, discriminatory, or harassing messages via the company e-mail system.

Two recent cases illustrate the types of fact situations that lead to arbitration in the unionized setting. In *Westcoast Energy Inc. v. Communications, Energy and Paper Workers Union of Canada Local 686B* (1999), the grievor[1] anonymously forwarded messages of a sexual nature to a female employee. The employer had a policy prohibiting such conduct, but was very lax in its enforcement. The grievor contended that another employee had told him that this female employee would not be offended by e-mails which contained the sexually explicit pictures. The arbitrator, in reaching his decision, determined that although the grievor had committed a serious employment offense, his long service and good employment record should be taken into account. The employee was therefore reinstated, given a six-month suspension, and ordered to write a letter of apology.

In *Canada Pacific Railway v. International Brotherhood of Electrical Workers* (2000), an arbitrator held that an employee's misuse of the company's computer system did not amount to theft nor did his e-mail messages, one of which contained an off-color joke, violate the employer's harassment and discrimination policy. The grievor who had an unblemished record of 9 years with the company was discharged for cheating on a correspondence course and for improperly using the employer's e-mail system. Some of the grievor's personal e-mails contained off-color jokes, a few derogatory comments about another employee, and disrespectful remarks about supervisors in general. The grievor was discharged and the union filed a grievance arguing that the employer's disciplinary response was excessive. The arbitrator allowed the union's grievance, holding that although the grievor's conduct called for discipline, a discharge was unwarranted. The arbitrator, having read all of the grievor's e-mail messages, noted that only one actually contained off-color jokes. On the whole, however, the arbitrator believed that the messages were neither disrespectful of authority nor harmful or harassing in nature. Consequently, the grievance was allowed and the grievor was reinstated.

Both of the above cases involved allegations of harassment and discrimination and reviewed the appropriateness of the employer's responses. Employers should be aware that they also may have been brought to a human rights forum where the issue of the employer's liability would likely have been dealt with in the nature of fines, apologies, and through the implementation of educational anti-harassment programs. Sexual harassment violates provincial and federal human rights legislation which prohibits discriminatory conduct on the ground of gender. Many human rights tribunals across Canada have held employers liable for sexual harassment in the workplace.[2]

In *Curling v. Torimiro* (2000), the complainant charged her employer and another employee alleging discrimination on the basis of gender, as well as both sexual harassment and sexual solicitation and for retaliatory conduct when the sexual advances were rejected by the complainant. The Ontario Human Rights Commission found that the parties had discriminated against the complainant and awarded damages against both the employer and the employee, jointly and severally. The Commission primarily awarded $10,000 as compensation for humiliation and loss of dignity; $10,000 as compensation for mental anguish; and $4,000 as compensation for her humiliation and loss of dignity in relation to the infringement of her right to be free from retaliatory treatment for the rejection of sexual advances.

In *Ryane v. Krieger* (2000), the complainant alleged that her employer had discriminated against her on the basis of sex/gender regarding a term of her employment and had refused to continue employing her. She alleged that she was subjected to unwelcome sexual jokes and comments about her appearance and requests for a sexual relationship. The British Columbia Human Rights Tribunal found that she had been discriminated against on the basis of sex and that the employer had refused to continue her employment on the basis of sex or disability. They ordered $4,000 for damages for injury to dignity, feelings, and self-respect. They also ordered the employer to pay $9,000 in lost wages.

Although the two cases above do not directly address Internet/e-mail issues specifically, it is easy to see how these types of sexual harassment could transcend into an electronic communication workplace.

Disclosure of Intellectual Property/Copyright Infringement. The ability of employees to transfer company information via e-mail that does not have sufficient confidentiality protection, such as a nondisclosure agreement, to outsiders puts that information at risk of losing its status as a trade secret and puts the employer at a distinct disadvantage with the loss of information. Employers might wish to discipline or discharge employees who jeopardize company proprietary information.

The Internet also contains content protected by copyright or other proprietary rights, opening up the potential for direct, vicarious, or contributory copyright infringement liability claims against employers should the information be downloaded and utilized without the proper authority. In Canada, if an employer has knowledge or facilitates or encourages the utilization of material in contravention of a copyright, it may be held liable for the employee's infringement.

Defamation. In Canada, defamation consists of any written, printed, or spoken words or any audible or visible matters or acts which tend to lower a person in the estimation of others or cause a person to be shunned, avoided, or exposed to hatred, contempt, or ridicule. Consequently, defamation claims against an employer may result from derogatory e-mail messages transmitted over the company e-mail system or discussions in chat rooms about other employees, customers, competitors, or third parties.

An example of a situation where defamation was alluded to was in the case of *Camosun College v. CUPE* (1999). The grievor was terminated for making a series of unwarranted allegations against other employees in the administration. The employee sent a lengthy e-mail to a Union "chat group" (one of several distribution lists that Camosun College maintained) on the College's computer network. The e-mail contained numerous allegations concerning the integrity, reputation, and competence of the faculty in his department. Specifically, it mentioned that three university professors were engaged in an underground enterprise and were using College resources to advance this private business. This message soon found its way to members outside of the network and the grievor was subsequently terminated.

The arbitrator stated that the expectation of confidentiality that attaches to letter mail cannot be applied to e-mail, and therefore a right to privacy was not involved. The arbitrator reasoned that the e-mail was communicated via a medium that presented it to be read and from which it could be conveniently copied and easily forwarded to be read by others, and thus, the e-mail was not confidential. As such the message could provide grounds for dismissal.

Thus, the arbitrator upheld the dismissal because the grievor's action breached his duty of loyalty to his employer. The arbitrator held that the employee is obliged to investigate and verify the concerns as far as possible prior to going public and to take every opportunity to correct the problem within the organization. Also, the grievor's statements within the e-mail were knowingly or recklessly false. The fact that the grievor knew his allegations were false or did not care whether they were false removed any possibility that the e-mail was privileged. Clearly, given this fact situation, it would have been easy for the affected employees (the professors) to have sued the grievor, along with the employer, for defamation.

Vicarious Liability of the Employer for the Employee's Tortious Acts. At common law, the employer is vicariously liable for torts committed by an employee in the course of his or her employment. Therefore, the doctrine attaches to the employer's responsibility for the tortious conduct of the employee without the existence of fault on the part of the employer. However, this doctrine does not absolve the employee from liability for tortious conduct, and the employer may, in fact, claim an indemnification against the employee for moneys paid to a third party due to vicarious responsibility.

Therefore, sexual harassment, copyright infringement, unauthorized disclosure of intellectual property, and defamation are just a few of the tortious acts of an employee for which an employer may be liable. This is a crucial concept for employers to understand when they are assessing the ultimate risks associated with employee Internet and e-mail access (Ball, 2000, p. 20–2).

In *P.A.B. v. Children's Foundation* (1997), the British Columbia Court of Appeal dismissed an appeal by an employer who had been found vicariously liable for acts of sexual abuse committed by one of its employees on a child who had been a resident with the employer. The employer was a nonprofit child-care organization. The Court held that an employer could be vicariously liable for a breach of trust and misconduct by its employee, especially where the breach was a breach of job-created authority.

Common Law Duty of Fidelity and Fiduciary Duties. Although an employer may find itself liable for the acts of its employees, an employee still owes a general duty of good faith and fidelity to his or her employer, even if the employees are not fiduciaries. Although the courts have not specifically addressed this duty in the context of Internet and e-mail use, courts have traditionally emphasized that employees are not allowed to use the time for which they are paid by the employer in furthering their own interests. This could be taken to include "surfing" the web and taking part in personal e-mail on company time.

Additionally, it is an implied term that an employee must at all times, during the employment relationship, protect the employer's interests. In *CRC-Evans Canada Ltd. v. Pettifer* (1997, p. 303), the Court held that "there is an implied obligation placed upon the employee to act in the best interests of his employer at all times." It has also been held that the duty of good faith and fidelity appears to exist even during an employee's own time. The obligation of fidelity subsists so long as the contract of service subsists, and even in the employee's spare time, the employee continues to owe that obligation of fidelity (Ball, 2000, p. 15-2).

Traditionally, employees in a management position or in the position of director or officer of a company are considered fiduciaries and are additionally held to a higher duty over and above that of the implied duty of fidelity. Determining which employees fit within the category is not always easy. Courts have characterized an employee as a fiduciary if he or she occupies a position at the uppermost part of the organization with effective power to make executive decisions concerning fundamental aspects of the organization itself (England and Christie, 1998, p. 11.89) That is, fiduciaries are placed in a position of trust by their employer and are entrusted with company property, confidential information, and customers. As such, they have a duty to act in the utmost good faith and in the best interests of their employer. A fiduciary must avoid conflicts of interest whereby their personal interests prevail over their fiduciary duty to their employer.

The Alberta Court of Appeal in *Wilcox v. G.W.G. Ltd.* (1985, p. 12) described the fiduciary obligation of employees as requiring that "upon the essential point of integrity to their employer their conduct must stand unimpeached" (England and Christie, 1998, pp. 11.84–85). Consequently, inappropriate Internet and e-mail access which results in harassment, defamation, copyright infringement, and unauthorized disclosure of confidential information, would likely be a breach of fiduciary duty.

A breach of the implied contractual obligation of good faith and fidelity, along with a breach of fiduciary duty is actionable in its own right, despite the fact that the employer may additionally have a good case for just cause for termination. There are a number of Canadian common law and arbitration cases where employees have been successfully sued by their former employer for breach of the duty of good faith and fidelity and breach of fiduciary duty.[3]

Canadian Aero Service Ltd. v. O'Malley et al. (1974), one of the leading cases from the Supreme Court of Canada, found former officers in breach of their fiduciary duty to their employer. The plaintiff company had been trying since 1961 to obtain an important contract in Guyana. The individual defendants, in their capacity as President and Executive Vice-President, were its top management for the two years prior to their resignation. When the defendants resigned from the company, they started their own company and pursued and eventually obtained the Guyana contract. The Court found the defendants liable for damages in the amount of $125,000. The plaintiff, the court held, was therefore entitled to compel faithless fiduciaries to answer for their default according to their gain.

In *Anderson, Smyth & Kelly Customs Broker Ltd. v. World Wide Customs Brokers Ltd.* (1996), the Alberta Court of Appeal found that a former employee, who was a director, officer, and minority shareholder of the plaintiff corporation, was in breach of his fiduciary duty when he resigned his employment with the plaintiff and commenced working with a new company and in turn, solicited the plaintiff's clients. The

Court also found the new employer liable because it knowingly benefited from the defendant's breach of duty. Consequently, the Plaintiff was compensated for lost profits.

In *Calgary Co-operative Association Ltd. and Union of Calgary Co-operative Employees* (*Townsend*), (1998), the grievor had been terminated from her position as cashier because she had participated with two other employees in a cheque kiting scheme. The union disagreed with the termination and suggested that the dismissal penalty was too severe under the circumstances. The arbitrator determined that the employee was in breach of her duty of good faith and fidelity when she was held to be in breach of the employer's trust. In doing so, the arbitrator upheld the employee's dismissal.

Discipline and Just Cause for Termination. In Canada it is becoming more commonplace for inappropriate and illegal Internet usage to be the determining factor in employee discipline and dismissals in unionized settings. The only question to be determined now is whether the inappropriate e-mails and Internet usage are just cause for dismissal.

Arbitrators weigh each fact situation to determine the extent of the disciplinary offense and the appropriateness of management responses in the context of the collective agreement. The following five cases illustrate how arbitrators have grappled with employee use of the Internet for personal reasons and have carefully attempted to balance management rights and the employee's right to privacy and job security.

In *Dhoot v. First Calgary Savings and Credit Union* (1998), an employee was put on a six-month probationary period after sending an e-mail message to "administrative staff" which pointed out that when all senior management were out of the office, there was great tranquillity and the employee could get more work done. Management were absent on the day the e-mail was initially sent, but they, along with two members of the Board of Directors, did receive a copy of it. The employee was issued a disciplinary notation putting her on probation and suspending her trading authority. The employee had been employed with the employer for four years and had previously only had positive evaluations. The employee chose not to accept the discipline and resigned. The employee sued for constructive dismissal. The Court found that the disciplinary memo constituted a fundamental change in the employment contract, and as such, the employee was found to have been constructively dismissed. The Court also found that the steps taken by the employer were an overreaction with little basis under the employer's existing policy. Although the employer had valid grounds to issue a warning, the employer's disciplinary response in this case was seen to be excessive. The Court awarded the employee damages based on a five-month reasonable notice period.[4]

In *Di Vito v. Macdonald Dettwiler & Associates* (1996), two employees were dismissed after circulating inappropriate e-mail. However, it wasn't the actual sending of the e-mail that amounted to cause. The e-mail consisted of derogatory and demeaning comments about an overweight female employee. The e-mail was sent out once, then stored for more than a year and then sent out again. When an investigation about the content, origin, and recipients of the e-mail occurred, the employees were less than truthful. The court held that while the employees were terminated for just cause, the court was not persuaded that the distribution of the e-mail alone was sufficient to terminate them. It was only their subsequent dishonesty that led the court to conclude there was sufficient cause for termination.

In *Re Public Service Employee Relations Commission* (*Johnstone Grievance*) (1999), the employer imposed a two-day suspension "for attempted inappropriate access to the Internet and inappropriate use of equipment." In this case, the grievor landed on a directory that had a large number of sex-related sites. However, he did not access any of these sites and the arbitrator found that the "breach" was technical in nature. The arbitrator found that a letter of reprimand was the more appropriate penalty.

In *Mount Royal College v. Mount Royal Support Staff Association* (*Horan Grievance*) (1998), the grievor, a 14-year employee, had been discharged for unsatisfactory work performance. Allegations included a substantial amount of work being done on personal matters on company time, persistent tardiness, and dishonesty. Specifically, the employer alleged overwhelming evidence that the grievor had received and reviewed numerous personal e-mails on company time. In upholding the discharge, the arbitrator concluded that the grievor did a substantial amount of personal work during business hours despite explicit warnings to cease this activity. The employer therefore had just cause to discipline and discharge the employee.

In *Chronicle Journal v. Thunder Bay Typographical Union, Local 44* (2000), the arbitrator overturned a discharge of a grievor who had been using company equipment on company time for personal and improper Internet access, specifically looking at pornographic material, some of which involved minors. Although the arbitrator agreed that the company did have cause to discipline the grievor, a discharge was an unwarranted disciplinary response given all the circumstances. Some of those circumstances were that although the company had a policy or rule in place regarding personal or non-work-related use of the Internet, the grievor, when confronted, had acknowledged that the amount of time he spent on the Internet was excessive and went far beyond what any employer could reasonably tolerate. Also the company had never disciplined other employees for use of the Internet for non-work-related purposes during working hours. Under the circumstances, the grievor was reinstated and the arbitrator substituted a four-month suspension without pay as a more appropriate disciplinary penalty.[5]

III. Electronic Communication Workplace Policies

Due to the rapid increase in the use of the Internet in the workplace, it is imperative that employers protect both themselves and the security interests of their company in relation to this means of communication. There are number of things that an employer can do in order to protect the company. Employers can acquire software packages which allow the network administrator to monitor and detect improper Internet and e-mail usage. Employers can also take preventative measures such as blocking the viewing of inappropriate or offensive sites or simply not allowing the transmission of e-mails which exceed a certain file size.

The most effective means of employer protection from misuse of computer resources by an employee, however, is still through the development and implementation of an in-house e-mail and Internet policy. These policies serve a variety of functions.

First, they serve as the basis for the employer's response to misconduct involving digital information and communications; and second, if consistently applied, the policy would serve as strong support for an argument for just cause in an action for wrongful dismissal or other forms of discipline imposed by the employer. Furthermore, if the policy itself is unambiguous in form and consistently applied, exposure to liability on the employer's side for acts performed by its employees could be avoided.

Employers should certainly ensure that their employees indicate that they have received and read the policy and also that they are reminded of its existence and advised of any revisions made to it.

Contents of Policies. The contents of these policies could include some of the following:

- Company e-mail must only be used for company purposes (attempts to maintain productivity);
- Any personal use is strictly prohibited or partial personal use is permitted (attempts to eliminate a reasonable expectation of privacy);
- The e-mail system should not be used to transmit pornographic, profane, or sexually explicit or otherwise offensive materials (attempts to protect against vicarious liability for harassment);
- The conduct expected of employees who engage in chat groups (examples: that they should act as the company's ambassadors and carefully review any contributions given the large potential audience);
- The company will not tolerate the use of the e-mail system to transmit offensive and derogatory remarks about a person's race, age, religion, color, place of origin, ethnicity, sex, sexual orientation, or disability (attempts to protect against vicarious liability for discrimination claims against the employer);
- E-mail should not contain defamatory statements about individuals or other companies (attempts to protect against vicarious liability for defamation claims);
- There could be guidelines regarding the appropriate use of computers, such as their use for business-related purposes only and that employees may access only information related to their job responsibilities;
- Information concerning a monitoring program which gives notice to employees that e-mail and Internet use may be monitored along with an explanation of the purpose of the monitoring; for example, to ensure a harassment-free environment; and
- Finally, notice to the employees of the disciplinary consequences of unauthorized or improper use of the computerized resources or breach of the policy itself.

Implementation of Policies and the Consent Issue. To achieve its effect, even the best written policy must be correctly implemented: It must be clearly understood, consented to by the employees, and consistently enforced by the employer. In relation to monitoring, the only way in which the employer can effectively avoid liability for monitoring a digital communication is for the employer to obtain the employee's consent.

This particular acknowledgement should indicate the employee understands the content of the Internet company policy and consents to monitoring under the terms of the policy.

This acknowledgement ensures that the employee has indeed turned his or her mind to the policy and thus understands its significance and that it will be strictly applied by the employer. Ideally all employees should be provided with a copy of the policy and be required to sign the acknowledgement as a condition of access to the company's Internet and e-mail accounts.

Finally, employers should ensure that any policy is rigorously applied and its terms are strictly adhered to. If the employer does not strictly adhere to its policy, or it has been inconsistently applied, it will be prevented from relying on it as the basis for discipline or discharge.

In *Consumers Gas v. Communications, Energy and Paper Workers Union* (1999), the grievor had been a senior clerk in the accounting department and had been employed for two years when he was dismissed. The arbitrator determined that the discharge of the grievor in relation to receiving and distributing pornographic material was too severe and excessive in light of the circumstances. The arbitrator did, however, determine that the distribution of two sexually explicit e-mails warranted serious discipline. The employer had a policy which prohibited the distribution of pornographic material, but this had been the first time in which any discipline had ever been imposed for a breach of the policy. The arbitrator noted that a "permissive atmosphere" had developed in the company. As a result, the arbitrator reinstated the employee and substituted a lengthy suspension as discipline for the employee's misconduct.

An interesting issue arises when employees who work from home, but with the employer's computers and communication facilities, are thus asked to sign the same workplace policy. The question remains: Can you have an e-mail or Internet policy that governs home-office workers? Relying on some of the cases to date, if the computer is owned by the employer and used by the employee simply as a tool of his or her employment, the employer would likely be able to monitor the Internet usage of that particular employee. Additionally, given an employee's duty of good faith and fidelity, an Internet and e-mail policy could likely govern those employees who work at home and through cyberspace. On the other hand, it may be difficult to prevent the employee from using that same computer for personal use. The courts will be very reluctant to uphold any employer discipline which is an unreasonable encroachment on the employee's personal privacy except in those circumstances where the employer establishes evidence of prejudice to its business interests.

Internet/E-mail Policies in the Unionized Setting. In some unionized settings in Canada, Internet and e-mail policies have been made part of the collective agreement. This can only occur where the union and management have expressly or implicitly made these rules part of the agreement or incorporated them by reference.

Even where such rules as an Internet/E-mail Policy do not form part of the agreement, it is now generally conceded and was held in *Crestbrook Forests Industries Ltd.* (1993) that in the absence of specific language to the contrary in the agreement, the making of such rules or policies lies within the prerogative of management, and arbitrators have held this to be so whether or not an express management's rights clause exists reserving the right of management to direct and "manage" the work force. Still, the rule-making power is not without limitation (Brown and Beatty, 2000, p. 4-19).

Arbitrators have set out a number of principles relating to the management's rule making power and have summarized them in *KVP Co. Ltd.* (1965). The "*KVP* test," as it is known, provides that:

I- Characteristic of Such Rule

A rule unilaterally introduced by the company, and not subsequently agreed to by the union, must satisfy the following requisites:

1. It must not be inconsistent with the collective agreement;
2. It must not be unreasonable;
3. It must be clear and unequivocal;
4. It must be brought to the attention of the employee affected before the company can act on it;
5. The employee concerned must have been notified that a breach of such rule could result in his or her discharge if the rule is used as a foundation for discharge; and
6. Such rule should have been consistently enforced by the company from the time it was introduced.

II- Effect of Such Rule re Discharge

1. If the breach of the rule is the foundation for the discharge of an employee such rule is not binding upon the board of arbitration dealing with the grievance, except to the extent that the action of the company in discharging the grievor finds acceptance in the view of the arbitration board as to what is reasonable or just cause.
2. In other words, the rule itself cannot determine the issue facing an arbitration board dealing with the question as to whether or not the discharge was for just cause because the very issue before the board may require it to pass upon the reasonableness of the rule or upon other factors which may affect the validity of the rule itself.
3. The rights of the employees under the collective agreement cannot be impaired or diminished by such rule but only by agreement of the parties (Brown and Beatty, 2000, p. 4-17).

A clear and properly implemented employee e-mail and Internet use policy will likely satisfy the scrutiny of arbitrators in Canada and be enforceable as a valid exercise of management rule-making power. As long as the policy addresses workplace use of the computer, arbitrators will most likely conclude that it is a reasonable policy which is necessary to address employee e-mail and Internet abuse and minimize the employer's risk of legal liability. However, to be enforceable the employer must follow the other requisites set out in the KVP test.

In determining whether it is appropriate to discharge an employee for violation of an e-mail and Internet policy, an arbitration board will weigh the seriousness of the breach, the prejudice to the employer and other employees, the remorse of the offending employee, and the employee's disciplinary record. While most breaches of the policy will likely merit a disciplinary response, it is very unlikely that discharge will be upheld except for very serious cases of abuse or repeated failure to follow the policy.

IV. Privacy Issues and Canadian Legislation

The pervasiveness and invasiveness of technology in tandem with increasing concerns by citizens over privacy, has resulted in federal and provincial legislative initiative to protect privacy in Canada. Employers are realizing that random monitoring of employee Internet use is important in assessing their own risk associated with granting their employees access to the Internet and e-mail as a tool of their employment. This raises even further issues related to the employee's right to privacy.

Canada has enacted legislation which protects the privacy of employee's personal information. The first legislative initiatives were in the public sector. However, the federal government has recently enacted legislation which covers the private sector in areas of federal jurisdiction. Monitoring of employee Internet and e-mail use will clearly fall under this legislation.

On January 1, 2001, Part 1 of the Protection of Personal Information and Electronic Documents Act ("Bill C-6") came into force in Canada and applies to the following:

- federal works, undertakings and businesses that collect, use, or disclose personal information in the course of commercial activities;
- personal information about the employees of a federal work, undertaking, or business that is collected, used or disclosed in connection with the operation of the federal work; and
- an undertaking, business, or organization that discloses personal information outside of the province for a consideration.

On January 1, 2002, Bill C-6 began to apply to personal health information of a federal work, undertaking, or business, or the disclosure of personal health information outside of a province for consideration.

On January 1, 2004, Bill C-6 will apply to organizations under provincial jurisdiction with respect to personal information collected, used, or disclosed within the province unless the province has an enacted substantially similar legislation and the Governor in Council has passed an order exempting organizations or activities from the application of the federal law with respect to intra-provincial collections, uses, and disclosures. It is not clear at this time whether this part of the Bill will withstand the constitutional scrutiny of the courts for federal jurisdiction covers only about 20 percent of the employers in Canada including interprovincial transportation (such as trucking, trains, buses, and airlines), interprovincial telecommunications, grain elevators, banks, postal service, atomic energy, radio and television stations, and the federal civil service. Most employers fall under provincial jurisdiction.

Therefore, until January 1, 2004, Bill C-6 does not apply to the majority of employers under provincial jurisdiction unless the company engages in an interprovincial or international commercial transaction involving the disclosure of personal information, for consideration. In our opinion this is quite narrow, i.e., the information itself must be the subject of the transaction and the consideration (or money paid) is for the information provided.

The province of Quebec already has privacy legislation in force that governs the private and public sector. Ontario and B.C. are expected to enact private sector privacy legislation soon following the same principles as Bill C-6. Alberta and Manitoba are considering such legislation. Alberta private sector privacy legislation is expected to be enacted within three years.

Why Privacy Legislation? In 1980, the Organization for Economic Co-Operation and Development (OECD) developed a set of guidelines on privacy. On October 24, 1995, the European Union passed Directive 95/46/EC of the European Parliament and of the council which embodied the guidelines of the OECD and stipulated that European countries were to cease transfer of the personal information of Europeans to countries that lacked adequate privacy protection on January 1, 2000.

In the early 1990s, the Canadian Standards Association (CSA) convened representatives from the public sector, business, consumer groups, and unions to begin work on a code to protect personal information. This work culminated in the development of the 1996 model code for the protection of personal information, representing a consensus among all of those stakeholders. The CSA encouraged its members and others in the industry to voluntarily adopt the model code for the protection of personal information. The code addresses two main concerns: the way in which organizations collect, use, disclose, and protect personal information and the right of individuals to have access to personal information about themselves and to have it corrected, if necessary. Voluntary implementation of the CSA Code by Canadian industries has not been overwhelming. Although a few major companies have voluntarily adopted the CSA code, many more have not.

Consumers in Canada are concerned about the protection of privacy. In a survey conducted by the Alberta Information and Privacy Commissioner's Office[6] in 2000, 78 percent of Albertans believed protection of privacy is important. Furthermore, 62 percent of Albertans are more concerned about privacy now than they were 5 years ago. A number of major companies, including Telus (a large telecommunications company), have adopted a privacy code out of commitment to the protection of its customer's and employee's personnel information.

The protection of privacy is also critical for successful and reliable e-commerce. There has been tremendous growth in e-commerce in the past few years, and it is expected to be a $220 billion dollar industry by 2001. If privacy is not protected, consumers will not trust e-commerce.

In response to the above public policy concerns and particularly to the European union directive, the federal government recently enacted Bill C-6.

Bill C-6. Bill C-6 applies to "personal information" which is collected, used, or disclosed in the course of commercial activities. These terms are broadly defined. "Personal information" means information about an identifiable individual, but does not include the name, title, or business address or telephone number of an employee of an organization. Consequently, this could include "personal information" in the form of information gathered from an employee by way of Internet and e-mail monitoring.

"Commercial activity" means any particular transaction, act, conduct, or any regular course of conduct that is of a commercial character, including the selling, bartering, or leasing of donor, membership, or other fund-raising lists.

The central theme of Bill C-6 can be summed up as follows:

- an organization must have the consent of an individual in order to collect personal information;
- the organization must disclose the purpose for collecting personal information and the information must only be collected for that purpose. If the purpose or use changes, then the organization must obtain a new consent;
- personal information cannot be disclosed without the knowledge and consent of an individual; and
- individuals may request to see their personal information and may correct errors.

The following are the exceptions to the above general principles regarding personal information which are permitted in Bill C-6.

- Personal information may only be retained for as long as is necessary to fulfill those purposes.
- Collection without knowledge or consent is permitted if it is in the interests of the individual; is reasonable for investigating a breach of an agreement or contravention of laws; is solely for journalistic purposes; and is publicly available and specified in the regulation.
- Use without knowledge or consent is permitted for investigation of breach of an agreement or contravention of laws; an emergency that threatens life; for statistical, scholarly study or research; where it is publicly available and specified in regulation; and where it was collected in the interests of the individual or was reasonable for investigating contravention of an agreement or law.
- Disclosure without knowledge or consent is permitted to a lawyer; for collecting a debt; to comply with a subpoena; on request, to government for national security, law enforcement, or administering the law; to the federal government's anti-money laundering agency; on the initiative of an organization to an investigative body or government for contravention of laws or national security; in an emergency that threatens the life of an individual; for statistical, scholarly study or research; to archives 100 years from creation of the record or 20 years after the death of an individual, whichever comes first; it is publicly available and specified in the regulation; by an investigative body; and when required by law.

It is unclear at this point whether breach of an Internet/E-mail Policy will be included in the exceptions to Bill C-6. In the nonunion sector an employee would have to agree to abide by the policy in order for it to be an "agreement." Then the employer could investigate a breach of "agreement" without the employee's consent. However, it is very unlikely that routine, ongoing monitoring of employee e-mails falls into the category of an "investigation for breach of an agreement." Therefore, it is prudent to obtain the employee's consent to monitor the Internet and e-mail use for the purpose of enforcing compliance of the policy. It is best to obtain that consent as a condition of granting the employee access to e-mail and the Internet.

In the union sector the only agreement that governs terms and conditions of employment is the collective agreement. It is an unfair labor practice to enter into an agreement with an individual employee without the union's consent. This suggests that an

Internet and e-mail use policy must have union consent. Otherwise monitoring or investigating employees for noncompliance is likely to violate federal privacy legislation which could make it particularly difficult for unionized employers to introduce Internet and e-mail use policies. Most unions will not likely agree to the policy because of the interference with employee privacy.

Application to Employees. Bill C-6 also applies to personal information about the employees of a federal work or undertaking that is collected, used, or disclosed in connection with the operation of the federal work or undertaking. The drafters of the legislation suggested that employee information in the context of the employer/employee relationship is not considered to be collected, used, or disclosed in the course of commercial activity. Therefore only the personal information of those employees who are under federal regulatory jurisdiction is covered by the law. Employees who are employed in federal works and undertakings include interprovincial telecommunications, grain elevators, flour mills, interprovincial pipelines, airlines, banks, interprovincial trucking companies, and atomic energy.

It is expected that several provinces will enact similar legislation soon and that this legislation will protect the personal information of employees under provincial jurisdiction as well. Therefore it is useful to discuss some of the privacy issues which may arise in the employment context.

Workplace Surveillance. Employers may use a variety of surveillance techniques to monitor employee behavior and job performance, including video surveillance, monitoring computer use and e-mails, or monitoring telephone use.

Video surveillance may involve overt or hidden cameras. Video footage and Internet and e-mail monitoring of an individual would be considered personal information, and therefore Bill C-6 will likely apply. As a general rule, employers will require the consent of the employees to conduct workplace surveillance. However, if there are reasonable and probable grounds to suspect that the employee is in breach of an agreement or law, surveillance is permitted, so there is no need for the employee's consent, and the information can be used to justify disciplinary actions in any subsequent legal proceedings. However, in many cases an Internet/e-mail policy will not be an agreement.

In *Re Calgary Regional Health Authority and HSAA (Dickinson Grievance)* (1999), the employer had put in place a policy disallowing personal use of the Internet, although a knowledgeable user could still access the Internet. The employer hired a contractor to monitor any access of the Internet and further determined to install a hidden video camera at one computer terminal that was being accessed. The grievor was taped at the terminal and initially denied accessing the Internet. The employer terminated the grievor, not so much for the accessing of the Internet against policy, but for the lack of candor and honesty when questioned initially by security and management. The arbitrator dismissed the grievance and upheld the termination.

With the introduction of Bill C-6 and the requisite provincial legislation that will likely be enacted in the next three years, employee consent will likely be required for monitoring electronic mail and computer use. As discussed previously, this may be part of a comprehensive computer and Internet-use policy with the consent obtained when the employee is given access to the computer. The purpose of the monitoring must be specifically explained to the employee. The information collected can only be used for that purpose unless the consent of the employee is obtained for another purpose. However, if the employer has reasonable and probable grounds to suspect that the employee has breached an agreement or law, then it may monitor the employee's e-mail and computer use without consent.

Employers must also be careful not to violate the *Criminal Code* provisions which prohibit the interception of private communications. Canada is similar to the U.S. in relation to the prohibition on "wire-tapping." Section 184(1) states: "Every one who by means of any electro-magnetic, acoustic, mechanical, or other device, willfully inter-cepts a private communication is guilty of an indictable offence and liable to impris-onment for a term not exceeding five years."

It noteworthy, given the mandatory consent provisions of the privacy legislation, that section 184(2)(a) of the *Criminal Code* holds that subsection (1) does not apply where the person has consented, expressly or implicitly, to the interception.

A private communication is defined in section 183 of the Criminal Code as:

> any oral communication, or any telecommunication, that is made by the originator who is in Canada or is intended by the originator to be received be a person who is in Canada and that is made under the circumstances in which it is reasonable for the originator to expect that it will not be intercepted by any person other than the person intended by the originator to receive it, and includes any radio-based telephone communication that is treated electroni-cally or otherwise for the purpose of preventing intelligible reception by any person other than the person intended by the originator to receive it.

"Telecommunication" is defined in section 35 of the Interpretation Act as " the emis-sion, transmission or reception of signs, signals, writing, images, sounds or intelligence of any nature by any wire, cable, radio, optical, or other electromagnetic system, or by any similar technical system." "Intercept" includes "listen to, record or acquire a communication or acquire the substance, meaning or purpose thereof."

Although e-mail is likely included in the definition of "telecommunication," the real issue lies in whether or not e-mail monitoring on a computer desktop or server falls within the definition of "intercept." Due to the way that e-mail is transmitted, it is unlikely that it could be intercepted as defined in the *Criminal Code*. "Intercept" means an interference between the place of origin and the place of destination of the com-munication (Rasky, 1998).

E-mail is transmitted from one computer through (usually) two Internet Service Providers onto a network server, and once that is complete so is the transmission. Consequently, the e-mail is simply just waiting to be retrieved by the recipient from the network. As a result, an employer that views a message which has been sent and saved onto a company's server is not really intercepting the message within the mean-ing of the *Criminal Code* (Coon and Cocker, 2001).

Another relevant provision of the *Criminal Code* is section 342.1(1)(b) which makes it an offense for a person, fraudulently or without "color of right" to intercept (or cause to be intercepted) either directly or indirectly any computer service by means of any device. Thus, as defined in section 342(2) of the *Code*, the monitoring of e-mail is implicitly, if not explicitly, encompassed by the technical aspects of the provision. The Courts, however, have held in construing these sections that an honestly asserted proprietary or possessory claim constitutes a "color of right" notwithstanding that it is unfounded in law or fact. Thus, while a court might one day find that an employer had no right to intercept its employees' e-mail, the employer's honest, yet mistaken belief, that it did have such a right, could serve to protect it (Morgan, 1999, p. 878).

At this point, there is no definitive Canadian ruling on who owns the e-mail in the issue of e-mail sent or received by an employee via his or her employer's computer system. This could be argued in two ways. One view is that e-mail sent or received in this context is property of the employer, to which an employee maintains no reasonable expectation of privacy. Thus, a search of e-mail in the workplace is really nothing more than a search of an employer's property (Rasky, 1998, p. 221).

A second perspective is to view sent or received e-mail as the property of the employee. Employers assign employees e-mail addresses and allow employees to have e-mail passwords. Thus, this approach suggests that employees have a reasonable expectation of privacy in their workplace e-mail (McIsaac, 2000, p. 2-86).

Canadian courts to date have not specifically addressed the issue of e-mail privacy within the workplace, although it was held in *R. v. Weir* (1998), that an individual's home e-mail via the Internet "ought to carry a reasonable expectation of privacy." Therefore, as Internet and e-mail monitoring becomes more commonplace in the workplace, the only deterrent to employers may be couched in terms of the new privacy legislation and the required consent that will be required of an employee when an employer wishes to monitor. The focus would then be shifted to one of the reasonableness of the substance of implementation of the consent and monitoring policy along with the various factors inherent in that implementation such as the notice given to the employee of the search policy, the clarity of the policy, and the fairness of the administration of the policy (McIsaac, 2000, p. 2-87).

V. Electronic Communication Issues in the Unionized Workplace

Legal issues surrounding the Internet have also affected the unionized workplace in Canada, but not to the extent as in the U.S. Monitoring of employees in the unionized setting has been addressed previously.

Arbitrators seem to have created a two-fold test with respect to an employer's right to utilize surveillance techniques with its unionized employees. First, an employer must have reasonable grounds to believe that its interests are being adversely affected before it can resort to any form of surveillance or monitoring beyond normal supervision, and second, an employer may monitor employees only to the extent necessary in order to protect its interest.

Although arbitrators in Canada have yet to deal with situations involving electronic monitoring in the unionized workplace, cases dealing with other forms of employee surveillance have raised identical issues. Employers in the unionized setting may face various challenges through the grievance and arbitration process if they initiate overly aggressive monitoring policies.

We believe that when faced with the issue, arbitrators will likely employ the same two-fold test described above. If the test is used to determine an employer's right to monitor, it may well result in arbitrators restricting monitoring to the most non-invasive methods possible. For example, with employee consent, an employer may monitor the date, time, and origin of an e-mail message to determine whether or not it is personal but be prohibited from accessing the message's content. Thus, what will become apparent is the need to balance the interests of employees in protecting their privacy from unreasonable intrusion along with the need of employers to protect themselves from liability issues related to the Internet and e-mail.

One of the easier ways of implementing an Internet/e-mail policy into the unionized workplace is to develop the policy in connection with the union and the collective agreement itself. The policy would outline that the Internet and e-mail could only be used for company purposes and on company time. It would also stipulate what sort of usage was proper and the consequences for improper usage, and finally, it would be a condition of access to the Internet and e-mail that the employee read and agree in writing to abide by the policy.

Another issue which has been addressed in the U.S. but has not been specifically raised in Canada at this point is the issue of union organizing on-line via the Internet and internal e-mail. In *E. I. du Pont de Nemours & Co.* (1993), the leading case in the U.S. on this issue, the Court held that the employer's practice of prohibiting its employees from using its e-mail system to distribute union information, such as meeting notices, violated the National Labor Relations Act. The employer had allowed employees to use the e-mail previously to discuss a wide variety of topics, but excluded all employees from using e-mail to distribute union literature, whether the employee was a union supporter or not. The Court held that because the employer had allowed its employees to use the e-mail system for other non-work-related purposes, it was a violation of the Act to deny use for union-related communications on the basis of discrimination. (This case seems to turn on the absence of an Internet/e-mail policy (Towns and Girard, 1998, pp. 17-18).)

One case of some significance in this area was addressed in Canada by the Ontario Labour Relations Board in *JDS Fitel Inc.* (1999). In that case, there was an application by the union alleging various unfair labor practices by the employer through its conduct during the union's organizing campaign. One of the complaints involved the apparent circulation of libellous material via the Internet by the employer, which was apparently extremely critical of the union. The address to that particular website was also posted on the employee discussion board.

The Court held that there was no need to comment on whether or not the information on the website would constitute interference and intimidation, thereby constituting an unfair labor practice, as they had determined, based on all the evidence, that the employer had played no part in the dissemination of the material. The Court also held that the posting of the location of the website on the discussion board could not be considered employer conduct, anymore than comments made from one employee to another in an employer-maintained lunch room would be attributed to management. Thus, this particular complaint of the union was dismissed.

Clearly, as electronic communications become more prevalent in unionized workplaces in Canada, the same struggle will ensue as in the more commonplace realm of the nonunion workplace — the need to balance the employee's rights of privacy and the right to organize with the employer's rights to manage and run the company without union interference on company time.

One issue is whether employees may use the employer's computer and its internal e-mail system to organize for the union. This brings into conflict the employee's right to organize in support of a union in the workplace and the employer's right to manage the workplace free from outside interference. Under Canadian law, unions and employees organizing on behalf of employees cannot organize on company time without management's consent. Unfortunately, when it comes to electronic communications, the determination of "company time" is not always so easily discernible.

An employee may send out an e-mail prior to that employee's "work hours," but the recipient may not access that particular union organizing e-mail until well within the recipient's work hours. Thus, the issue is whether the employee is organizing on company time. This has been addressed by Malin and Perritt (2000, p. 22) who state,

> With electronic solicitation, however, the recipient controls when he or she will actually read the message. Even though the recipient receives the message during working time, the recipient need not read it immediately. The recipient can recall the message during break time or even remotely from home after departing the premises. Moreover, remote site workers tend to exercise greater control over their time and can determine whether any given moment is "working time" or not.
>
> .   .   .   .
>
> Similarly, once an employer licenses the employees to use the e-mail system, or other electronic communication devices, it may not prohibit the employees from using the system to solicit co-workers to support a union without a showing of special circumstances. There is no principled reason to treat employee use of the computer system differently from the use of the employee parking lot, cafeteria, locker room or entry hall for the same purpose.

We suggest that the reason employees will likely be able to use the company computer resources to organize is the following where they state,

> The starting point of analysis in both instances is recognition that, as a property owner, an employer has a right to exclude anyone from its premises. Once it invites employees onto the premises, however, albeit, for the limited purpose of performing their job responsibilities, it may not prohibit or restrict them from soliciting their co-workers to join a union unless the prohibition or less restriction is necessary to ensure order and prevent disruption of the business operation. Similarly, an employer has a property right to exclude all employee use of its bulletin boards. Once it invites employee use of the bulletin boards, however, albeit for the limited purpose of posting for sale notices, it may not prohibit or restrict them from posting union meeting notices unless the prohibition or lesser restriction is necessary to prevent disruption or interference with the employer's business purpose (Malin and Perritt, 2000, p. 19).

As the workplace is a forum for union activity, so is the computer. However, the employer provides the computer to facilitate productivity not to promote trade unionism. The rights of employees to organize and participate in lawful union activities is protected under the labor relations legislation of each Canadian jurisdiction. However, this is a qualified right. An employer has the right to mange its affairs and maintain an efficient business enterprise. An employee has an obligation to perform work in return for compensation. Therefore, the labor relations legislation in each Canadian jurisdiction prohibits unions (and employees acting on behalf of unions) from persuading an employee to become or refrain from becoming a member of a trade union at the workplace during working hours. Provisions attempt to balance an employees statutory right to engage in union activity and employer's proprietary and commercial interests (Maklim, 1990).

In *Consolidated Fastfrate Ltd.* (1980) , the Ontario Labour Relations Board stated that "The right to engage in trade union activity, and the right to pursue business efficiency, are both recognized parts of the statutory scheme. Neither right is unlimited, and accommodation between the two must be obtained, with as little destruction of the one as is consistent with the maintenance of the other. It follows, we believe, that the formulation of general rules in this area must be undertaken with some caution for differing fact situations may call for differing accommodations."

In considering whether unions should be allowed access to a company e-mail, labor boards must weigh these competing rights — a delicate balance. On the one hand, it permits unions access to computers which will enable unions to distribute literature and effectively communicate with every employee in the workplace both during and after working hours. This could detrimentally impact business efficiency and cause considerable workplace disruption. Unions could literally jam the employees' e-mail. Under the circumstances, most labor boards will likely hold that such activity is prohibited unless there is no other effective means for the union to communicate with the employees.

Another issue is whether an employer can use the Internet to bypass the union and distribute literature and information to its employees. Although this is fast becoming a hot labor issue in the U.S., it remains virtually untested in Canada, perhaps due to the fact that Canada's unions traditionally organize blue-collar work forces where the Internet and e-mail do not play a big role in the daily activities of the employees. Outside of the public service, most organizational drives of professional employees have been unsuccessful.

Under federal jurisdiction, and in the provinces of Alberta, Manitoba, New Brunswick, Nova Scotia, Ontario, and Prince Edward Island, there is an express provision in the labor legislation which provides that an employer is free "to express his views" so long as the employer does not use coercion, intimidation, threats, promises, or undue influence. Pursuant to British Columbia labor legislation, an employer may "communicate to an employee a statement of fact or opinion reasonably held with respect to the employer's business." In Saskatchewan, there is a general prohibition against employer interference and coercion in the union organizing process, but this is modified with a statement that "nothing in this Act precludes an employer from communicating with his employees." However, Canadian labor boards must balance the employers freedom of speech with the competing employee's interest in associating with and organizing a trade union.

All labor boards in Canada must find the delicate balance between employer free speech and the employee's rights to organize and associate with the trade union. These issues most frequently arise during negotiations for a collective agreement or during an organizing campaign.

During an organizing drive, an employer is free to communicate with its employees provided that it does not use intimidation, coercion, or undue influence. Whether this takes place over the Internet or e-mail will make little difference in the assessment of the labor relations board.

Direct employer communications with employees during negotiations is also permitted provided that this does not interfere with the union's right to represent its members. In *AN Shaw Restoration Ltd.* (1978) at p. 219, the Ontario Labour Relations Board stated:

> Where communications occur between employer and employees during negotiations, the board must draw a line dividing legitimate freedom of expression from legal encroachments upon the union's exclusive right to bargain on behalf of the employees. The line is not an easy one to find, and can only be discovered by asking whether such communications in reality represent an attempt to bargain directly with the employees. If employer communications can be characterized in this manner, they must be regarded as unduly influencing employees and, therefore, falling outside the protection provided to freedom of expression. . . .

Therefore, if direct employer communications with employees during bargaining bypasses the union and undermines its right to represent its employees, this may violate the statutory duty to bargain in good faith and amount to an unfair labor practice. This is the same balance that will be found with respect to direct employer communications with employees through e-mail and the Internet.

VI. Conclusion

The rapidly increasing use of Internet and e-mail in the workplace has introduced complicated issues related to the areas of potential liability of employers arising from the improper use of the Internet and e-mail by employees, as well as creating numerous privacy issues which must soon be addressed by all employers — union and nonunion. If employers specify and disseminate clear and concise e-mail and Internet use policies, they will be able to significantly reduce the risk associated with employee misconduct in this area. Not only should the policies be clear and concise, but they should also be communicated to the employees in such a fashion that all employees understand the policy and the consequences of breaching that policy.

Employers can be concerned that their investments and information technology tools are being misused by employees, but at the same time clear communication and respect for the rights of employees and their privacy will encourage a positive, healthy work environment along with a decreased risk for potential liability for all parties involved. We agree that the Canadian Courts and arbitrators will need to make a concerted effort to understand the new technology and the various problems that arise as a result of that technology and then strike a balance between employee rights to engage in concerted activities vs. employer property and entrepreneurial rights.

Notes

1   Note that Canadians use the term "grievor" rather than the American term "grievant."
2   Each province and the federal government in Canada has enacted human rights legislation. This legislation typically prohibits discrimination on the grounds of gender, race, country of origin, age, family and marital status, sexual orientation, and other grounds. The legislation is administered by a human rights commission which may direct an unresolved complaint to a hearing before a human rights tribunal. A human rights tribunal has statutory hearing and remedial powers which, within its jurisdiction, are similar to a provincial or federal court.
3   In the union sector, the common law courts do not have jurisdiction over grievances between employees and their employers. Therefore, a case against an employee for breach of duty or fidelity would be advanced through the grievance and arbitration procedure set out in the collective agreement between the union and the employer.
4   In Canada, damages for constructive dismissal and wrongful dismissal are assessed by multiplying compensation for loss of salary, other compensation, and benefits over the period of reasonable notice, and subtracting any sums earned during the notice period through mitigated employment.
5   In Canada, unionized employers under both federal and provincial jurisdiction are subject to a grievance arbitration procedure where unresolved grievances go to a binding, consensual arbitration board of one or three members. The arbitration board has the ultimate discretion to reinstate an employee grievor and to substitute the employer's penalty of discharge with a lessor disciplinary penalty such as a suspension or warning. Discharge of an employee is seen by most arbitration boards as workplace "capital punishment" which is reserved only for the most extreme cases and where employees have a very poor progressive disciplinary record. Therefore, many arbitration boards will reinstate an employee even where discipline is warranted and will usually substitute the penalty with a period of suspension without pay.
6   The Province of Alberta has followed most other jurisdictions in Canada by enacting legislation governing the protection of privacy and access to information in the public sector. The Privacy Commissioner in Alberta administers the Freedom of Information and Protection of Privacy Act which applies to the Provincial government, municipalities, hospitals, school boards, and their agencies.

References

Ball, Stacey Reginald. *Canadian Employment Law*, Vol. 1. Aurora: Canada Law Book, 2000.
Brown, Donald J.M. and David M. Beatty. *Canadian Labour Arbitration*. Aurora: Canada Law Book, 2000.
Coon, Kevin and Jonathan Cocker. "Legal Issues of E-mail and Internet Access in the Workplace." *Internet and E-Commerce Law in Canada* 1 (January 2001): 81–87.
England, Geoffrey, Innis Christie, and Merran Christie. *Employment Law in Canada*, Vol 2. Toronto: Butterworths, 1998.

Leone, Daniel L. "Inappropriate Use of E-mail and the Internet on Company Time." *Mathews, Dinsdale & Clark LLP Newsletter* (July 2000): 1–3.

Maklim, P. "Property, Status and Workplace Organizing." *University of Toronto Law Journal* 40 (1990): 74.

Malin, Martin H. and Henry H. Perritt, Jr. "The National Labor Relations Act in Cyberspace: Union Organizing in Electronic Workplaces." *University of Kansas Law Review* 49 (November 2000): 1–41.

McIsaac, Barbara. *Law of Privacy in Canada.* Scarborough: Carswell, 2000.

Morgan, Charles. "Employer Monitoring of Employee Electronic Mail and Internet Use." *McGill Law Journal* 44 (1999): 849–902.

Rasky, Holly L. "Can an Employer Search the Contents of Its Employees' E-mail?" 220 *Advocates Quarterly* 20 (1998): 221–28.

Towns, Douglas M. and Jeana Girard. "Superhighway or Superheadache? E-Mail and the Internet in the Workplace." *Employee Relations Law Journal* 24 (Winter 1998): 5–29.

Cases

Anderson, Smyth & Kelly Customs Broker Ltd. v. World Wide Customs Brokers Ltd. [1996], A.J. No. 475 (Alta. C.A.).

AN Shaw Restoration Ltd. [1978], 2 Can L.R.B.R. 214 (Ont.) (Burkett).

Calgary Co-operative Association Ltd. and Union of Calgary Co-operative Employees (Townsend) (1998), 72 L.A.C. (4th) 248 (Moreau).

Canada Pacific Railway v. International Brotherhood of Electrical Workers (Lahaie Grievance) [2000] , C.L.A.D. No. 151 (Picher).

Canadian Aero Service Ltd. v. O'Malley et al. (1974), 40 D.L.R. (3d) 371 (S.C.C.).

Chronicle Journal v. Thunder Bay Typographical Union, Local 44 (Barichello Grievance) [2000], O.L.A.A. No. 575 (Marcotte).

Consolidated Fastfrate Ltd. [1980], O.L.R.B. Rep. April 418 (MacDowell).

Consumers Gas v. Communications, Energy and Paper Workers Union (Primiani Grievance) [1999], O.L.A.A. No. 649 (Kirkwood).

CRC- Evans Canada Ltd. v. Pettifer (1997) 26 C.C.E.L. (2d) 294 (Alta. Q.B.), affd 80 A.C.W.S. (3d) 39 (Alta. C.A.).

Crestbrook Forests Industries Ltd. (1993), 38 L.A.C. (4th) 89 (McEwan).

CUPE v. Camosun College (Metcalfe Grievance) [1999], B.C.C.A.A.A. No. 490 (Germaine).

Curling v. Torimiro (2000) O.H.R.B.I.D. No. 16 (Laird).

Di Vito v. Macdonald Dettwiler & Associates (1996) 21 C.C.E.L.(2d) 137 (B.C.S.C.).

E. I. du Pont de Nemours & Co., 311 N.L.R.B. 893 (1993).

JDS Fitel Inc. [1999], O.L.R.D. No. 3471 (Chapman).

Mount Royal College v. Mount Royal Support Staff Association (Horan Grievance) [1998], A.G.A.A. No. 12 (Ponak).

P.A.B. v. Children's Foundation [1997], B.C.J. No. 692 (B.C.C.A.).

R. v. Weir (1998) 213 A.R. 285 (Q.B.).

Re Calgary Regional Health Authority and HSAA (Dickinson Grievance) [1999], Alta G.A.A. 99-085 (Moreau).

Re Public Service Employee Relations Commission (Johnstone Grievance) [1999], B.C.C.A.A.A. No 359 (Hope).

Ryane v. Krieger (2000) B.C.H.R.T.D. No. 41 (Patch).

Westcoast Energy Inc. v. Communications, Energy and PaperWorkers' Union of Canada, Local 686B (Bourdon Grievance) (1999), 84 L.A.C. (4th) 185 (Albertini).

Wilcox v. G.W.G. Ltd. (1985), 8 C.C.E.L. 11 (Alta. C.A.).

Index